Iris Murdoch and the Ancient Quarrel

Bloomsbury Studies in Philosophy and Poetry

Series Editors: Rick Anthony Furtak, Colorado College, USA and James D. Reid, Metropolitan State University of Denver, USA

Editorial Board:
Daniel Brown, University of Southampton, UK
Kristen Case, University of Maine Farmington, USA
Hannah Vandegrift Eldridge, University of Wisconsin–Madison, USA
Cassandra Falke, University of Tromsø, Norway
Luke Fischer, University of Sydney, Australia
John Gibson, University of Louisville, USA
James Haile III, University of Rhode Island, USA
Kevin Hart, University of Virginia, USA
Eileen John, University of Warwick, UK
Troy Jollimore, California State University, USA
David Kleinberg-Levin, Northwestern University, USA
John Koethe, University of Wisconsin–Milwaukee, USA
John T. Lysaker, Emory University, USA
Karmen MacKendrick, Le Moyne College, USA
Rukmini Bhaya Nair, Indian Institute of Technology, India
Kamiyo Ogawa, Sophia University, Japan
Kaz Oishi, University of Tokyo, Japan
Yi-Ping Ong, Johns Hopkins University, USA
Anna Christina Soy Ribeiro, Texas Tech University, USA
Karen Simecek, University of Warwick, UK
Ruth Rebecca Tietjen, University of Copenhagen, Denmark
Íngrid Vendrell Ferran, Goethe University Frankfurt, Germany

Bloomsbury Studies in Philosophy and Poetry explores ancient, modern and contemporary texts in ways that are sensitive to philosophical themes and problems that can be fruitfully addressed through poetic modes of writing, and focused on questions of style, the relations between form and content, and the conduciveness of literary modes of expression to philosophical inquiry. With a keen interest in the intertwining of poetry and philosophy in all forms, the series will cover the philosophical register of poetry, the poetics of philosophical writing and the literary strategies of philosophers.

The series provides a home for work on figures across geographical landscapes, with contributions that employ a wide range of methods across academic disciplines, and without regard for divisions within philosophy, between analytic and continental, for example, that have outworn their usefulness. Featuring single-authored works and edited collections, curated by an international editorial board, the series aims to redefine how we read and discuss philosophy and poetry today.

New Titles:
Maurice Blanchot on Poetry and Narrative *Ethics of the Image* by Kevin Hart
Philosophy of Lyric Voice *The Cognitive Value of Page and Performance Poetry* by Karen Simecek
Heidegger and Poetry in the Digital Age *New Aesthetics and Technologies* by Rachel Coventry

Iris Murdoch and the Ancient Quarrel

Why Literature Is Not Philosophy

Lyra Ekström Lindbäck

BLOOMSBURY ACADEMIC
LONDON • NEW YORK • OXFORD • NEW DELHI • SYDNEY

BLOOMSBURY ACADEMIC
Bloomsbury Publishing Plc, 50 Bedford Square, London, WC1B 3DP, UK
Bloomsbury Publishing Inc, 1359 Broadway, 12th Floor, New York, NY 10018, USA
Bloomsbury Publishing Ireland, 29 Earlsfort Terrace, Dublin 2, D02 AY28, Ireland

BLOOMSBURY, BLOOMSBURY ACADEMIC and the Diana logo are
trademarks of Bloomsbury Publishing Plc

First published in Great Britain 2024
This paperback edition published 2026

Copyright © Lyra Ekström Lindbäck, 2024

Lyra Ekström Lindbäck has asserted her right under the Copyright,
Designs and Patents Act, 1988, to be identified as Author of this work.

For legal purposes the Acknowledgements on p. xiii constitute
an extension of this copyright page.

Series design: Ben Anslow
Cover image: *Amor Sacro y Amor Profano (Sacred and Profane Love)*,
Tiziano Vecelli (1514) (Galería Borghese, Roma) (Public domain)

All rights reserved. No part of this publication may be: i) reproduced or transmitted in any form, electronic or mechanical, including photocopying, recording or by means of any information storage or retrieval system without prior permission in writing from the publishers; or ii) used or reproduced in any way for the training, development or operation of artificial intelligence (AI) technologies, including generative AI technologies. The rights holders expressly reserve this publication from the text and data mining exception as per Article 4(3) of the Digital Single Market Directive (EU) 2019/790.

Bloomsbury Publishing Inc does not have any control over, or responsibility for, any third-party websites referred to or in this book. All internet addresses given in this book were correct at the time of going to press. The author and publisher regret any inconvenience caused if addresses have changed or sites have ceased to exist, but can accept no responsibility for any such changes.

A catalogue record for this book is available from the British Library.

A catalogue record for this book is available from the Library of Congress Cataloging

ISBN: HB: 978-1-3503-3291-1
PB: 978-1-3503-3295-9
ePDF: 978-1-3503-3292-8
eBook: 978-1-3503-3293-5

Series: Bloomsbury Studies in Philosophy and Poetry

Typeset by Integra Software Services Pvt. Ltd.

For product safety related questions contact productsafety@bloomsbury.com.

To find out more about our authors and books visit www.bloomsbury.com
and sign up for our newsletters.

Contents

Preface		viii
Acknowledgements		xiii
List of abbreviations		xiv
1	The ancient quarrel: *A background story*	1
2	What is (not) a philosophical novel? *The sensory illusion of sense*	37
3	The feel of muddled thinking: *Conceptual content in literature following Kant's aesthetics*	75
4	Real characters and fictional people: *Stanley Cavell and the epistemology of fiction*	95
5	Problems purged: *The consolations of tragedy*	109
6	Playing with fire: *The immorality of literature*	133
Concluding remarks		167
Notes		172
Bibliography		207
Index		217

Preface

1. It's personal

As a fiction writer, I have never set out to write a philosophical novel. On the contrary, I have been troubled by a feeling that my literary work would somehow be threatened if I allowed for philosophy to 'get into' it. Why do I nurse this worry? After all, 'philosophical' is more commonly used as a compliment to literature than an insult. Why have I then been feeling that my philosophical thinking should be regarded as a dangerous temptation when writing fiction, in order not to compromise the 'properly artistic' aspects of my work?

This discomfort might easily be dismissed as a private matter; perhaps just a symptom of the difficulty to uphold two professional identities. But – and probably much philosophical work begins this way – one day I asked myself: What if this malaise is not just personal, but a symptom of a more general problem? What if there may be something off not with my intuition, but with the currently widespread notion that literature could only have something to gain from being mixed up with, or interpreted as, philosophy?

When I came across the work of Iris Murdoch (1919–99), I finally found this problem spelled out properly. An accomplished novelist and an intriguing philosopher, this Anglo-Irish woman insisted throughout her double careers that they should be considered as two distinct practices. Indeed, not just regarding her own work: Murdoch is also a remarkable aesthetic thinker who has made many attempts to describe what makes art so peculiar. Instantly when I opened the collected volume *Existentialists and Mystics*, and began reading the interview with Murdoch by Bryan Magee, I knew that I had stumbled upon the place to start digging.

Magee asks Murdoch whether she considers her literary and philosophical writing to be 'radically different kinds of writing'. Unfashionably enough, Murdoch answers a definite yes. She lists a number of differences between the disciplines. 'Literature is read by many and various people, philosophy by very few.' Bad philosophy is not really philosophy, 'whereas bad art is still art'. Literature 'does many things, and philosophy does one thing'.[1] Offhandedly, in this transcribed television interview, she speaks of literature as sensuous, formal, entertaining, arousing of emotions, mimetic and connected with sex. 'It might take a long time to "define" literature,' she says, 'though we all know roughly what it is. It is the art form which uses words.'[2]

I had found my ally. Indeed, as Murdoch is keen to point out, even the forefather of Western philosophy, Plato, agrees with us here.[3] He initiated what has since become known as 'the ancient quarrel': the opposition between literature and philosophy. In Murdoch's writings on literature, art and aesthetics (often treated together with other topics), she touches upon the problem of the distinction between literature and philosophy repeatedly.

But when I looked at the scholarship on Murdoch to find a lengthier explication of her position in the ancient quarrel, I was greatly disappointed. Most of her interpreters seemed instead eager to contradict her distinction between the disciplines, often in order to read her own novels as philosophical. No one really grappled with what I took to be the most interesting problem: What is it about literature which makes it unfortunate to regard it as philosophical? And so, I set out to make my own little contribution to the quarrel.

2. Problem definition and delineations

In this book, I argue for why literature is not philosophy.

This may strike some as a battle against a straw man. After all, I have not a single named opponent who claims that literature *is* philosophy. As you will read in the first chapter, not even the 'poetic thinker' Heidegger considered the two practices to be completely conflated. The blurring of the boundaries between the disciplines is usually performed in a much more sophisticated manner than that. Arguing that literature is philosophically interesting, or that philosophy is conducted through fiction, is indeed not the same thing as stating that literature *is* philosophy. However, what I seek to counter with the claim that literature is not philosophy is not one specific argument, but the pervasive spirit that literature would only have something to benefit from epithets like 'philosophical' or 'doing philosophy'. As a disciple of Murdoch, I also prefer illuminating generalizations over minute reconstructions of arguments. Like she says in *Metaphysics as a Guide to Morals*: 'To see the whole picture one may have to stop being neat.'[4] Precision must sometimes take a backseat for the bigger picture to arise.

One of the most common hostile assumptions I have been faced with when presenting the topic for my book is that my goal would be to create a failproof taxonomy that would define, limit and police the categories 'philosophy' and 'literature'. Perhaps this assumption is founded on what I take to be one of the most harmful principles in contemporary academic philosophy: the refusal to speak in general terms. Terminological precision has become a universal golden standard, whether it comes in the analytic form of isolating concepts from their contexts and endowing them with artificially fixed technical meanings in distinction from near-synonyms, or in the continental exegetical form of analysing how a certain word is used in the work of a certain philosopher or tradition. Not only does this principle result in terribly boring articles and books – it also serves to make an already difficult discipline further isolated from how the rest of the world lives and reflects. Ordinary language philosophy has attempted to remedy this illness by looking at how words are used in lived contexts. But, in the anxiety to create a new standard of verification in the confusing reintroduction of the flux of life into philosophical language, the investigations done in the name of ordinary language philosophy often tend to become too localized, as if accuracy here could only mean being as particular as possible.

However, speaking in general terms about philosophy and literature is not only possible, it is something we regularly do. In everyday life, we have no trouble with terribly vague concepts such as 'life', 'everyday' and 'trouble'. Nonetheless, in philosophy, a heightened awareness of what we mean when we say something is perhaps needed to create a functional academic dialogue. Some historical understanding is essential here too. But this does not mean that it would be impossible to talk about 'philosophy' and 'literature' in general and make oneself understood.

That being said, this is my problem: Why is literature not philosophy? Why would it be misleading, unnecessary, distortive, misguided and/or unfruitful to regard it so? What is it about literature that conflicts with the purposes, focuses and methods of philosophy – broadly and generally understood as a theoretical, truth-seeking, conceptually clarifying, hermeneutical, rational and/or critically discerning practice? What does it mean that literature is an art, and not philosophical thinking?

I expound this not by placing literature in contrast to any definite definition of philosophy, but by providing an aesthetic-philosophical description of literature as the art form which uses words. Some might react with a frown already to this. The art form which uses words; well, other arts may use words as well, and literature has many subgenres that are not best described as artistic. Another way of naming my object might be: the fine art of literature. Probably most of you have some sense of what is indicated by this. But to prevent further disappointment, it might as well be spelled out: the description provided by this book is not intended to be exhaustive, essentialist or determining. My aim is not to fixate the object that is literature. 'Literature' is a porous, general category; 'philosophy' as well. That the categories may be permeable and unstable does not imply that there is no relevant distinction to be drawn between them.

From this also follows that the works of literature cited in this book are not meant to be ideals of the category at large. My examples do not make up a representative bouquet of different genres, periods and styles. There are, for instances, remarkably few examples from poetry. Why is that? Well, poetry is more evidently distinct from philosophical discourse, and in any case, actual works of literature and how to interpret them is not the focus of this book. The aesthetic-philosophical understanding of what literature, as an art form, is, is.

The attentive reader will find a certain bias for novels, more specifically realist fiction, even more specifically the fiction by Iris Murdoch. I have greatly enjoyed rereading them. But this is not a study of Murdoch's fiction. Some of the earlier interpretations of her novels as philosophical are discussed at length, since these often come together with the wish to rebut or weaken her insistence on the distinction between literature and philosophy. In contrast to them, I propagate a reading that applies her view of the distinction to her own works, that is, reading the novels as art, and not as philosophy. Nonetheless, my main focus is not these novels, but the general and abstract philosophical category known as 'literature'. Some of the things I say about literature will in one sense or another apply to many, or even most, texts known under this name; some will only apply to some, and some will also apply to the other arts (or certain works from the other arts). Therefore, some conceptual fluctuation between 'poetry', 'literature' and 'art' will be permitted.

Nor is this book strictly an exegetical investigation of Murdoch's philosophical aesthetics. She is my guide, and not my topic. I intend to follow her backwards and forwards where I think that she was right, a method which entails a number of deviations from the more narrow path of interpreting her arguments. That the book entails lengthy discussions of Kant and Plato may be unsurprising, since it is widely acknowledged that these two are important for Murdoch's understanding of art. But I also discuss more contemporary scholars, such as Stanley Cavell and Martha Nussbaum, who Murdoch did not engage with, but who are now prominent figures in the debate regarding the distinction between philosophy and literature. My question is: Why is literature not philosophy? Rather than: Why did Iris Murdoch think that literature was not philosophy? But since Murdoch is a good guide on the topic, these two questions will often tend to merge.

Many more disclaimers, to delineate the focus and purposes of this book, could probably be made. But let me now say a couple of words of what I *will do* instead, and in what order.

3. Chapter overview

The book is divided into six chapters. The first, 'The ancient quarrel: *A background story*', asks: How has the ancient quarrel developed since Plato's time? This chapter provides a historical (but non-chronological) background to the philosophical understanding of the distinction between literature and philosophy and aims to situate Murdoch's (and mine) view in relation to ancient, modern and contemporary approaches.

In Chapter 2, 'What is (not) a philosophical novel? *The sensory illusion of sense*', some preliminary aspects of Murdoch's distinction between the disciplines are introduced, especially in relation to the concept 'philosophical novel'. With Kant and Hegel, I explicate what I call 'the sensory illusion of sense' in art. A philosophical reading of Murdoch's novel *The Black Prince*, by a philosopher who claims to be respecting her distinction between philosophy and literature, but nonetheless ends up claiming that literature is 'doing philosophy', is criticized. Then, Murdoch's own appreciation of Sartre's *La Nausée* as a good philosophical novel is discussed, and I describe both what kind of philosophical work I take this novel to do, by relating it to Stanley Cavell's notion of reasonable doubt, and what some of the limitations that come with doing philosophy in the form of fiction may be. Finally, Murdoch's novel *The Philosopher's Pupil* is described as a novel that is about philosophy and a philosopher, without being philosophical.

Chapter 3, 'The feel of muddled thinking: *Conceptual content in literature following Kant's aesthetics*', takes the discussion of Kant's aesthetics further, and asks what the non-conceptuality of the aesthetic judgement might mean in relation to literature, an art which obviously makes use of concepts. Murdoch's quarrel, and subsequent reconciliation, with Kant on this topic is touched upon, after which the chapter mainly follows Kant's arguments directly. Kantian notions like the intellectual interest in the beautiful, sublimity and aesthetic ideas are clarified. To exemplify how his notion of non-conceptuality might be understood in relation to literature, 'muddle' in Murdoch's fiction is described as an aesthetic idea.

Chapter 4, 'Real characters and fictional people: *Stanley Cavell and the epistemology of fiction*', asks: What is a fictional character? The chapter takes off from the contemporary postcritical debate about the status of fictional characters in literary studies and moves through the epistemological problem of fiction unto Stanley Cavell's usage of fiction to question the epistemological approach. With some support from Coleridge and Freud, I criticize Cavell's understanding of the character Othello as a 'literary fact' and his attempt to question the boundary between literature and philosophy. Our engagement with fictional characters is described as deep and meaningful, yet as different from our relations to actual people. At the end of the chapter, I discuss Murdoch's insistence on the difficulty of creating fictional characters.

The next and fifth chapter, 'Problems purged: *The consolations of tragedy*', asks: Why is tragedy not philosophy? Through Murdoch's Kantian notion of 'form' as a way to describe the differences between literature and philosophy, I approach the philosophical popularity of the genre. The fluctuations in Murdoch's own philosophical understanding of the concept of tragedy are also discussed. Aristotle's description of tragedy as a highly ordered art form then provides the means for a questioning of Martha Nussbaum's attempt to use the genre to question the distinction between literature and philosophy, in what I call Nussbaum's paradox of clarified muddle. Finally, I confront the genre with Socrates' description of philosophy as practising dying.

In the sixth chapter, 'Playing with fire: *The immorality of literature*', some lengthy attention is finally devoted to the Platonic origins of Murdoch's view of the distinction between literature and philosophy. This last chapter asks with Murdoch 'the not uninteresting question whether Plato may not have been in some ways right to be so suspicious of art'.[5] Some of the notions that have been central in the attempts of previous research to read Murdoch's fiction and view of art as philosophical and/or morally edifying are explicated as more ambiguous than meets the eye: attention, the distinction between fantasy and imagination, bad art and great art, and art as love. Finally, I provide my own interpretation of what Murdoch calls the 'unique truth-conveying potential of art', as something I with Murdoch, Kant and Freud conceptualize as 'sublime sublimation'.

It might indeed take a long time to explain what literature, the art form which uses words, is and does. Subsequently and somewhat unfortunately, this book spans over hundreds of pages. But, as Murdoch says, we all already know roughly what it is going to show. Despite the at times quite technical discussions that will follow, I invite the reader to hold onto her intuitive, general feeling for what literature is. Ordinary assumptions can be very useful in philosophy, especially in an age when the practice of this discipline has become more and more specialized and academized. It is those sophistic interpretations of the philosophical character of literature I seek to quarrel with; not the ordinary reader's experience of being entertained, immersed, confused, stimulated, disturbed, awed or pleased.[6]

Acknowledgements

Doing philosophy properly is impossible without dialogue. It has been my privilege to discuss everything in this book with my PhD supervisor Hugo Strandberg. Among many other things, he has shown me how fierceness and humility, historical knowledge and open-mindedness, dependence and originality, can and should coexist. Needless to add, any faults still left in this text are my own.

I am also grateful for my years at the Centre for Ethics as Study in Human Value, Pardubice University, Czech Republic. My PhD colleagues there have continuously inspired and provoked me with their quirky and diverging perspectives. A generous donation from the Sixten Gemzéus Foundation, for young Swedish scholars studying abroad, made my time there possible. Another donation from the Helge Ax:son Johnson Foundation provided the means for putting this book together after my graduation.

My thanks also to the philosophy department at Södertörn University College, for making me feel completely at home there as a visiting scholar and allowing me to linger there when the pandemic otherwise would have left me isolated. I am especially grateful to Ulrika Björk for giving me the kind of female empowerment and mentoring which is so unfortunately rare in academic philosophy. My friends and conversation partners in Stockholm, especially my pseudo-colleagues Mats Dahllöv and Anna Enström, have given me so much inspiration and support. I am especially thankful for our endless conversations about Kant and aesthetics.

I want to thank the Iris Murdoch Society for their encouragement of all kinds of scholarship on Murdoch, even by green and arrogant scholars such as I was at my first conference with them. The Iris Murdoch Library at Kingston University has also been very welcoming and helpful.

This book could not have been written without the support and encouragement I have received from people who do not agree with me. Here, I especially owe thanks to Niklas Forsberg, Nora Hämäläinen, Miles Leeson (who works tirelessly to connect scholars through the Iris Murdoch Society) and Rick Anthony Furtak, who was good enough to invite me to contribute to this book series on poetry and philosophy. I am also grateful to Suzie Nash, Alexander Bell and Lucy Harper at Bloomsbury Academic UK.

But most important for anyone doing anything is to have a place in the world to do it from. My deepest gratitude is to my friends and family. They have been astoundingly helpful with keeping both me and my work together. Especially Emil: without you there would have been no twins, no PhD and a much less evolved Lyra. Thank you for opening me to the passion in and beyond quarrels, both ancient and new.

Abbreviations

Iris Murdoch

AD	'Against Dryness'
AIN	'Art Is the Imitation of Nature'
FS	'The Fire and the Sun: Why Plato Banished the Artists'
LP	'Literature and Philosophy: A Conversation with Bryan Magee'
MGM	*Metaphysics as a Guide to Morals*
SG	'The Sublime and the Good'
SGO	'The Sovereignty of Good over Other Concepts'

Immanuel Kant

CJ	*Critique of the Power of Judgment*
CPR	*Critique of Pure Reason*

1

The ancient quarrel: *A background story*

1.1. Picking a fight

When I tell people outside of academia what my project is about, they are usually surprised. That literature is not philosophy? Well, does not everyone already know this? Why would you feel the need to research that?

They are right of course. Even what has been argued to be more dubious cases do not have us confused. When we go to the library to search for the novels by Fyodor Dostoevsky, Marcel Proust, J.M. Coetzee, Clarice Lispector or Iris Murdoch, we know where to look. We are also quite confident that Friedrich Nietzsche's *Thus Spoke Zarathustra* or Søren Kierkegaard's pseudonymous work can be found in another section than that of fiction, where Jean-Paul Sartre's and Simone de Beauvoir's theoretical works are also located; but we know to leave this section if we want to borrow the Existentialist novels, perhaps *Les Mandarins* or *La Nausée*. When poetry collections and novels are reviewed in newspapers and journals, we do not expect them to be judged by philosophers by merit of their truth-telling, conceptual accuracy or logical consistency (or whatever evaluative standard philosophy is expected to conform to these days). Likewise, no one goes to the defence of their philosophical dissertation dreading to be cross-examined on banal metaphors, unrelatable characters or stylistic clichés. In short, we seem to have no trouble keeping these disciplines apart in our ordinary and/or professional lives.

To the extent that this book may further anyone's understanding of why literature is not philosophy, it will then probably mainly strengthen and confirm what they already know. This does not seem to me to be a superfluous accomplishment. Although philosophy today often either, in the analytic context, seeks to provide an argumentative solution to a clearly defined problem; or, in the continental context, grapples with exegetical and hermeneutical issues in relation to a history of texts, I believe that simply attempting to grasp what we already know (or not know) is a good old philosophical practice. My aim is to provide an aesthetic description of literature as an art, and thus as distinct from philosophy.

When I tell people within academia, especially those who are working in philosophy and/or literary studies, that my book is subtitled 'Why Literature Is Not Philosophy', they are surprised in an entirely different manner. Some are annoyed; many feel provoked; a couple are piquantly amused. In comparative literature and philosophy, at least in continental departments, it seems to be a commonly held belief that it is more meaningful and fruitful to seek to dissolve the boundaries between the disciplines than to insist on keeping them apart. Why this should be so is a question I have grappled with throughout my PhD years. What do these people wish for or fear that they think could be attained or avoided by conflating literature with philosophy? Why do they so often assume that 'philosophical' would be a universal compliment to literature? And who are they, in their own efforts to describe that literature *is* philosophy or philosophical, so united against? Has the ancient quarrel today become so one-sided that it is hardly a quarrel anymore, merely a new dogma, stating that any attempt to insist on a distinction is reactionary, naïve and/or harmful, for literature as well as for philosophy?

If such a dogma exists, and it is my impression that it does, the purpose of this book is to challenge it. I believe that this dogma obscures many important characteristics of literature, under the fatal guise of seeking to elevate its status. Those who are provoked may thus be justified: I am indeed picking a fight.

In the chapters that follow, I seek to give a philosophical description of literature that enforces the distinction between philosophy and literature. I shall do so mainly by explicating Murdoch's view, with occasional recourse to other thinkers such as Kant, Plato and Stanley Cavell. Murdoch's perspective on art can somewhat reductively be described as a Neo-Platonist aestheticism, and it largely coincides with my own. In order to situate this approach before we get into the more detailed discussions of the following chapters, this introduction will offer an overview of some of the perspectives that have shaped the ancient quarrel, with a focus on those thinkers who have been important to Murdoch. This is not intended as a detailed genealogy, but as a general sketch of the background for her thinking and for the writing of this book. The quarrel that will be recapped is one-sided, in the sense that it only covers the philosophical understanding of literature, without attempting to see philosophy from the eyes of literature (whatever that would entail, since literature does not have views or theories in any comparable way).

Another and perhaps too obvious disclaimer: the discussions in focus in this book are not universal. They concern literature and philosophy as understood and practised in the Western tradition, from the backward-reaching perspective of today. Literature and philosophy are historical and cultural constructs. What defines those two categories has fluctuated a great deal over time and place, and still does. However, this does not make literature and philosophy completely relative, or ungeneralizable. I believe that many of the marvellous things that literature is and does can be better brought out by highlighting the distinction, rather than blurring the lines between the two disciplines. This is of course not to say that it would always be wrong to mix them up or that some traditions that do – outside of the post-Enlightenment, secular Judeo-Christian academic philosophy and fine arts, making no distinction between myth, philosophy and poetry – would be inferior. The literature and philosophy discussed in this book are, in an extremely broad sense, local phenomena, and so are the arguments concerning them.

I have chosen to order this chapter thematically rather than chronologically, to give the reader a feel for the wide variety of perspectives that may inform the philosophical distinction between literature and philosophy, instead of constructing an illusion of a linear development. Problems of metaphysics, historicity, psychology, technology, aesthetics, religion, freedom, power, economy and institutionality are intertwined with how the understanding of the relationship between philosophy and literature has shifted throughout the centuries. Some of these problems will simply be touched upon here, for the sake of indicating the manifold of different aspects that may play into the distinction; others will continue to arise throughout my text. The history of philosophy is internalized in every philosophical problem, but not necessarily chronologically so. As we shall see in the next section, the quarrel may even be said to begin with a questionable invention of its own origin.

1.2. The first stone: Socrates and Plato

Even if there among academics today may be a considerable consensus that the boundaries between the disciplines should be questioned, these scholars are nonetheless right to feel that they are working against a powerful resistance, inscribed in the very self-understanding of philosophy. Their original opponent is of course Plato, so foundational for Western thought that it is often said, quoting A.N. Whitehead, that '[t]he safest general characterization of the European philosophical tradition is that it consists of a series of footnotes to Plato.'[1]

More decisively and vigorously than perhaps anyone else, Plato (428–348 BC) insists that poetry is not philosophy. In his dialogues, he provides many good arguments for the untruthfulness and moral dubiousness of art, has Socrates (470–399 BC) question and ridicule poets and rhapsodes, and advocate for censorship as well as banishment of non-compliant poets from his ideal philosophical state. This does not arise out of any simple disdain. Even though Plato can at times be very harsh with the poets, Socrates' suggestion of banishment is in fact done with outmost politeness, even gushing friendliness:

> Now, as it seems, if a man who is able by wisdom to become every sort of thing and to imitate all things should come to our city, wishing to make a display of himself and his poems, we would fall on our knees before him as a man sacred, wonderful, and pleasing; but we would say that there is no such man among us in the city, nor is it lawful for such a man to be born there. We would send him to another city, with myrrh poured over his head and crowned with wool, while we ourselves would use a more austere and less pleasing poet and teller of tales for the sake of benefit, one who would imitate the style of the decent man and would say what he says in those models that we set down as laws at the beginning, when we undertook to educate the soldiers.[2]

As Murdoch says, his suggestion of censorship can indeed be seen as a compliment,[3] and a quite emphatic one at that. The power of poetry is hardly underestimated here. Plato, rumoured to himself have been an aspiring playwright in his youth, sees the poets as formidable rivals to philosophers. For the explicit purpose of not seeming to be too unwarrantedly harsh on them, he has Socrates refer to what he calls an ancient quarrel or old opposition between philosophy and poetry.[4] To not let this quarrel appear one-sided, Socrates cites a couple of denigrating comments on philosophy made by the poets, or at least in their plays, such as calling the philosophers 'great in the empty eloquence of fools'.[5]

However, whether this quarrel actually existed before Plato is uncertain. In fact, some scholars suggest that it seems more likely to have been invented by him, in order to further define and distinguish his new philosophical practice from the historical storytelling and entertaining theatre of his past and present. Andrea Wilson Nightingale sees the invention of the quarrel as a 'part of a bold rhetorical strategy designed to define philosophy and invest it with a near timeless status'.[6]

Glenn W. Most demonstrates in his article 'What Ancient Quarrel between Philosophy and Poetry?' that there is scant evidence of any philosophers attacking poetry as a whole before Plato, and even less of poets attacking philosophy or philosophers. The sources of the passages quoted by Socrates in the dialogue have not been identified, and so might as well have been made up by him. Nevertheless, Most analyses these in great detail, considering their meter and possible context. He concludes that the quotations are almost certainly not invented, but that they remain very obscure as proofs of a pre-existing quarrel, especially an ancient one. Most writes that

> there is nothing to prevent us from supposing that all four quotations derive not only from the same genre, Old Comedy, but also from the same author and even from the same text. For all we know, what we find in this passage of Plato's *Republic* might be four fragments of the lost first version of Aristophanes' *Clouds*.[7]

In Aristophanes' *Clouds*, Socrates is indeed satirized, in a way which provoked so much ill will that he thought it was pivotal for bringing up the charges against him that eventually resulted in his execution.[8] That there have been poets holding serious grudges against philosophers is undoubtable, even though 'philosophy' was not really a defined discourse before Plato. But Most concludes that 'Plato is generalizing so broadly from the evidence of poetry that he comes very close to a full-scale invention – without, however, quite getting there.'[9] Rhetorically, Plato reshapes a couple of more or less recent utterances from Old Comedy, perhaps only concerning one philosopher, into a generalized and long-standing opposition between 'poetry' and 'philosophy'.

Why does Plato feel the need to invent such a feud? As Martha Nussbaum states, he is not just inventing a quarrel, he is primarily inventing a genre: 'Before Plato's time there was no distinction between "philosophical" and "literary" discussion of human practical problems.'[10] Neither did Plato, in all probability, have access to any philosophical treatises in prose, such as the later writings of Aristotle. The poets were viewed by his contemporaries as 'philosophers', Nussbaum writes, 'if by this one means seekers for wisdom concerning important human matters'.[11] Socrates didn't write, because he was sceptical to the truth-conveying ability of text in general. As a philosopher, he did definitely not have a secure and established position in the city: he was ridiculed, accused of corrupting the youth and subsequently executed. After his death, Plato strove to establish a place for philosophy in society, partly by founding his Academy, and partly by producing texts. The genre he developed is shaped by Socrates' suspicion towards writing, in that their dialogical form demands an interactive interpretation, and does not present any straightforward accounts that seek to convince through beauty, rhetoric or entertainment. Nussbaum calls the genre 'a theater constructed to supplant tragedy as the paradigm of ethical teaching'.[12] She describes Plato's dialogues as unemotional versions of antique drama, designed to speak to the intellect alone, and (mistakenly in her view) rejecting poetic tragedy as philosophically relevant. Later in this book, I shall quarrel a bit with her understanding of tragedy.[13] For now, it suffices to say that there was indeed something new and threatening with what Socrates called philosophy, obviously not welcome in the city on the same terms as poetry.

In this light, Plato's reasons for 'inventing' the opposition to establish a new authoritative genre for seeking and testing wisdom start to make more sense. Philosophy, as he wants to define and pursue it, is for him evidently distinct from poetry. It does not really have an audience except for its participants, it does not take the form of plays that could compete and win laurels at the dramatic festivals, and so the insufficiencies of poetry as philosophy must be demonstrated to make the new form of writing, thinking and discussion appear legitimate. As Nightingale writes:

> To people in the fourth century BCE, the notion of a quarrel between philosophy and poetry would have probably appeared rather ludicrous – an unknown stripling brashly measuring himself against a venerable giant. Indeed, philosophy was no real match for poetry in this period. For, in Plato's day, poetry was addressed to large groups of people in a variety of oral/performative contexts, whereas philosophy reached a relatively tiny group of literate elites.[14]

The invention of the 'ancient quarrel' can thus be said to have been foundational for philosophy's self-understanding as a practice in its own right. Ironically enough, for us today, Plato's texts trouble us primarily with their literary character. We have come to expect philosophy – no matter how different it can be stylistically, taking the form of confessions, treatises or letters – to at least have an identifiable authoritative voice. But it is notoriously difficult to read Plato's dialogues doctrinally. What did he really mean? What are we to make of all the action, what is the philosophical import of the historical and spatial placing of the *Republic*, or the drunken commotion at the end of the *Symposium*? And is Socrates always right, is he Plato's mouthpiece? Murdoch has been accused of somewhat naïvely following the doctrinal reading of Plato of her time, in which what Socrates says is interpreted as the right opinions. Catherine Rowett speaks of 'her remarkable blindness to the question of how the author's views are to be extracted from a discussion between fictional characters in a dialogue'.[15] Indeed, Murdoch may at times be too hasty here, but there is also a risk for the philosophical problems to get dissolved into investigations of historical and/or textual accuracy in these discussions. As Debra Nails points out: whether Socrates actually is the voice of Plato or not may be irrelevant, since 'the truth is no truer when uttered by Socrates'.[16] Attention to form may become an evasion from doing the philosophical work ourselves: the important question is not 'what can Plato have meant' but 'how shall we live' or 'what is real'. With that said, such problems may of course also be enriched by closer attention to the structures of the dialogues, and I apologize in advance to the philologically minded reader for the – perhaps efficient, but at times careless – mix-ups between Plato and Socrates that this book has inherited from Murdoch.

Enough with the caveats. Since Western philosophy undoubtably has its roots in Plato (no matter if one wants to see this as simply a historical fact or regard the rest of the canon as mere footnotes), it has also, despite what can look like an overwhelming consensus to hold the poets in higher philosophical esteem, been unable to shake its foundation on his distinction between the disciplines entirely. Quarrelling with Plato's banishment of the poets has therefore often gone hand in hand with attempts to redefine his views of philosophy, wisdom and truth. I shall now continue my recap of the quarrel, by making a jump thousands of years ahead, and look at two philosophers who were self-declared fierce opponents to Plato's metaphysics.

1.3. Quarrelling with 'truth'

The ancient quarrel cannot even with the most generous of generalizations be described as a long-standing tournament between two self-identical opponents. At best, it can be reconstrued as a story between two interrelated shapeshifters. Refuting an earlier claim in the quarrel has usually meant attempting to redefine the forms and purposes of philosophy, literature, art and truth.

1.3.1. Friedrich Nietzsche

Two of the thinkers that might first come to mind here are Nietzsche and Heidegger. Both are easily identified as philosophers – they are taught in philosophy courses, and their books can be found in the philosophy section in the library[17] – but both argued, although in quite different ways, that Plato was wrong on art and truth, and that philosophy should move closer to poetry. Murdoch read both of them extensively, and even worked on a book on Heidegger towards the end of her life. She was impressed by the force of their thought, but critical to both, especially to their disregard for morality. As a self-declared Neo-Platonist, she implicitly and explicitly sought to absorb and counter their arguments, so a brief account of their views on the ancient quarrel will provide an important piece of the background to Murdoch's.

Plato's reasons for banishing the poets have not yet been discussed here – I shall return to this matter[18] – and are somewhat more complex than his critics at times make them appear. But let us follow Nietzsche's interpretation for a moment, in a brief summary of his contribution to the ancient quarrel.

Already in his first book, *The Birth of Tragedy*, Nietzsche positions himself explicitly against Plato's views of art and truth. Nietzsche accuses Socrates of an exaggerated rational optimism: that the ultimate and transcendent truth of life is not only knowable, but also good. Art, on the contrary, stays on the level of appearances, and is deceptive and immoral. In what Nietzsche sees as wishful thinking and life-denying metaphysics, Plato confuses virtue with understanding. Rather than being synonymous with the good, Nietzsche thinks that truth requires honesty and courage, since the search for it may lead to some quite ugly discoveries. In order to live with these horrid truths, we need the 'metaphysical consolation' of art. Nietzsche wants to reawaken our delight in existence, but he also thinks that the untruthfulness of art paradoxically can make it capable of a higher truthfulness: 'for all life is founded on appearance, art, illusion, optic, the necessity of perspectival and of error'.[19]

This prompts a rapprochement between philosophy and poetry. Nietzsche claims that the Socratic life-avoiding optimistic overvaluation of dialectical reasoning has eventually reduced poetry into an ancillary of philosophy, just like philosophy was in the middle ages to theology.[20] What Nietzsche will later suggest as the new centre focus is not philosophy as truth-seeking, but an understanding of life as a will to power, which is a creative pursuit. Thinking and artistic creation thus become one and the same. Especially in his later work, the proposed new relationship between poetry and philosophy is tied up with a new role and character of truth in life, which becomes more and more of an open question for Nietzsche.[21] In *On the Genealogy of Morality*, he even wants to call 'the *value* of truth' into question.[22] Is he thereby abandoning philosophy?

Nietzsche's own writing often borders on the poetic, aphoristic and novelistic, which can make him hard to interpret, and at times has called his position in the philosophical canon into question. Considering that his philosophical project is mounted against what he sees as an unbroken tradition of metaphysical speculation, it is not so strange that some have hesitated to locate his place in it.

1.3.2. Martin Heidegger

However anti-metaphysical Nietzsche takes himself to be, Martin Heidegger calls him the last metaphysician (which Derrida in turn has said of Heidegger). Heidegger sympathizes with Nietzsche's attempt to overturn Platonism but criticizes him for remaining stuck in the same logic. Flipping the Platonic logic into an overvaluation of the sensuous over the suprasensuous still presupposes some kind of metaphysical division of being, which Heidegger accuses Nietzsche of maintaining.[23] In Heidegger's own ontology, appearances and reality instead exist on the same level. Truth is not a matter of referential correctness but is brought out for us in events of *disclosure*. Hiddenness is also a part of true being, which makes 'truth' into a name for the strife between elucidation and concealment. According to Heidegger, this strife assumes *Gestalt* (structure) in the work of art, and this makes art prominently philosophically important.

Heidegger goes against (what may be argued to be an oversimplification of[24]) the Platonic view of mimesis and says that art does not merely produce a likeness. Instead, art is 'the reproduction of things' general essence'.[25] All art is '*in essence poetry*';[26] that is, the bringing forth of the being of things through language, which is a *founding* of truth rather than a reference to it. Without going in too deeply into his descriptions of how, it suffices for our purposes here to say that poetry remains closer to the thingness of things than philosophy. This is why Heidegger argues for a poetizing of philosophy. In the philosophical tradition of speculative metaphysics, abstraction transforms what it names and thus fails to capture the 'essence' of things which great art brings out.

Therefore, as David A. White puts it, 'thinking must remain near to poetizing in order to receive assistance in counteracting the representational biases inherent through the history of metaphysics'.[27]

However, claiming that philosophy must pay attention to the truth-disclosure of art is not, even to Heidegger, the same as confusing it with poetry. Even in the cases where the divide between the disciplines is crossed over, such as with 'Nietzsche who as a thinker is a poet, and with Hölderlin who as a poet is a thinker',[28] the divide is not thereby erased. Instead, Heidegger is interested in the relationship between the two, because '[b]y distinguishing thinking from poetizing, thinking steps out into its essence more sharply'.[29] He is also aware that this discussion becomes one-sided, since the thinking on the relationship is done through thinking rather than poetizing.[30] In White's words: 'it is thinking which will supervise the conversation between thinking and poetizing'.[31]

Indeed, even if Heidegger attempts to redefine poetry as another way of disclosing the truth, he does not aim to conflate the disciplines. Rather than arguing for seeing literature as philosophy, he advocates for a philosophical interest in poetry, and even for philosophy to make use of poetic means. White interprets him as saying that 'thinking needs poetry to be truly thoughtful, but poetry does not need thinking to be truly poetic'.[32]

Murdoch quarrels quite a bit with Heidegger's advocation for a poetization of philosophy in her unpublished manuscript on his work. She accuses him of having initiated the move away from ordinary, intelligible language into the kind of jargon that (post-)structuralist theory has made so unfortunately influential. At the same time, she acknowledges that philosophical works may also have the beauty of art without any loss to the quality of their thinking (naming the *Tractatus* and Plato's dialogues as examples[33]). Here, we may note that the question of whether philosophy may be seen as literature is a different one from why literature is not philosophy, and the former question shall remain largely unexplored in this book. Even though philosophical works may have literary qualities, they must also be something else. Murdoch implies, somewhat obscurely, what is at stake: 'There must be something in philosophical argument of which we are persuaded that it is in some sense "necessary". What sort of "necessity" this is is in itself a philosophical question. To put it so is to attempt to indicate how odd and almost impossibly difficult philosophy is.'[34] In what follows, I shall instead approach the problem of the ancient quarrel from the perspective of what it is about *literature* that is threatened to get lost or obscured if literature is seen as philosophy. If 'the art form which uses words' may also be truth-conveying, this generally happens in a more ambiguous and uncontrollable way than that of philosophy, something I will return to in the last chapter.

What do Nietzsche's and Heidegger's views on art and truth bring to the ancient quarrel? First of all, an illumination of how interconnected the attempt to redefine the relationship between poetry and philosophy is with Plato's founding of the self-understanding of Western philosophy as a metaphysical pursuit. Secondly, both their works show how difficult it is to wrestle a new philosophical practice out of this metaphysical logic, without just ending up with a negative image of it, and how the attempts to free oneself from referentiality and abstraction risk turning into mysticism, jargon and unintelligibility. Most importantly, their preoccupation with 'truth' reveals how narrow a philosophical revaluation of literature perhaps inevitably becomes: recognizing literature as meaningful or valuable is for Heidegger the same thing as seeing it as truth-disclosive, while for Nietzsche art reveals the untruthfulness of truth. As 'the last metaphysicians', they relocate the hitherto transcendent truth to happenings in our lives in appearances.

But what if literature was not discussed in terms of truth-telling? What if it was instead described as an art form with another standard of correctness than that of philosophy? Such an approach would make the problems of metaphysics irrelevant to the discussion of poetry. We shall now return to antiquity and look at someone who has often been called the first defender of poetry after Plato: his own pupil.

1.4. Aristotle's appreciation of poetry

1.4.1. The *Poetics*

Let us rewind the ancient quarrel a bit. In fact, let us go back all the way to 335 BC, when it is estimated that Aristotle's *Poetics* was written. This book, which to this day has remained the key text on dramaturgy and narration, is a series of lectures on the structure and interest of antique tragedy. A second half, on comedy, is believed to have been lost. Aristotle (384 BC–322 BC) was Plato's direct pupil in his Academy, and it is popularly assumed that the *Poetics* is written with the purpose to rebut Plato's scepticism against poetry. Thus, it is taken to be the prominent second step of the ancient quarrel and a powerful strike against Plato's wish to banish the poets from his ideal philosophical state.

However, the *Poetics* contains little that explicitly argues for the philosophical value of poetry. Neither are there any explicit references to Plato, so those who want to regard it as a direct rebuttal to Plato are required to do some exegetical work in order to 'bring out' such an argument from Aristotle's quite technical description of tragedy. What definitely separates him from his teacher is instead that Aristotle recognizes poetic excellency to have an intrinsic value, or at least that it should be judged on its own terms rather than those of what makes a good city, improves morals or develops a philosophical understanding. He writes that '[t]he criterion of correctness is not the same in poetry as in ethics, and not the same in poetry as in any other art'.[35]

But there are other quotes that keep recurring in discussions of Aristotle's place in the ancient quarrel, frequently called upon by those who want to claim that he sought to defend the philosophical value of poetry, such as that 'poetry is more philosophical and serious than history' and that there is a 'universal pleasure in imitations' because 'understanding is extremely pleasant'.[36] What are we to make of these?

It is difficult to enter into these scholarly debates without being a classical philologist, since what exactly might have been meant by the original Greek is not only dependent on mastering an ancient language from a long-lost society and discourse, but also on the fact that what we call Aristotle's text is not really Aristotle's, but an original that has been deductively reconstructed on the basis of a long history of transmission through potentially faulty copies and translations of his lecture notes into Latin and Arabic. Since many of these discussions tend to revolve around the interpretation of specific concepts, they cannot easily be countered without an understanding of ancient Greek and the entire history of transmissions of the text. For example, some scholars have argued that the so-called central concept of 'katharsis' is not even original to the text but a later insertion, and of questionable importance for the *Poetics* as a whole.[37] I am certainly unequipped to judge the veracity of such arguments.

Nonetheless, what exactly Aristotle wrote or not is perhaps less important for our present purposes than how his contribution to the ancient quarrel has been interpreted. Socrates says in the *Republic* that if someone was to have a good argument for why poetry is not only pleasant but also beneficial, he would 'listen benevolently'.[38] Stephen Halliwell opens his influential book *Aristotle's Poetics* with the speculation that this line might be a challenge from Plato to his young pupil Aristotle, who already when Plato wrote the *Republic* might have attempted to argue against his teacher's view of the art.[39] According to Halliwell, it was in 1986 (when his book was published) widely held that 'Aristotle's concern is only to show that there is a legitimate pleasure to be taken in poetry'. Halliwell instead seeks to explain how 'it has the moral and educational value which Plato seems to expect the true … defender of the art to claim for it'.[40] This appears now to have become, if not the received view, then at least a quite widespread interpretation of the *Poetics*.[41]

Without going into the moral and educational value of poetry yet,[42] and without claiming any exegetical expertise when it comes to Aristotle, I might at least suggest that this does not strike me as the main difference between his and Plato's view of poetry. Nor does Aristotle seem to take poetry more seriously or to appreciate it more. Socrates confesses to be a charmed admirer of Homer, and it is precisely because he considers the poet's work to be so powerful that he wants to ban it from the city.[43] The main difference between Plato and Aristotle is that Aristotle does not consider the poets to be *rivals* to the philosophers. He seeks to determine the criteria for poetry's own kind of excellence. The *Poetics* as a whole is a manual in how to write and judge good drama. That drama may be excellent by its own standards is not to say that poetry must be morally or intellectually educational; it is not even calling it beneficial.

But did we not just quote Aristotle as saying that 'poetry is more philosophical and serious than history'? Yes, and he follows this by explaining that this is because poetry 'tends to express universals, and history particulars'.[44] (As we shall see later, many who today argue for the moral philosophical value of literature instead stress how prose can make us attentive to 'particulars'.[45]) A universal for Aristotle is 'the kind of speech or action which is consonant with a person of a given kind in accordance with probability or necessity'; in other words, poetry shows us what might be expected to happen to someone like this in a situation like this, not what has happened to a specific person.[46] As Jonathan Lear remarks, 'it is tempting to read him as saying that poetry provides us with deeper insights into the human condition. This is a temptation which ought to be resisted.'[47] Rather than showing us a kind of human 'essence', Lear argues, Aristotle simply means that poetry proceeds from generalization, and thus 'has emerged from the mire of particularity in which history is trapped'.[48]

Some more attention will be given to Aristotle's account of tragedy in Section 5.3. For now, it suffices to say that he sees poetry as a separate art, requiring specific skills, and with its own standard of excellence. Focus lies not on how art creates good understanding or good morals, but on how great drama is constructed. His *Poetics* is a philosophical and technical description of poetry as poetry, and not an argument for the philosophical value of poetry. Whether or not this makes his account into an aesthetics remains a contested point, depending on how one defines what aesthetics is.

1.4.2. A historical note

Aesthetics is a Greek word, but, in contrast to metaphysics and ethics, the ancients did not consider it a field of inquiry in its own right. It is etymologically derived from *aisthetikos*, which means 'of or for perception by the senses'.[49] This is not what is meant by aesthetics today. Since the eighteenth century, aesthetics has been a name for the branch of philosophy interested in beauty, art, taste, genius and creative imagination. To call Plato's or Aristotle's writings on these subjects an aesthetics would be an anachronism, but that is not necessarily a problem. A more substantial hinder for any direct comparison with modern aesthetics is that Plato's philosophy of beauty is never connected to art, and Aristotle's writings on poetry concern more technical aspects, and are centred on the making of rather than reflections upon art.

But it might nonetheless be fair to say that the aesthetic approach to literature is foreshadowed by their work, perhaps especially by Aristotle's view of poetry as an art with its own standard of quality. The ancient quarrel enters into a new phase with the explicit separation of the purposes and forms of poetry from those of philosophy. In the eighteenth century, when the term 'aesthetics' is coined, the dominant tendency becomes to discuss literature together with the other 'fine arts' (also a relatively new concept at the time), as art in general becomes a separate focus for philosophical treatment. But just as with the 'arts', which for the ancients was a group name for everything from shipbuilding to medicine, what is meant by the terms 'philosophy' and 'poetry' has by the eighteenth century also undergone some considerable historical changes, in more tangible ways than just conceptually.

First of all, poetry for Plato and Aristotle did not mean written texts, it meant performed lines and lyrics. Tragedies were never studied in writing; they were enacted by a small number of male actors, partly sung, and watched at festivals by populous audiences. Rather than invoking disinterested aesthetic appreciation, they were entertaining and political, or at least a part of civic life. Poetry was always sung, often at the accompaniment of a lyre, and recited by rhapsodes. Homer did not hold a pen; he composed in his head. Texts existed to support the oral performances, and were not treated with any reverence, rather with distaste.[50]

What about philosophy then? Before Plato, we have only fragments of philosophical writings, and naturally no audio records of how philosophy was conducted orally. What we do know is that the distinctions between philosophy and other sciences, such as medicine, astronomy and politics, were largely irrelevant. Early philosophers, like Parmenides and Empedocles, used versification, and these didactic epics cannot be easily separated from poetry. Socrates did, as has been mentioned, not write.

Plato did, with explicit reservations against the written word. He did not invent the Socratic dialogues out of nothing – earlier prose dialogues by the minor Socratics Antisthenes and Aeschines exist – but he developed them into a new genre.[51] Perhaps more importantly, Plato founded an academy for philosophy that served as a centre for discussions and research for three centuries (from 387 to 386 BC). Here, his pupil Aristotle developed a new genre of philosophical text, but even though his writings are somewhat more similar to our academic articles, they were probably not intended for 'publication' (which would have entailed producing a few papyri rolls to be copied and passed forward by readers) but supposed to serve as lecture notes.

As I will get into quite soon in this chapter, a secular understanding of both literature and philosophy is also a relatively young phenomenon. In Plato's dialogues, the reservations against poetry are often explicitly religious ones. It is rather surprising, almost shocking, that Aristotle singles out this art from its religious and political functions, and thus, as Nickolas Pappas comments, 'positively sets the tone for later philosophies of art, especially modern ones, that cut art from its religious roots to examine, as it were, only half of the original organism'.[52]

This is merely to indicate some of the historical problems with regarding the ancient quarrel as a sustained, self-identical argument. 'Literature' and 'philosophy' are not ahistorical categories. Their respective inner developments are bound up with social, ideological and technological changes. But looking at the historical development of literature and philosophy does not just help us see how the disciplines have differed; it also shows how the writing of that history is shaped by what we now take literature and philosophy to be. An awareness of their transformations thus becomes an increased awareness of what we mean when we say 'literature' and 'philosophy' today.

We shall now continue on the route implied above, by introducing the dominant perspective for this book, which has been immensely influential for the philosophical understanding of art: aesthetics.

1.5. The aesthetic approach

1.5.1. Immanuel Kant

First off, it is important to note that Kant's aesthetics is not mainly a theory of art. True, after his long account of the beautiful and the sublime, he presents a taxonomy of the fine arts, describing, ranking and comparing them, but as he explicitly warns in a footnote: 'The reader will not judge of this outline for a possible division of the beautiful arts as if it were a deliberate theory. It is only one of the several experiments that still can and should be attempted.'[53] To put it otherwise, Kant's description of painting, music and poetry is an experimental sketch. What is to be read as an authoritative theory is instead that which made him turn to aesthetics in the first place: the strive to complete his description of the human mind.

My writing will allow a certain amount of switching between speaking of literature, poetry and art. I thereby follow Murdoch's way of discussing the distinction between literature and philosophy, where individual texts are less important than a general understanding of what characterizes (the literary) art. Murdoch's stance is very Kantian, in the sense that her thinking on art entails a metaphysical understanding of the aesthetic judgement as a certain state of mind. Even though she also quarrels a bit with Kant, his aesthetics is undeniably foundational for her distinction between the disciplines. It is therefore motivated to introduce his perspective properly here.

What does it mean to regard literature aesthetically as an art? What is so special about art? Kant was not so much fascinated by individual artworks as our capacity to experience and make judgements about beauty and sublimity in general. What kind of relation to the world and ourselves does this capacity entail? It is clearly very different from our rational understanding or moral freedom.

Aesthetics as a field of inquiry was opened up by Alexander Gottlieb Baumgarten's *Aesthetica* from 1735, where the Greek word aesthetics is first used for our appreciation of art instead of (as the Greek word originally means) our sensuous impressions. Baumgarten considers the artistic to be a specific kind of knowledge, a sensuous cognition. Important for Kant was also Edmund Burke's 1757 *A Philosophical Enquiry into the Origin of Our Ideas of the Sublime and the Beautiful*, which through a focus on the psychological and physiological aspects of this appreciation strives to find principles of material causation for our judgements of taste. However, Kant was critical to both, and for a long time he considered the endeavour to make aesthetics into any kind of lawful science futile.[54] He thought that our appreciations of beauty were based solely on subjective pleasures. Eventually, his decision to write a critique of taste comes as a response to a problem that needed to be tackled in order to complete his philosophical system.

The *Critique of the Power of Judgement*, also referred to as the third Critique, is published in 1790, when Immanuel Kant (1724–1804) is sixty-six years old. It follows the *Critique of Pure Reason* (1781) and the *Critique of Practical Reason* (1788), where Kant presents his metaphysics and moral philosophy respectively. Kant was not – it has been said – very interested in art. His Critiques were initially only intended to be two.

'Critical' for Kant concerns the boundaries for knowledge that reason can discover by reflecting upon its own limitations. In the first Critique, he performs his famous Copernican turn: that is, instead of looking to the world in order to understand it, looking to reason itself to see how it prescribes its own order to whatever appears to it. Reason is thus subjected to a transcendental criticism by Kant, or, in less grandiose words, put in its place. In the second Critique, a similar operation is performed in the field of morality. It is the absolute most fundamental conditions of our free will which concerns Kant here. He claims that we must postulate a freedom which goes beyond our inclinations and desires, since we have the capability for making completely disinterested moral choices.

There is, as Kant points out himself in the introduction to the third Critique, an insurmountable chasm between these two projects. How can the inescapable, determinate principles for our pure reason be understood together with our suprasensible free will? How can a world of causation be the same as a world of freedom? What makes experience into a whole? Kant finds himself in need of an even more basic foundation of our being in the world than what our pure reason and our free will can provide. There seems to be a reflective, *a priori* capability that contributes nothing to understanding and does not intend to change anything in the world, but which nonetheless tunes our consciousness to it. He discovers the paradigmatic case for this reflective capability in our judgement of beauty, and thus moves on to undertake a third critical project, this time concerning the aesthetic (and the teleological judgement, which the second half of the book is occupied with).

Kant is striving to identify the bottom line of beauty: its necessary, transcendental, critical conditions. Thus, he separates it from everything which makes it 'impure', such as emotion, conceptual understanding and moral interest. This makes his aesthetic philosophy very illuminating when it comes to identifying what is so special about art in general, but less useful for analysing individual artworks. There is also not very much about literary specificity to be found in the third Critique.[55]

For now, it suffices to conclude that literature for Kant differs from philosophy by being an art, and our appreciation of art is based on feeling, not thought. These feelings are however neither pathological (emotive) nor wilful to him, but disinterested and reflective. Briefly, we could say that reading a poem for Kant means that our mental faculties are put into a free, purposeless play which is pleasurable without being gratifying. Writing great poems is an inspired activity, where the inexplicable and unwilled originality of genius is combined with an education of taste and craft. Philosophy, on the other hand, or more specifically the transcendental criticism, is for Kant the deduction of the *a priori* principles for our cognition, will and judgement. There is thus no risk whatsoever of him ever confusing the two.

1.5.2. Georg Wilhelm Friedrich Hegel

Hegel (1770–1831), on the other hand, sees the literary art as the last outpost between the rest of the arts and philosophy. This does not mean that he considers literature to *be* philosophy: rather, he intuits in its similarity to philosophy an end to art. When poetry turns into speculative thinking, it stops being poetry, and becomes irrelevant as art. But this is not considered a loss. For Hegel, (simplifying him slightly) everything in the world is meant to lead up to philosophical understanding, or what he calls conceptual spiritual self-recognition. Together with all other human practices, such as the natural sciences, religion and social organization, art is thought of as a more primitive and material kind of what we might call the self-consciousness of consciousness. Philosophy is pure consciousness conceptually grasping itself *as* consciousness. Art, on the other hand, is spiritual self-recognition through sensuous materials.

This is not to say that Hegel disvalued art. In contrast to Kant, he was very interested in art, knew a great deal about the development of painting and sculpture, and was well versed in music and poetry alike. His aesthetics is not a transcendental critique, but takes the form of a history of art. From the pyramids to Goethe, he describes the development of the arts as a self-reflection that becomes progressively abstract. It is not a disinterested pleasure he is occupied with, or any specific kind of aesthetic judgement, but a historical development of spiritual self-understanding.

Hegel may on the surface appear to side against Plato in the ancient quarrel, since he judges all the arts on the merit of their spiritual self-reflection, and thus always has an eye on their philosophical value. But there is also a great deal of attention to artistic and literary specificity in his aesthetics that can aid an investigation into what differs literature from philosophy, which is why I shall return to him in the next chapter.

'Aesthetics' is a word that Hegel is quite ambivalent to. He prefers to use the term 'philosophy of art', which is also more accurate for his project. For him, art is spiritual self-recognition in and through the sensuous. If Kant takes little interest in the actual art object, Hegel pays close attention to many specific artworks and genres. His system of the individual art forms includes architecture, sculpture, painting, music and poetry. These forms are characterized by different mediums (i.e. sensuous materials), and different relationships between form and content. For example, architecture and sculpture are both very much related to physical space and directly perceptible forms, whereas the colours and sounds of painting and music are suggestive of more abstract, in themselves imperceptible, unities or extensions. (A symphony is not made up by the sounds, but their organization.) With poetry, this imaginative dimension of the work of art becomes its very medium. What we sensuously perceive is less important than what we imagine when we read. It is thus not primarily language which Hegel takes to be the medium of poetry, but imagination.

Poetry is the highest form of art for Hegel. It is the culmination of art's 'making itself independent of the mode of representation'.[56] Indeed, anything can be drawn into poetry and fashioned by it. It is much more independent of its sensuous manifestation than the other arts. Poetry can also be translated; a building cannot. As such, it approximates the dissolution of art, since this abstract inwardness threatens the unification of the sensory and the spiritual which defines art and brings it closer to both pictorial thinking, that for Hegel characterizes the religious, and the abstractions of philosophy.

He makes a clear distinction between poetry and prose, and by the latter he does not mean the novel form. The novel was not yet (Hegel held his lectures on art between 1818 and 1829) a very popular and widespread or, even less, esteemed literary art. Even though the genre of prose narratives had begun to develop a self-consciousness during the eighteenth century, it was the industrialization of printing which began in the 1820s that was to reshape the literary landscape and eventually make oral recitation of poems into an oddity and page-turners into the new standard. For Hegel, prose is not a name for a fine art.

In poetry (which includes epic, lyric and drama), the particulars (such as the individual words, or the verse form) are not separable from the topic but embodies it. As Hegel puts it, for it to be poetry, 'every part, every feature must be living and interesting on its own account'. It is art and must thus 'absolutely preserve the appearance of that lack of deliberation and that original freedom which art requires'.[57] (Here, Hegel echoes clearly of Kant.) Prose, on the other hand, is expressive of ordinary or scientific thinking. In ordinary thinking, everything is just expressed arbitrarily and contingently, without any inner organizing principle. In Hegel's words, the ordinary prosaic mind 'is content to take what is and happens as just this bare individual thing or event'.[58] In scientific prose, what Kant calls the determining judgement is operative. It aims at understanding, in the sense of sorting particulars under given universals or laws.

However, scientific prose is not what Hegel considers his own writing to be. Real philosophy is according to him better described as speculative thinking, which surpasses ordinary and scientific thinking and approximates poetry in that it considers the organic unity of the thing at hand. But it is still distinct from poetry for Hegel, in that its medium is not imagination but concepts:

> Thinking, however, results in thoughts alone; it evaporates the form of reality in the form of the pure Concept, and even if it grasps and apprehends real things in their particular character and real existence; it nevertheless lifts even this particular sphere into the element of the universal and ideal wherein alone thinking is at home with itself.[59]

In contrast, the subject matter of poetry is still something individualized, finite and sensuously manifested, even if only in an abstracted, imaginative way. This differs it from philosophy for Hegel, which aims at something more universal than particular human feelings and actions and seeks to be the self-consciousness of spirit itself. And so, even if Hegel looks to art in order to find the seeds of speculative thinking, his aesthetics contain very detailed descriptions of what differs art from philosophy. His definition of art as sensuous spiritual self-recognition introduces an ineradicable difference between the disciplines, which many might be tempted to overlook with such an indirectly sensuous art as literature.[60]

1.5.3. A further note on German Idealism

To conclude: if Kant's aesthetics describes our relation to art as pertaining to a different state of mind than that of understanding or will, Hegel develops this into a specific kind of historical progression of self-reflection. But they both see art as separate and distinct kinds of object and activities, and they provide us with rich accounts of an aesthetic appreciation which clearly differs from philosophical understanding. For Kant, art is such a separate thing from the transcendental criticism of philosophy that he barely comments upon how poetry can contribute to our thinking. They are not in any way considered to be rival disciplines. Indeed, precisely because they are not, he finds in the aesthetic a different mode of cognition which allows him to bridge the insurmountable chasm between necessity and freedom that his two first *Critiques* have left him with. For Hegel, the quarrel is more closely at hand, since he sees the formation of the arts as a preliminary stage of philosophical reflection. Yet, art in itself is not and cannot be philosophy. This perspective eventually brings him to pronounce art to be a thing of the past, something we can enjoy for entertainment and diversion, but the importance of which now pales in comparison to the latest (i.e. his own) development in speculative thinking.

However, characteristic to both Hegel and Kant is a way of looking at art as something with its own and specific kind of excellence; as autonomous in the sense that individual works should be judged as art, and not as proto-philosophy, moral lessons or illustrations of thoughts. This is the aesthetic perspective that dominates Murdoch's view of literature, and which I intend to stay with throughout the arguments that will develop in this book. But the autonomous perspective is not the only kind of aesthetic philosophy, not even among Hegel's direct peers. A further note on German Idealism is needed in order not to leave the account of this part of the ancient quarrel too conspicuously incomplete.

In the 'Oldest System Programme of German Idealism', written in Hegel's handwriting but believed to have been authored or co-authored by Schelling and/or Hölderlin, a desire for a greater unification of understanding than that which rational thought can accomplish is proclaimed. What this manifesto-like paper seeks to unify is both all free men and all Ideas. Philosophy must utilize mythology to unite the enlightened and the unenlightened and strive for a total and therefore also sensuous grasp of the world. In this short document, probably written around 1796 when the three thinkers mentioned above were students together, the distinction between literature and philosophy is proposed to be dissolved in the name of an idealistic aesthetic rationality: 'The philosopher must possess just as much aesthetic power as the poet [Dichter].'[61]

German Idealism contains more complex and nuanced descriptions of how this might be achieved, especially in the writings of Schelling. Schelling insists that philosophy must include the productive activity of nature in its account of our ability to think, and therefore questions the subject/object distinction. To put it extremely briefly, this is how art becomes 'the organ of philosophy' for Schelling. Whereas philosophy's self-reflection on thinking lacks an external object, 'the production in art is directed outwards, in order to reflect the unconscious through products'.[62] Schelling thus, in contrast to Hegel, sees an insufficiency in conceptual philosophy in comparison to art.[63] Through the partly unconscious activity of genius, art goes beyond what the finite intellect can represent to itself. Poetry reaches higher than philosophy, in that its insights are incarnate, particular and actual.

This is close to Hegel's (somewhat later) description of poetry. But Schelling's contribution to the ancient quarrel can be described as the inversion of Hegel's, in that Hegel sees the freeing of conceptual thinking from material restraints as beneficial, whereas Schelling seeks to undermine the sole authority of conceptual philosophy with the sensuously particular actuality of poetry. But later Schelling eventually loses interest in art as a manifestation of the absolute, since he increasingly begins to think that any creation by finite spirits (like men) is merely finite, and only God is capable of revealing himself.[64] Here, the totalizing mythological thinking of the early System Programme is echoed in his mature thought, but now pessimistically rather than with naïve optimism. Philosophical metaphysics as well as his own metaphysics of art appears incurably insufficient in the light of a transcendent absolute (God).

Schelling is mentioned here not because of any particular importance for Murdoch, but because his early perspective on the ancient quarrel is perhaps one of the most distinction-resistant, and because he has been foundational for some of the thinkers in this chapter, primarily Heidegger and Kierkegaard. In his early as well as his later philosophy, Schelling has been a precursor for several modern anti-metaphysical and/or religious philosophers. By stressing the unconscious, and regarding the sensuousness and particularity of art as a beneficial challenge to philosophy, Schelling's proto-Romantic position in the ancient quarrel challenges the Enlightenment's more authoritative taxonomies and paves the way for many of the following approaches to the ancient quarrel. In the next section, the attentive reader may find some echoes of his challenging philosophy through poetry, and his view of both as lamentably finite in relation to God, in the writings of Kierkegaard.

1.6. A higher purpose

1.6.1. The religious background

Introducing God into the mix might to a secular philosopher seem like a strange move, but as was mentioned before, the ancient quarrel was from the beginning very much a religious issue. Socrates' strict suggestions of censorship in the *Republic* arise out of concern for how the poets portray the gods, and what effect this has on the spiritual and moral development of the citizens. Should the poets really be allowed to portray the gods as jealous, mourning or hysterical with laughter? What kind of spiritual corruption might follow from this?[65]

Compared with the aesthetic perspective, the religious (and in what will follow, Christian) approach to the ancient quarrel may look like an instrumentalization of poetry and philosophy alike. Both are to be judged in the light of a higher purpose. But for a believer, the matter is more complicated than that – God is never an external issue – which also makes the entire history of the distinction between literature and philosophy into a more complex triangular affair. Western thought has been dominated by Christian theology for thousands of years, and almost everything we know about the ancients has been sifted through the knowledge and interpretations of Muslim scholars and Christian monks in the Middle Ages. Neither philosophy nor literature as we understand them today is thinkable without the Scripture; the communication, study and publication of which have literally created the literary culture we live in.

The Middle Ages are often skipped over in discussions of the ancient quarrel – the usual approach is, like in the beginning of this chapter, to go straight from Plato to Nietzsche. Historical overviews are rare. But one notable such is Thomas Barfield's *The Ancient Quarrel between Philosophy and Poetry*, which extensively covers the thoughts of Plotinus, Augustine, Varro, Boethius, Dionysius the Areopagite and Thomas Aquinas, before moving on to the moderns. At stake for many of these religious thinkers is the relationship of poetry to sin, worship and the truth beyond the finite human intellect. The role of language in faith and the textual and pictorial religious arts is also crucial here, as well as how the general populace is influenced by the entertaining arts. Generally, we find among the theologians much more agreement with Plato's banishment of the poets than in later writings. As Barfield writes about Augustine, he 'thinks we should "award the palm" … to Plato, who would not tolerate the corrupting influence of the poets on the citizens and who threw the poets out as the root cause of the problem.'[66] The beauty of the arts is an ambiguous problem, and philosophy is often called upon to keep poetry in check. Barfield writes: 'The poets are hedged in at this point – exiled from the Republic, accused of serving demons by Augustine, limited to the philosopher's Muse by Boethius: and so through the Middle

Ages the voice delivering divine wisdom will have to be a voice other than the poet's.'[67] But poetry can nonetheless be justified, if taken as a spark of beauty rather than the voice of reason, awakening our love and wonder – if, as Barfield says with Thomas Aquinas, we recognize that 'the poets do not speak for God'.[68]

That there is no ethical and/or religious standard of veracity for the frivolousness of the arts and that they are, as a whole, thus untrustworthy, is a perspective that echoes in almost every later agreement (partial or not) with Plato's banishment of the poets. Murdoch, though secular, inherits this perspective from Plato of course, but also from two Christian thinkers who she read widely and deeply throughout her life, namely Søren Kierkegaard and Simone Weil.

1.6.2. Søren Kierkegaard

Kierkegaard (1813–55) is a difficult thinker to characterize, perhaps especially in the light of the ancient quarrel. He was a philosopher who wrote pseudonymous, fictitious, ironic texts, with the ultimate purpose of demonstrating how hard it is to be a true Christian. In his work, literary and philosophical methods are simultaneously utilized and parodied, and he has his alias Johannes Climacus ending his *Concluding Unscientific Postscript* by stating that anyone who invokes this book as an authority has thereby misunderstood it.

Kierkegaard's texts are constructed as indirect communication, creating a double reflection through which the reader is meant to go against his or her own understanding in order to perceive some of the absurd paradoxes that may be religiously enlightening. This is Kierkegaard's way to escape an instrumentalizing dogmatism, since instrumental dogmatism is precisely that which in his view leads to a falsely self-reliant Christianity. But there is still a purpose here. His aim is not to state a quotable truth, but to invoke a subjective process in the reader by confronting him or her with unresolvable paradoxes. And so, one might say that it is the very untrustworthiness of poetry that is activated philosophically by Kierkegaard in order to reveal the insufficiencies of philosophy and poetry alike.

Much more could be mentioned about the 'literary' aspects of Kierkegaard's writing – the pseudonyms, the irony and the paratexts – but I shall refrain from going into that complex ongoing debate here.[69] Nonetheless, a few more words on Kierkegaard's radically existentialist Christianity are necessary to bring out his peculiar perspective on the ancient quarrel. In contrast to Saint Augustine, who relies upon the distinction between poetry and philosophy to keep the former in check, Kierkegaard intentionally dissolves the distinction in his own work in order to rob the reader of any other authority than that of divine grace. The best philosophy can do when it comes to metaphysics is, according to him, the Socratic confession of ignorance. For Kierkegaard, being a Christian means believing that true understanding is something deeper than understanding alone can achieve. As he has Anti-Climacus state in 'The Sickness unto Death': 'Does this mean, then, that to understand and to understand are two different things? They certainly are, and the person who has understood this – but, please note, not in the sense of the first kind of understanding – is *eo ipso* initiated into all the secrets of irony.'[70]

Where the philosopher is at risk of overestimating his own profundity, the poet is playing a dangerous game of relativizing profundity as such. Kierkegaard's famous tripartite division of the stages on life's way throws a certain light of this distinction: the esthetic, the ethic and the religious. The esthetic is described in 'The Seducer's Diary' as a kind of self-centred doubling of life: to 'personally enjo[y] the esthetic' and to 'esthetically enjo[y] [one's] personality'.[71] We may already intuit from this how useful poetry can be to expose the illusory self-sufficiency of philosophy. A self-consciously ironic poetization of philosophical discourse, as the one Kierkegaard himself employs, can break up the authority of the philosophical and make negative room for the sole truth of God. Faith is absurd and can never be construed logically. Thinking and writing is very little compared to the act of accepting God's forgiveness.

Some of his pseudonyms call themselves poets. We are not meant to take this as an instruction to read them only for pleasure – but as a warning for taking their word as gospel. Poetry and philosophy alike are utilized to become superfluous. As Kierkegaard writes under his own name in 'On My Work as an Author': 'Christianly, one does not proceed from the simple in order then to become interesting, witty, profound, a poet, a philosopher, etc. No, it is just the opposite; here one begins and then becomes more and more simple, arrives at the simple.'[72]

1.6.3. Simone Weil

The focus in this part of the chapter lies on two Christian thinkers with philosophical backgrounds and rich literary educations, who are both very important to Murdoch. They are alike in that they both advocate for a strictly anti-dogmatic, almost apophatic Christianity. In other respects, however, they differ significantly from each other. Kierkegaard was brought up Danish Puritanical Protestant; Simone Weil (1909–43) was from a secular Jewish-French family and later became a Catholic mystic. Weil's thinking has had a profound impact on Murdoch, an influence that has been treated extensively in earlier scholarship.[73] She will be brought up again several times in this book. The following passages will situate Weil in the ancient quarrel at large, raise some flags regarding the reception of her work and describe her view of literature.

First: the flags. Most of Weil's religious writings were not published during her lifetime. One of the most popular volumes today, *Le pesanteur et la grâce* (*Gravity and Grace*), is in fact not written by Weil herself, but compiled out of selected and rearranged quotes from her notebooks by her friend the Catholic philosopher and writer Gustave Thibon. *Le pesanteur et la grâce* is an aphoristic and exclusively Christian book, and it gives a somewhat misleading impression of Weil's thought. The notebooks it has been assembled from have been published later, and they contain a much richer and ambiguous theological account, with Hindu, Buddhist and ancient Greek faith being of almost equal importance to the Gospels. The notebooks also consist of more or less chaotic fragments in development, and the presentation of these as aphorisms grouped together under thematic headlines can give the misleading impression of a systematic Christian thinker providing semi-poetic sentences for meditation. Even in academic work, *Le pesanteur et la grâce* is often quoted as a direct source, and since much of the scholarship on Weil is Christian in nature, a kind of confessional white-washing of this eclectic, multi-interested theological philosopher who declined to be baptized has indeed continued to take place since her death.

Another dominant perspective that has skewed the reception of Weil is an exaggerated reliance on biographical information. Her biography is indeed captivating: she was a brilliant co-student of Jean-Paul Sartre and Simone de Beauvoir at Sorbonne, became involved with the worker's movement, took a year-long leave from her job as a philosophy teacher to take up work in the factories to share the conditions of the working class, clumsily attempted to participate in the Spanish Civil War, experienced a mystical conversion, fled from France together with her family as Jewish refugees during the war, starved herself in sympathy with the soldiers at the front even though she suffered from tuberculosis, which eventually led to her dying of cardiac arrest, only thirty-four years old.[74] Weil is often seen as someone who voluntarily took the suffering of the world upon herself, and although it might to some extent be true, it also gives an unfortunate character of hagiography to much of the research on her work. The dazzling storytelling of her saintly (or, as some non-believers have characterized it, insufferably masochistic) life streamlines the philosophy of an intensely self-critical and continuously evolving aesthetical and political thinker, into that of a Catholic spokesperson.

It is however undoubtably true that all of Weil's later work is thoroughly shaped by a Neo-Platonic Christian conviction. This is also the case regarding her view of literature and philosophy. Unfashionably enough for someone who studied alongside the Existentialists, Weil is not afraid of appearing moralistic. Fiction is for her dubious in itself, since it entails a reversal between the good and the bad. The good becomes boring and the bad becomes interesting.[75] Immorality is thus so inseparable from literature that it would be wrong to reproach writers for being immoral, if one would not at the same time also reproach them for being writers. Weil writes:

> On that account, one could condemn all literature *en bloc*. And why not? Writers and readers for their part will passionately cry out that immorality is not an aesthetic criterion. But here they need to prove, which they have never done, that one should apply only aesthetic criteria to literature.[76]

Still, Weil devotes some considerable attention to the revelatory power of literature. She makes a sharp distinction between works of genius and the rest (echoed in Murdoch's somewhat more generous and blurry division of good and bad art). Her Platonic reinterpretation of Kant contributes with a remarkably original perspective in the ancient quarrel, in which art becomes aesthetic, erotic and epiphanic at the same time.

Weil maintains Kant's formalistic description of beauty as a purposiveness without a purpose (finality without an end in the older translation) and a disinterested pleasure. But she sees this tension between absence (of purpose) and presence (of completion) as a revelation. In artworks of genius, the transcendent final end shines through:

> All human creations are adjustments of means in view of determinate ends, except the work of art, in which there is adjustment of means, where obviously there is

completion, but where one cannot conceive of an end. In a sense the end is nothing but the very arrangement, the assembling itself of the means employed; in another sense the end is completely transcendent.[77]

Thus, she makes theological metaphysics out of Kant's aesthetics. 'We always look upon aesthetics as a special branch of study,' she writes in her notebooks, 'whereas it is actually the key to supernatural truths.'[78]

Beauty is also understood by Weil in terms of the ladder in Plato's *Symposium*, where sensuous beauty leads the soul towards the superior and transcendent beauty of truth. But for Weil, this progressive revelation never really leaves the ground. Patrick Sherry notes that Weil 'does not seem to manifest Plato's anxiety to mount from the bottom rungs of the ladder of beauty to transcendent beauty as quickly as possible.'[79] In Weil's thought, we are never liberated from mortality and carnality. Suffering and desire play a part in the experience of beauty, as it brings about a kind of splitting of consciousness, in that our finite and corporeal existence is contrasted with a purposeless beauty.

The ability to create this kind of beauty cannot be compelled. Those writers who are not geniuses only create immoral fantasies, which may seem fascinating, but do not bring about the splitting of consciousness that only true beauty can. Genius is a divine grace. 'To seek a remedy for the immorality of letters is an entirely vain enterprise. Genius is the only remedy, and accessing the source of genius is not within the reach of our efforts.'[80] Yet, Weil also seeks to describe the kind of endeavour that may bring great art about: 'That poem is good which one writes while keeping the attention orientated toward the inexpressible, *qua* inexpressible.'[81]

Philosophy, on the other hand, is not seeking beauty but truth.[82] In contrast, literature is desire-driven, partly unconscious and in pursuit of beauty. It is only accidentally truth-conveying and usually way too immoral, since it so unrestrictedly is concerned with fantasies. Only in rare instances may it direct our love towards that which is without any fathomable end.

In explaining the desire-driven part of this, Weil makes a Platonic reversal of Freud. 'Freud's doctrine would have been absolutely true,' she writes, 'if he would not have viewed the most base in our sexuality as the grand cause.' We love God with our carnal eros: 'We haven't anything else with which to love.'[83] Mad, immoral and occasionally divine, the artist attempts to reorientate his sexual energy towards beauty. This is not a sublimation for Weil, but the true direction of our eros. It is precisely because it cannot be willed that it may constitute a revelation.

One might sum up the perspective on the ancient quarrel that is implicitly or explicitly expressed by religious thinkers, also more modern ones like Kierkegaard and Weil, as a mistrust in the omnipotence of reason and/or will. Poetry may help us towards insight just because it is *not* philosophy; it can break up our rigidified self-knowledge and make it possible to experience the paradoxes of transcendent love. But it is an uncontrollable and ambiguous force and might as well make us immoral and falsely convinced as enlightened.

As modernity develops, literature as a distortion of ordinary discourse becomes an increasingly popular idea. Formal experimentations and the breaking of conventions start to be regarded as important artistic qualities. This reflects and develops a general view of literature as able to express something other than what can be said with the voice of didactic reason. Central for this development is the psychoanalytic tripartite division of man's consciousness. The analysis of ideology in Marxist and post-Marxist thinking also sets a new standard for interpreting art, where disruptive qualities are valued as important challenges to a false consciousness. In the section below, I have somewhat roughly grouped together three thinkers who I believe are important for framing Murdoch's place in the ancient quarrel: Freud, Sartre and Adorno. They are very different, but their views of literature can all be understood in terms of expressing the suppressed.

1.7. Expressing the suppressed

1.7.1. Sigmund Freud

When Plato suggests that the inspired poet, like the lover, reaches his great heights through his madness, he plants a seed in the quarrel that is not to fully blossom until more than two thousand years later.[84] The connection between these two otherwise so different thinkers is indeed explicitly indicated by the latter. The Austrian neurologist Sigmund Freud (1856–39) claims to be developing 'the Eros of the divine Plato' in his analyses of the sexual psychopathology of ordinary and extraordinary consciousness, known as psychoanalysis.[85] If Plato has Socrates ask the poet in the *Ion*: aren't you a madman? Freud's counter would be: Well, if we look closely enough, who isn't? In fact, the marvellously semi-intentional activity known as poetic writing can perhaps teach us a great deal about the delusional fantasies we all live by, as well as their libidinal origins.

Even though it is no exaggeration to say that Freud's theories have revolutionized the humanities, he was a clinical practitioner rather than a philosopher. Endlessly intellectually curious, he nonetheless sought to understand man for the purpose of improving his health, on an individual as well as a cultural level. This makes his contribution to the ancient quarrel rather angled, if not to say restricted. Take beauty for example, which somewhat mysteriously brings happiness to mankind. Freud is not really interested in analysing what characterizes it, or what kind of relation it has to our understanding of the world. Even when he speaks of aesthetic matters, he is not philosophically interested in them. Freud dismisses aesthetics as an unsuccessful science hiding behind high-sounding, empty verbiage, but admits that: 'Unfortunately psychoanalysis too has scarcely anything to say about beauty.'[86] There is no use for beauty, but it seems evident that it has something to do with sexual desire, he notes; and then rapidly provides a concluding musing over the curious fact that the genitals themselves, although arousing, are rarely considered beautiful.

No matter how philosophically interesting his theories may be, it is important to note that Freud himself does not operate as a philosopher. As Lionel Trilling puts it, his concern is to help the patient, not to train him in metaphysics or epistemology, and so the distinction he draws between reality and illusion is the one which practically leads to a liveable life.[87] This perspective would have troubled Plato, who thought that the lower parts of the soul did not merit much attention, and that truth became more accessible if these were left to wither.[88] But if most of the philosophers in this quarrel are approaching literature from the bias of truth-seeking, Freud is shifting the conversation by approaching literature and philosophy alike from the bias of cause and cure. What lies behind these human activities? Do the productions of these texts help, or do they cover over something that more urgently needs our attention? Are they distorted expressions of more fundamental drives? The famous theory of art as sublimation of unacceptable fantasies suggests that art may, just as Plato feared, be the privileged outlet for things that a decent man should learn to suppress.[89] Freud is however less concerned with decency, truth and goodness; he is occupied with curing neurosis.

He applies a similar perspective on philosophy. As Jonathan Lear puts it, some of Freud's case studies indicate how 'philosophical reflection can be used as a defense, blocking the self-understanding it purports to deliver'.[90] However, there is an important distinction to note here: that kind of philosophy might easily be categorized as somewhat flawed, whereas a 'discovery' of sublimated desires in the poet does not render his poems any less brilliant. A poet may well be a madman; the philosopher should, following Freud's positivistic view, be more like a scientist.

I shall have reason to come back to Freud's understanding of creative writing, with its basis in fantasies, day-dreams and sexual desire, and so these paragraphs are mainly intended to situate him in the ancient quarrel.[91] Perhaps one could say that it is precisely as a non-philosopher that he brings such a decisive new philosophical perspective on literature. Even though Schelling, as we saw, also sees art as closer to the unconscious than philosophy, he values and describes it in relation to what kind of truth it brings. Freud does no such thing, which has led some to say that he has a contempt for art. From a critical perspective, it might be true that Freud has no 'adequate conception of what an artistic meaning is', as Trilling complains.[92] Hamlet might be interpreted in the light of the Oedipal complex: if we think with Freud that this analysis completes our understanding of the play, we miss what Trilling calls its 'artistic meaning'.[93] But art does not just present a meaning. It is also extremely pleasant, even when it is about horrible things, something that fascinated Freud endlessly.

Freud picks up on Plato's complaints that the poets indulge the lower parts of our soul – but in contrast to Plato, he studies rather than judges their art for this. His essay 'Creative Writers and Day-dreaming' sets out to 'discover in ourselves or in people like ourselves an activity which [is] in some way akin to creative writing.'[94] As paradigmatic texts for this purpose, he takes not literary classics but popular hero-stories and romances. If it was not already difficult for the serious poet to feel addressed here, it gets even more so when he compares these stories to children's play and day-dreams. Imagining oneself as the hero, in an easily sortable world of good and evil, is a central aspect of all these human activities, Freud suggests.

This escapist quality might be more pronounced in pulp fiction, but similar characteristics are not hard to find in critically esteemed works either. Literature can be pleasant by providing a way to deal with that which social life offers no outlet for. Thus, it may show us what men suppress in their daily lives. It is no coincidence that Freud has taken the names for some of his most central concepts, such as the Oedipus complex, from Greek tragedies. The dramas that are played out in great works of art express the dramas we play out in our lives. And so, even though art might not teach us about a higher truth, it can – with some help from the psychoanalytical interpretation – show us a lot about what it is to be human.

Murdoch read Freud extensively.[95] When she combines Plato's harshness against art with a more tolerant humanism, it echoes clearly of Freud. Men are flawed, they have shameful desires and they live most of their lives in fantasies. Is not that also interesting? Cannot art be appreciated as a place where veracity and critical self-reflection are not the guiding principles, but where we instead may find some harmless enjoyment?[96] But as the study of literature becomes less of a bourgeois pastime, and more of an academic job, enjoyment seems to have become more difficult to defend as a primary characteristic of the art. Instead, a regrettable consequence of Freud's influence has been that many literary scholars began approaching works of fiction almost like case studies, as if the real meaning of the work was its hidden neuroses. Literature is of course very psychologically interesting, and 'artistic meaning' is not an unambiguous concept;[97] but I also doubt that a novel is made justice by being treated as a patient awaiting diagnosis.

1.7.2. A brief Marxist bridge

This hermeneutics of suspicion, as Paul Ricœur has named it, or the practice of digging out disguised meanings from a text, dominates literary analysis during the first half of the twentieth century. It develops out of primarily two influential new ways of thinking: psychoanalysis and Marxism. If one has read nothing but the tombstone of Karl Marx (1818–83), one already knows that he brought a critical, new perspective on philosophy: 'The philosophers have only *interpreted* the world in various ways; the point is to *change* it.'[98]

I shall not discuss Marx here,[99] merely squeeze him in as an unpassable bridge between two thinkers that are important to Murdoch. Except for a brief interest in communism in her youth (which later made it impossible for her to gain a visa to the States, something she much regretted), Murdoch never really held Marxism in high esteem.[100] But some of the thinkers she engaged most deeply with, such as Simone Weil and Jean-Paul Sartre, certainly did, and his influence on the understanding of the relationship between literature and philosophy during the twentieth century can hardly be overrated. As Marx transformed philosophy from within, into a critical endeavour to understand and change the exploitation and oppression that formed the economic basis for that thinking itself, many wanted to bring a similar kind of political self-consciousness to literature. In what remains of this section, we shall look at two very different ways of doing that: Sartre's and Adorno's.

1.7.3. Jean-Paul Sartre

Jean-Paul Sartre (1905–80), in dialogue with primarily Simone de Beauvoir, Maurice Merleau-Ponty and Albert Camus, developed what was to become famous as French *Existentialism*.[101] Murdoch wrote the first English monograph on Sartre when she was in her early thirties, and although her admiration for him was packed with critical reservations already in her youth, he remained very important for her thought, not in the least on the distinction between literature and philosophy. The Existentialists were central propagators of the term 'philosophical novel', and thus reinvigorated the ancient quarrel with the explicit idea of seeing the two disciplines if not merged, then at least as having the same aims; right before Murdoch felt pressed to argue the opposite.[102]

The liberational Existentialist view of literature is heavily influenced by Marxism, psychoanalysis and Heideggerian ontology.[103] It sees the literary work as activating a peculiar kind of authentic consciousness. Existentialism promotes what may be called an anti-metaphysical metaphysics: it is rejecting metaphysics in the sense of a truth preceding existence that could be grasped by pure understanding, but regards the self-consciousness of man as a fundamental condition of being. Sartre thus prefers to speak of ontology instead of metaphysics, but Simone de Beauvoir talks about 'the metaphysical attitude, which consists in positing oneself in one's totality before the totality of the world'.[104] To bring out the self-consciousness of our unavoidable freedom, in having to choose our actions and our worldview, is the ultimate aim of literature and philosophy alike. This revelation is often anxiety-inducing, since it entails facing the absurd contingency of existence, because there is nothing to guide us except our own choices.

However, man is not an isolated solitary will for the Existentialists. He exists in specific historical situations, where power structures often seek to deny him his self-conscious freedom. Bad faith occasions our cooperation in these because it is more comfortable to avoid facing the absurdity of existence. Thus, there is no purely metaphysical problem; it is always a political problem too. This becomes more pronounced for the Existentialists after the Second World War. The occupation of Paris confronts them with the reality of political force, indeed violence, at a very close angle. What is the point of literature and philosophy in times like these? Sartre, de Beauvoir and Merleau-Ponty start the journal *Les Temps Modernes* in October 1945. This is where the notion of engaged literature, *littérature engagé*, gets articulated.

In Sartre's introduction to the first issue of *Les Temps*, he rallies against the self-concerned, world-ignorant middle-class writers who think they can write about life, society and even themselves without recognizing their political responsibility. Faced with the current crisis in Europe, literature suddenly appears to be a frivolous luxury, a pointless activity to be ashamed of. So Sartre writes:

> We do not want to be ashamed of writing and we don't feel like writing so as not to say anything. Moreover, even if we wanted to we would not be able to: no one can. Every text possesses a meaning, even if that meaning is far removed from the one the author dreamed of inserting into it. For us, an author ... is 'implicated,' whatever he does – tainted, compromised, even in his most distant retreat.[105]

Both philosophy and literature count here as engaged literature. But the Existentialists nonetheless differ between their novels and their theoretical work. Both are concerned with experiences, but fiction is more about mimicking experiences than analysing them. As Simone de Beauvoir writes: 'While the philosopher and the essayist give the reader an intellectual reconstruction of their experience, the novelist claims to reconstitute on an imaginary plane this experience itself as it appears prior to any elucidation.'[106]

A very realistic, if not naturalistic, ideal for prose writing follows from this view. Sartre indeed affirmed in his *What Is Literature?* (1948) that he would not dream of regarding poetry as engaged literature. Poetry is the alienation of language as a sign-system; it turns the material of ordinary speech into objects of sounds and moods. Prose, on the other hand, is more like speaking. It is human interaction with the world. By naming things, the writer changes our consciousness of them, and thus changes our behaviour:

> If you name the behavior of an individual, you reveal it to him; he sees himself. And since you are at the same time naming it to all others, he knows that he is seen at the moment he sees himself. The furtive gesture which he forgot while making it, begins to exist beyond all measure, to exist for everybody; it is integrated into the objective mind; it takes on new dimensions; it is retrieved. After that, how can you expect him to act in the same way?[107]

It is very clear here that the existentialist philosophical novel is not supposed to bring a disinterested pleasure. It is meant to mimic our behaviour in reality and change our actions by disclosing them for us. Sartre's description of what is known as 'transparent prose', immersive story-telling in which the language becomes invisible, draws our attention to how novels inevitably rework our perception and interaction with the world.[108] Later post-Marxist aesthetics, such as that of Rancière and Adorno, tend instead to stress the opposite: it is only the kind of art which challenges our naturalized perceptions that entail a politically potent resistance to our habitual and ideology-infused modes of being.

1.7.4. Theodor W. Adorno

We shall only briefly look at Adorno's highly complex aesthetic theory here. As one of the central instigators of critical theory, Adorno is perhaps more famous for his criticism of the capitalist culture industry than his aesthetic theory, which was published posthumously. Nonetheless, Adorno is a notable heir of Schelling, Hegel and (perhaps especially) Kant, and attempts to reconcile some of their characterizations of art with a post-Marxist critique of society. The influence of Adorno's work on Murdoch's ethical and aesthetic philosophy has, at least to my knowledge, never been investigated, but we know that she read him quite thoroughly and with (a sometimes reserved) admiration. The sparse references to him in her work are enough to make one suspect that he had a greater impact on her than is usually acknowledged, or even mentioned. In her book on Sartre, for example, she contrasts Sartre's optimistic faith in the reason and agency of the individual with the pessimistic attitude to reason and the primacy of the object in Adorno's thought. Adorno 'pictures knowledge as an attentive truthful patience with the contingent', she writes.[109] Although Murdoch expresses irritation with Adorno's unnecessarily specified terminology, her view of attention and contingency is clearly not simply Weilian in nature but has also been informed by his negative dialectics.

To call Adorno a pessimist is perhaps not completely accurate. In *Negative Dialectics*, he speaks of using 'the strength of the subject to break through the fallacy of constitutive subjectivity'.[110] This roughly means that even though our subjectivity has been constituted by the historic productive forces of capitalism, there are ways to shatter this rigidified apparent rationality by critical reflection. Art offers one of the most privileged ways of doing this, which does not mean that art would be intentionally political or 'engaged' for Adorno. Instead, the more disinterested and aimless art is, the more it is free of the interests and aims that usurps everything into the dominant ideology. It is precisely by not presenting theses or making rational claims that art can be a powerful reminder to philosophy not to trust its own rationality. Even though art is in this sense free, or autonomous, it is bound up with society through this autonomy: it has a designated place that renders it harmless. But in this historically determined role, it can also allow us to glimpse something of the non-identical that is lodged within the hegemonic discourse. To put it bluntly, it is only by being pointless that art has a point for Adorno.

Literature is in a sense particularly interesting and ambiguous here, since its medium is language. In the *Dialectic of Enlightenment*, co-written with Max Horkheimer, language is described as a central part of man's illusory rational control over nature; illusory since it makes man a slave under precisely the system he has erected for his liberation. Stewart Martin describes this role of language well:

> Here language is understood to emerge from the primal attempt to overcome fear by controlling it through a unified system of representation, in which shock and its attendant sense of powerlessness are converted into power through knowledge of what caused that shock; a knowledge which will thereby defend the subject from future shocks. The emergence of language is hereby associated intrinsically with the constitution of rationality and subjectivity as an attempt to control nature through its representation.[111]

In *Aesthetic Theory*, Adorno develops the liberational potential of art within this logic. Instead of speaking the controlling language of Enlightenment reason, art intentionally gives up its own intentionality, and instead of controlling what it names, it seeks to bring otherness into the act of naming. 'With human means art wants to realize the language of what is not human', Adorno says.[112] Thus, he is less interested in the kind of transparent prose that Sartre privileged, and tends instead to speak of art's truth content as emerging from the point where language most evidently fails us:

> If the language of nature is mute, art seeks to make this muteness eloquent; art thus exposes itself to failure through the insurmountable contradiction between the idea of making the mute eloquent, which demands a desperate effort, and the idea of what this effort would amount to, the idea of what cannot in any way be willed.[113]

This entails a privileging of absurd literature, such as the plays by Beckett, since 'it is precisely the so-called literature of the absurd ... that proves that understanding, meaning and content are not equivalents'.[114] In terms of the ancient quarrel, then, literature is of interest to philosophy precisely to the extent that it is not philosophy (intentional critical self-reflection) but art.

The perspectives introduced by the thinkers in this part – Freud, Marx, Sartre and Adorno – might seem new to the ancient quarrel, but questions like: How should we live? What is a healthy consciousness? and How should society be organized? were already inimical to Plato's treatment of the problem in *The Republic*. What is new is rather a certain *mistrust* – of society, of the individual's self-knowledge and of rationality itself – which introduces novel kinds of oppositions and interrelations between philosophy and literature. By not being philosophy, and instead more like fantasies, lived experiences and/or unintentionally created objects, art is in various ways looked upon as capable of expressing the suppressed and of liberating man's consciousness from inauthenticity. But if literature has this ability, why should not philosophy be more like literature? If rational discourse is somehow inauthentic, would it not be better if the philosopher spoke with the same kind of enigmaticalness and creativity as the poet, creating disruption rather than reasserting a falsely stable meaning? We seem to have paved the way for an introduction of Murdoch's nemesis: Jacques Derrida.

1.8. The influence of deconstruction

1.8.1. Jacques Derrida

As the title of this section indicates, my main concern here is not Jacques Derrida (1930–2004) himself, but his influence on the ancient quarrel. More or less perverted versions of his thought have had a profound impact, especially on literary studies, and might even be said to be the origin of the currently widespread notion that it would somehow be wrong or even harmful to make a firm distinction between literature and philosophy. Murdoch also poses some of her perspectives on literature in explicit opposition against what she takes to be the Derridean view. Whether she gives a just characterization of his thought or simply attacks a straw man has been the target of some scholarly grumbling.[115] I shall not get into detail regarding the validity of her offhand dismissal of Derrida here, only say a couple of words on what position in the ancient quarrel she takes him to occupy.

When it comes to literature, Murdoch's main accusation (and perhaps also the main source of her annoyance) is that deconstruction (as Derrida's philosophy and its following is often called) has brought about a lamentable critical-elitist focus on language to the detriment of more 'ordinary' engagements with fiction. This removes the humanist aspects of reading – 'treating a tale as a "window into another world", reacting to characters as if they were real people' – because 'the ideal deconstructionist is more like a scientist who shows that things are *absolutely not* what they seem (they really are made of atoms)'.[116] To admire or to care for a novel and its characters, to be caught up by its story, and to find that it mirrors something in life, is something the deconstructionists have delegated to the naïve laymen. Instead, they see literature 'as a network of meanings esteemed for its liveliness, originality, ability to disturb'.[117] They are specialized professionals, scientists. The literature that gets written to impress them and their own critical analyses of it (which now seem to have become the main artworks) is obscure, difficult and 'provides the consoling feeling of having a special private expertise'.[118]

Murdoch's criticism is evidently sweeping – she unhesitantly groups together 'post-structuralism, deconstruction, modernism, postmodernism'[119] – but it is not completely unfounded. What she seeks to describe is an attitude in the Zeitgeist that threatens to turn literature and the study of it into a dry and pseudoscientific discipline for professionals, while ordinary enjoyment of fiction is dismissed as naïve. The origins of this threat can indeed be traced in Derrida. For example, he says in an interview: 'I must confess that deep down I have probably never drawn great enjoyment from fiction, from reading novels, for example, beyond the pleasure taken in analyzing the play of writing, or else certain naive movements of identification.'[120] The analysis is the real feast; almost the only thing of importance.

But this gives no more than a caricature of what Derrida actually thought about the relationship between literature and philosophy. Primarily, he (informed by Heidegger) argues that Plato's invention of the ancient quarrel creates an artificial separation between poetry and philosophy, where the concept of mimesis establishes a false inferiority for art. 'It is in the name of truth, its only reference – reference itself – that mimesis is judged, proscribed or prescribed according to a regular alternation', he writes.[121] This, in Derrida's view, also means that these two disciplines remain determined by each other: by casting literature as frivolous, emotional and caught up in appearances, philosophy gives itself a misleading air of being concerned with transcendent truths. This binary hierarchy is dependent on a constructed opposition, in which the seemingly opposite poles in fact constitute each other.[122] In contrast to Nietzsche and Heidegger, however, Derrida does not think that this metaphysical logic can be escaped so easily: turning to poetry as if it was philosophy will not help us. We must instead deconstruct what gives rise to the seeming metaphysical foundation of the distinction.

This is an ethical project, bound up with a more general dominant logic: 'the hierarchically ordered opposition between the intelligible and the sensible: between mind and body, idea and manifestation, signified and signifier, content and form, male and female, and so on', as Leslie Hill puts it.[123] Derrida's influence on social and political theory is thus concurrent with his position in the ancient quarrel, and can be summed up as an insistence to dismantle rather than overthrow hierarchical binaries. He foreshadows, for example, Judith Butler's famous critique of the presupposed binarity of gender in *Gender Trouble*, when he says that 'feminist discourse risks reproducing very crudely the very thing which it purports to be criticizing'.[124]

In other words, deconstruction is driven by an imperative to do justice, and this also goes for literature and philosophy. For Derrida, doing justice here entails a number of things, such as understanding how literature and philosophy are arbitrary and historical categories, removing the 'naïve belief in meaning or referent',[125] suspending the transcendent reading, discovering how meaning is constituted by discourse rather than the other way around, and not being deceived by logocentrism (the notion that a present truth is lost or perverted by being turned into writing). In the light of this, insisting on a distinction between literature and philosophy appears to be a stupid defence of false metaphysical essences. The main inheritance of Derrida in the ancient quarrel is to engender literature and philosophy alike with a suspicion against themselves as definable disciplines.

1.8.2. Postcritique

After the hermeneutics of suspicion was followed by Derrida's massive popularity, the eagerness to dissolve any apparently stable or natural meanings has become the norm in literary studies. Ironically, what was proposed as an ever-moving questioning of the validity of rigid methodological thinking has itself rigidified into an established method: 'deconstruction' has become a method to pick for your paper, a recognizable dissection of the word-play of a text that predictably shatters any naïve perception of its apparent 'meaning'. I am speaking of this as if this is the currently dominant trend – in fact, it is more and more becoming the hegemony of the past. If Derrida grew up under the Existentialists and questioned how Sartre in *What Is Literature?* could assume that there is a given object for that question, a 'what' of literature;[126] today's scholars have grown up under the influence of the anti-naïve critical attitude of deconstruction, and they question it in various ways.

In literary studies, there is a (for a philosopher) slightly incomprehensible general approach referred to as 'theory'. Theory encompasses everything from New Criticism to the Frankfurt School, deconstruction and New Materialism, and it can perhaps be summed up as an approach to the meaning of a literary work as discursively constituted, as well as a self-critical awareness of the bias inherent in the act of analysis. Rita Felski, professor of English, describes it thus: 'Theory simply is the process of reflecting on the underlying frameworks, principles, and assumptions that shape our individual acts of interpretation.'[127] Felski is one of the main proponents of a new, influential movement in not just literary studies but the humanities in general, known as postcritique. Postcritique questions the hegemonic authority of theory: 'We are called on to adopt poses of analytical detachment, critical vigilance, guarded suspicion; humanities scholars suffer from a terminal case of irony, driven by the uncontrollable urge to put everything in scare quotes.'[128] Felski (in line with other scholars such as Toril Moi, Christopher Castiglia and Elizabeth S. Anker) instead proposes 'to risk alternate forms of aesthetic engagement',[129] which may entail 'to lay oneself open to charges of naïveté, boosterism, or metaphysical thinking'.[130]

This is an obviously anti-Derridean posturing, which seeks to defend precisely that which he dismissed as unscholarly. In their recent book *Character: Three Inquiries in Literary Studies*, Felski, Moi and Amanda Anderson 'consider the taboo on treating characters as if they were real people, what it means to identify with characters, and the experience of thinking with characters'.[131] A distinctly Murdochian echo can be heard here, and her critique of the overemphasis on choice and action in morality is indeed discussed in Andersons essay. Considering this, and the fact that Moi has worked extensively on Murdoch as well, it is somewhat surprising that they name Alex Woloch's book *The One vs. the Many* (2003) as 'one of the first to recognize that the taboo on "treating characters as if they were real people" placed undesirable restrictions on literary critics'.[132] One might even suspect the proponents of postcritique of constructing an intentionally shallow history in order to launch their thoughts as part of a new and fresh movement.[133]

If so, this approach has been very successful. Postcritique has in itself become a 'method', where affective aspects such as enchantment and shock (both titles for two chapters from Felski's *Uses of Literature*) are described, investigated and appreciated, instead of deconstructed away. It has had a great impact on the interpretive humanities, such as literary studies and art history, but has not attracted as much attention in philosophy. Since this book takes its guidance from Murdoch, it does not have any direct link to postcritique, but some kind of affinity in approach, occasioned by a common Zeitgeist, can perhaps be discerned. I share the postcritical view that the value of literature is not best determined or brought out by critical suspicion, and that the 'naïve' approach of taking the work at face value might be more fruitful and just. What this book does not share with the postcritical approach is, however, a defence of literature as a form of knowledge.[134]

1.8.3. Artistic research

The view of literature as knowledge is more forcefully expressed in the new field of artistic research, and its subgenre research in creative writing. In contrast to postcritique, artistic research can be said to affirm theory by practising it as indistinguishable from art. It is very difficult to generalize about artistic research, since it has no established tradition, no standard of veracity, a very short history and is usually enmeshed in the artist's/scholar's individual artistic practice. This boundlessness is often highlighted by its proponents as a strength, and as bringing a productive challenge to the clearer scientific standards of other kinds of research. The much-criticized traditional separations of subjective and objective, practice and theory, artwork and interpretation, are sublated in artistic research, in an approach that has been described as a return to the holistic multi-disciplinary practices of the Renaissance.[135]

Artistic research began to be established as an internationally institutionalized education roughly around the turn of the millennium – but practical research in design is older than that, creative writing slightly younger, and the time of origin for PhD programmes has varied greatly across the world. Although these programmes have provided funding for the work of many artists, as well as job opportunities as teachers for earlier graduates, there is a certain unclarity about what differs these scholarly projects from the art made outside of academia. A similar perspective might apply to philosophy as well – who is to say that you cannot think, and perhaps even think better, if you are not employed as a philosopher? – especially since philosophy has a tradition of incorporating into its canon works that were written outside of academic institutions. Nonetheless, philosophy has a long history, and it is usually quite easy to see whether someone approaches certain problems informed by it or not, even if they write as enigmatically as Wittgenstein or as poetically as Nietzsche. To put it differently, philosophy has a standard (or several standards) of verification; art has its historical standards of quality, originality, or taste as well; even though both of these traditions may be hard to pin down and are continuously shifting. But what about artistic research?

A much-quoted definition of artistic research is given by Henk Borgdorff:

> Art practice qualifies as research when its purpose is to broaden our knowledge and understanding through an original investigation. It begins with questions that are pertinent to the research context and the art world, and employs methods that are appropriate to the study. The process and outcomes of the research are appropriately documented and disseminated to the research community and to the wider public.[136]

Whether the wider public ever has displayed any interest in artistic research remains highly doubtful, but that is perhaps beside the point. Borgdorff's formula is created as a distillment of institutional guidelines and is meant to define the difference between art and artistic research. The first sentence is, I think, the most interesting. Artistic research has a *purpose*, which is to *broaden* our knowledge. Attributing art production with a purpose is a very controversial move, especially since it is an institutionalized purpose (and not the result of a personal conviction) tied to the distribution of funding. But this is not, the proponents of artistic research explain, in any way *restrictive*. The metaphorical language effectively covers over the instrumentalization of art. After all, how could a broadening be limiting?

Artistic research is not to be understood as *governed* by any standard of research – rather, it is described as revolutionizing our idea of knowledge from within. In the introduction to *The Routledge Companion to Research in the Arts*, Helga Nowotny talks about how 'the space of possibilities – and the human imaginative capacity to open them up – is vast, if not infinite; and ... more and more means and instruments, mostly but not entirely scientific and technical, are at our disposal to expand the space of imagination'.[137] There is productive uncertainty in all kinds of knowledge production, she notes. 'Artistic practices, just like scientific practices, will thereby widen the scope of research, with the enormous potential to enrich all fields of research.'[138] Borgdorff similarly speaks of 'a fundamental openness for the unknown, the unexpected, which can also form a corrective to what is currently regarded as valid research'.[139] Through a rhetoric littered by contemporary value-words like creativity, widening, expansion, cross-fertilization, imagination, originality, subversion, critique and, yes, research, this new scholarly field is described as bringing a boundless indeterminacy to knowledge – a deliberately unclear standard and purpose. This institutionalized artistic practice seems to have become precisely the jargon-ridden professionalized pseudo-science Murdoch feared would follow in the surges of deconstruction, where an ordinary enjoyment of art becomes disdained as naïve and art is instead 'esteemed for its liveliness, originality, ability to disturb' which obscurely contributes to an ungraspable production of knowledge.[140]

Although something might occasionally be gained from the blurring of boundaries between theory and practice, and some interesting works may of course also be produced under the name of artistic research, I believe that there are several reasons to be suspicious. Besides my gut feeling that the pseudo-scientific approach dulls and deadens the (literary) artwork by restricting its accessibility to a specialized elite, and that the 'creative' method for theorizing might mean a non-disciplined flow of difficult verbiage,[141] there are several ways to argue that the removal of disciplinary distinctions risks undermining art and philosophy alike. From an Adornian perspective, artistic research could be criticized as an attempt to divest art of its power to be pointless, and instead institutionalize it under the hegemonic parameters of knowledge-production. From a Freudian perspective, the unconscious need for expression of suppressed desires that fuels artistic inspiration might be suspended by the demand to make every step of the artistic production self-conscious through the parallel writing of a dissertation. From a Platonic perspective, practising research in and through art risks eroding the vigorous reality-testing of philosophy and instead makes us content with an apparent achievement of understanding. From the very simplest Murdochian perspective, turning art into a scholarly production of knowledge might make us end up forgetting how enjoyable, social and fun art is, and how very difficult philosophy is. 'One might say that bad philosophy is not philosophy, whereas bad art is still art.'[142]

1.9. Continental and analytic: The contemporary divide

In the previous section, we saw how the influence of deconstruction has given rise to two notable contemporary positions in the ancient quarrel: postcritique and artistic research. However, since the former is mainly a trend in literary studies and entails a certain kind of defence of a separation between literature and theory, and the latter is a development within the arts, and proposes a blurring of the boundaries between art practice and scholarly work, it still remains to be said what the main current philosophical perspectives on the distinction between literature and philosophy are, and how Murdoch's view relates to these.

Philosophy today, since the early twentieth century, is divided into two traditions: continental and analytic. Continental philosophy is sometimes known as phenomenology (although it usually encompasses much more than the inheritance from Husserl) and analytic philosophy is sometimes referred to as the Anglophone tradition (although not everything in English is analytic philosophy, and not all analytic philosophy is written in English). There are no clear demarcation lines between the two, and some might even argue that nothing does or should keep them apart; but a trained eye can quite easily sort a piece of writing into one or the other of the discourses. Any description of the divide is of course the product of gross generalizations, but in order to move on towards an overview of the present state of the quarrel, let me nonetheless name a couple of characteristics.

There are stylistic differences: continental philosophy tends to be more essayistic, and analytic philosophy is more argumentatively construed. There are different canons and different ways of relating to the canon: continental philosophy is more rooted in German Idealism, phenomenology, post-Marxism and/or psychoanalysis, and it tends to reach further back, tracing exegetical inheritances and historical developments of thought from Plato onwards; whereas analytic philosophy has its roots mainly in linguistic analysis, utilitarianism and logic, and it is often more centred around specific problems, detaching them somewhat from their historical contexts. Analytic philosophy is divided into several subfields, whereas continental philosophy tends to treat problems of, say, metaphysics, aesthetics, language and politics as intertwined. Most important for my purposes, analytic and continental philosophy have traditionally very different relationships to literature. Continental philosophy is closer to fiction and poetry both stylistically, methodologically and institutionally (in that it is more read outside of academia and often put into dialogue with literature), whereas analytic philosophy is more obviously a completely different kind of text. Analytic philosophy is far, far bigger (and richer, at least monetarily), especially but not exclusively in the English-speaking world.

It would here also be appropriate to situate my own approach. I did my graduate and postgraduate studies in aesthetics at two different continental institutions (in Sweden and the UK), and this book is written while I am doing my PhD at a centre for ethics in the Czech Republic that is refusing to sort itself into either tradition (and has therefore been labelled 'analytic' by some visiting continental scholars, as well 'continental' by analytic scholars). Iris Murdoch, my main guide, studied and worked within a very analytic milieu in Oxford and Cambridge, but had an unusually deep interest in both the continental canon and the contemporary debates on the continent. She began a doctoral dissertation on Husserl at Cambridge, which she eventually abandoned. She was a Fellow at St. Anne's, Oxford, from 1948 until 1963, and later taught at the Royal College of Art until 1967. She read French fluently and German well enough. Her thought was mainly shaped by Plato, Kant, Wittgenstein, Existentialist philosophy (primarily Kierkegaard, Heidegger and Sartre) and Simone Weil, although many of her arguments were explicitly made in reaction to the analytic debates surrounding her. Her philosophical writing is often essayistic in style, although she claims to prefer an argumentative and impersonal tone. She is remarkably difficult to sort into any of two traditional categories of philosophy. Scholarship on her work thus has the potential to address both, but may also risk falling short of the internal standards of either: the exegetical carefulness of one, or the argumentative clarity of the other.

Many have objected to the divide between analytic and continental philosophy, and attempts have been made, especially from the analytic side, to conduct a rapprochement. These thinkers are often, as was Murdoch, inspired by Wittgenstein.[143] Stanley Cavell (1926-2018) explicitly states that he wants to 'write as though these paths had never divided'.[144] Cora Diamond (1937-), another post-Wittgensteinian, describes Cavell and Murdoch as 'speaking my language in that they are analytic philosophers, but they are also very deeply outside analytic philosophy ... It's that sort of being inside and outside analytic philosophy which I think is so important for the way I try to do philosophy'.[145] Martha Nussbaum (1947-) criticizes what she refers to as the Anglo-American tradition for assuming that 'the ethical text should, in the process of inquiry, converse with the intellect alone; it should not make its appeal to the emotions, feelings, and sensory responses'.[146] All of these three thinkers are, in different ways, propagating a turn to literature in order to widen the scope and methods of philosophical thinking.[147] They are (or in the case of Cavell, were) educated and employed by analytic departments; their claims for the philosophical value of literature arise out of an analytic tradition, where the distinction between literature and philosophy is taken for granted. In contemporary continental philosophy, a similar claim would not raise any eyebrows since it is generally (especially after Heidegger and Derrida) held that philosophy benefits from keeping close company with creative writing.

And yet, as Murdoch's thought (and hopefully this book) will show, the continental canon offers plenty of foothold for a firmer distinction between the disciplines. Primarily by reading Plato's banishment of the poets in conjunction with Kantian aesthetics, a wide range of characteristics that make it difficult, misguided and unfruitful to read literature as philosophy or philosophical shall be brought out. I believe that I am contradicting a general trend in making these arguments, in continental philosophy as well as in that kind of (often post-Wittgensteinian) analytic philosophy that works in opposition to its own tradition; even though, as this introductory chapter has shown, the ancient quarrel was neither then nor now a consistent struggle between two unchanging opponents.

We have now reached the end of the introductory chapter and its historical overview of the ancient quarrel. My purpose has been to situate Murdoch's perspective, and I have thus neglected to bring up several other important contributions to the quarrel at large.[148] All of the thinkers mentioned in this chapter could also have been given a much more thorough treatment. But his has been but a prelude, a background for the show that shall follow. Iris Murdoch may seem like its lead character, but the main star is her life companion: the beautiful, muddled, morally dubious, fantastical, shameless, consoling, accidentally educational and erotic character of literature.

2

What is (not) a philosophical novel?
The sensory illusion of sense

2.1. Introducing Iris Murdoch's distinction between philosophy and literature

2.1.1. Mocking poetry

Philosophy, says Iris Murdoch, is in general 'witty rather than funny',[1] whereas the artist is more free to joke around. So, even though this method may eventually grant literature the upper hand, examining the jokes philosophy and literature make about each other could give us a good preliminary sense of their differences as well as their point of contact. After all, making fun of someone is usually as much a case of separating yourself from them as it is an act of paying close attention and wanting to provoke a reaction.

The quarrel between philosophy and literature was referred to as ancient already by Plato, but it has been argued that this opposition was invented by him to establish the seriousness of his own philosophical pursuits.[2] If Plato did indeed throw the first stone, the quarrel can be said to begin with a mocking.

In the early dialogue *Ion*, the rhapsode with the same name is thoroughly questioned (i.e. made fun of) by Socrates, who claims that he wants to find out what the pretty Ion is actually skilled at. He is obviously good at dressing up in nice clothing and capturing the attention of his audience – but what kind of understanding does he convey to them when he recites and talks about Homer? In *The Fire and the Sun: Why Plato Banished the Artists* Murdoch sums up the exchange as follows:

> Ion lays claim to knowledge, but is dismayed when Socrates asks him what Homeric matters he is expert on. What, for instance, does he know about medicine, or sailing or weaving or chariot racing, all of which Homer describes? Ion is forced to admit that here doctors, sailors, weavers, and charioteers are the best judges of Homer's adequacy. Is there then any Homeric subject on which Ion is really an expert? With unspeakable charm Ion at last says yes, generalship, though he has not actually tried it of course: a conclusion which Socrates does not pursue beyond the length of a little sarcasm.[3]

The person under attack here is the rhapsode, but the poet himself is later going to receive a more respectful, but no less harsh, version of the same treatment in the *Republic*. In any case, '[t]he question is raised ... of whether or how artists and their critics need to possess genuine expert knowledge'.[4] Here Murdoch steps into the dialogue herself and suggests, 'Ion, looking for something to be expert on, might more fruitfully have answered: a general knowledge of human life.'[5]

The pathetic Ion, who would no doubt have made a disastrous general, is at the end of the dialogue asked by Socrates to choose 'how you wish us to consider you: as a wrongdoer or as divine'?[6] (Guess which one he picks.) Murdoch, however, wants us to consider that the rhapsode might in fact be a completely different *kind* of expert, and not just the scoundrel Plato takes him as. Making his audience weep and laugh, even magnetically drawing them out of their senses, he is troublingly suspicious for Plato, who does not consider him to be a serious person. Ion does not know anything about anything. He is obviously not very good at thinking. And yet, he has a kind of power which makes Socrates feel the need to question and tease him with an almost desperate insistence ('You refuse even to say what things you're clever about, though I keep begging you'[7]), something Socrates himself fails to see, something Murdoch sums up with the puzzlingly vague 'a general knowledge of human life'.

2.1.2. 'Now, here you are – a philosopher *and* a novelist'

Iris Murdoch's (1919–99) interest in the distinction between literature and philosophy spans over her entire productive years.[8] In her first book, the monograph on Sartre, the conflict is constantly bubbling under the surface. At this time (1953), she has not published a novel of her own and has thus not yet been confronted with the eager insistence of critics and scholars to regard her philosophical and literary writings as intertwined. This first book is also the only place where Murdoch provides a lengthy discussion of a novel she considers to do significant philosophical work, namely Sartre's *La Nausée*. Later on, Murdoch will maintain this judgement, even though she is generally sceptical to the label 'philosophical novel' and firmly refuses it for her own work.

In this first chapter, I shall discuss and elaborate on her reasons for considering this label unhelpful in the consideration of most literature, as well as inappropriate for her own novels. I shall begin to suggest what I take it to mean to read literature as literature, by refuting an interesting philosophical reading of her novel *The Black Prince*. With Kant and Hegel, I shall describe the art of literature as producing a sensory illusion of sense. Then, by coupling Murdoch's interpretation of Sartre's novel with an unsolved problem in Stanley Cavell's *The Claim of Reason*, I shall describe what I take to be the philosophical work of *La Nausée* and suggest some limitations that come with doing philosophy as fiction. Finally, I shall make use of Murdoch's novel *The Philosopher's Pupil*, a non-philosophical novel centred around a philosopher, to shed some more light upon the distinction between an artistic and a philosophical approach.

Murdoch's refusal of the label 'philosophical novelist' often comes across as merely defensive. Throughout her career, she is continuously asked questions like: 'Can you make any observation on the sort of role philosophy can play in novels?',[9] 'Are you not the only well-known novelist who is a trained philosopher?',[10] 'Do you express a philosophy in *your* novels?',[11] 'Is it a philosopher's novel?',[12] 'How does it work as a double career? Would you say that it's complementary or conflicting, or both?',[13] 'You don't think you impose your own philosophical theories on your novels in a different way?',[14] 'Now, here you are – a philosopher *and* a novelist – and the matter continually arises: but, do you see yourself as a "philosophical novelist", whatever that means?'[15] and eventually an interviewer even comments: 'I chose to avoid her Platonist preoccupation with the search for Truth and Goodness, suspecting that she was tired of pointing out that she does not write philosophical novels.'[16]

Prompted by questions like these, Murdoch repeatedly states: no, her fiction is not philosophical. She answers that she thinks that imposing her own philosophical theories on her novels is 'a very dangerous thing to do, and I certainly don't want to mix philosophy and fiction – they're totally different disciplines, different methods of thought, different ways of writing, different aims'.[17] Literature, she says, 'is full of tricks and magic and deliberate mystification. Literature entertains, it does many things, and philosophy does one thing.'[18] She returns many times to the 'absolute horror' she feels 'of putting theories or "philosophical ideas" as such into [her] novels'.[19] 'I mention philosophy sometimes in the novels because I happen to know about it, just as another writer might talk about coal mining; it happens to come in.'[20] She views the intention to write a 'philosophical novel' as mostly misguided:

> [O]n the whole I think it's dangerous writing a philosophical novel. I mean, this is not a thing writers can easily get away with. Take the case of Thomas Mann, whom I adore, for instance. When his characters start having very long philosophical conversations, one feels, "Well, perhaps we could do without this." My novels are not "philosophical novels".[21]

And yet there is that kind of haunting whiff of philosophy in Murdoch's view of art as well, when she states things like that 'though they are so different, philosophy and literature are both truth-seeking and truth-revealing activities';[22] that art 'is the most educational of all human activities';[23] that poets could claim to have an expert knowledge of human life in general; and that 'a good writer can't help having a philosophy in a certain sense of the word, in that he has wisdom about the human condition'.[24]

Scholars have grasped at these relatively rare statements like straws, in order to justify their reversal of Murdoch's firm insistence on the distinction between literature and philosophy. To quote Niklas Forsberg, whose own argumentation for the philosophical import of literature I shall quarrel with later in this chapter: 'there is a strong tendency among Murdoch's readers to portray her philosophical and her literary writings as intertwined',[25] a received view which 'leaves no room for Murdoch's fear, her absolute horror' of putting philosophy in her fiction.[26]

For a more extensive account of this general tendency, I happily refer my reader to Forsberg's criticism of the received view, which is still largely adequate and relevant. Discussions of other Murdoch scholars will otherwise occur in a scattered form throughout this book. For now, I shall simply offer some quotes to show how common this starting point of ignoring or contradicting Murdoch's distinction between literature and philosophy has become: Maria Antonaccio claims that 'any reader of Murdoch's philosophy is bound to notice its deep literary character, just as any reader of her novels cannot fail to recognize their constant philosophical preoccupations'.[27] Gary Browning begins his book on Murdoch by stating that 'I am convinced that her work fits together like a whole and that it is a mistake to separate her novels from her philosophy',[28] and Anna Victoria Hallberg explicitly skips arguing against Murdoch's own insistence on the distinction and says: 'I do not approach Murdoch's novels with a "neutral" question of investigating whether or not her novels are indeed philosophical; I have already made up my mind, so to speak, that they are.'[29] Rowe and Horner begin their introduction to an anthology by claiming that Murdoch has sparked a lot of interest primarily because of 'her unique position as a working moral philosopher and practising novelist whose fiction tests and contests the moral stances to which she commits herself in her philosophical essays (despite the fact that she said repeatedly that she did not want philosophy to intrude into her fictional writing)'.[30] In an introduction to another anthology, Sofia de Melo Araújo says that 'in all truth, literary and philosophical aspects have always come hand in hand when reading Iris Murdoch'.[31]

Disregarding what a novelist says about her own work in an interview is one thing; for I am on no account intending to argue that an author's intention should be taken as gospel for the interpretation of her novels. But Murdoch is not just a literary writer posing with a phobia for theory in fiction. She is also a profound and original aesthetic philosopher who provides many in-depth discussions of why literature, as an art form, should be considered as distinct from philosophy, and these will be expounded throughout the following chapters. Plato and Kant shall also be given plenty of attention, not just because Murdoch called them her 'personal gods',[32] but because their remarkable thoughts on beauty and art help us discern the specificity of art and the aesthetic experience. My aim is to defend my subtitle (*Why Literature Is Not Philosophy*) by discussing certain aesthetic characteristics which make it misguided, unnecessary, misleading and/or reductive to regard literature as philosophical.

In this chapter, I will discuss that ineradicable but elusive whiff of sense through which the poet might appear as, and in some ways also is, an expert on human life. Following Murdoch's general suspicion of the concept 'philosophical novel', but also her admiration for one specific philosophical novel, I will attempt to give an account of when this vague expertise can be said to be compatible with philosophical work, and why it is nonetheless at large better understood as proper to literature. Making too much sense out of this sensory illusion of sense risks, I shall argue, leaving behind precisely that which makes the literary art so enjoyable, beautiful and special.

2.2. Forced to ask questions? The sensory illusion of sense in *The Black Prince*

2.2.1. 'If nothing sensuous is present no art is present'

One of the characteristics of art which in Murdoch's view distinguishes it from philosophy is its sensory qualities. In her conversation on literature and philosophy with Bryan Magee, she brings this up several times. 'If nothing sensuous is present no art is present',[33] she says, and '[o]f course literature does not look like "analysis" because what the imagination produces is sensuous, fused, reified, mysterious, ambiguous, particular. Art is cognition in another mode.'[34] This 'sensuous thingy element' is proper to 'every art form',[35] even if Murdoch also states that '[a] work of art is of course not a material object'.[36] The artwork consists of an imagined, projected unity, 'a sustained *experienced* mental synthesis',[37] which is in a sense a hoax, an illusion, a mere feeling of coherence.

In literature, where nothing sensuous is immediately present except for written language, the illusoriness of its material unity can be more pronounced. Murdoch's thinking is here clearly influenced by Hegel, who reflects on this peculiar character of poetry in his *Aesthetics*:

> [Poetry] has to keep the middle way between the extremes of what is directly visible or perceptible by the senses and the subjectivity of feeling and thinking. This central element of imagination [*Vorstellung*] therefore draws something from both spheres. From thinking it takes the aspect of spiritual universality which grips together into a simpler determinate unity things directly perceived as separate; from visual art it keeps things juxtaposed in space and indifferent to one another. For imagination is essentially distinguished from reason by the fact that, like sense-perception from which it takes its start, it allows particular ideas to subsist alongside one another without being related, whereas thinking demands and produces dependence of things on one another, reciprocal relations, logical judgements, syllogisms, etc.[38]

In thus marking the distinction between poetry and thinking, Hegel continues with adding that poetry produces an imagined, inner unity of the things juxtaposed which nevertheless 'remain[s] hidden'.[39] There is a kind of inaccessible wholeness of the artwork, which gives its disparate sensuous parts an illusion of coherence; whereas thinking demands and produces relations and causality. Thus, a literary work can 'go together' without really 'making sense' – attempts to sort out and explain its inner relations may entail leaving its quasi-sensuous imagined unity behind.

2.2.2. Niklas Forsberg on *The Black Prince*

This Murdochian-Hegelian description of the sensory and experiential character of literature provides the foundation for my criticism of Niklas Forsberg's interpretation of Murdoch's novel *The Black Prince*. In his book *Language Lost and Found: On Iris Murdoch and the Limits of Philosophical Discourse*, Forsberg presents a rare and interesting exception to the dominant tendency among Murdoch scholars to contradict or simply disregard her distinction between literature and philosophy. He claims to stay with her division between the disciplines, and he also provides a very good criticism of the problems with the received view.[40] Nonetheless, he proceeds with a declaration of his own: that literature, as an art, *is* doing philosophy, albeit in another way than has been commonly assumed. Purportedly grounded in Murdoch's own view of art, he gives an interpretation of *The Black Prince* which exemplifies his idea that understanding 'literature *qua* literature' means understanding it 'as a form of philosophical expression in its own right'.[41]

Since he claims to be, in contrast to many Murdoch scholars, recognizing her distinction between literature and philosophy, and yet sees the artistic as a philosophical expression in another form, examining his interpretation more closely may be fruitful for my purposes. What does it mean for Forsberg to read a novel as a work of art? Let us begin with following his description of what it is not.

His criticism of earlier research becomes most devastating in his discussion of Martha Nussbaum's[42] and Michael Weston's[43] interpretations of *The Black Prince*. Both regard the novel as an elaboration of Murdoch's Platonism. To put it briefly, Forsberg points out that what Nussbaum and Weston take to be straightforward philosophical statements are in fact conveyed to us by an unreliable narrator. When the confused and unsympathetic writer Bradley Pearson, in love with a girl thirty-eight years his junior, says that 'Love brings with it … a vision of selflessness',[44] Forsberg suggests that this might more reasonably be read as a part of Bradley's narcissistic self-deception than as a philosophical proclamation by Murdoch. But Nussbaum and Weston read the novel as 'a more or less unproblematic expression of Murdoch's philosophical ideas and the fact that it is a literary work of art turns out to be a fairly unimportant detail' for them.[45]

So, what is literature, understood as a work of art? In Forsberg's book, we find a complex and nuanced account of Murdoch's view of artworks as mimetic, autonomous wholes that are 'teaching us density and distance'.[46] Distance is here not to be understood as detachment, but in the perfectionist sense: as distance to the unattainable good. Forsberg quotes from Murdoch's 'Against Dryness': 'With this, renewing our sense of distance, we may remind ourselves that art too lives in a region where all human endeavour is failure.'[47] I understand this to mean, in Forsberg's interpretation of Murdoch, that art can make us aware that we are sunken in an unclear, messy, constantly shifting existence of confused relations and self-deceptions. We are effused in this muddle and can never fully separate ourselves from our world or our world from our words or our words from our constant interactions with each other. This is why '[t]he understanding of distance is (also) the understanding of togetherness and intimacy'.[48]

This unusually accurate description of one aspect of Murdoch's view of art provides the basis for Forsberg's more daring suggestion of the philosophical significance of literature. In the introduction, he says that he 'aims to show that literature … can do philosophical investigations'.[49] Even though he later 'caution[s] the reader not to make too much of these claims, for I am not attempting to put forward a theory about the philosophical significance of literature in general',[50] his reading of *The Black Prince* is not simply aimed to be a novel-specific investigation but is meant to carry implications for how literature in many cases could be seen as doing philosophy. While admitting that 'when a philosophically inclined mind approaches literature, it might not be an entirely innocent approach',[51] he nonetheless wants to show that 'literature is (often) philosophically significant precisely because and to the extent that it is not philosophy (as we know it)'.[52]

Literature does philosophy, according to Forsberg, by being these mimetic, autonomous wholes in the medium of language. 'What literature brings', he says, 'is a way to see how sentences come to life, or fail to come to life in the context of a human life. This is rare in philosophy.'[53] Literature mirrors the world in words. As such, argues Forsberg, it challenges the security of the philosopher who thinks that he can discuss concepts outside of their lived situations. This approach is inspired by ordinary language philosophy, but it is also unwittingly close to the naturalistic insistence of the Existentialists.[54] Exchange 'object' for 'concept' here, and I believe Simone de Beauvoir's description of the philosophical relevance of literature comes quite close to Forsberg's:

> In the real world, the meaning of an object is not graspable by pure understanding. Its meaning is the object as it is disclosed to us in the overall relation we sustain with it, and which is action, emotion, and feeling. We ask novelists to evoke this flesh-and-blood presence whose complexity and singular and infinite richness exceed any subjective interpretation.[55]

However, de Beauvoir's insistence on the 'flesh-and-blood presence' of fiction differs her account from Forsberg's. A good novel, she writes, 'allows one to undergo imaginary experiences that are *as complete and disturbing as lived experiences*. ... A true novel, therefore, allows itself neither to be reduced to formulas nor even to be retold; one can no more detach its meaning from it than one can detach the smile from a face'.[56]

Even though this could be implicit in Forsberg's understanding, his interpretation of *The Black Prince* still entails a detachment from the sensory, experiential character of the story, and attempts to see through its illusion of sense. With Hegel, we could say that he creates reciprocal relations and abstract syllogisms of things that in the novel merely are juxtaposed. Since letting literature have its say for him means attending closely to what meaning a particular utterance by a particular character can have in a particular situation, Bradley's sudden exclamation 'What's that bloody smell?' in a conversation with Julian comes to leave the smell itself aside. Instead, Forsberg takes his interruption to indicate that Bradley is not attentive to Julian, that he does not care about her and 'does not really love her':[57] 'Bradley is completely unable to attend to his love, because the smell of strawberries matters more to him than Julian does.'[58] The sweetish, sickly smell of strawberries is thus reduced to bearing a relational, conceptual content, showing a man out of tune with his own concept of love.

But the meaning of Bradley's statement can no less be detached from the smell of strawberries than a smile from a face. The 'unique but unidentified smell, carrying awful associations' entering Bradley's mind 'as a swarm of bees', and enclosing him and the reader in the 'smell of youthful illusion and feverish transient joy'[59] is not merely a telling interruption to the dialogue – it is a part of the novel as a sensuous whole. Here, we find a problem not specific to Forsberg's reading but to all acts of interpretation. 'The obvious problem is', as Charles Bernstein puts it, 'that the poem said in any/other way is not the poem.'[60] Does this mean that one should never interpret, and protect the sacred integrity of the artwork at any cost? No, of course not. But saying that the artwork independently does what is in fact dependent on an interpretation is a problematic move. In order to have this statement of Bradley's do the philosophical work he wants to see in it, Forsberg must detach the conceptual relations from their sensuous muddle, thereby isolating and changing them. And this is not what he claims to be doing.

On the contrary, it is very important for Forsberg to stress that the novel does this completely independently; that he is simply 'letting literature have its say'.[61] 'The philosophical strength of literature is certainly not its capacity to illustrate or exemplify philosophy; its strength is that it is the other of philosophy: a contrast fluid.'[62] Here, he almost (as does de Beauvoir) seems to be describing literature like an immediate instantiation of life. Through literature, he claims, we can discover

> what place these words and sentences have in *a life as a whole*. Literature is one of the art forms that can do this. We can attain a picture of what a particular kind of life may look like and we *can* look at it from a distance; a distance impossible to attain regarding one's life as a whole. Indeed, it is utterly unclear what it would mean to claim to have such a distance to oneself and one's life.[63]

There is an obvious paradox here. Forsberg recognizes that life never comes in the kind of finished whole that a story does, allowing for this kind of distance. Yet, he does not consider the kind of wholeness the artwork presents as illusory. In separating literature from philosophy, he seems to suggest that literature can serve the purpose of isolating a piece of life. His interpretation of Murdoch's view of art as mimetic spells this out explicitly: 'Rather than making pictures, I think of Murdoch the novelist as someone *taking* pictures, recording us as it were.'[64] Indeed, the work of ordinary language philosophy he claims to be done by literature might just as well, or probably better, be done by an actual recording. If we wanted to study 'how our conceptual tissue looks'[65] or 'where words come from',[66] would we not be better off studying texts that are embedded in lived practices (such as transcriptions of real conversations, or chatlogs)? Why turn to those texts which give us an illusory sense of being complete little lives in themselves, providing us with a pleasing imaginary experience of grasping something that cannot really be grasped?

2.2.3. Illusion of sense and indirect communication

The answer here is, unfortunately, rather long and complicated. It is related to the exaggerated reliance on Kierkegaard and the skewed interpretation of Kant that Forsberg claims to find in Murdoch, through which the literary work becomes a self-contained turning of concepts we can peer into as a looking glass. According to this view, the novel offers us an opportunity to step back into 'a distance impossible to attain regarding one's life as a whole',[67] making it into a sort of refractory laboratory for human sensemaking, liberated from the usual intersubjective hustle of life. Forsberg describes it thus:

> An indirect communication, as an artwork, that is, *as a self-sufficient whole* (Kant is here necessary!) deliberately removes the authorial intention and forces its reader to relate to the world presented, to the muddled and the emotionally charged, and makes him/her try to sort out just how these words, as uttered by this person, at

this time, in this light, fit (or do not fit) into this kind of life (this "context" if you like).[68]

This quote summarizes his views of Murdoch's reliance on Kierkegaard and Kant, and I shall explain my issues with both in a moment. But let us begin with the novel. What does 'sort out' mean here?

Forsberg's reading of *The Black Prince* is centred around what he calls Bradley Pearson's 'illusion of sense'.[69] This means, for example, that Bradley is mistaken when he thinks that he means 'love' when he says 'love'. He has the word for it, but not the concept. It is thus not a 'philosophical novel' in the sense of being a series of statements or arguments:

> Rather it works with its reader in a way similar to the way Kierkegaard wanted his pseudonymous texts to work. That is, this is a mirror of our world, our times – where some of the concepts (not words) Murdoch wants to reawaken are almost impossible to invoke. This means that I take Bradley Pearson to be under the illusion of meaning them, and that Murdoch counts on us seeing that.[70]

To Forsberg, it is 'obvious that Bradley is not in attunement with himself and his feelings; that he does not know what he talks about when he talks about love'.[71] So, if we are 'to get something out of reading' this story, 'if we are to learn anything philosophical' from it[72] (which to Forsberg is the same thing as reading it as a work of art), we must look at the story in a way we could never look at ourselves within life, and yet partly recognize ourselves in the picture. We see the illusion of sense in all its power, yet we uncover it as an illusion.

But what happens with the experience of reading after we have 'discovered' such a lack of attunement? Try reading the following passage from *The Black Prince*, when Bradley has first realized that he is in love with Julian:

> I am not sure how long I lay upon the floor. Perhaps an hour, perhaps two or three hours. When at last I pulled myself up into a sitting posture it appeared to be afternoon. It was certainly another world and another time. Of course there was no question of eating anything, I should instantly have been sick. Sitting on the floor I reached out and drew towards me the chair upon which she had sat and leaned against it. I could see my own sherry untouched upon the table, hers half drunk. A fly was drowned in it. I would have drunk it fly and all, only I knew I could keep nothing down. I clasped the chair (it was the tiger lily one) and stared at her copy of *Hamlet*. The pleasure of picking that up and fingering it, perhaps seeing her name written in the front, was hundreds of years ahead in a delightful future of perfectly satisfying preoccupations. There was no hurry. Time had already become eternity. There was a huge warm globe of conscious being within which I moved with extreme slowness, or which perhaps I was. I had only to gaze, to stretch my hands out slowly like a chameleon. It no longer mattered where I looked or what I did. Everything in the world was Julian.[73]

When I first read this, it did not matter to me in the slightest whether Bradley 'really loves'[74] Julian. There was no question about clarity or failure involved in partaking of this 'illusion of sense'. I did not feel, as Forsberg did, 'invited, nearly forced, to think through how the same words are "turned" differently and thus "linked" to different concepts'.[75] We (especially if we are not philosophers) are perfectly able to read *The Black Prince* and share Bradley's experiences without reflecting in the least upon this.

By breaking the suspension of disbelief[76] and taking the presence of an unreliable narrator to be the most important factor of the story, Forsberg approaches the novel as a text with a certain purpose, comparable to Kierkegaard's use of *indirect communication*. Let us 'ask what the novel looks like if it is *not* an expression of Murdoch's philosophy', he begins;[77] and then sets out to explain how it is 'a Kierkegaardian work' instead.[78] Forsberg has identified many characteristics that indicate a Kierkegaardian inspiration in the structure of *The Black Prince*: its layers of pseudonyms, for instance, and its meta-reflective passages. He has also noted that Murdoch in one place calls art indirect communication. But does this really mean that her novel is a piece of Kierkegaardian indirect communication?

In falsely taking themselves to be true Christians (having lost the concept, but not the word), Kierkegaard felt his contemporaries in need to be shown that they were living in an illusion of sense. They thought they believed in God, but what they meant by the word God was not really God.[79] But you cannot remove such an illusion by simply pointing it out. As Forsberg puts it, indirect communication is instead 'a strategy that aims to be non-dogmatic in a fairly radical sense, since it aims not to present any views of its own, but merely to display where and how one can go (or we have gone) wrong'.[80]

Radically non-dogmatic seems to me an exaggeration here. Kierkegaard explicitly uses indirect communication to do away with illusions: 'In relation to pure receptivity, like the empty jar that is to be filled, *direct* communication is appropriate, but when illusion is involved, consequently something that must first be removed, indirect communication is appropriate.'[81] Seeking to effect a very Lutheran change of heart, Kierkegaard aims his texts to do away with the false faith that is already filling up the jar. He wants to '*deceive into the truth*'.[82] The 'indirect method', he says, works 'in the service of truth' and 'dialectically arranges everything for the one ensnared'.[83] It may be anti-dogmatic, but only methodically so: the goal intended is true, Christian faith. But Murdoch, precisely after one of the sentences Forsberg quotes to enforce his view that she 'employs Kierkegaard's distinction between direct and indirect communication to mark out the difference between her philosophical and her literary works',[84] says:

> Art is artificial, it is indirect communication which delights in its own artifice. … *The art object is a kind of illusion, a false unity,* the product of a mortal man who cannot entirely dominate his subject matter and remove or transform contingent rubble and unclarified personal emotions and attitudes.[85]

In the case of literature, the illusion of sense is not a method but a characteristic, akin to the quasi-sensory juxtaposition described by Murdoch and Hegel in 2.1. There is no purpose, only a feeling of purposiveness. It is not a form designed with a pedagogical aim of deceiving into truth, but the result of a (sometimes naïve, sometimes wilful) partial failure to be objective. This marks a sharp contrast to Kierkegaard's indirect communication, about which Forsberg says: 'There is a goal here, but there is no "trickery".'[86] In the novel, there is instead trickery, but no goal. That Murdoch plays with a Kierkegaardian structure in the narrative of *The Black Prince* is no ground for stating that the novel has a philosophical aim, not even the vaguer 'to reflect upon and understand our own morality'.[87] The novel might just, as Murdoch suggests in the quote above, be delighting in its own trickery. Kierkegaard, on the other hand, talks about indirect communication as a strategic move to be adopted when the audience cannot be compelled into awareness, and compares it to martyrdom.[88]

Indeed, rather than being 'radically anti-dogmatic', the indirect communication is for Kierkegaard intended to lead to a devastating clarity. Even if Forsberg evades the comparison with martyrdom, another kind of intentional destructiveness echoes in his Kierkegaardian understanding of Murdoch's aesthetics. His account of Murdoch's view of art as mimetic tellingly culminates in an appeal to smash the reflections:

> Murdoch holds up her mirror to nature and lets us see how concepts such as art, love, marriage, transcendence (among others) are modulated in this form of life. But since a mirror holds no doctrines of its own, we must now reflect on her reflection. We must learn to look behind the mirror. Bradley did not know just how right he was when he said: "We are *for* breaking, our smash is what it's for".[89]

2.2.4. Kant and the autonomy of art

In this appeal to look behind or smash its reflections, what has happened with the self-sufficiency of art? What, for that matter, does Forsberg mean with 'self-sufficient wholes', a concept he claims to be Kantian but which cannot be found in Kant?[90] Forsberg has, as he mildly puts it, his 'reservations concerning Murdoch's understanding of Kant',[91] and argues that she 'misses the details – even to such an extent that she obscures the strong affinities between her own view and Kant's'.[92] His own understanding of Kant provides good support for his view of literature as inviting us to reflect upon the turning of our concepts.[93] However, I believe that there are some problems with this reading, which skews not only Kant, and Murdoch's use of Kant, but the specificity of art, which Forsberg claims to respect in his description of its philosophical import.

With 'self-sufficient wholes', Forsberg has created his own (purportedly Kantian) definition of the autonomy of art. In his brief explanation of Kant's aesthetics, Forsberg departs from the famous proposition of the first Critique: 'Intuitions without concepts are blind; concepts without intuitions are empty.'[94] 'Since it is not really possible to separate concepts and intuitions', Forsberg continues, 'making an experiential judgment and having an experience are both matters of conceptualization.'[95] Seemingly unaware of the difference between the aesthetic, reflective judgement of the third Critique and the conceptual, determining judgement of the first, he then takes the aesthetic to be subsumed under the famous proposition, and understands the artwork as conceptually autonomous:

> To simplify: in art, the expression is its own idea; the "word" is its own concept – there is no distinction to be drawn between exemplarity and ideality. It does not

stand and fall in relation to something outside of it. If we think of it as a concept in its own right, it is not, as it were, true or false depending on how it relates to an empirical fact. It is what it is, and now it is up for us to relate to it. When we see an artwork, we see its concept (for, as he [Kant] made clear already in the first critique, *all* cognitions are conceptual).[96]

If this would have been the case, Forsberg's reading of *The Black Prince* as a turning of concepts could indeed have been called approaching it as a work of art. However, as Kant makes explicit at numerous places in the third Critique, the aesthetic judgement is *not* conceptual.[97] It is a specific and different kind of judgement than the ones he has previously described, which also means that the aesthetic object is a very different kind of object. It is a representation which we do not seek to understand, but the judgement of which is made in relation to pleasure and displeasure.

The feelings of pleasure (in the experience of beauty) and displeasure (in the experience of the sublime) belong to a distinct faculty, explicitly separate from the faculty of desire as well as the faculty of cognition.[98] This is also what Kant means with *autonomy*: these feelings are independent of us wanting to effect a change in the world or seeking to understand it.[99] As such, the aesthetic judgement is autonomous from the understanding not in the sense of being disconnected from it, but in being free from conceptual determination. It is an 'intermediate faculty'[100] that occasions a free play between understanding and imagination, which makes us intuit what Kant calls the 'feeling of life'.[101] Thus, it is not in any sense a conceptual autonomy which Kant describes as proper to art. The pleasure and displeasure of the aesthetic judgment 'grounds *an entirely special faculty for discriminating and judging that contributes nothing to cognition* but only holds the given representation in the subject up to the entire faculty of representation, of which the mind becomes conscious in the feeling of its state'.[102]

This 'feeling of its state' is a pleasurable harmony between the faculties of the mind, that is, that which holds all of our experiences together. The aesthetic judgement is a reflective capability which, in contrast to the determining judgement, does not 'sort out' anything, but instead makes us intuit a purposiveness without a purpose. We *feel* like there is a point to the beautiful, but it has no point besides its own form.[103] Furthermore, even if our opinions clearly differ, there is a subjective universality to the judgement of taste: we *feel as if* everyone should agree with us, even though there is no objective basis for making this claim. For Kant, this subjective universality is the intuition of a common sense (*sensus communis*), a non-conceptual presupposition that our minds share the same basic structure. Murdoch is highly aware of, and also probably alluding to, this Kantian fundament to aesthetics when she suggests that Ion could perhaps lay claim to being an expert on 'human life in general'. This concerns something so general and subjective that it is more akin to having a feeling for the form of perception – a sense of the common sense – than possessing any useful knowledge.

I shall soon return to Kant again. For now, it suffices to note that this reflective harmony, which he sometimes refers to as a feeling of unity of the manifold, could be described as an illusion of sense, but not the kind that can be broken. As Hegel puts it, echoing Kant, '[t]he beautiful [*Schöne*] has its being in pure appearance

[*Schein*]'.[104] There is no looking behind its sensuous appearance. To Hegel, however, beauty therefore also points beyond itself and makes us strive for making the same idea apparent in thinking. He is very clear that this progression entails leaving art behind. 'For precisely on account of its form, art is limited to a specific content. ... In order to be genuine for art, such truth must in virtue of its own specific character be able to go forth into [the sphere of] sense and remain adequate to itself there.'[105] Hegel's lectures on aesthetics subsequently end with the dissolution of art, which through its historical progression of spiritual self-knowledge in the sensuous eventually frees itself from 'anything objective and particularized'.[106] In contrast to Hegel, Murdoch rejects a view of art where the point would be to progress beyond it and make sense of it.[107] However, against the background of either of these accounts, Forsberg's understanding of literature as nearly forcing us to engage in a sorting out and a smashing of mirrors can only be understood as leaving the domain of the aesthetic and moving into that of the understanding.

In a way, Forsberg comes close to acknowledging this himself: 'One might say that if novels can be philosophy, in the sense developed here, a great deal of philosophical work is still to be done when we are done with a novel: it falls back on how we relate to what we read. Conceptual clarity requires conceptual responsiveness.'[108] This kind of philosophical, conceptual responsiveness is not, in my opinion, what it means to let 'literature have its say'.[109] It is Forsberg's philosophical investigation, not simply *The Black Prince*, speaking in his interpretation of the novel, and it is a 'clarification' which leaves important aspects of the experience of reading it behind. So when he says that 'Literature as literature, as having a philosophical import of its own, means: *This* sentence, as uttered *here*, by *this* person, under *these* circumstances is what is important – *that* is letting literature have its say,'[110] I fundamentally disagree with him, and I believe Murdoch would too. That kind of placing and sorting out requires a specific kind of approach which seeks to go beyond the novel's sensory illusion of sense, as in the telling translation of the sweetish, feverishly youthful smell of strawberries into the conclusion that 'Bradley does not really love her and that he is torn by that knowledge at some, though not necessarily conscious, level.'[111]

So, if *The Black Prince* is not doing philosophy, what would a properly philosophical novel look like? Or, put otherwise: could philosophy fruitfully take the form of a sensuous illusion of sense, offering us reflection on something that is experiential and particular but at the same time thought? To answer this, we shall now turn to what Murdoch saw as a very rare example of a successful philosophical novel: Jean-Paul Sartre's *La Nausée*.

2.3. *La Nausée*: The philosophical novel

2.3.1. Encountering *La Nausée*

Let us get back to the artist's expertise on human life in general. What holds our experiences together? Within the abundance of contingent particulars that make up our existence, how is it possible that we can make sense of it at all? Do we even make sense of it, or does it only feel like it; do we to a large extent rely on illusions of sense, vulnerable to the impulse of sceptical doubt?

Jean-Paul Sartre's *La Nausée* is one of the strongest reading experiences of my life. I came across the novel in my late teens, just when I had been going through a (social? emotional? psychological? philosophical?) dissociative crisis of sorts, which took form as recurring experiences of sensory impressions detaching themselves from my conceptions and becoming overwhelming, boundless and arbitrary. I remember, for example, how faces could look to me as weirdly construed as if I were regarding them upside down. The symbolic coherence of nose, mouth and eyes was suddenly nonsensical for me, and all I saw was a fleshy presence of cartilage, skin and muscles. Even this characterization does not do it justice, because it presents 'cartilage, skin and muscles' as classifiable materials.

These experiences were as terrible as they were marvellous. Terrible because they made me fear that I was losing my mind, that I was stuck in a lonely, senseless and abnormal processing of the world that I could not really communicate to my friends or my girlfriend at the time. Marvellous because I felt as if I was discovering something. Even though these episodes made me giddy and sick, I had a suspicion of occasioning them myself, perhaps by (something every clever girl has been accused of enough times) 'thinking too much'.

Reading Sartre's novel, I was infinitely moved at discovering that I was not alone. Other people had had these experiences too, and what was more: without losing their inherent terror, they could be given a beautiful form, could be presented through the artwork's semblance of sense, its purposiveness without a purpose. The narrator of *La Nausée* was very other to me indeed: an isolated and discontent, mid-century middle-aged Frenchman who, after years of travel, has settled down in the small, bourgeois village Bouville[112] to write a historic monograph about a marquis. Still, it was as if I shared his state of mind exactly when he was gazing at his own face in the mirror:

> My glance slowly and wearily travels over my forehead, my cheeks: it finds nothing firm, it is stranded. Obviously there are a nose, two eyes and a mouth, but none of it makes sense, there is not even a human expression. Yet Anny and Velines thought I looked so alive: perhaps I am too used to my face. When I was little, my Aunt Bigeois told me "if you look at yourself too long in the mirror, you'll see a monkey." I must have looked at myself even longer than that: what I see is well below the monkey, on the fringe of the vegetable world, at the level of jellyfish. It is alive, I can't say it isn't; but this was not the life that Anny contemplated: I see a slight tremor, I see the insipid flesh blossoming and palpitating with abandon. The eyes especially are horrible seen so close. They are glassy, soft, blind, red-rimmed, they look like fish scales.[113]

If artworks are structured as illusions of sense, they are in equal measure (at least since modernism) concerned with unsettling or criticizing our habitual sensemaking illusions. Sartre's novel explores this topically with perhaps unparalleled force, whereas primarily formal explorations are countless. By reshaping that which gives our experiences unity, some artworks can be so deeply formally disturbing that they have been regarded as immoral. D.H. Lawrence, in discussing the public's repugnance for Cezanne's still lifes, suggests that these are perceived as so *wrong* precisely because they disturb the social, habitual organizing patterns we rely on for perception. Lawrence compares these patterns to the drawings of children:

> When a child sees a man, what does the child *take in*, as an impression? Two eyes, a nose, a mouth of teeth, two straight legs, two straight arms: a sort of hieroglyph which the human child has used through all the ages to represent man. … Is this what the child actually *sees*?[114]

Somehow, it all usually goes together for us. The 'hieroglyphs', to use Lawrence's word, provide unities for our experiences. To see someone drawing against or outside these patterns upsets us. If we somehow lose faith in those unities, we experience a dissociation like the one depicted and reflected upon in Sartre's novel. If that is philosophical, could not all artistic formal experiments be called philosophical? Can the perceptive illusions of sense, that artists like Cezanne challenge, somehow be distinguished from our conceptual sensemaking? Put in slightly more Kantian terms: is the aesthetic form of appearances qualitatively different from the comprehension of our understanding?

2.3.2. Kant's rainbow

Yet another excursion on Kant might here be necessary, before we dive into the artistic and intellectual sensemaking of *La Nausée*. In 2.2.4, I noted that Forsberg formulates his allegedly Kantian basis for the philosophical import of literature on a conflation between the determining and the reflective judgement. To clarify what I mean by saying that an illusion of sense differs from sensemaking, the distinction between these must be explained.

Kant calls our ability to order the manifold of appearances *synthesis*, 'the action of putting different representations together with each other and comprehending their manifoldness in one cognition'.[115] For example, by synthesis, we can comprehend the manifold of rain: the wetness, the cold and the round form of the drops, into one cognition: it rains. The ground for synthesis is the power of judgement. Kant writes that 'all actions of the understanding [can be traced] back to judgments'.[116] In the 'First Introduction' to the third Critique, Kant divides judgements into determining and reflective. Determining judgements are logical subsumptions of particulars under concepts.[117] If we know that gravity pulls everything towards the earth, when we see raindrops falling from the sky, we can conclude that they are falling down because of gravity.

Thus, we can make sense of the manifold, a manifold that is sometimes called intuitions (immediate, sensuous appearances[118]), sometimes appearances (intuitions as they appear to us), representations (our mental representations of the appearances) or forms (a certain aspect of appearances that corresponds not to their sensations but the order of them[119]). Above all, it is most important to remember that 'we have nothing to do with anything except appearances anywhere'.[120] Kant explains it like this:

> Thus, we would certainly call a rainbow a mere appearance in a sun-shower, but would call this rain the thing in itself, and this is correct, as long as we understand the latter concept in a merely physical sense, as that which in universal experience and all different positions relative to the senses is always determined thus and not otherwise in intuition. ... [N]ot only these drops are mere appearances, but even their round form, indeed even the space through which they fall are nothing in themselves, but only mere modifications or foundations of our sensible intuition; the transcendental object, however, remains unknown to us.[121]

Everything we see is appearances, formed by our cognitive make-up. But there is a peculiarity to this quote. Why does Kant feel the need to explain that the raindrops are appearances, while it goes without saying for the rainbow? It is like the appearance-character of the rainbow would be exceptionally apparent. Even though we can grasp the manifold of its colours with the concept rainbow; yes, we might even know the meteorological process behind it and be able to give a detailed account for the process of reflection and refraction of light in water, the appearance-character of it still remains before us. Or rather, the *beauty* of the rainbow remains.

It is like the rainbow (a popular metaphor for illusions) presents a unity of the manifold on its own, a unity that is not dependent on our conceptual synthesizing. Even if we know what it is, we marvel at another kind of unity of its manifold than that of knowledge. This is a judgement based on pleasure, or what Kant calls an *aesthetic judgement*. The aesthetic judgement is a reflective judgement, which means that the manifold of intuitions is not subsumed under a given concept. Instead, '[t]he reflective power of judgment thus proceeds with given appearances, ... not schematically, ... but artistically'.[122]

Sartre's *La Nausée*, I will argue, depicts a break-down of the determining judgement through an artistic presentation. As such, it is an artwork doing philosophical work to a degree at which it becomes justified and relevant to classify it as a philosophical novel. Some of my readers will probably indignantly object here that countless artworks present similar challenges to our habitual illusions of sense (such as Lawrence describes in his defence of Cezanne). Why, then, is it not justified to call them 'philosophical' as well?

In what follows, my account of the import and the limitations of the philosophical work of *La Nausée* shall attempt to meet this objection implicitly. This novel is not singled out as the only possible philosophical artwork. But it is discussed as an exception that proves the rule: even if terms like 'philosophical' and 'poetic' would, in theory, be applicable to everything, widening their scope of meaning risks diluting rather than broadening their force. *La Nausée* is not just formally, but topically and self-consciously reflecting on these problems, which makes it into more of an independent (as in independent from interpretation) piece of philosophical discourse.

2.3.3. 'One good philosophical novel'

Iris Murdoch cherished Sartre's first novel throughout her life. She, who was so resistant to regarding novels as philosophical, said, for example, in an interview in 1977:

I can think of one good philosophical novel that I admire very much, Sartre's *La Nausée*. That does manage to express some interesting ideas about contingency and consciousness, and to remain a work of art which does not have to be read in the light of theories which the author has expressed elsewhere.[123]

For it to be meaningful to call a novel philosophical it is not enough, according to Murdoch, to know that the author had a philosophical ambition in writing it: 'Tolstoy or someone may say that he is writing to "express a philosophy", but why should we think he has succeeded?'[124] He might instead have written a brilliant novel *despite* this intention (and the religious world-view presented at the end of *Anna Karenina* can indeed be difficult to square with the novel as a whole).

In general, Murdoch is sceptical to the existentialist ambition of writing philosophical novels. While admiring Sartre as well as Simone de Beauvoir on other grounds, she considers most of their fictional work partly failed:

[T]hese characters and the universes which they inhabit are made excessively transparent. We can see a little too precisely what is being done. These people are appealing, but they are never enchanting – and the worlds in which they live are without magic and without terror. There is here none of the enticing mystery of the unknown …. Sartre's nightmares are thoroughly intelligible. … [This literary tradition produces works which] lack the concreteness and the opaque character of poetry. They are designed to show and to persuade. They are not ends in themselves. They are like thoughts and not like objects.[125]

Note the words she is using here to describe the lackings of the existentialist novel. It is too transparent, too consciously and rhetorically designed. It is too much like a thought and not enough like an object. It is deficient in magic, enchantment and mystery. '[A]s soon as the "existentialist voice" is switched on', she says in another place, 'the work of art rigidifies.'[126] But Sartre's first novel is a rare exception. Why?

Murdoch's first book, a monograph on Sartre from 1953, starts off with an enraptured chapter on *La Nausée* entitled 'The discovery of things', which may well be her best piece of literary criticism. She stays very close to Roquentin's experiences but rotates them in the light of philosophical reflection. She describes the central pulse of the novel as 'a certain discovery, of metaphysical interest': 'that the world is contingent, and that we are related to it discursively and not intuitively'.[127] We partake in this discovery through the break-down of Roquentin's discursive understanding, his (to put it in Kantian terms) failure to subsume appearances under concepts. This is how Murdoch (primarily by quoting) summarizes the climax of the novel, where 'its metaphysical character is made more clear':

Roquentin is staring at a seat in a tramcar. "I murmur: it's a seat, as a sort of exorcism. But the word remains on my lips: it refuses to go and rest upon the thing …" "Things are delivered from their names. They are *there*, grotesque, stubborn, huge, and it seems crazy to call them seats or to say anything whatever about them." He continues his reflections in the public park: though he has often said, for instance, "seagull", he has never before felt that *that* which he named existed. "Existence had lost the inoffensive air of an abstract category: it was the very stuff of things. ... I understood that there was no middle way between non-existence and this swooning abundance."[128]

Indeed, this experience could be described as a discovery of the fundamental contingency of the world, and the arbitrariness of our discursive understanding of it. But what exactly is made clear here, save Roquentin's experience? The prose has at the same time a concreteness and an obscurity, which makes it enchanting, but not very explanatory.

Murdoch sums up the philosophical 'point' of the novel in many different ways. She says that it 'gives expression to a pure metaphysical doubt'.[129] She says that it is 'an epistemological essay on the phenomenology of thought'.[130] Elsewhere, she says that it 'describes what one might call a sort of logical loneliness'.[131] None of these descriptions do exactly conflict with one another, but together they allow for a certain vagueness as to what kind of philosophical investigation *La Nausée* actually performs. This vagueness, I believe, does not stem from any uncertainty of Murdoch's. Instead, she recognizes that 'the descriptions ... constitute the argument',[132] so that a reiteration of the former cannot fruitfully be detached from the sensory impressions it is invoked through:

> These evocations of the viscous, the fluid, the paste-like sometimes achieve a kind of horrid poetry, calling up in the reader – as do so many passages in the work of Sartre – *une espèce d'écœurment douceâtre*, the sweetish disgust which is a form of *la nausée* itself. Yet the effect is not always unpleasant.[133]

To understand *La Nausée*, we cannot *progress* from its enchanting juxtaposition of sensory experiences into an abstract analysis of them. We must stay with the horror and the delight in reading the novel, as its 'consistently reflecting, self-consciously philosophical'[134] character takes form on a perceptual level. The ideational content is represented precisely *as* a breakdown of perception: '[B]efore me, posed with a sort of indolence, was a voluminous, insipid idea [*une idée volumineuse et fade*]. I did not see clearly what it was, but it sickened me so much I couldn't look at it [*je ne pouvais pas la regarder tant elle m'écœurait*].'[135, 136] This nausea becomes incomprehensible if we do not feel it. We must stay within the spell of the artwork: experiencing it becomes, in this rare case, the same thing as becoming aware of the discursive arbitrariness of our understanding.

Even though Murdoch's reading of *La Nausée* presents such a detailed and nuanced account of what a properly philosophical novel could look like, it has been curiously ignored or misrepresented by several Murdoch scholars who insist on calling *her* a philosophical novelist. Instead, they construct their account of how her fiction is philosophical in contrast to Sartre, who they seem to think that she considered failed. Miles Leeson, in *Iris Murdoch: Philosophical Novelist*, skips over the chapter about *La Nausée* (and all the other occasions at which she has professed her admiration for the novel) and quotes from the end of her book on Sartre where she says that he 'has an impatience, which is fatal to a novelist proper, with the *stuff* of human life'.[137]

However, right before this, Murdoch has said that Sartre's longing for a 'reduction to the intelligible' is a 'dread' which he shares with Roquentin.[138] In *La Nausée*, Sartre has created a character who experiences his '"I" that goes on existing ... [as] merely the ever-lengthening *stuff* of gluey sensations and vague fragmentary thoughts'.[139] Clearly, the novel is in Murdoch's eyes deeply engaged with this *stuff*, even though it simultaneously expresses a horror for it. But according to Leeson, Murdoch's 'distinction between "proper" novel writing and philosophizing' is drawn by her '[i]n order to distance herself from Sartre'[140] – the only author she admired for having written a successful philosophical novel.

This complete disregard for the philosophical work of *La Nausée* is re-ascribed to Murdoch by Anna Victoria Hallberg, who presents a similar argument to Leeson's. Instead of relying on Murdoch's description of the novel, she turns to Peter Lamarque:

> Roquentin often personifies existentialist-philosophical arguments. And Peter Lamarque, expresses the following on Sartre's *Nausea*: "That novel is a philosophical novel in the sense that it uses a fictional (and literary) context to provide an imaginative realization of a conception of consciousness that Sartre presents in his non-fictive philosophical writings." That Sartre uses a fictional context to provide a philosophical conception, in Lamarque's words, gives us a first clue to how Murdoch's method of hybridisation uses a different direction. The existentialist novel starts in the abstract and makes up something particular-like in order to illustrate the abstract idea. Murdoch's hybrid novels, on the other hand, have a direction of ascesis that suggests that the upward movement starts from the particular. The hybrid begins in the picture of the particular (a happy event, the behaviour of dogs, emotional reactions, chance encounters, falling in love), which is enlightened in a way that, concerning the characters, leads to insights of a moral nature.[141]

I am repeating this passage in full because I believe it exhibits two kinds of widespread carelessness regarding the philosophical 'content' of novels. Let us begin with the fictive realization of a philosophical conception that Lamarque takes Sartre's novel to be. To illustrate what is meant by this, Hallberg quotes a paragraph from *La Nausée* in which Roquentin takes himself to be 'alone in the midst of ... happy, reasonable voices' which he experiences as 'fishy-eyed men who look as if they are turned upon themselves and with whom no agreement is possible'. Hallberg concludes: 'This echoes Sartre's famous line "l'enfer c'est les autres" (hell is other people) which is one conclusion of philosophical weight in the collection of philosophic essays *Being and Nothingness* (1943).'[142]

Indeed, constructing a fictional realization of the philosophical conclusion 'hell is other people' sounds like a stupid thing to do, artistically as well as intellectually. But besides the fact that Roquentin from time to time experiences a social malaise and hates the bourgeoisie, this does neither describe the novel nor Sartre's philosophy, and especially not the relationship between them.[143] In fact, the 'conclusion of philosophical weight' quoted above is nowhere to be found in *L'Être et Le Néant* – it is a line from a play by Sartre called *Huis Clos*.[144]

This is almost the opposite of how Murdoch reads *La Nausée*. Furthermore, it is precisely this facile, careless way of approaching the 'content' or 'point' of literature which makes her mistrust the notion of philosophical novels. She is well aware of how delighted critics and scholars are to be discovering this sort of 'philosophical weight' in fiction, and how the pomp of those discussions risks blinding us to the sensory, experiential and enchanting character of literature, while at the same time lowering the bar for what is to count as philosophical work. 'When we ask what a novel is *about* we are asking for something deep', she says; something both mysterious and erotic. 'What is Proust about, and why not just read Bergson?'[145] An account of its presumed philosophy of time will never explain *La Recherche* for us. Philosophy, on the other hand, requires a 'patient relentless ability to stay with a problem'[146] – it is not just a throwing around of statements like 'hell is other people'.

Hallberg's other claim, that Murdoch's 'hybrid novels' present us with particular situations intended to lead to more general moral insights, is equally problematic. I shall return to this in Chapter 6. For now, I will just mention a couple of things on particularity. As Nora Hämäläinen remarks, 'a certain emphasis on particularity is ubiquitous' in contemporary ethical discussions on literature.[147] 'Literature is brought into the philosophical discussion to illustrate the particularity of moral situations.'[148] Hämäläinen questions this dichotomous approach by stating that '[l]iterature, as well as philosophy, is a product of highly processed thought'.[149] In her discussion of Murdoch, she also points out that 'the particularistic, perception-centered aspect of her thought is only one aspect of her overall picture'.[150]

While I agree with Hämäläinen that the characterization of Murdoch as a particularist is misguided (e.g. the pictorially generalizing role of metaphor in her great philosophical work *Metaphysics as a Guide to Morals* can hardly be exaggerated) and share her mistrust to viewing literature as necessarily more particularized than philosophy, I should hesitate to describe novels as 'product[s] of highly processed thought'. While art can present us with sensuous particulars in a way which is rarely useful for philosophy, art can also be sensuous in a generalizing and sweeping way.[151] As Kant's distinction between the reflective and the determining judgement implies in the example of the rainbow, the reflective judgement of beauty can be described as 'respecting the illusion' of the whole. Similarly, novels might often be more like spells of totality than exhibitions of precision. As with an optical illusion or a mirage, 'sensory' does not automatically mean 'more attentive to the minute details of what is really there'.

Before we move on to a more philosophical discussion of *La Nausée*, any account of Murdoch's strict exclusion of most works from the category of philosophical novel must also take note of her (in the eyes of some) frustratingly limiting definition of philosophy. Approached not from the perspective of literary studies, where simplifications of what counts as philosophical 'content' are commonplace, but from academic philosophy, where the field as Forsberg says has (quite recently) rigidified into being overly institutionalized and narrowly 'academic',[152] it might easily be felt that her distinction between literature and philosophy implies a far too constricted understanding of what philosophy should look like. In contrast to literature, philosophy requires a 'strictness of ideas and arguments'.[153] And because it 'is so difficult', it 'is very small'.[154] Murdoch does not even count Kierkegaard and Nietzsche as philosophers.[155] She says that '[p]hilosophy aims to clarify and explain, it states and attempts to solve very difficult highly technical problems and the writing must be subservient to this aim.'[156]

Clearly, this is not true of *La Nausée*, so Murdoch must in some sense be exaggerating the characteristics here in order to make the general difference between the philosophical and the literary more discernible.[157] Her reasons for this are not, I believe, founded on a belief in some sort of timeless, transcendent essences of 'philosophy' and 'literature'. Rather, it is out of concern for the incomparable achievements of the great works of each of these disciplines. Of course there is at bottom here a normative view of what and how excellent philosophy and literature should look like – but departing from specific works rather than proposing a taxonomy. Murdoch is at times very explicit about this, as when she begins her essay 'The Sublime and the Good' by suggesting that we should 'start by saying that Shakespeare is the greatest of all artists, and let our aesthetic grow to be the philosophical justification of this judgement.'[158] Similarly, her strict limitation of the category of philosophical novel (which seems to consist almost solely of *La Nausée*) departs not from a taxonomy of definable criteria, but from the sense of it being excellent both as literature and as philosophy. 'Of course', she says about this novel, 'it is still philosophically "fresh".'[159] I shall now attempt to make my own account of how and why it could be considered as such.

2.3.4. Reading *La Nausée* as Stanley Cavell's missing justification of reasonable doubt

Raising the burden of proof for legitimating the use of the label 'philosophical' about a novel may be tricky, but I shall nonetheless try to demonstrate how I (with Murdoch) think that Sartre's first novel lives up to this standard. Please note that I am talking about a philosophical standard here; *Anna Karenina* is no less excellent as literature if we question the value of the 'philosophies' Tolstoy thinks he has put into it.

Philosophy may in general be described as being in a more direct dialogue with its own history than literature. For example, it is difficult to imagine a great philosophical work being written by someone completely unfamiliar with the philosophical canon, whereas radiant literature might more plausibly be created by an uneducated ignorant. Testing the validity of a philosophical 'freshness' can be achieved by putting a work into dialogue with others, backwards as well as forwards, to see if it contributes anything to the presentation, solution or dissolution of their problems. By contributing, I here mean something stronger than just exemplifying or illustrating; something more akin to providing a missing piece. I shall attempt to argue that *La Nausée* does this with the reasonable doubt of scepticism in Stanley Cavell's *The Claim of Reason*. In this anachronistic interpretation, the philosophical book from 1979 provides a context that brings out the importance of the phenomenological and epistemological investigations of the novel from 1938.

In *The Claim of Reason*, Cavell is occupied with the validity of the doubt of the sceptic. The philosophical investigation of the sceptic (also called the traditional epistemologist) departs from the question of how we can know anything at all. Does the world really exist (as we know it)? Might not our senses be playing tricks on us? If you see an object, how can you be sure that you see all of it? The oddness of questions like these is made apparent to us by ordinary language philosophers like Austin, who points out that they are not being raised in any real situations, and so the questions become empty and forced. Knowledge of what? The epistemologist invents the problem he then professes to solve.

But Cavell does not want to be so quick to dismiss the 'reasonableness of doubt', as he calls it.[160] According to him, Austin partly trivializes the epistemologist's problem. Could we not imagine a case where such a doubt might be reasonably raised? This would be 'a case where there is *some reason to think* that what you claim may not be so; the sense, or fact, that *something is amiss*'. And so, the question becomes: 'whence comes this sense of something amiss about the simplest claim to knowledge under optimal conditions, where there is no practical problem moving us?'[161] He then proceeds with attempting to give us some examples of situations in life that could occasion fundamental doubt.

However, the examples Cavell gives in order to demonstrate the reasonableness of doubt are frustratingly insufficient. As commentators like Robert Mankin have complained, 'one feels that the examples given in discussing knowledge (a misconception in regard to a telephone number, a misidentification of a Big Band number) are close to trivial'.[162] A confusion about a telephone number[163] is indeed unlikely to cause us to doubt our knowledge of the world in general. Moving on from this example (which in its banality rather seem to strengthen than contradict Austin's dismissal of the sceptic's doubt), Cavell eventually concludes that 'an experience of a different order is needed, an experience that philosophers have characterized, more or less, as one of realizing that my sensations may not be *of* the world I take them to be at all, or that I can only know how objects appear (to us) to be, never what objects are like in themselves'.[164] He confesses to have had such experiences himself. But the account of them that follows is as arbitrary and inaccessibly abstract as the generic object of the traditional epistemologist:[165]

> I can only here attest to having had such experiences and, though struggling against them intellectually, have had to wait for them to dissipate in their own time. It seems to me that I relive such experiences when I ask my students, as habitually at the beginning of a course in which epistemology is discussed, whether they have ever had such thoughts as, for example, that they might, when for all the world awake, be dreaming; or that if our senses, for example our eyes, had differently evolved, we would sense, i.e. see, things other than we see them now, so that the way we see them is almost accidental … ; or that the things of the world would seem just as they now do to us if there were nothing in it but some power large enough to … arrange the world for our actions as a kind of endless stage-set, whose workings we can never get behind, for after all consider how little of anything, or any situation, we really see. I know well enough, intellectually as it were, that these suppositions may be nonsense, seem absurd, when raised as scruples about particular claims to knowledge. But if these examples have worked in the initial motivation of particular claims, then the attempt to prove intellectually that they have no sense is apt to weaken one's faith in intellectuality.[166]

Could there be an experience that reveals us to be under an illusion of sense, which in itself makes perfect sense? As Forsberg puts it, recognizing that an illusion of sense is real 'involves taking a researcher to a place where she recognizes that "I, a researcher, do not know what is meant with the word "research" anymore".[167] We are indeed at the boundaries of reason (or the reasonable) here, where philosophers like Cavell (and Forsberg, who calls himself a 'follower of Cavell of sorts'[168]) think that the most fruitful philosophical investigations might take place.

But since *The Claim of Reason* leaves us without any satisfying account of such an experience, it is tempting to conclude, as, for example, Anthony J. Cascardi does, that 'Cavell regards skepticism not as rooted in doubt but as stemming from the avoidance of truths that we are unwilling to accept'.[169] According to Cascardi, the doubt is *merely* a cover that the traditional epistemologist resorts to because it 'provides a way of "disowning" knowledge that would bear too heavily upon us, that would leave us too exposed, or without defense'.[170] Certainly this is part of Cavell's argument concerning scepticism. But the reasonableness of the doubt lies *not only*, as Cascardi argues, in it being some sort of psychological avoidance of the tragic truths of the human situation (that we are mortal, that we are dependent on each other for life and meaning, that we are faced with the other even though we can never completely know her).[171]

Cavell's famous claim that '[o]ur relation to the world as a whole, or to others in general, is not one of knowing, where knowing construes itself as being certain' brings together two strands of thought:[172] that scepticism can be seen as an 'attempt to convert the human condition ... into an intellectual difficulty, a riddle'[173] *and* that part of the predicament of being human is to experience such fundamental doubts as give rise to scepticism. To put it simply, there is a real doubt even if there cannot be any real certainty. Indeed, Cavell uses this quote from the preface to Kant's first Critique as an epigraph for the chapter on the reasonableness of doubt:

> Human reason has this peculiar fate that in one species of its knowledge it is burdened by questions which, as prescribed by the very nature of reason itself, it is not able to ignore, but which, as transcending all its powers, it is also not able to answer.[174]

Thus, what is required to complete Cavell's account and support the notion of the reasonableness of doubt is an illusion of sense which would show what it would be like to experience our habitual way of relating to the world as an illusion of sense. It might be described as a metaphysical discovery that we are related to the world discursively and not intuitively. In other words, Murdoch's interpretation helps us see how *La Nausée* could be read as a detailed, complex and nuanced experience of the sort Cavell failed (or refused?) to conjure up.

The story about Roquentin stays with both the pressing doubt *and* the kind of avoidance it brings with it/is caused by. As Cavell says, 'the cost of our continuous temptation to knowledge' is 'suggestive of madness', of being outside of human conventions, and thus the cost is also a 'loss, or forgoing, of identity or of selfhood'.[175] And as Murdoch points out, '[i]t is important that Roquentin has no *être-pour-autrui*, no close connexion with other people and no concern about how they view him; it is partly this that enables him to be such a pure case'.[176] Roquentin thinks that 'both social conventions and linguistic conventions are there ... to cheat us'.[177] Sartre's account of his experiences presents us with the illusion of seeing through language into the contingent overflow of being itself. In attempting to describe his experience of the root in the park, its overwhelming existence makes Roquentin vainly grasp after words, and finally he settles on 'absurd':

> The word absurdity is coming to life under my pen; a little while ago, in the garden, I couldn't find it, but neither was I looking for it, I didn't need it: I thought without words, on things, with things. Absurdity was not an idea in my head, or the sound of a voice, only this long serpent dead at my feet, this wooden serpent. Serpent or claw or root or vulture's talon, what difference does it make. And without formulating anything clearly, I understood that I had found the key to Existence, the key to my Nauseas, to my own life. In fact, all that I could grasp beyond that returns to this fundamental absurdity. Absurdity: another word; I struggle against words; down there I touched the thing. But I wanted to fix the absolute character of this absurdity here. ... This root out there was nothing in relation to which it was absurd. Oh, how can I put it in words? Absurd: in relation to the stones, the tufts of yellow grass, the dry mud, the tree, the sky, the green benches. Absurd, irreducible; nothing, not even a profound, secret upheaval of nature could explain it. Evidently I did not know everything, I had not seen the seeds sprout, or the tree grow. But faced with this great wrinkled paw, neither ignorance nor knowledge was important: the world of explanations and reasons is not the world of existence. ... This root ... existed in such a way that I could not explain it. Knotty, inert, nameless, it fascinated me, filled my eyes, brought me back unceasingly to its own existence. In vain to repeat: "This is a root" didn't work any more. I saw clearly that you could not pass from its function as a root, as a breathing pump, *to that*, to this hard and compact skin of a sea lion, to this oily, callous, headstrong look. The function explained nothing: it allowed you to understand generally that it was a root, but not *that one* at all. This root, with its colour, shape, its congealed movement, was ... below all explanation. Each of its qualities escaped it a little, flowed out of it, half solidified, almost became a thing; each one was *In the way* in the root and the whole stump now gave me the impression of unwinding itself a little, denying its existence to lose itself in a frenzied excess.[178]

Roquentin is not involved in any social or practical situation; he is alone with an overwhelming sense that there is something absurd with existence. Objects are not what he habitually took them to be when he was busy in the world – now, it is as if he has discovered that we cannot know what they are in themselves. He and the readers feel like he has gained some sort of privileged access to being as it really is, beyond words and human interactions. These are philosophical problems reflected upon (but by no means 'solved', or even defined) through the text as a work of art.

As a work of art, it calls upon our reflective, aesthetic judgement. There is a kind of unity to the manifold of Roquentin's impressions (and Sartre's choice of words) which cannot be sorted out. Compare the lengthy quote above to this passage from Kant's third Critique:

> Flowers are free natural beauties. Hardly anyone other than the botanist knows what sort of thing a flower is supposed to be; and even the botanist, who recognizes in it the reproductive organ of the plant, pays no attention to this natural end if he judges the flower by means of taste. Thus this judgment is not grounded on any kind of perfection, any internal purposiveness to which the composition of the manifold is related.[179]

As we might reasonably expect, there is a philosophical self-awareness to Sartre's choice to approach his problem, which I here call the problem of reasonable doubt, through art. The *purposiveness without a purpose* of the aesthetic judgement allows for a kind of account where what is illusory or not, making sense or presenting nonsense, does not really matter. Roquentin's root can be read as a repetition of, a reflection upon and an expansion of Kant's example with the flower. Knowing its function and classifying its parts cannot help us understand 'what sort of thing a flower is supposed to be' in relation to its beauty, just like the illusory promises of a rainbow do not disappear when we know what optical conditions cause it. That which holds the manifold of our experiences together is something other than conceptual understanding. As Sartre writes: 'neither ignorance nor knowledge was important: the world of explanations and reasons is not the world of existence.'[180]

Here, the partly frustrated attempts to understand (which we go through together with the narrator) form part of the experience as a whole, and its lack of purpose is both experienced as pleasing, through the beauty of the prose composition which gives us the sense of purposiveness, and unpleasurable, in that it invokes the sublime terror of what the imagination is unable to hold together.[181] It now becomes possible to see more clearly how Murdoch could criticize Sartre as a philosopher so harshly, while confessing her unmixed admiration for *La Nausée*. The novel is of course not disconnected from the rest of his oeuvre – Murdoch actually describes it as an 'instructive overture to Sartre's work'[182] – but in being a successful artwork it manages to stay with an enchanting and unstable illusion of sense. It is an instructive overture in more than just a positive sense. Murdoch holds Sartre's philosophical work largely in suspicion. She thinks that a revealing question to ask about any philosopher is: 'what is he afraid of?'[183] This is indeed a question she asks and answers often enough about Sartre. Just like Roquentin, she says, he dreads the chaos, 'the irreducibility of man and the world of thought ..., the *stuff* of human life'.[184] In *La Nausée*, he stays with this dread. Most of the novel is played out at the point of doubt, the pressing impulse to thought, which makes it perfectly possible to read without the explanations his philosophical work later presents us with.

Murdoch finds that the novel's 'interest lies in the powerful image which dominates it'.[185] This 'image' gives us a fuller account of the kind of experience Cavell fumbled after when trying to defend the reasonableness of the sceptical impulse. As such, it is also (as Cavell so well has explained about this kind of doubt) an avoidance of love, a lonely, frantic and deeply unsettling story about a man unable or unwilling to share in the life of other people, who continuously loses his grasp of the ordinary meanings of situations, acts and things. A philosophical justification of the reasonableness of doubt might therefore not be communicable more determinately than as a self-aware aesthetic illusion of sense.

2.3.5. Some philosophical limitations of Sartre's novel

Moving on, this implies some limitations to the philosophical work performed by the novel, especially when read in relation to Sartre's theoretical writings. Naturally, there are countless philosophical interpretations of *La Nausée*. Most seem to take for granted that Sartre's fiction (as he himself also claimed) should be read as continuous with his philosophical propositions. One interesting exception is Richard Kamber, who in the article 'Sartre's Nauseas' instead identifies an important disjunction between Roquentin's nausea and the nausea briefly alluded to in *L'Être et le Néant*.[186]

In the novel, Kamber says, nausea is 'a special way of apprehending external objects ... which nullifies the categories, concepts and instrumental associations in terms of which we ordinarily perceive the world'.[187] In his philosophical work, however, Sartre has reinterpreted the term into an aspect of self-consciousness, a 'dull and inescapable nausea [which] perpetually reveals my body to my consciousness'.[188] Roquentin's experiences instead constitute a revelation of *things* that are forcing themselves on his almost defenceless consciousness. Kamber shows how Sartre nursed a hope to be able to refute idealism by proving this immediate 'being' philosophically, and reads *La Nausée* as an 'elaborate account of what it would be like to have a direct revelation of the independent existence of perceivable objects'.[189] In *L'Être et Le Néant*, this 'being' is not correspondent to nausea but to 'l'être-en-soi' (being-in-itself), something Sartre according to Kamber fails to explain any immediate access to.

Kamber does not consider this to be a problem of the novel:

> It is clear ... that Roquentin's revelation is genuine; we have no reason to suspect that he is deluded or deceived about the significance of his experience. But the same can be said of Jonathan Harker in *Dracula*. Mr. Harker is quite right to believe in the transformation of corpses into blood-sucking bats.[190]

Since fiction entails no claims to reality, Kamber says, 'Sartre was under no obligation to verify the existence of Nausea' in the novel; only if he philosophically wanted 'to complete his case against idealism'.[191] The experiences of Roquentin, which in my Cavellian interpretation enforces the reasonableness of sceptical doubt, should in Kamber's eyes be read as completely belonging to another world. According to him, *La Nausée*'s failure to fill a gap in Sartre's philosophy seems to make it unable to serve any philosophical function whatsoever. Fiction, even though it might 'present us with a world that is very much like our own', cannot according to him 'present us *with* our own'.[192]

The parallel to *Dracula* might appear ridiculous, but I nonetheless believe that it (albeit a bit bluntly) says something about the limitations for doing philosophical work through a literary work of art. Fiction does not belong to another realm, but when we take part of it, we treat it *as if* it did. To sort out and make sense of its 'propositions' we must break the suspension of disbelief.[193] When we begin to discuss what kind of representations of bodily desires blood-sucking vampires symbolize or invoke, for example, we have moved away from the 'reality' of *Dracula*. And if we want to evaluate Roquentin's doubt as a revelation of philosophical precision and force, we must stop being so drawn into his experiences that we share them on a sensory and emotional level; we must shatter the illusion of sense in order to question it. (What *kind* of fundamental doubt have I stated Roquentin's experiences to be an example of in the account above? Ontological, epistemological, metaphysical, or even moral doubt? Terminological precision could bring, as I suggested earlier, more of a distortion than an explanation of a novel – the philosophical 'work' it is able to perform must perhaps remain vague in order to retain its concrete, sensory, object-like, character as a work of art.[194])

However, this does not mean that Kamber dismisses the experience of the novel as necessarily false. 'That Sartre failed to make the case for "quelque moyen d'accès immédiat" to the transphenomenal being of external objects (and failed to acknowledge his failure) would not preclude the possibility of a private revelation – a unique encounter with being inaccessible to philosophical generalization.'[195] Such experiences are not irrelevant to philosophy (we have seen Cavell grasping for them), but they are also not enough. Sartre seemed to recognize this himself; in an interview which Kamber quotes, he says that he wrote *La Nausée* as a novel because 'the idea was not solid enough for me to write it as a philosophical book; it was a quite vague thing, but it still had me in a very strong grip'.[196]

This vagueness makes the novel difficult to meet like an argument. In another article which questions the philosophical importance of the novel, David Pole goes so far as to suggest that Roquentin's metaphysical doubt (as well as, incidentally, his hatred for the bourgeoisie) is rooted in Sartre's psychological issues ('an anger and a hatred, obscurely born'[197]). What gives the novel its power is exactly what makes Pole doubt its philosophical validity.

> 'The effect is enclosing, hence hypnotic; but its vision, of course, narrows correspondingly. It serves literature well, but prophecy [a name Pole gives to philosophy that seeks to convince through suggestiveness rather than argumentation] badly; for it forces us powerfully to identify with a certain unusual mental state – in fact, as I suggested, a pathological one. It discourages, *unless we deliberately disengage ourselves and step back,* any survey that would place it in perspective.'[198]

This suggests some important limitations for philosophical fiction. In order to engage with a novel philosophically, we are tempted to break its spell, extract thoughts or statements from their sensuous, particularized and experiential contexts, so as to be able to comment or respond in the language which is 'proper' to philosophy: what we, here and now, take philosophy to be, as a contemporary academic discipline and a canon of texts. Of course one can quarrel with the boundaries of philosophical discourse, but this is always at the risk of intelligibility and community. A philosophical work must 'hold up' in a way that a novel need not; the latter is not disvalued by the accusation that its sense is just illusory.

Stanley Cavell's *The Claim of Reason* famously ends with the question: 'But can philosophy become literature and still know itself?'[199] *La Nausée* is indeed both literature and philosophy. But I am not, and Murdoch never seemed, completely convinced that it really knew itself philosophically. She took Sartre's subsequent theories to be conceived partly in flight from some of the implications of his own first story. As a novelist, he was able to stay with his disgust for the stuff of human life, which he then took refuge from in his philosophy, where (in Murdoch's words) '[h]is gloom is superficial and conceals elation'[200] at explaining the condition of man as a solitary freedom. This does not describe the predicament of Roquentin, who has no similar 'insights' but is despairingly overwhelmed by the world.

Where does that leave us with the concept 'philosophical novel'? As Murdoch indicates, it is very rare (and not necessarily desirable) that a work can hold the magic of a great artwork while at the same time being an independent piece of philosophical discourse. Rather than arguing for their interwovenness, I have turned to *La Nausée* in order to show that even though literature and philosophy can on rare occasions make a common case, they are nonetheless in general better understood as different disciplines. As a sensory illusion of sense, art delights in a trickery which thinking strives to go beyond. But if Kant is right that these questions of reason are as unavoidable as they are unanswerable, life is lived within an illusion of sense which we are never able fully to trust, but also never able to figure out. In that sense, art may indeed be said to entail a different kind of general knowledge of human life than that of philosophy. To conclude this chapter, we shall look at Murdoch's story about a philosopher's struggles with some of those aspects of his existence.

2.4. The surface of philosophy in *The Philosopher's Pupil*

2.4.1. Mocking philosophy

George is a middle-aged bungler, who blames his former philosophy teacher John Robert Rozanov for having ruined his life by advising him to give up philosophy. Now, rumour has it that Rozanov is returning to their common hometown, after many years abroad. One day at the baths, George notices a 'fat man whose swimming trunks clung almost invisibly beneath his paunch. The fat man had a big bony puckered face and stiff flat brush of grey hair which was evidently still dry. As he now turned his head George recognized John Robert Rozanov.'[201]

The Philosopher's Pupil is the only one of Murdoch's novels which has 'philosophy' (albeit as an agent noun) in its title, and yet it has received comparatively little attention among the critics who want to see her as a philosophical novelist. Perhaps this is because, as I shall argue in this last part, the story is occupied with those things about and around philosophy and the philosopher which are *not* philosophy. Any reader afflicted with a Derridean spirit will here surely protest that pointing out what is not philosophically relevant, that is, branding something as 'the other' of philosophy, is tantamount to actualizing its latent philosophical potency. But I shall stick with my initial claim in this chapter, which was that examining the jokes philosophy and literature make about each other serves to give us a sense not only of their point of contact, but also of their differences.

Just like Plato taunted Ion for his prettiness, Murdoch is obsessed with John Robert Rozanov's ugliness. The gorgeous rhapsode was mocked into admitting that he lacked any tangible skills, and that the only way to not dismiss him as mad was to regard him as a tool for the divine. The unattractive Rozanov has a knack for lucid reasoning, but he is deficient precisely of that knowledge which Murdoch sought to emphasize in the rhapsode and the poet, which she somewhat vaguely referred to as a general knowledge of human life. It is the feeling of life as a whole which eludes him; a grasp of it all which might, 'deep down', just as well be illusory, but which our existence among our fellow humans nonetheless requires us to sustain. In this last section, I shall allow myself to dwell a bit on the lost and ugly philosopher, as well as some aspects of how others perceive him, and thus use a non-philosophical novel which revolves around a philosopher to tease out some of the differences between literature and philosophy.

It might seem as if we get a good picture of who Rozanov is as a philosopher. We are told that he has taken an interest in philosophy of science, written a book on Kant's view of time, and another one called *Kant and the Kantians*, studied Descartes and Leibniz, become obsessed with Greek history, published a study on the Peloponnesian war, and after having been more of 'a sceptic, a reductionist, a linguistic analyst' in his youth later on having 'become a neo-Platonist' – in brief, a hotch-potch of philosophical interests. Murdoch has even gone so far as to borrow a title from one of her own essays to his 'seminal work, *Nostalgia for the Particular*',[202] something scholars wanting to question her distinction between literature and philosophy have been quick to pounce on.[203] Surely that must indicate some connection between her novels and her philosophical work! I think it is safer to assume, as Murdoch herself has suggested in interviews, that this is rather to be taken as a joke.[204]

Would Murdoch really joke about Plato? Miles Leeson seems at least to consider it unthinkable. In his book *Iris Murdoch: Philosophical Novelist*, he states that '[i]t is central to the novel that Platonism is discussed by Rozanov', exemplified by Rozanov's thought: 'Who could fathom Plato's mind?'[205] The 'Platonism' is also for Leeson underlined by other supposedly Platonic themes in the novel such as '[i]ncest, unrequited love, homosexuality and sexual violence'.[206] When Rozanov is ignorant and distracted towards others, Leeson comments that he displays 'a lack of Platonic vision', as well as being deficient of 'Simone Weil's concept of attention', two complex philosophical concepts that here seem to have been conflated to simply mean 'being nice to other people'.

Bran Nicol takes *The Philosopher's Pupil* to be 'the novel which explores the relationship between philosophy and literature perhaps more deeply and more contradictorily than any of Murdoch's other'.[207] He sees in the title of Rozanov's seminal book an 'implicit sense of confession' regarding the connection between Murdoch's philosophical and literary work.[208] Subsequently, he takes Rozanov as a direct representation of her neo-Platonic philosophy, opposed to George as 'an embodiment of a quasi-Nietzschean ideal of "beyond good and evil"'.[209] The repulsive unworldly man in bathing trunks plays the part of Socrates; the bungler with an aggression problem is Nietzsche. This is not supposed to be taken as a joke.

But these characters can in no deeper sense be understood as representative of philosophical positions. If they have anything to do with the history of philosophy, it is rather as caricatures of popularized stereotypes (Plato was a detached homosexual idealist, Socrates was ugly and Nietzsche eventually went mad). This is not just a dismissive remark. In a way, I agree with Nicol that *The Philosopher's Pupil* can be read as expressive of Murdoch's notion of the relationship between literature and philosophy: but contrary to him, who interprets her as unconsciously wanting to see them merged, I think it strengthens her insistence on the distinction.

Consider this depiction of Rozanov philosophizing:

> Now every morning as he assumed burden of consciousness he reflected upon its strangeness: the mystery of mind, so general and so particular. Why do thoughts not lose their owners? How does the individual stay together and not stray away like racing water-drops? How does consciousness continue, how can it? Could the curse of memory not end, and why did it not end? Did not the instant, of its nature, annihilate the past? Was not remorse a fiction, an effect of a prime delusion? How could a feeling be evidence of anything? All those days and nights he had spent with the many and the one, how little wisdom they had brought him, now when thoughts were changing into living sensa, and appearance and reality contended inside his frame which seemed at times as huge as the universe, and racked with as large a pain. The point of solipsism, often missed, was that it abolished morality. So if the pain he felt seemed like a spiritual pain, must he then not be the victim of a mistake? How little it all helped him now when he was pitchforked back into this mess of tormented being. The Other, whose hard fine edge he had aspired to trace, and in whose very absence he had sometimes gloried, was no more than an amoebic jelly, an unsavoury ectoplasm of wandering ideation. Truth was just a concept which had attracted him once.[210]

It is not what Rozanov thinks that is interesting and relevant here. It is his almost sensory experience of thinking, his feeling of life, which is in focus: being 'pitchforked back into this mess of tormented being', feeling a pain which 'seem[s] like a spiritual pain', fumbling at a concept like 'an amoebic jelly, an unsavoury ectoplasm of wandering ideation'. A couple of pages later, we are told that he 'needed, like a drug, someone to talk to, preferably another philosopher. ... All his life he had talked with pupils and colleagues. He felt ill now with the deprivation.'[211] Philosophy is here portrayed as something akin to psychosomatic malaise and substance abuse.

The story takes place not when Rozanov is in his full power, but when he feels like his mind is deteriorating and he is unable to write. He can no longer properly do philosophy and is thus confronted with his mind and body as mere sensory, contingent stuff, and with his history and present of messy relationships, which he is defencelessly sunken in. As George accurately reflects: 'There was a kind of helplessness about the philosopher, some absolutely monumental lack of common sense.'[212] In contrast to the attractive Ion, who is not an expert at anything, except perhaps human life in general, Rozanov is made the ugly figurehead of a philosophical knowledge which is clumsy and idiotic precisely when it comes to human life in general.

Of course he is not thus representative of *all* of philosophy. He is a specific character, the depictions of whose specific life and consciousness can be read as an implicit commentary on some of the boundaries of philosophy; the points at which the philosopher is confronted with something other than philosophy. One of these points is George's, his former pupil's, relation to philosophy. George's passion for thinking is more like a manic pursuit of hidden significance. He finds meaning in random details, not from reflecting upon them, but in immediate, flash-like (and arguably mad) intuitions:

> Was it not *significant* that the philosopher had returned to Ennistone? Why had he returned? There were meanings in the world. He had just seen his own double in the Botanic Gardens. Perhaps it was just someone very like him, but that had meaning too. Twice now he had seen this double, capable of anything, walking about and at large. Once, talking to someone in his office, he had seen through the window a man fall from a high scaffolding. He had immediately apprehended that man as himself. He said nothing about this at the time or later. There were meanings in the world. He had seen the number forty-four chalked on a wall.[213]

Instead of the 'patient relentless ability to stay with a problem', which Murdoch in an interview describes as the mark of a philosopher,[214] George is approaching philosophy almost like astrology.[215] He is desperate for some kind of immediate explanation, but at the same time desires to be mystified and dazzled. His obsession with Rozanov is evidently bordering on insanity ('He had heard the pigeons saying "Rozanov, Rozanov" in the early dawn.'[216]). It is the idea, or perhaps even the fetish, of philosophy he is after when he feverishly questions his former teacher:

> 'Are you writing your great book, I mean the final one?'
> 'No.'
> 'Well, I don't mean the final one, you're not all that old, I suppose. I hope you're writing philosophy?'
> 'No.'
> 'What a pity! Why not, are you tired of it at last? I often wondered if you'd ever get tired of it and give it up.'
> 'No.'
> 'Look, there's an awful lot I'd like to talk to you about, an awful lot I'd like to ask. You know I always felt there was something *behind* everything that you said.'
> 'I don't think there was,' said John Robert. He was now regarding George with his pale fierce eyes.
> 'I mean a sort of secret doctrine, something you only revealed to the initiated.'
> 'No.'[217]

These are not 'philosophical debates', as Nicol would have them, and they do not form 'the heart of the novel'.[218] On the contrary, Rozanov seems to be correct in telling George that 'in your case philosophy is just a nervous craving'.[219] There is no 'depth' of philosophy here, but a very interesting depiction of its surface. At the heart of the novel lies not the philosopher's thoughts, but the philosopher's appearance. Numerous, slightly repetitive, but surprisingly vivid and captivating depictions of his charismatic ugliness practically flood the story.

Apart from the shock glimpse at the Baths, it was some years since George had seen his old teacher and … Rozanov had changed a good deal. He had become fatter, slower in his movements and stiffened by arthritis. The shabbiness and shagginess was now clearly that of old age. A little saliva foamed at the corners of his protruding lips as he talked. His once-smooth brow had grown soft pitted flesh, humped between deep lines of wrinkles. Coarse hairs were growing from his nose and ears. Grey braces, visible under his gaping jacket, supported his uncertain trousers half-way up his paunch. He had always looked rather dirty and now looked dirtier. He filled the little room with his bear-like presence and his smell. He stared gloomily at George.[220]

This is not just George's impression, but a picture which is repeated in the eyes of others. His granddaughter's Hattie's companion Pearl, to mention just one other example, regards the philosopher in a similar light:

How charmless that big, awkward man was, careless about Hattie, egoistically absent-minded, consulting always his convenience and oblivious of theirs. How ugly he was too, fat and flabby and wet-mouthed with jagged yellow teeth. (This was before he had acquired the false ones commented on by George.) His big head and big hooked nose made him look like a vast puppet in a carnival. His movements were graceless and clumsy. His stare was startled and disconcerting, as if, when he looked at someone, he simultaneously recalled something awful which had nothing to do with the person looked at.[221]

Both Pearl and George are, as most of the other characters in the novel, obsessed with the philosopher. Despite his ugliness, he has a magnetic and enchanting effect on the people around him, generating strong emotions he seems as unaware of as (when they are confessed) disinterested in, even disgusted by. The philosopher is depicted as taking the sensuous, the relational, the social and the emotional as completely irrelevant. What is irrelevant to him is, in order words, himself, as a social person and a body.

Even though this is to some extent meant to be a criticism of a certain strand of philosophy,[222] the novel also highlights a difference between literature and philosophy which is difficult to shake completely. Without going as far as Plato, who at times seems to equate true knowledge with abstraction and who in the *Timaeus* describes the body as a mere 'vehicle for the head',[223] it is hard (if at all desirable) to get away from an understanding of philosophy as having a different relation to the sensuous, the personal and the experiential than literature. This is not to say that embodied, lived experience would be irrelevant to philosophy. But even in phenomenology, the method and the aim of philosophy differ significantly from the artistic approach, a distinction I shall attempt to highlight by returning briefly to Hegel.

2.4.2. Reason individualized and toothless

As was explained before: in Hegel's account of the end of art, we find a remarkably clear account of the distinction between literature and philosophy ('speculative thinking').[224] Art is spiritual self-recognition in and through the sensuous. It is defined by having the sensuous as its medium. However, in literature, the sensuous material at hand is not clay or colour, but language and the imagination. It treats these constituents almost like sensuous objects, even though they are more immaterial.[225] Thus, poetry 'keep[s] to the mean between the abstract universality of thought and the sensuously concrete corporeal objects'.[226]

This 'mean' means for Hegel that the expression of a poetic work can never be abstracted from its imaginative sensuousness, in contradistinction to philosophy:

> Thinking, however, results in thoughts alone; it evaporates the form of reality into the form of the pure Concept, and even if it grasps and apprehends real things in their particular character and real existence, it nevertheless lifts even this particular sphere into the element of the universal and ideal wherein alone thinking is at home with itself.[227]

Again, even if this would be argued to be a specific view of philosophy, it is hard to imagine a philosophical approach which would not attempt to move beyond the imaginative and sensuous into a more generalizable and abstract understanding.[228] But this 'mean' also means that literature *is* balancing against the immateriality of thought. What is expressed in poetry is, according to Hegel, 'reason individualized'.[229] A poem put in other words is not the poem, but a philosophy explained differently is the same philosophy. They have different relations to their 'bodies'.

Murdoch's descriptions of the ugly, charismatic philosopher can be said to toy with this distinction in an almost parodic fashion. Rozanov, 'reason individualized', is a caricature of reason swallowed by its sensuous embodiment. George, sneaking up on the philosopher asleep, finds him literally toothless:

> John Robert was clothed, but with his shirt open and the waist of his trousers undone. ... George ... looked at the sleeping face. John Robert's face did not look calm in repose. The open moist lips, through which the slightly bubbling snore emerged, were still urgently thrust forward in the dominating moue which was their customary expression. The closed eyes, in their stained hollows, were slightly screwed up. The cheek-bones still protruded upon the flabby face, and the furrows on either side of the large hooked nose were like violent scourings. Upon the forehead, above which the frizzy grey hair had not yet started to recede, the flesh rose soft and pink in little regular pipings between the deep lines. A dirty grey stubble covered the chin and thick much-folded saurian neck. Only the chin seemed weaker, less formidably decisive. George realized with a little shock the reason for this. John Robert had taken out his false teeth, which were to be seen glinting upwards in a shallow white cup upon the bedside table.[230]

This is – like a meta joke – reason individualized and sensuously concretized to the point of barely not being reason anymore; reason defenceless, reason asleep. But faced with the body of the philosopher, we are not simply faced with a sensuous impression. The imaginative medium of literature invokes open-ended reflections and thoughts (such as the ones laid out in this interpretation of *The Philosopher's Pupil* as highlighting the distinction between philosophy and literature). The step from admitting this, and

Forsberg's claim that *The Black Prince* is 'forcing us to ask questions'[231], or Nicol's view that *The Philosopher's Pupil* is 'forcing us to become suspicious readers',[232] might seem slight, but is, I believe, decisive. A novel is a free play, not a forced incitement to scepticism.[233] Any philosophical interpretation, such as this one, is not compelled by the story, but rather makes use of certain aspects of it for its own purposes.

2.4.3. 'A very odd unnatural activity'

In many scholarly accounts, it seems to be a given presumption that something would stand to be *gained* from reading literature as philosophy. But is it not more likely that something could get *lost* on both sides by blurring the lines between the practices? Murdoch's insistence on the distinction is partly meant to remind us of how terribly hard philosophy is. Philosophy is not a name she considered to be applicable to thinking in general, but 'a very odd unnatural activity. … Philosophy disturbs the mass of semi-aesthetic conceptual habits on which we normally rely. … It is an attempt to perceive and tease out in thought our deepest and most general concepts.'[234]

The unnaturalness of such a philosophical conceptual sorting-out can, again, be hyperbolically illustrated by the example of Rozanov. He is in a sense an inversion of all the non-philosophical characters in the novel. For him, the habitual approach *is* the philosophical. Eventually unable to resist his incestuous love for his granddaughter, he feels driven to attempt to understand it, to tease out the most general concept behind his uncomfortable feelings:

> Other people solved such problems without even noticing them, or else lived thoughtlessly without their ever arising; he could not. Was it that he loved her? Was this love? Did he after all know so little of the world as not to have thoroughly understood this concept? Was it the same thing now as what he had felt when she was eight (or was it nine)? Perhaps the thing he felt, and thought he could identify, was always changing. Had it, in especial, changed lately, as Hattie grew – older? To say that John Robert was "in love" with his grand-daughter was to employ too vague and dubious a concept. What was certain was that he was obsessed with her.[235]

Needless to say, the pressing problem here is not the philosophical one. Instead of participating in this conceptual sorting out and asking whether he 'really loves her', the reaction of the reader is probably closer to that of his granddaughter, who, when the awkward confession of his incestuous desires suddenly surfaces, is struck again by his ugliness:

> Hattie stared at the huge face of the philosopher which seemed suddenly like a relief model of something else, a whole country perhaps. She stared at the flat head, the lined bumpy fleshy brow and the very short electric frizzy hair, the big birdlike nose framed by furrows in which grey stubble grew, the pouting prehensile mouth with its red wet lips and the froth of bubbly saliva at the corners, the fiercely shining rectangular brown eyes which seemed to be trying so hard to send her a

signal. The soft plump wrinkles of the brow, pitted with porous spots, so close to her across the table, gave her especially the sense of something so sad, so old. She felt frightened and full of pity.[236]

Just like Hattie, most readers probably take the deviant philosopher and the story about him at (forgive the pun) face value. The natural reaction to his unnatural desires is not a deconstructive theorizing. But, as was mentioned, Nicol argues that the explicit mention of the narrator forces us to become suspicious readers. Early in the story, the narrator N introduces himself and his town (which he gives the fictious name 'Ennistone'), and towards the end, he says that he 'also had the assistance of a certain lady', indicating presumably Murdoch herself.[237] This renders the artificially constructed character of its realism especially apparent, Nicol remarks, which makes everything 'seem pregnant with some extra meaning, the exact nature of which is unclear'.[238]

It is difficult for a critic to resist the impulse to make too much of this vague, hidden, seeming meaning. Even if the illusion of a deeper sense is highlighted as such, it does not mean that there would be any complex significance behind it, or that an ordinary reader must be on a tense look-out for it (I, at least, was not). An explicitly present, perhaps unreliable, narrator does not necessarily break the suspension of disbelief. We already know that a novel is made up – being reminded of that does not stop us from being enchanted by its characters. Nicol, however, takes this reminder as a directly philosophical prompt:

> Realist fiction is thus founded upon an implicit ideology or *philosophy* – not something as consciously or clearly thought-out as, say, a romantic or post-modernist aesthetic manifesto, but a philosophy nonetheless. The implications of this fact for Murdoch's fiction is that it complicates the relationship between the "philosophical" and the "literary" in her work.[239]

Briefly, Nicol claims that Murdoch's making explicit the 'literariness' of her fiction is what becomes expressive of her philosophical understanding of what literature is and should be. This would perhaps more fittingly be called a poetics than a philosophy, but besides that, I do not disagree. Naturally, her practice as a novelist is informed by her aesthetic understanding of art, and vice versa. This does not make her novels 'governed by her philosophy'[240] any more than it makes her aesthetic philosophy into an ornament on her literary writing. But Nicol views her insistence on regarding literature and philosophy as 'opposites' as neurotic.[241] To support this interpretation, he claims that: 'the single most characteristic feature of her philosophical rhetoric is its preference for oppositions: the sublime and the beautiful, the crystalline and the journalistic, existentialism and mysticism, low and high Eros, the necessary and the contingent, fantasy and imagination, appearance and reality.'[242]

In fact, Nicol is the one exaggerating these into (supposedly neurotic) oppositions. The sublime and the beautiful, not even considered opposites by Kant,[243] are by Murdoch suggested to be much more intertwined than his aesthetics allowed;[244] the low and the high Eros are different points on a sliding scale; and fantasy and imagination are not as opposite as much of the Murdoch scholarship would have them be.[245] Nicol exaggerates these oppositions in order to be able to present her insistence on the distinction between literature and philosophy as an expression of a general neurotic need for oppositions, culminating in a lamentable self-denial, as if she secretly and against herself wanted nothing more than to write a brilliant philosophical novel. 'After all', Nicol says,

> we could easily imagine a parallel version of literary history in which Iris Murdoch devoted herself to a brilliant revitalisation of the philosophical novel after Sartre. The pertinence of these questions suggests that one of Murdoch's defining characteristics as a writer can be explained by the Lacanian notion of "giving way" [*céder*] on one's desire, that is, continually frustrating or failing to recognise it.[246]

Contrary to Nicol, I do not think that Murdoch considered a philosophical novel to be a higher achievement than a 'merely' artistic novel, and unless one embarks on a very dubious psychoanalysing of her person, there is no support in her work for that claim. Coupled with the Lacanian analysis, Nicol makes a Derridean diagnosis of Murdoch as a clear case of a 'logocentric' metaphysical thinker who places philosophy in the dubious position of an oppositional supplement to literature.[247] Again, Nicol exaggerates the distinction into an opposition in order to strengthen his claim:

> As befits a metaphysician, Murdoch makes the typical philosophical move that Derrida has repeatedly exposed and challenged in metaphysics: she defines literature as the realm of contradiction and irreducibility, of chaos and muddle. But this move, Derrida demonstrates, is precisely the means by which philosophy creates its own other, placing the literary outside the boundaries of philosophy and thereby implying that philosophy is not all about contradiction and unchecked rhetorical play.[248]

A philosophy all about unchecked rhetorical play was indeed a nightmarish vision to Murdoch, something which made her hold especially Derrida in suspicion. This is also the sense in which she thought that 'bad philosophy is not philosophy, whereas bad art is still art'.[249] If we think of art as creating a sensuous illusion of sense, there is not really a way for it to fail (even if there are still ways in which it could be more or less interesting, enjoyable and beautiful). An artwork cannot be dismantled by arguments. Grasping at its sense, attempting to get behind the 'play' of the story, entails leaving the work behind by dispelling the illusion of sense. The disillusion of the reader becomes the dissolution of the artwork. In Hegel's words: 'the beauty of art does in fact appear in a form which is expressly opposite to thought and which thought is compelled to destroy in order to pursue its own characteristic activity.'[250]

As we have seen with the example of *La Nausée*, Murdoch does not think that sensuous impressions or emotions (such as nausea) must be inimical to philosophical work. But a properly philosophical novel is a rare case and not a universally desirable achievement. She considered *The Philosopher's Pupil* to be a non-philosophical novel about (among other things) the almost insurmountable difficulty of philosophy, as a way of showing how 'if you're not doing philosophy pretty well you're not doing it at all'.[251] It is about the anguish, the ugliness, the obsessions, the charisma, the emotions and the relationships in, around and on the surface of philosophy.[252] The feeling of helplessness is doubly illustrated when George, finally, gives in to his dark desire and attempts to drown Rozanov. Sneaking up on him sleeping again, George is faced with a defenceless, senseless body, which is again minutely depicted:

> The philosopher was snoring more quietly now with a faint bubbling sound. This time he had left his teeth in, and his mouth and chin had not collapsed, but his sleeping face looked to George huge and senseless, a pile of flabby layers of soft folded skin, pitted and porous, old, like the remains of something which had failed to be cooked, or a collapsed heap of blanched dead plants deprived of light. The eyes had vanished into hooded wrinkled holes. It was not like a face but a chaotic mess of flesh spread out where a face might have been. The skin was coarse and patchily discoloured, dirtied by a grey growth of beard. George moved his gaze to where the open neck of the starchily clean shirt revealed a rising slice of pink hairless chest. The genitals were covered, the knobbly knees visible, red and smooth and curiously touching as if they had not aged and were still the knees of a boy. Beneath them the legs were a livid white, with prominent blue veins, and sparsely covered with extremely long black hairs. The philosopher's feet were covered by a towel.[253]

Rozanov does not wake up when George heaves him into the bathtub and pushes his face down because he has already taken 'an effective mixture' in order to commit suicide. No one eventually triumphs or gets the upper hand in their relationship. Killing off her philosopher might be read as Murdoch indicating that literature 'wins out' over philosophy,[254] which in turn may be interpreted as a desperate attempt to ward off the unavoidable 'tension' between them, but since she claimed to feel no such tension,[255] the explanation could also be much easier. This is a novel about the relationship between philosopher and his pupil, not a philosophical novel. It deals with philosophy just like the rhapsode Ion deals with wars and medicine – portraying their auras without providing any genuine understanding. The audience is enchanted into feeling and imagining these lives, an achievement which demands implicit knowledge of how human life rests upon such sensory illusions of sense. Philosophical work worthy of its name should, according to Murdoch, grapple more thoroughly with its problems than these artistic 'magical' presentations, and I for one am much inclined to agree.

2.5. Chapter summary

In this chapter, I have discussed the concept 'philosophical novel' from the perspective of approaching the literary art as a sensory illusion of sense. Departing from the mocking of a pretty rhapsode and his poetry, and ending with the caricature of an ugly philosopher, I have intended to give a preliminary feel for the distinction between literature and philosophy. Murdoch's insistence on this distinction has been introduced: not just as a novelist's squirmy attempt to divert the interpretations of her own work, but as the well-grounded claim of an aesthetic thinker wishing to safeguard the integrity of two different practices which are only rarely mutually enforcing. To exemplify what this can mean, I have looked more closely on what I take to be one of the more interesting philosophical readings of Murdoch's fiction, Niklas Forsberg's interpretation of *The Black Prince*, and questioned his claim that literature is doing philosophy also when read as art. He wants to see the novel as an instance of Kierkegaardian indirect communication, but I have argued that its illusion of sense is not instrumental and not intended to be broken. Together with Hegel and Kant, I have shown how the fundamentally sensuous and reflective dimension of literature risks being neglected when it is approached as coercing the reader into a conceptual sorting-out, as Forsberg would have it.

However, staying with a sensory illusion of sense must therefore not entail that literature can never make a common case with philosophy. Jean-Paul Sartre's *La Nausée*, by Murdoch admired as a rare example of a good philosophical novel, has been discussed as being both a significant artwork and a valuable phenomenological-epistemological justification of the reasonableness of sceptical doubt. Based on this example, some of the philosophical limitations of the novel form have also been indicated. Finally, I have turned to Murdoch's novel *The Philosopher's Pupil*, which I have read as a portrayal of the obsession, appearance, fatigue, enchantment, sensory impressions and relationships surrounding and permeating a philosopher. I have argued why this novel 'about' philosophy is not better understood as a philosophical novel, and thus provided a further criticism of the prevalence and desirability of that concept.

While this chapter has suggested a somewhat rough (but in no sense definitive or exceptionless) delineation of the practices of literature and philosophy, the next chapter will look more closely at the role of conceptual thinking in the literary art. As Kant was quoted on already in this chapter, the aesthetic judgement is non-conceptual. But clearly, reading fiction and poetry is not a conceptless activity – so how can we understand the kind of thinking that is involved without conflating literature with philosophy? I shall take off from Murdoch's quarrel and subsequent reconciliation with Kant, to investigate how the concepts of and in aesthetic and artistic experiences can be said to differ from the conceptual determining judgements of the understanding.

3

The feel of muddled thinking: *Conceptual content in literature following Kant's aesthetics*

3.1. The purity of the aesthetic judgement

'Kant prefers bird-song to opera', Murdoch complains. He exemplifies beauty with tulips and wallpapers, instead of Shakespeare. His pure judgement of taste describes an immediate and non-conceptual pleasure, which, Murdoch remarks, might be true for the appreciation of a rose, but hardly for *King Lear*, which demands a much more complex cognitive engagement. Indeed, it sounds like almost all of literature would have to be excluded from 'the extremely narrow conception of art which is implicit here'.[1]

In this chapter, I will explain why this understanding of Kant's aesthetics is misleadingly simplistic and show how Murdoch's own view of the art of literature can be squared with the non-conceptual judgement of taste. At the centre of this discussion is the role of conceptual understanding in our appreciation of art and literature. We shall travel from the pure judgement of taste to specific examples from Murdoch's fiction, a road which entails going through what Kant means with concepts, discussing the relevance of knowing whether something is a product of nature or an artwork, describing the sublime and explaining the Kantian notion of aesthetic ideas. The focus is Kant's aesthetics, but Murdoch will also play a prominent part here. Beginning with her relatively early (1959) quarrel with him, which was indicated in the paragraph above, going through her later (1992) reconciliation with and reinterpretation of his notions of beauty and the sublime, and ending with an exposition of what I take to be an important aesthetic idea in her fiction, my main question is: How can we understand the non-conceptuality of the aesthetic judgement in relation to literature, an art which obviously makes use of concepts?

In the essay 'The Sublime and the Good' (quoted above), Murdoch is critical of Kant's notion of a pure judgement of taste. The pure judgement of taste is described in the third Critique as a judgement which is not mixed with any interest (§2), independent from charm and emotion (§13) and any empirical sensations (§14), and not understood under a concept or as conforming to any end (§16). Instead, it is based on a 'feeling of life … which contributes nothing to cognition but only holds the given representation in the subject up to the entire faculty of representation, of which the mind becomes conscious in the feeling of its state'.[2] Here, Kant describes an *a priori* capacity of the mind to feel the form of its own powers. What is intuited by the aesthetic judgement is thus not an object, but our own cognitive powers, which are here felt and not (as in philosophy) thought about.

Murdoch's offence with the notion of purity is based on a misreading. After having described the non-conceptuality of the judgement of taste according to Kant she concludes: 'We note at once that pure art or true art, according to Kant, is a very small area of what we normally think of as art.'[3] In fact, Kant nowhere speaks about 'pure' or 'true' art. Since the third Critique also entails a good number of paragraphs on art, it is tempting to read it as an art theory.[4] However, even when explicitly discussing the arts, Kant cautions the reader to refrain from this: 'The reader will not judge of this outline for a possible division of the beautiful arts as if it were a deliberate theory. It is only one of the several experiments that still can and should be attempted.'[5] Art is a complex, quasi-intentional creative activity, and relating the pure judgement of taste to its empirical products will always have something mixed, provisional and experimental about it. The purity Kant is after does not concern the birdsong or the opera, but a certain way we relate to our being in the world, a *feeling* of a *state of mind* which, when all interest, understanding, will and sensation have been removed, can become apparent as an *a priori* faculty. In other words, his aesthetics is primarily a transcendental critique, not a theory of art.

In Murdoch's later discussion of Kant in *Metaphysics as a Guide to Morals*, this distinction has become more apparent. She now speaks about aesthetic enjoyment as a certain kind of awareness which does not necessarily form the entirety of an experience, in saying that '[w]e can recognize the idea of "switching" from ordinary awareness to aesthetic contemplation'.[6] Her margin notes in the exemplar of the third Critique that has been kept by her archive suggests that she did not read, or at least not read attentively, the passages on genius, the different arts and aesthetic ideas until a later date.[7] In any case, it is clear that her view has been modified during the more than thirty years that passed from the publication of the essay mentioned above.[8] In the later work, Murdoch states, 'Kant's exaltation of spontaneous creative imagination in fine art felicitously extends or amends his characterization, earlier in the *Critique of the Power of Judgement*, of art generally in narrower formal terms as the production of conceptless objects, and the experience of beauty.'[9] In fact, what has been amended is Murdoch's narrower initial interpretation of his aesthetics, where she took his description of the *a priori* aesthetic judgement as a direct characterization of empirical art objects.[10]

As was explained earlier, Kant's judgement of taste is a specific feeling which in itself does not contribute to the understanding or fulfil any other purpose.[11] However, Kant does in fact recognize that it can be mixed up in various ways, in the arts as well as concerning other kinds of beauty (such as the purposive beauty of a human being, or the intentional attempts to convince in rhetoric).[12] Rather than delineating what is proper art and not, the notion of an *a priori* purity makes the contrast to the (potentially endless) empirical instances of beauty obvious. Recognizing that an artwork can be and do other things (convey information, or be a building with other purposes, such as a temple) is not a contradiction to stating that the aesthetic judgement entails a specific state of mind which is distinct from conceptual understanding (among other things).

Understanding artworks in relation to the aesthetic judgement, while at the same time seeing them as separate things, appears to be surprisingly tricky. An artwork, such as a literary text, is an object which can be approached in many different ways. It is perfectly possible to make use of a novel for historical, philosophical, sociological, psychological and many other purposes. Indeed, doing so might be very fruitful and illuminating. My quarrel in this book lies only with these approaches to the extent to which someone claims that this is tantamount to understanding it aesthetically, as a work of art.[13] Making philosophical use of a novel is not the same as appreciating it as art. The notion that art in itself would constitute a kind of thinking or knowledge in another form, as if the point of art would be to prompt philosophical speculation, in fact devalues the aesthetic feeling while claiming to explain it. To better clarify what makes the aesthetic judgement distinct from conceptual understanding, I shall now criticize an example of a purportedly Kantian attempt to conflate them.

3.2. Making sense of beauty

Cognitivist interpretations of Kant's aesthetics are common, but they vary greatly in degree. One of the most extreme examples is Angela Breitenbach, who speaks about the 'cognitive value of art' and how experiences of art contribute to 'achievements of the understanding'.[14] Her article 'One Imagination in Experiences of Beauty and Achievements of Understanding' clearly advocates for understanding the aesthetic judgement as a kind of thinking, which is the opposite view of Kant's aesthetics to the one I take in this chapter.[15] Countering her arguments may therefore be an effective way to illuminate what is meant by the non-conceptual basis of the aesthetic judgement.

In the judgement of taste, the faculties of the mind are put into a free, harmonious play which is felt as a subjective pleasure. Breitenbach reads this as a kind of preparation for understanding, where imagination produces

> representations that can be conceptualized, even though they need not be conceptualized in any particular way. ... More generally, for Kant this means that an artwork strikes us as beautiful when it makes possible an inexhaustible wealth of thoughts that are not fully determined by the artwork itself, yet adequate to what it expresses.[16]

It is true that Kant says that some artworks may put the imagination and the understanding into a free play which stimulates 'so much thinking that it can never be grasped in a determinate concept, hence which aesthetically enlarges the concept itself in an unbounded way'.[17] He says (quite beautifully) that such an artwork 'gives more to think about than can be grasped and made distinct in it'.[18] Breitenbach, however, has reconstrued the causality, implying that beauty *is an effect of* the inexhaustible wealth of thoughts. That would reduce the aesthetic pleasure into a mere symptom of the furthering of conceptual understanding. But as Kant makes clear in §9, 'the key to the critique of taste', the feeling of pleasure in the aesthetic judgement does not proceed from an intellectual understanding, but from an inner sensation of harmonious play.

Breitenbach exemplifies her understanding of the third Critique by discussing a dance (*Vollmond* by Pina Bausch), the beauty of which 'lay in pointing me to ideas of great significance whose content went beyond any particular representation of what was shown by the dance itself'.[19] She claims that these attempts to 'make sense of what [she] saw and heard' lie at the heart of the aesthetic experience.[20] As she quotes in her article, Kant writes that 'an artwork "expands ... the mind by setting the imagination free" and by connecting the representation of a concept with "a fullness of thought to which no linguistic expression is fully adequate"'.[21] Breitenbach takes this to mean that the dance will 'point us to important and far-reaching ideas', and that this is what induces the aesthetic pleasure.[22]

Here, she reduces the pleasure that constitutes the judgement of taste to a mere symptom of its prompting of intellectual activity.[23] What Kant is talking about in the passage quoted and shortened by her above is not beauty in general but poetry, which undeniably works with concepts, but which uses them not in a determining but reflective way. In poetry, every given concept invokes 'the unbounded manifold of forms possibly agreeing with it, the one that connects its presentation with a fullness of thought to which no linguistic expression is fully adequate, and thus elevates itself aesthetically to the level of ideas'.[24] (I shall return later to Kant's notion of aesthetic ideas.)

Poetry is self-declared illusion, and Kant differs it from the purposive art of rhetoric, in which the 'pure enjoyment' and 'honesty' get lost (in a touching footnote, he confesses that the enjoyment of rhetoric for him 'always [has] been mixed with the disagreeable feeling of disapproval of a deceitful art'[25]). In rhetoric, it is *as if* the orator would merely be playing with ideas in an amusing way, when in fact, his purpose is to convince the audience. In poetry, the relationship is reversed. It might seem as if a poem is intended to further our understanding of something, but the poem is free from all purposes. Paradoxically, it is this very freedom which enlivens our faculties and enriches our concepts in the unbounded and directionless way he describes. A poem presents a kind of illusory sense, 'yet without thereby being deceitful; for it itself declares its occupation to be mere play'.[26]

In claiming that the artwork is pleasurable *because* it makes her think, Breitenbach is reducing the free, disinterested play of the aesthetic judgement to a side-effect of cognitive progression, interpreting the choreography basically as a more sensuous and confused form of rhetoric. But there is no such progression implied in the judgement of taste. As Hannah Ginsborg remarks, pleasure is 'a state of mind which tends towards its own perpetuation';[27] it wants to *stay* with itself, not progress towards conceptual understanding. Nonetheless, this state of mind may bring about the peculiar kind of fullness of thought that Kant seeks to describe with his notion of aesthetic ideas.[28]

In what follows, I shall explicate more closely what it can mean to stay with this aesthetic pleasure in contrast to conceptual understanding, especially in literature. In order to do that, it must first be clarified what conceptual understanding is, and how it is possible for us to have and share experiences which are other than that.

3.3. Blind or empty?

Concepts are the products of the human mind's capacity to make 'one's own representations into objects of one's own thoughts'.[29] In contrast to intuitions, concepts are general, reflected mental presentations. As Howard Caygill explains, Kant differs between the *a priori* concepts that are foundational for experience and the derived or empirical concepts that 'are drawn from experience by means of comparison, reflection and abstraction'.[30] The *a priori* concepts are those aspects of our cognitions that all experiences must conform to, such as causality,[31] whereas the derived concepts form our self-aware mental representations. For the purposes of this discussion, only the derived concepts are relevant. Conceptual understanding occurs when an intuition is coupled with such a concept, which is how Kant describes cognition in general.

But the aesthetic judgement is not a cognition of an object. It is based on a

> feeling of pleasure or displeasure, which grounds an entirely special faculty for discrimination and judging that contributes nothing to cognition but only holds the given representation in the subject up to the entire faculty of representation, of which the mind becomes conscious in the feeling of its own state.[32]

When I look at something beautiful, my imagination and my understanding are put into a harmonious play, and this is a pleasurable awareness of my ability to form judgements in general, without actually cognizing anything. To simplify: beauty is the mind enjoying itself, not understanding the world. As Kant spells it out:

> If the given representation, which occasions the judgment of taste, were a concept, which united understanding and imagination in the judging of the object into a cognition of the object, then the consciousness of this relationship would be intellectual (as in the objective schematism of the power of judgment, which was dealt with in the [first] critique). But in that case the judgment would not be made in relation to pleasure and displeasure, hence it would not be a judgment of taste.[33]

The aesthetic pleasure is purely subjective and tells us nothing about the object that has occasioned it. Nevertheless, the judgement of taste is universally communicable. This is a critical insight for Kant, effectively saying that the limits of our rational understanding are more narrow than our ability to share a world. As Hannah Ginsborg points out, '"mitteilen" in the eighteenth century does not have a specifically linguistic connotation, but means "to share with others", so that a state of mind which is "universally communicable" is not one that can be described or made comprehensible to all others, but one which everyone can, or perhaps must, have in common.'[34] Pleasure and displeasure, Kant writes, 'are not kinds of cognition [and thus] cannot be explained by themselves at all, [they] are felt, not understood; hence they can only be inadequately explained through the influence that a representation has on the activity of the powers of the mind by means of this feeling.'[35] Through pleasure and displeasure, the artwork communicates something that we cannot fully conceptualize to each other, a feeling of a state of mind, which we can never be sure has been adequately shared, but whose very possibility we are nonetheless strongly inclined to assume to be universal.

This non-conceptuality of the aesthetic judgement, which Kant even speaks of as occasioning a certain 'embarrassment',[36] is perhaps not obviously reconcilable with the famous proposition of the first Critique: 'Thoughts without content are empty, intuitions without concepts are blind.'[37] Indeed, if we try to analyse it as a cognition, the aesthetic judgement could come across as both a bit like an empty thought, in that our capacity for cognition in general is activated without any object being determined, and a bit like a blind intuition, in that it is a non-conceptual feeling. Kant continues: 'The understanding can intuit nothing, the senses can think nothing. Only from their unification can cognition arise.'[38] He also makes clear that cognition is the only thing that can be universally communicated. So how is a non-conceptual universally communicable feeling like the aesthetic judgement possible?

To begin with, as Robert Hanna explains in his illuminating article 'Kant and Nonconceptual Content', what Kant has in mind with 'cognition' in the famous proposition is not consciousness as a whole, but only *'objectively valid judgements'*.[39] Empty thoughts and blind intuitions *do* exist. In fact, Kant gives examples of empty concepts in describing noumena, and as Hanna remarks, it is perfectly possible to imagine bogus or nonsensical thoughts, such as 'the concept of a furiously-sleeping colourless green idea or of a round square'.[40] Hanna quotes Kant in saying that 'appearances can certainly be given in intuition without functions of the understanding',[41] and his article provides a rich flora of examples of nonconceptuality of various degrees in Kant, demonstrating that even when a concept is present, it does not account for the entirety of a cognition.

One of his examples is when Kant notes that an astronomer cannot 'prevent the rising moon from appearing larger to him, even when he is not deceived by this illusion'.[42] '[S]uch illusions', Hanna notes, 'perceptually persists *even after the acquisition of conceptual sophistication about them*.'[43] Early in the evening, the astronomer sees the moon as larger than when it has travelled to the top of the sky, even though he (as most grown-up non-astronomers as well) knows that the size of the moon is always the same. The relationship between intuitions and concepts is never 1:1, even though they are cognitively complementary and interdependent. This is because there is more to consciousness than objectively valid judgements. Or, as Hanna puts his main point: 'the underlying nature of cognitive content [is not] exhausted by its functional or its purely logico-rational components.'[44]

The Critique of the Power of Judgment in its entirety concerns the reflective judgement[45] – an *a priori* principle of formal purposiveness. Briefly put, it describes our ability of not just subsuming objects under concepts (as the determining judgement does) but of having a feeling of unity of our experience altogether.[46] Through this feeling, we do not make objectively valid judgements, but intuit how 'fitting' (or, as in the case of the displeasure in the sublime, how unfitting) the disposition of our mind is to the world. It is a reflective feeling of our capacity for cognition in general. As Andrea Kern explains, the aesthetic thus differs from philosophy in that it is not a conceptual analysis of the disposition of our mind, but an *experience* of it.[47]

By now, it should be clear that this feeling or state of mind is not departing from, or aimed at furthering, conceptual cognitions. However, this does not mean that it cannot coincide with them. Kant actually spells this out: 'even if the given representations were to be rational but related in a judgement solely to the subject (its feeling), then they are to that extent always aesthetic.'[48] The aesthetic in itself is neither rational nor irrational. We can understand something (or not) and make an aesthetic judgement of it at the same time. So, does the knowledge of what we have in front of us not matter at all when we appreciate its beauty?

3.4. Nature, art and intellectual interest

As soon as we leave the metaphysical analysis and turn to actual aesthetic experiences,[49] the picture gets more complicated. There are certain things we need to know. For us to appreciate *King Lear*, we need to know how to read, or at least understand what a theatrical performance is. But as we shall discover, not even our appreciation of tulips presents a straightforward case of nonconceptuality, even though it may seem so at a first glance.

Flowers are free natural beauties according to Kant: '[h]ardly anyone other than the botanist knows what sort of thing a flower is supposed to be; and even the botanist ... pays no attention to this natural end if he judges the flower by means of taste.'[50] There is no scientific knowledge relevant to the beauty of a flower, just as there is no profession which makes one immune to the marvel of a rising moon. In relation to the aesthetic judgement, no one *knows* any better.

As Robert Hanna says, it does not even matter if we would mistake a rose for a tulip. '[E]ven though the object falls under some concept or another (we not only see the rose but also see it as a rose), this conceptual fact is wholly irrelevant to its being beautiful, since its being beautiful consists merely in the relation between its phenomenal form and the pleasure we experience in the harmonious interplay of our cognitive faculties.'[51] Suppose that I am completely unable to tell different kinds of flowers apart, that I do not understand what a rose is, or that I am only having a hallucination of a crossbred tulip-rose: 'still the aesthetic judgement of taste has a direct object and remains valid', Hanna concludes.[52]

Murdoch is more sceptical to the abstract absoluteness of this claim:

> This strict and illuminating definition is of course not necessarily easy to apply to the vast area of our *experiences* of beauty, wherein all kinds of "extraneous" knowledge seems to play an indissoluble part. To take an example, although botanical studies are distinct from aesthetic pleasures, it may be difficult to dissociate our delight in a tree from our perception of what kind of tree it is! ... Strictly, [for Kant,] to class it as a beech tree is to leave the realm of the aesthetic.[53]

It is true that conceptual classification for Kant is separate from the aesthetic judgement. It makes no difference *in beauty* whether this particular pretty flower is a tulip or not. If it would, the integrity of our aesthetic judgement would be endangered. If someone upon learning that an until now disregarded little scrawny thing is, in fact, a tulip, then suddenly exclaims 'how pretty!' this judgement of taste would be as empty as that of someone who pronounces a painting to be beautiful when he finds out that it is painted by a great artist. Understanding can be of no help to us in making aesthetic judgements:

The understanding can make a universal judgement by comparing how satisfying the object is with the judgements of others, e.g. all tulips are beautiful; but in that case that is not a judgement of taste, but a logical judgement, which makes the relation of an object to taste into a predicate of things of a certain sort in general; but that by means of which I find a single given tulip beautiful … is the judgement of taste alone.[54]

However, things are not entirely that simple in the third Critique. Kant does care whether the tulip is real or not. In the curious §42, 'On the intellectual interest in the beautiful', Kant talks about a man who walks away from fine art, 'those beauties that sustain vanity and at best social joys', and instead 'turns to the beautiful in nature, in order as it were to find here an ecstasy for his spirit in a line of thought that he can never fully develop'.[55] This man takes 'an immediate and certainly intellectual interest in the beauty of nature', and the thought that awes him is that nature has indeed produced these astonishingly pretty wildflowers and birds. '[I]t is worth noting here', Kant writes,

> that if someone had secretly deceived this lover of the beautiful and had planted artificial flowers (which can be manufactured to look entirely similar to natural ones) or had placed artfully carved birds on the twigs of trees, and he then discovered the deception, the immediate interest that he had previously taken in it would immediately disappear.[56]

This is indeed an intellectual interest taken in the beautiful. The man's awe is dependent on a conceptual cognition (this bird is a product of nature) and the enlivening thoughts that he can never fully develop are stemming from that understanding. However, Kant is very clear about the causality here. The judgement of taste is not dependent on any moral or intellectual interest, '**although it produces one**'.[57] Reason takes an interest in the correspondence between the harmony of the faculties of our mind, which is what we feel in beauty, and the occurrence of such beautiful objects in nature. It is an experience of the appropriateness between our consciousness and the world that the strolling man attempts to comprehend, and thus it naturally matters to him whether what he is admiring has been produced by another human or not.

That nature can look to us like intentionally produced art is a marvel, and an interestingly unstable marvel. The judgement of beauty is not a conclusion following from knowing that this is a real tulip, but the insight that what we perceive is *not* natural might nevertheless upset our judgement. Kant gives another example in §42, where the knowledge that it is a real nightingale is described as crucial for the charming beauty of its song:

> What is more highly extolled by poets than the bewitchingly beautiful song of the nightingale, in a lonely stand of bushes, on a still summer evening, under the gentle light of the moon? Yet there have been examples in which, where no such songbird was to be found, some jolly landlord has tricked the guests staying with him, to their complete satisfaction, by hiding in a bush a mischievous lad who knew how to imitate this song (with a reed or a pipe in his mouth) just like nature.

But as soon as one becomes aware that it is a trick, no one would long endure listening to this song, previously taken to be so charming; and the same is true with every other songbird.[58]

In this (utterly charming) passage, the beauty (or the charm; it is not entirely clear whether Kant mainly sees this as an empty cliché) of the song seems to rest upon the assumption that it is always lovely to hear a nightingale in the evening. Since this would merely be a logical judgement, I believe it is safe to assume that Kant also has a real experience of beauty in mind. Even though it can easily be overthrown (perhaps this practice of employing mischievous lads was common in his circles), Kant expects every upstanding citizen to find not just pleasure in this enchanting song, but also a kind of intellectual satisfaction in the insight that nature has produced it. People who lack feeling for the beauty of nature (which is here rather puzzlingly described as 'the receptivity to an interest in its contemplation') are characterized by him as stupid, hedonistic drunkards, who 'confine themselves to the enjoyment of mere sensory sensations at table or from the bottle'.[59]

Art, which the nature-loving, strolling gentleman of the previous example had turned away from as a vanity, is then in the following paragraphs 'saved' by Kant.[60] Art is described as a kind of mediated nature. It is separated from the effect-seeking or purposive practice of crafts (like the mischievous lad with the flute), it is beautiful when it is unintentionally like nature; it is given its rules by geniuses who do not understand and cannot explain why or even how they create what they create. It is not supposed to mimetically trick us that it is nature. On the contrary, our conceptual understanding of it as art is fundamental for our aesthetic judgement of it: 'art can only be called beautiful if we are aware that it is art and yet it looks to us like nature'.[61]

Thus, the concept of art and the concept of nature seem both to be implicated in all experiences of beauty. Furthermore, they are always intertwined with each other: nature is beautiful when it looks as purposive as art, and art is beautiful when it seems as spontaneously created as nature. How to understand this nature/art-chiasm in Kant is well explained (and expanded upon) by Adorno. Nature and art are in his view conceptually mediated by each other, and must be understood through their dialectical relation:

> Wholly artifactual, the artwork seems to be the opposite of what is not made, nature. As pure antitheses, however, each refers to the other: nature to the experience of a mediated and objectified world, the artwork to nature as the mediated plenipotentiary of immediacy.[62]

To understand what it means that nature is mediated, we can think of the experience of the nightingale, which reveals itself to be dependent on a poetic cliché. As Adorno puts it: 'something frightening lurks in the song of birds precisely because it is not a song but obeys the spell in which it is enmeshed.'[63] The talented boy with the flute shakes us into an upsetting awareness of this. Turning our pleasure into displeasure, the intellectual interest produced by the beautiful ('interest' meaning for Kant here 'desire for it to exist') is a question of us being at home (or alienated) in the world. In more Kantian terms, the possibility to mirror the harmony of our faculties (which is fundamental for cognition in general) in an object which exists independently of our intentions is giving us an indication that our feeling of life may not just be subjective, but objective too. Similarly, our ability to create such an unintentionally purposive object (art) out of some ungraspable source in ourselves (the inspiration of genius) shows us the connection between us and nature in another way. Thus, the intellectual interest produced by the beautiful is dependent on an absence of purpose – we cannot intentionally create this indication of objective harmony.

So, even if the feelings of pleasure and displeasure are in themselves non-conceptual, actual aesthetic experiences are not disconnected from our cognition of what kind of object we have in front of us. Together with our conceptual understanding (this is art, or this is nature) a special kind of inexhaustible, contemplative interest is produced by the aesthetic feeling. The man who finds 'an ecstasy for his spirit in a line of thought that he can never fully develop'[64] when walking in nature is not making objectively valid judgements, but his understanding and imagination are certainly engaged. The guests discovering that they have been tricked into a clichéd enjoyment of a non-existent nightingale are shaken into an uncanny consciousness, inducing a correspondingly vague and boundless reflection.

Here, we see how taking an intellectual interest in aesthetic experiences differs from the prompting of imaginative activity that Breitenbach describes. She says that the 'achievement of the performance ... relied on my drawing out ideas that were suggested, but only suggested and never made fully explicit, by the artwork itself'.[65] Even though she recognizes an (at least initial) indeterminacy of the thoughts, she makes it sound as if the beauty of the artwork would have remained dormant without her active intellectual engagement. On the contrary, Kant's notion of beauty is an immediate feeling. His account of the intellectual activity prompted by the aesthetic judgement is not a 'drawing out', but something more akin to losing oneself in an intuition of a mysterious sense unattainable for the understanding (an intuition in which, if we are to believe Adorno, something frightening always lurks). Since we can be tricked by fake flowers, the aesthetic state of mind is not a reliable foundation for determinate judgements. Rather, beauty upsets the authority of our conceptual understanding, making us aware that we can only ever *have an indication in feeling* of whether our general cognitive disposition is adequate to the world or not. The intellectual interest in the beautiful thus becomes not just boundless but recursive, too: by offering an ecstatic delight in recognizing these thoughts as something we can never fully develop.[66]

3.5. Sublime boundlessness

This recursiveness of intellectual interest also pertains to the sublime. As was mentioned before, when Murdoch criticizes Kant for not allowing conceptual content in art, she confuses the judgement of beauty with experiences of art. In order to widen what she takes to be his understanding of art, she suggests a merging of the beautiful with the sublime. She describes the Kantian sublime as the failure of imagination to compass an abstractly conceived ... totality which is not given but only vaguely adumbrated by reason. The sublime is a segment of a circle, grasped by imagination, with the rest of the circle demanded and as it were dreamt of by reason, but not given. The sublime is only occasioned by natural objects ..., and the imaginative understanding the lack of which occasions the pain-and-pleasure of sublimity is a kind of vast systematic perception of nature which space and time and the nature of our sensibility forbids.[67]

Artworks, especially tragedies, give us such a sublime segment of a circle, she suggests. In his notion of the sublime, 'Kant is concerned, though in a very narrow way, with the helplessness of human beings',[68] a concern he should not have kept hermetically sealed from his understanding of art. Again, Murdoch believes herself to be speaking against Kant more than she is. She subscribes to the surprisingly common view that Kant considered the sublime to have no place in art. But not only does he speak of the sublime in relation to art; he even states that 'the presentation of the sublime, so far as it belongs to beautiful art, can be united with beauty in a verse tragedy'.[69] Using the sublime to question the non-conceptuality of art might have been fruitful if Kant really considered conceptual understanding to be as absent from art as it is from the pure judgement of taste. The following discussion will show that he did not; even though, as we shall eventually see, the kind of thinking he described as proper to poetry might be said to have more to do with the sublime than he explicitly recognized.

The aesthetic experiences of beauty and the sublime are for Kant similar in that they are not dependent on any determinate concepts, but are 'nevertheless still related to concepts, although it is indeterminate which'.[70] They are connected to a certain presentation [*Vorstellung*], but conceptually indeterminate. Beauty, however, is immediately pleasing and compatible with charms, and makes us feel as if our minds would be harmoniously tuned to the comprehension of the world, whereas the sublime is 'contrapurposive for our power of judgement, unsuitable for our faculty of presentation, and as it were doing violence to our imagination'.[71] In the paragraphs where Kant is treating the sublime, he explicitly confines his discussion to nature because the sublime 'in art is, after all, always restricted to the conditions of agreement with nature'.[72] Art can in other words be sublime, but only in the sense in which it is like nature (which, as we saw in the previous section, it in some sense always is). Indeed, not even nature can properly be called sublime, because the sublime experience is not dependent on any quality of an object but occurs in the feeling when we cannot grasp what we have in front of us, so that 'the mind is incited to abandon sensibility and to occupy itself with ideas that contain a higher purposiveness'.[73]

The sublime is that 'which is great beyond all comparison'.[74] Being beyond comparison here for Kant means that we cannot measure it with a logical judgement (such as that an orange is bigger than an apple) but an aesthetic, which makes us attempt to enlarge the imagination beyond its bounds. The feeling of being unable to grasp it in intuition or imagination reminds us of the potential infinitude of our power of judgement, '**a faculty of the mind that surpasses every measure of the senses**'.[75] Thus, the initial displeasure becomes a pleasure, in that we are somehow still capable of imagining it as a given totality (without intellectually or sensuously comprehending it), as with the idea of the infinite.

This positing of a totality is not an objectively valid judgement. Neither is it imaginative in the sense of constructing stories. Fantasies, knowledge, conclusions and external purposes are all irrelevant to the sublime, as Kant makes clear while again explicitly connecting it to art:

> Thus, if someone calls the sight of the starry heavens **sublime**, he must not ground such a judging of it on concepts of worlds inhabited by rational beings, taking the bright points with which we see the space above us to be filled as their suns, about which they move in their purposively appointed orbits, but must take it, as we see it, merely as a broad, all-embracing vault; and it must be merely under this representation that we posit the sublimity that a pure aesthetic judgment attributes to this object. In just the same way, we must not take the sight of the ocean as we **think** it, enriched with all sorts of knowledge (which are not, however, contained in the immediate intuition), for example as a wide realm of water creatures, as the great storehouse of water for the evaporation which impregnates the air with clouds for the benefit of the land, or as an element that separates parts of the world from one another but at the same time makes possible the greatest community among them, for this would yield merely teleological judgments; rather, *one must consider the ocean merely as the poets do*, in accordance with what its appearance shows, for instance, when it is considered in periods of calm, as a clear watery mirror bounded only by the heavens, but also when it is turbulent, an abyss threatening to devour everything, and yet still be able to find it sublime.[76]

Here, we can recall the child and the astronomer appreciating the beauty of the moon, that is, taking it as they see it. This is by Kant considered analogous to judging an appearance 'merely as the poets do', which is taking an impression (such as the surface of the ocean) as imaginatively overflowing its conceptual determination. Beauty and sublimity can evidently be combined here. We can also recall Roquentin's horror in Sartre's *La Nausée* in experiencing how the boundless unique particularity of existence was not 1:1 with his discursive comprehension.[77] If conceptual understanding is irrelevant to the beautiful, the sublime exposes it as powerless. The aesthetic is in both cases a feeling of the inner organization of our abilities of comprehension, as harmonious or as insufficient. If we take both kinds of aesthetic feeling as relevant to art, the beautiful can be understood as that which presents the pleasing form of purposiveness without a purpose, whereas the sublime haunts us with an awareness of the instability of that form. In Murdoch's words:

> The work of art may seem to be a limited whole enclosed in a circle, but because of contingency and the muddled nature of the world and the imperfections of language the circle is always broken. ... Kant's concept of the sublime, though he did not himself apply it to art, suggests something essential to the nature of serious art: how the world overflows the art object, how it transcends it, how emotions attend the experience of this.[78]

We are now in a better position to see how conceptual complexity could coincide with an aesthetic experience. By pleasing us with its formal non-conceptual beauty, while also invoking what Kirk Pillow refers to as 'feelings of sublime incomprehension',[79] a play by Shakespeare is read or watched with an aesthetic state of mind. No matter how much our linguistic or historical knowledge is partaking in the experience: as art, it simultaneously offers a reflection of the insufficiencies of conceptual understanding. As Murdoch suggests, it is this violence done to our imagination which makes 'for instance the reading of *King Lear* ... indeed exhilarating. It is also, if we perform it properly which we hardly ever do, painful.'[80]

The diligent reader of Kant might here be waiting for a complete account of sublimity to be presented. Indeed, the sublime is not simply a painful feeling of threatening boundlessness; for Kant, it is also pleasurable, since we can always counter this feeling of being overwhelmed by a magnitude or power with an imaginative idea of its greatness. If we feel faint by looking out into the infinite void of the universe, we may find an exhilarated repose in the insight that we can nonetheless form an idea of its infinitude. As Kant says, 'the subject's own incapacity reveals the consciousness of an unlimited capacity of the very same subject.'[81] With the sublime, he does not stay with the aesthetic judgement, but instead describes how 'the aesthetic judgment itself becomes purposive for reason, as the source of ideas, i.e., for an intellectual comprehension for which all aesthetic comprehension is small.'[82]

The consolatory aspect of this ambiguity in Kant's account of the sublime, as Melissa Merritt describes it, bothers Murdoch. As Merritt writes, 'Murdoch denies that "our supersensible destiny" comes into clear view simply by reflecting on the universal reason within out breasts.'[83] Murdoch agrees that the shock of the sublime may awake our morality, but she is sceptical of the eventual triumph of reason in sublime experiences.[84] Rather than seeing the aesthetic comprehension as small in comparison to the intellectual, she argues that it humbles us by exposing the limits of our understanding. 'Good art', she writes in *Metaphysics as a Guide to Morals*, 'accepts and celebrates and meditates upon the defeat of the discursive intellect by the world. Bad art misrepresents the world so as to pretend that there is no conflict.'[85]

If one thinks, as I do with Murdoch, that the aesthetic comprehension is not small in comparison with the intellectual, the displeasure inherent in the sublime will never be completely overturned. Instead, the marvel of the aesthetic state of mind lies in enabling us to nonetheless appreciate these feelings: to enjoy the limitations of our conceptual understanding. In order to do that, art presents us with a kind of overflowing placeholders for intellectual conclusions, invoking both a harmonious pleasure of beauty and a straining sublime boundlessness. These placeholders can be understood with the Kantian notion of aesthetic ideas.

3.6. Aesthetic ideas

Kant calls an aesthetic idea 'that representation of the imagination that occasions much thinking though without it being possible for any determinate thought, i.e., concept, to be adequate to it, which, consequently, no language fully attains or can make intelligible'.[86] It is really in literature 'in which the faculty of aesthetic ideas can reveal itself in its full measure', when the writer aims to make things like death, love, heaven and hell visible to us through sensible representations.[87] Aesthetic ideas are 'inner intuitions' of something that lies beyond experience, and 'no concept can be fully adequate to them', even though they are associated with a given concept.[88] As such, they are intuition's counterpart to the unpresentable ideas of reason suggested by the sublime. Where the experience of the sublime consists in imagination's failure to present that which corresponds to reason's idea (e.g. of infinity), the aesthetic idea is a successful imaginative elaboration of an indeterminate concept:

> In a word, the aesthetic idea is a representation of the imagination, associated with a given concept, which is combined with such a manifold of partial representations in the free use of the imagination that no expression designating a determinate concept can be found for it, which therefore allows the addition to a concept of much that is unnameable, the feeling of which animates the cognitive faculties and combines spirit with the mere letter of language.[89]

The poet (or another kind of artist) gives the imaginative representation of this concept a sort of fake-intuitiveness which it never has in life. He makes us feel that we can intuit it as a unity without giving us any determinate understanding of it, and thus 'aesthetically enlarges the concept itself in an unbounded way'. (We can feel like we know what hell is like after having read Dante's *Inferno*.) An aesthetic idea does not really make us understand anything but serves 'really only to animate the mind by opening up for it the prospect of an immeasurable field of related representations'.[90]

In *Sublime Understanding*, Kirk Pillow argues convincingly for what he admits to be 'an unorthodox reading of Kant's doctrine of aesthetic ideas', namely 'that reflection on them assumes the form of a judgment of sublimity'.[91] Aesthetic ideas 'arouse in imagination a feeling of being overwhelmed'[92] similar to the experience of the sublime. They are not to be misinterpreted as more vague, confused or preliminary ideas of reason. Rather, as Pillow explains, 'they express an indeterminate and expansive range of meaning that no rule, concept, or rational idea can encompass'.[93] In a novel, for example, the excessive wealth of connotations and associations that its descriptions invoke may overwhelm us – and this is not an artistic failure. On the contrary, an aesthetic idea can never become a determinate cognition. Neither are they mere symbols for rational ideas, since, as Pillow points out, they are not rule-bound or determinable.[94] Formally, the work may appear harmoniously complete, but its material nonetheless overwhelms imagination's capacity for comprehension in a sublime way.

Simone Weil's reading together of the beautiful and the sublime expresses a similar view, when she says in her lecture on Kant that: 'The unity of a work of art must be ceaselessly in peril and still be preserved at each instant.'[95] Beauty stabilizes the artwork formally, while the sublime reflection allows for a boundless overflow, constantly threatening the unity of its own presentation. With this understanding, it becomes evident that art does not have to be void of thoughts and concepts, even though the aesthetic entails an entirely different approach to conceptual content.

This also helps us see how a literary work can use the medium of language to present something which 'no language fully attains or can make intelligible', as Kant says about the aesthetic ideas.[96] Using language to invoke overwhelming images, boundless connotations and formal beauty, this arrangement of words becomes expressive of another state of mind than that in which we make objectively valid judgements. Remembering that universal communicability for Kant is not limited to determinate understanding, but also encompasses the reflective pleasure and displeasure in which the mind feels itself, we can also understand how art can be communicative and be about our lives in the world, without having as its aim to further our understanding of it.

3.7. Muddle

To conclude this chapter's discussion of conceptual content in the art of literature, I shall now give an example of what I take to be a frequently occurring aesthetic idea in Murdoch's fiction: muddle.

Muddle can be used both as a verb (to muddle), a noun (a muddle) and an adjective or adverb (muddled). Etymologically, it is derived from Dutch *moddelen* ('to make (water) muddy') and originally means to 'destroy the clarity of' something.[97] According to a couple of dictionaries, muddle can mean 'an untidy or confused state',[98] 'to behave, proceed, or think in a confused or aimless fashion or with an air of improvization', being drunk or stupid and confused as if drunk, an 'embarrassing condition; mess',[99] 'to identify wrongly; to mix up in the mind', 'to make (speech) blurred or garbled', 'to bewilder, to make (a person) unable to think clearly; to confuse (a person's mind)'.[100] Synonyms include: jumble, to bungle or mishandle, to bewilder, to perplex, disorientation, mix-up, scramble, disorder, etc., but none of these bring us the same metaphorical sense of a sediment stirred through water, making it impossible not only to see the bottom but even to distinguish the bottom from the surface.

Muddle is a word used in almost everything Murdoch ever wrote. If one expands the concept beyond the word, to include the many scenes with mud, bogs and drownings in her fiction, the metaphorical use of muddle becomes wider still. It occurs often in her philosophical writings as well, especially in descriptions of how art relates to the world. As was previously quoted from *Metaphysics as a Guide to Morals*: 'The work of art may seem to be a limited whole enclosed in a circle, but because of contingency and the *muddled* nature of the world and the imperfections of language the circle is always broken.'[101] Or in *The Fire and the Sun*: 'But because of the *muddle* of human life and the ambiguity and playfulness of aesthetic form, art can at best only explain partly, only reveal almost: and of course any complex work contains impurities and accidents which we choose to ignore.'[102] Muddle has in other words a double function in Murdoch's oeuvre: as an aesthetic idea, and as an idea of importance for the aesthetic.

If we return for a moment to Kant's nature-loving gentleman, who during his walk in the forest finds an ecstasy for his spirit in a line of thinking he can never fully develop, his aesthetic state of mind seems indeed to be describable as muddled. The clarity of conceptual thinking is here stirred in an indeterminate feeling of life.

This upsettingly ungraspable jumble is by art made into an object for prolonged reflection, the form of which invokes a pleasure which makes us want to stay with the conceptually undetermined reflection. In fact, the 'revelations' and 'explanations' of art which Murdoch speaks of are irrevocably tied to this 'almost'; of giving us a feel for our embeddedness and alienness in life, something we cannot fully think – no matter how much thinking might otherwise be involved. This is what the concept seems to entail in her philosophical aesthetics.

Muddle, as an aesthetic idea in Murdoch's fiction, mirrors this 'stirredness' – the feeling of how the world overflows or disturbs our attempts to make sense of and create order in life. In an abstract determinate description like this, it naturally seems like something awfully vague. In art, however, a 'thing' like muddle can achieve a strikingly expressive force, through the reflective feelings invoked rather than its conceptual clarity. To see what that can be like, let us look at a couple of examples from some of her novels.

In *The Time of the Angels*, the word occurs as an adjective twice in the same scene to describe the feelings that the Russian refugee Eugene has for his grown-up son Leo. In this first paragraph, Leo has just entered the room:

> [Eugene] contemplated his tall slim son with a surprise that never diminished, a surprise at seeing him so grown-up, so large, so handsome, so impertinent. With the surprise came timidity and the *muddled* pain of an inexpressible love. Always they blundered at each other, there was no technique of contact, no way of taking hold. On Leo's face Eugene read the equivalent of his own amaze: a look of uncertain apprehensive boldness. They were present to each other in the room as unintelligible, unmanageable objects. Eugene hunched himself.[103]

At the centre of this paragraph is 'the *muddled* pain of an inexpressible love'. Still, this unspeakable love is being well expressed through the depiction. Eugene and Leo are 'blundering' against each other. They both mirror the bold apprehensive amaze of the other. Even though they are standing still here, just gazing at each other, they are presented as formless forces in motion, as 'unmanageable objects'. They are deeply interconnected, but still 'there [is] no technique of contact, no way of taking hold'.

On the next page, Leo confesses to have stolen and sold Eugene's precious icon, which had belonged to his mother in St Petersburg:

> Eugene was silent. He felt an immediate and intense pain of humiliation. He could not look at Leo, it was as if he himself were ashamed. He stared at the floor. Leo had taken the icon and sold it. It was not the clean loss that he had imagined and tried to make terms with. It was something *muddled* and ugly and personal, something twisted back into him, something that disgraced him. He drooped his head and continued to be silent.[104]

Eugene is not angry, but something worse. The shame and guilt of Leo become his own humiliation. This muddled disgrace is private but shared, and the blurring of identities in the first paragraph, which at the same time entails a distance, here becomes acutely insufferable. As readers, we feel like we know exactly what that kind of painful, indistinct, shame-infused love feels like. The idea would look small if it was conceptualized in an explanation – Eugene experiences messy feelings – but is enlarged by the artistic presentation. Part of the power of an aesthetic idea lies in its falling short of providing a conceptual grasp of the boundless imaginative responses it provokes, which induces the sublime reflection described by Pillow.

As was said, muddle is both an aesthetic idea and an idea about a certain aspect of the aesthetic. Sometimes in her fiction, this other connotation is also involved. In *The Philosopher's Pupil*, a quite meta-reflective story, the word is often invoked to reflect upon that which escapes our phantasmatic imaginings.[105] Muddle here points to how life, in its boredom and meagreness, exceeds the stories we tell ourselves about it. As such, the idea reflects back upon the story we are reading, invoking a feeling of (in Murdoch's words) 'how the world overflows the art object, how it transcends it'.[106]

At times in the novel, muddle is connected to mediocrity and poverty, that which is too mundane to stir our imagination. For example, one of the women of the family sees herself as inferior because she used to be a '"poor Bowcock", one of the *muddled* ones who had no grasp on life'.[107] It gets explicitly connected to poverty again when the grand dame, Alex, looks at her son and discovers something more material and mortal than she usually sees:

> Now the older face appeared, George as he would be when he was sixty or seventy, less plump, more gaunt, more lined. The lines were already faintly sketched on the brow which had been smooth so long. Alex looked, feeling the pain of her love for him. She thought, I have somehow relied on George being invulnerable, untouchable, youthful, somehow like myself, a guarantor of myself. But now he looks just like an ordinary worried *muddled* mediocre shop-soiled man. She saw his shabby suit, his dirty shirt, his need of a shave.[108]

Muddle is here used to indicate a reality which becomes visible when a more idealized image gives way. The same sense is repeated in another place in the novel, when the young man Tom finds himself in the midst of a series of event which he has no hold over. At first, 'he had acted instinctively at each moment as he felt he must. But now the dream-like unfolding of destined action seemed to have come to an end, the magic was switched off, and he was returned to the clumsy perilous *muddle* of ordinary life'.[109] Here, muddle represents that which resists his self-narrativization. The formlessness of experience is invoked as bulging inside the story, self-consciously reflected upon by a novelist who is also a philosopher, and who sees the art object as essentially pierced, 'whereby its sense flows into life'.[110] We are given, and reminded that we are given, a sense of a grasp of something which cannot be made complete sense of. If there is any philosophical understanding implicit here, it is the philosophical self-consciousness of the conceptual indeterminacy of art.

In many of her novels, the word 'muddle' is used about a formless aspect of relationships. It can point to that which habit makes us see less clearly ('the warm muddle of my wife' in *A Severed Head*[111]) or how the secret nature of infidelities makes them more shapeless, when the interconnectedness with other people (such as the betrayed spouses, or children and the like) dilutes the love of the illicit couple with indistinct guilt and fears and imaginings. In *The Nice and The Good*, John exclaims to Jessica, whom he has refused to marry but kept seeing even after they have broken up: 'We can't go on in this sort of emotional *muddle*. We've got no background, no stability, no ordinariness. We're just living on our emotions and eating each other. And it's so rotten for you.'[112]

The eating each other is, together with 'rotten' and 'emotional muddle', an almost uncanny incantation of how deeply but unclearly human beings can reach into each other. When rejection and desire are mixed up, as they are for John and Jessica, an experience of bodily disintegration can accompany love. In an earlier passage, their relationship is described as 'the familiar *muddled* atmosphere of pity and passion'.[113] Pity invokes a distance, and passion closeness. The other is *other* but at the same time deeply inside of oneself, in a muddle that could perhaps best be described as a closeness-to-otherness.

To explain aesthetic ideas is tricky, since any attempt to 'clarify' them falls back on conceptually determinate judgements. As we have seen, it is not simply by the concepts that are used, but in relation to them and through feeling, that art communicates.[114] In association with a given concept, much that is unnameable is stirred up by the imagination, which gives us an enlivening feeling for our capacity for cognition in general.[115] Thus, what Murdoch calls the 'intense showing' of art[116] refers to something other than the clarification of philosophy, at least if one by philosophy means a kind of conceptual understanding, by Kant understood as making our representations into objects of our own thoughts by comparison, reflection and abstraction. What is shown by muddle as an aesthetic idea can (because of the boundless character of the aesthetic imagination) only be exemplified, never exhaustively explained or defined. It makes it more 'muddled' what a word like 'muddled' might mean, not more definite.

I shall give one final example of what this can look like in Murdoch's fiction. In *An Unofficial Rose*, muddle is depicted as resisting narrative grasp when a scene from the past emerges into the present. The retired gentleman Hugh, when walking through the garden with his old friend Mildred, has a Proustian experience of a smell which throws him out of the present into a memory he cannot at first place: 'The smell of citronella troubled Hugh exceedingly. What a *muddled* state he seemed to be in today. Why was that particular smell in that particular place so oddly disturbing?'[117] They keep on walking, and when they reach the little bridge, the memory hits him:

> Hugh leaned on the parapet and looked down. He descried in the sunny water the long waving of the green weed. Then moving his gaze, and by a change of focus, he saw just below him in the stream the reflection of himself, and of Mildred who was leaning close beside him and also looking down. With that, and with a wild rush of distressed emotion the memory came up and he recalled the kiss. It had been here, exactly here, and at just such a moment they had both paused and seen their reflections in the glass below them. They had seen their reflections; and then, as if prompted by those shades below, turning to each other, with a naturalness, pallidly and in silence they had kissed.[118]

The smell, as well as the reflection of them in the water, and the park in its entirety, is caught up in an almost contourless muddled memory overlapping the present moment. Again, it is in the clash between images (their own shadows, physically as well as temporally) that muddle is intuited, an aesthetic idea invoking the very lack of containment in life.

3.8. Chapter summary

In this chapter, I have given an account of the role of conceptual content in the aesthetic appreciation of literature.

By tracing early Murdoch's misunderstanding of Kant's aesthetics, I have first shown how the pure aesthetic judgement differs from experiences of actual artworks. As later Murdoch also acknowledges, the aesthetic can be recognized as a specific state of mind without claiming that it exhaustively defines our ways of engaging with art. I have gone through what Kant means with concepts and shown how they can be present in art without its aim being an achievement of the understanding. We can intuit beauty without understanding it – but beauty can produce a boundless intellectual interest, and conceptual cognitions can affect our appreciations of beauty as nature or art. The landlord's jolly prank changes our appreciation of 'the nightingale', and it is impossible to think that the experience of watching an enormous, blood-red moon would not be slightly different for an astronomer than a child. But the child and the astronomer are sharing a profound feeling, which may sublimely overflow their attempts to grasp and understand what they are witnessing.

Whether harmonious or violently disruptive, aesthetic experiences *relate* to our conceptual understanding, but they are not simply prompts to it. A man walking through a field of lilies, finding an ecstasy for his spirit in a line of thinking which he can never fully develop, can stumble upon various insights, true or false – but an account of these can never exhaust the significance of his aesthetic state of mind. He is simply enjoying the free play between his imagination and understanding. Similarly, aesthetic ideas are (in Kant's words) 'representation[s] of the imagination that occasions much thinking though without it being possible for any determinate thought, i.e., concept, to be adequate to [them]'.[119] They give us an imaginative and quasi-pictorial grasp of things that the imagination and the understanding cannot form a conceptual knowledge of, such as infinity or hell. I have described how 'muddle' functions as such an aesthetic idea in Murdoch's fiction.

To conclude: thinking is of course not absent from art. But the aesthetic experience does not point us towards conceptual understanding. Rather, literature can allow for a muddling of concepts in the sense of letting them disintegrate in the feeling of life, as mud is stirred in water. By being in relation to our conceptual understanding, while not being governed by it, aesthetic states of mind allow us to intuit the harmony which makes conceptual understanding possible as well as the disturbances that remind us of its arbitrary limitations. There are no completely pure experiences of beauty since neither birdsong nor opera can be *a priori*. Instead, all aesthetic experiences are unstably related to our conceptualizations of nature and art as separate and intertwined.

With aesthetic ideas, Kant formulated an example of how art can work with concepts without leading towards an understanding, in serving 'really only to animate the mind by opening up for it the prospect of an immeasurable field of related representations'.[120]

This aesthetic 'opening up' can take many different forms. The pleasure and displeasure of an indeterminate representation, which makes a flower in a poem unidentical to our conceptual understanding of it, can be pleasingly beautiful as well as sublimely overwhelming. If Shakespeare was right that 'a rose/by any other name would smell as sweet',[121] Gertrude Stein was also correct to write that 'A rose is a rose is a rose.'[122] In both phrases, something more indeterminate and enlivening is at stake than actually knowing what a rose is, without any of these ways of relating to the concept being blind or empty.

4

Real characters and fictional people: *Stanley Cavell and the epistemology of fiction*

4.1. 'Reacting to characters as if they were real people'

What kind of relation can we have with fictional characters? Caring about them, as people rather than as textual constructs, has long been unfashionable in literary criticism. It has been dismissed as naïve to relate to, say, Othello or Anna Karenina, as if they were entities in their own right, instead of, say, deconstructing how the illusion of their subjectivity is constituted by the text. Recently, this dogma has been challenged, most notably in the postcritical book *Character: Three Inquiries in Literary Studies* by Amanda Anderson, Rita Felski and Toril Moi. Against the formalist tradition, they set out to take the ordinary reader's interest in character seriously and describe why characters matter. We often relate to characters as we would to real people, Moi claims and makes a Wittgensteinian refutation of the philosophical habit of taking their fictional status as a logical problem.[1] Felski exclaims in her essay: 'Another possibility presents itself: it is their fictional qualities that make characters real. Characters are not real persons; they are real fictional beings!'[2]

However refreshing these essays are, they are aimed at literary studies and leave the philosophical problem of fictionality[3] largely unresolved. What is a 'real fictional being', as Felski puts it? Her main explanation seems to be that they are aesthetically mediated – but what does this mean? Moi, explicitly following Stanley Cavell's criticism of the taboo on talking about character, attempts to dismiss the philosophical conundrum at the epistemological status of fiction by describing talk about characters 'as a language-game in its own right, on a par with others (praying, begging, asking, questioning, for example)'.[4] But Moi neglects to describe the specific challenge to epistemology that Cavell utilizes fiction to make, as well as the special status of fiction. Granted, this falls outside the scope of literary studies. Their essays are mainly concerned with reading and interpreting literature, not describing it philosophically. More surprising is that they seem to have missed how Iris Murdoch has predated the raising of some of their concerns with almost forty years, even though Moi has previously worked on Murdoch, and Anderson's chapter contains an extensive discussion of how Murdoch's moral philosophy is compatible with a closer engagement with character.[5]

In the essay 'Against Dryness' from 1961, Murdoch wants to make a case for 'the now so unfashionable naturalistic idea of character'.[6] Here, she objects to both the journalistic tendency of contemporary prose, and its counterpart, what she calls the 'crystalline' and mythical fiction, since neither of them succeeds in giving us more than a flimsy and shallow idea of human personality. Creating characters that appear real to us is for Murdoch one of the most important achievements of fiction, and a good critic should remain responsive to them. In *Metaphysics as a Guide to Morals* from 1992, she criticizes the paranoid and deconstructive readings of contemporary literary theory, and pronounces instead her appreciation for

> The "old", and in my view, proper, literary critic, [who] approaches a literary work in an open-minded manner and is interested in it in *all sorts of ways*: which certainly does not exclude treating a tale as a "window into another world", reacting to characters as if they were real people, making value judgements about them, about how their creator treats them, and so on.[7]

Note the 'as if', 'reacting to' and the 'how their creator treats them'. What Murdoch is arguing for here is of course not that we should really, in every sense of the word, treat or think of fictional characters as real or uncreated. This is a superfluous remark – we already know that they are imaginary. But what is it that we know when we know this? And what does it mean to acknowledge a character, or to treat a story as a window into another world? What does the 'deeper' relationship to imaginary characters entail that she thinks is so important? Here, she leaves some threads hanging in the air.

In this chapter, I shall pick up the slack that both Murdoch and the recent postcritical voices have left us with and attempt to unravel these threads a bit longer, through a discussion on Cavell, Coleridge and Freud. I shall focus on character and the problem of fictionality, two issues that I consider as entangled. Fiction, I shall argue, suspends our reality testing, and reacting to characters as if they were real means something very different from being amongst real people. In analytic philosophy, the problem of fiction has often been (unfruitfully) examined as an epistemological issue. In Stanley Cavell's work, fiction is instead presented as a challenge to the entire epistemological approach, leading up to a very interesting attempt to question the distinction between literature and philosophy. By following his reasoning on character more extensively than Moi, I will describe the challenge he finds to epistemology in fiction, but also argue that he fails to sufficiently account for the specificity of fiction. Thereafter, I shall turn to Coleridge and Freud to explain how suspension of disbelief and artistic form allows for another way of relating to characters than to actual people. Finally, I will criticize how Cavell reads Othello as a 'literary fact' of the tragic human condition, and thus makes use of fiction to question the distinction between literature and philosophy. At the end, I shall also return to Murdoch's notes on character. The main aim of this chapter is to explain how the fictional status of literature makes it difficult to utilize *as* philosophy, even though the philosophical study of fiction can powerfully challenge a philosophical approach.

Cavell's essay 'The Avoidance of Love' is published in 1967, close in time to Murdoch's 'Against Dryness', and expresses a similar discomfort with the loss of a deep imaginary relation to fictional characters. Cavell begins the text by describing the development in Shakespeare studies from a discussion of characters to a discussion of words. He suggests that this distinction is absurd, since paying attention to what the characters say should be indistinguishable from paying attention to them, and vice versa. The reason behind this development might be, Cavell says, that the critic 'has been made to believe or assume, by some philosophy or other, that characters are not people'.[8] Does Cavell then think that characters are people, in every sense of the word? The answer to that is complex, and never completely resolved. Throughout the essay, Cavell presents us with an ambulating discussion of what it means that Shakespeare's characters are fictional, that is, what difference it makes that we cannot climb onto the stage and stop Othello from murdering Desdemona.

But in Cavell's magnus opus *The Claim of Reason* from 1979, this question has somehow dissipated. Here, Othello reappears, now presented to us not as an imaginary character, but as a 'literary fact', expressive of the fundamental tragedy of the human condition. His fictional status has now somehow been bypassed, which gives Cavell the possibility to present him as a proof of the conclusion 'that skepticism concerning other minds is not skepticism but tragedy'.[9] Using Othello to refute sceptical doubt, Cavell is both exposing a fundamental deficiency of the epistemological approach, and, I will argue, leaving us with the problem of the untouchable Othello unresolved. But before we take a closer look at Othello, let us begin with digging deeper into the problematic relationship between epistemology and fiction.

4.2. Epistemology and the problem of fiction

In what sense are fictional characters not real? The difficulty of asking this question properly can be discerned in most philosophical investigations of the epistemology of fiction. These often have something quite unnatural, even slightly ridiculous, about them. In reading them, one might feel inclined to suspect that the problem of fiction threatens to expose some essential and embarrassing deficiency of epistemology. Nonetheless, the epistemological status of fiction has since the seventies been one of the most popular problems of literature in analytic philosophy.[10]

As Arthur Danto writes, 'pretty much the only way in which literature of the non-philosophical kind has impinged upon philosophical awareness has been from the perspective of truth-or-falsity'.[11] Theories of truth and referentiality seem to struggle with the problem of fiction worse than Don Quixote with his weather mills. Danto gives a parodical but accurate summary of the discussions. For a character like Don Quixote to be meaningful to us, his name must refer to a substantial entity, although clearly not to a specific existing Spaniard in La Mancha. Can Don Quixote thus be said to live in an entirely different realm? Well no, 'for the relation of [this realm] to ours and finally to us remains as obscure as that between Don Quixote and us when he was a homeless wraith, an ontological ghost wandering in worlds undreamt of by poets'.[12] All of the attempts to solve this referential riddle raise, as Danto points out, the problem of why 'we, as readers, should have the slightest interest in Don Quixote if what it is about is an unactualized thin man in a region of being I would have no reason to know about save for the interventions of semantical theory'.[13] As Danto almost indicates, the matter of who and what Don Quixote is seems then to be tied up with the problem of why, and indeed how, we care.

That we in novels, plays and films repeatedly find ourselves moved and upset by things which are not real seems to puzzle some philosophers profoundly. They tend to bring up the problem of made-up stories as if faced with something very alien – the standard approach of epistemology: to make the habitual into a problem – and not something they have been accustomed to since early childhood. This creates a plethora of almost incomprehensible referential questions. Are novelists *really* making assertions, or are they just 'pretending to'?[14] Do movie-goers *really* think that the characters, whose fates they are so absorbed by, *really* exist?[15]

As these arguments proceed, it usually gets more and more confusing what words like 'really' and 'pretend' are supposed to mean. And so the philosophers entangle themselves in weird comparisons, not seldom creating fictional examples of their own to illustrate the problem. Imagine for example, says Kendall L. Walton, the movie-goer Charles enjoying a scary tale about a monstruous slime. When can we say that he is *really* afraid?

> If Charles is an older movie-goer with a heart condition, he may be afraid of the movie itself. Perhaps he knows that any excitement could trigger a heart attack, and fears that the movie will cause excitement, e.g., by depicting the slime as being especially aggressive or threatening. This is real fear. But it is fear of the depiction of the slime, not fear of the slime which is depicted.[16]

What is so ridiculous about this example? Is it a bad example, or is the problem of knowing what is real and not perhaps irrelevant for our enjoyment, indeed even our understanding, of fiction? We already know that Charles has no real reason to be afraid (just like we are not really worried about his heart condition), but we also know that he is not pretending. What is it that we know in knowing this? It seems like epistemology, the self-knowledge of knowledge, gets flustered by running up against fiction. Fiction casts a new light over the fundamental concerns of the epistemologist, suggesting that the very unquestioning mode of perceiving the world that he tries to take apart constitutes the heart of our engagement with imaginary stories.

In Cavell's work, the traditional epistemologist is described as driven by this refusal or inability of taking things at face value. He transforms everyday life into an intellectual problem. He refuses to rely on habit, he craves proof that we can trust the world, that it and other people 'really' exist, and that he is not just dreaming or being played tricks on by a superior intelligence. The human condition of living in a shared world, where we are both endlessly connected with and separate from other people, is by the epistemological sceptic converted into an intellectual riddle. And when the epistemologist discovers that we 'really' cannot know anything for certain, this is according to Cavell not a discovery of the world but an attempt to escape it.

Cavell's engagement with the relationship between philosophy and literature could be said to arise out of his criticisms of sceptical doubt. In fiction, knowledge does not present itself as this kind of forced intellectual problem. So, Cavell seems to think, literature might paradoxically give us a better understanding of what knowledge is than philosophy – even though this literary knowledge might perhaps, as he phrases it, not 'know itself'.[17]

Indeed, with a work of art, what is real and important cannot be proven intellectually. True understanding of an artwork does not arise when we have certainty that what we are witnessing is real, but when we are prepared to give up that quest and the epistemological problem disappears. As Cavell puts it with Wittgenstein: 'Believing it is seeing it.'[18] Fiction becomes in this sense the epitome of art. But even though the belief we place in it is not equivalent to taking what we are witnessing as irrelevant or even unreal, believing it here still means something different than treating it as real.

It means, as I shall claim with Coleridge's old concept, to suspend our disbelief. And so, while fiction might cast a certain light over the unnaturalness of the sceptic's concerns, it does not resolve his doubts; it merely suspends them. This suspension is not applicable to our engagements with people outside of made-up stories, something which severely undermines Cavell's attempt to question the boundaries between literature and philosophy. To understand how, we must zoom in on the untouchable Othello.

4.3. The untouchable Othello

Othello is an upstanding general of the Venetian army in the sixteenth century, of Moorish race. He gets manipulated to doubt the faithfulness of his white, young, beautiful wife Desdemona. These doubts are eventually intensified into an unbearable rage, culminating in him murdering Desdemona.

In 'The Avoidance of Love', Cavell asks us to dwell for a moment on the joke about the Southern yokel who wants to rush up to the stage and save the pretty lady from being smothered by Othello. How can we explain to him that he shouldn't; or rather, that he can't? The uneducated brute thinks that someone is actually being killed on stage. 'Yes', Cavell answers, 'and that is exactly what's happening.' But it is only play acting. Desdemona will be alive again tomorrow night, and then she will be killed again. 'The trouble is,' Cavell says, 'that I really do not know what I am being asked, and of course I am suggesting that you don't know either.'[19] The problem with Othello's, for lack of a better word, 'unreality', seems impossible to phrase properly. How can we explain to the Southern brute that no actual murder is taking place?[20]

> 'They are only acting; it isn't real.' But we may not be perfectly happy to have had to say that. Not that we doubt that it is true. If the thing *were* real … But somehow we had *accepted* its non-factuality, it made it possible for there to have been a play. … 'They are only pretending' is something we typically say to children, in reassurance; and its no happier a thing to say in that context, and no truer. The point of saying it there is not to focus them on the play, but to help bring them out of it. It is not an instructive remark, but an emergency measure.[21]

We only say that it is not real when we want to make the play seem less meaningful to someone, or even make it vanish altogether. If a child is scared that a monster from a film will be hiding under her bed, or if someone thinks that he can save Desdemona, this is the only explanation we can offer. If the Southern yokel doesn't accept that, we must restrain him. Or remove him from the theatre. Or stop the play.

> *That* is something we can do; and its very extremity shows how little is in our power. For that farthest extremity has not touched Othello, he has vanished; it has merely interrupted an evening's work. Quiet the house, pick up the thread again, and Othello will reappear, as near and deaf to us as ever.[22]

Othello is unreachable and untouchable, impossible for us to interact with. Yet, if we would not feel as if he were about to smother his wife, he would not be Othello to us, just a bad actor. The problem here, which has been troubling Cavell for over ten pages, 'is brought out by asking: How do I know that I am to do nothing, confronted with such events?'[23] Or: 'What is the state of mind in which I find the events in a theatre neither credible nor incredible?'[24] Or: In what sense do we 'believe' in fiction?

4.4. Suspension of disbelief

Coleridge's concept of *suspension of disbelief* has long been the most popular way of describing the peculiar (in)credibility of fiction. Or rather, over the last couple of decades, it has served as the most popular starting point of refutation for many analytic epistemologists, who seem to compete in finding faults with Coleridge.[25] As Freeman points out: even though 'he provides us with a possibility for solving the paradox, no post-1975 theorist has aligned himself with this possibility'.[26] This would be because Coleridge is not 'taking the paradox of fiction seriously enough to bother about solving it'[27] – indeed, he does not even find fiction to present us with any kind of logical paradox. Since I believe that our relation to fiction is better described as a state of mind than an epistemological problem, I shall attempt to explicate what Coleridge may mean with his famous concept.

In fact, *suspension of disbelief* is not so much a theory as merely a descriptive term, occurring only once in Coleridge's writings. It is introduced in a paragraph in his *Biographia Literaria* from 1817, where he compares his own phantasmatic poems to Woodsworth's more realistic ones. No matter how supernatural the story is, Coleridge suggests, it becomes 'real' to us while we are reading it, because we

> transfer from our inward nature a human interest and a semblance of truth sufficient to procure for these shadows of imagination that willing suspension of disbelief for the moment, which constitutes poetic faith.[28]

This is basically all he says about the concept as such, and so it is more of a fleeting phrase than a proposed model for understanding fiction. But as the durability of the phrase suggests, it nonetheless captures something. Coleridge's subsequent account of the nature of lyrical imagination develops what may well be said to be inherent in his notion of poetic faith. Phantasmatic or realistic, he says, all lyrics can 'produce the pleasurable interest, which it is the peculiar business of poetry to impart'. This interest functions

> by awakening the mind's attention to the lethargy of custom, and directing it to the loveliness and the wonders of the world before us; an inexhaustible treasure, but for which in consequence of the film of familiarity and selfish solicitude we have eyes, yet see not, ears that hear not, and hearts that neither feel nor understand.[29]

Thus, poetic faith can be understood as an immersive enchantment, a kind of heightened presence in perception. Suspension of disbelief is, in other words, something else than a lack of doubts and should not be confused with our habitual, unquestioning acceptance of our surroundings. The playgoer is not like a stressed parent preparing breakfast, numbly going about his business, nor is he a slacking epistemologist. In our enjoyment of fiction, we do not forget our doubts, like Hume did when he left his study: we place them on hold, and let the phantasmatic appear real and the real phantasmatic. The argument that Coleridge wants to make with suspension of disbelief is that there is no crucial difference between his way of writing and Woodsworth's, because our desire to differentiate between the actual and the made up is, in fiction, converted into a desire to conflate them. If he is right, fiction is indeed not best explained in terms of knowledge. It is not even the element of fantasy that is crucial, but a kind of immersion that suspends the impulse to sort information after degrees of reality. Rather than being a logical problem for the epistemologist to resolve, fiction seems to challenge his entire approach.

To understand how fiction undermines the epistemological approach, we shall turn back to Cavell. In *The World Viewed,* he describes the enjoyment of film as a reversion of the myth of Faust.[30] Faust, as Cavell writes in *The Claim of Reason,* 'is the Midas of knowledge'.[31] Everything he touches loses its value as it is turned into understanding. The misery of Faust makes us realize that reason alone cannot provide us with a sufficient access to meaning, or in Cavell's words, that 'this success … is not humanly satisfying'.[32] Fiction is not here immediately contrasted to the Faustian approach, but we find an extension of the discussion in Cavell's writings on film. In contrast to the dissatisfaction of Faust, when movies 'reproduce the world magically' they allow us 'to view it unseen'. This is 'a wish not to need power, not to have to bear its burdens. It is, in this sense, the reverse of the myth of Faust.'[33] By temporarily relieving us from the need to understand and act in the world, fiction can turn everything it touches into what Coleridge calls 'an inexhaustible treasure'.

But Cavell's approach is not entirely aligned with Coleridge's. The latter's poetic faith, which renders phantasmatic settings as present to us as realistic ones, is not the same as the presence Cavell places in opposition to sceptical doubt. Cavell does not use the term 'suspension of disbelief', probably because he wants to suggest that the problem of credibility is *irrelevant* rather than suspended – in fiction as well as in life. He describes how in epistemological investigations, 'the world normally present to us (the world in whose existence, as it is typically put, we "believe") is brought into question and vanishes',[34] as it is turned into an intellectual problem. And thus, scepticism involuntarily shows us that the presentness of the world 'cannot be a function of knowing'.[35] The kind of presentness that Cavell describes is already there. Thus, it is not the same as the immersion created momentarily by poetic faith. In other words, Cavell is not attempting to hold forth suspension of disbelief as a solution to the problem of sceptical doubt.

Quite the contrary. As we shall see, Cavell wants to present Othello as a literary fact about the human condition, and to propose the tragedy of human life as the real and necessary condition which the traditional epistemologist attempts to escape. Othello thus becomes the counterproof to scepticism and Cavell's suggested solution to the problem of other minds. To achieve this, Cavell must undo Coleridge's unification of the phantasmatic and the realistic. He wants to suggest that we relate to Othello like we would relate to a person, and not like we would relate to a fairy or an alien. He claims that 'science fiction cannot house tragedy because in it human limitations can from the beginning be bypassed'.[36] But even if there were no supernatural elements in Shakespeare's tragedies, such as the ghost in *Hamlet* or the witches in *Macbeth*, Cavell never really clarifies how the belief we place in a play would be of the same kind as our belief in the world, which is evidently what he wants to suggest.

Cavell says about the theatre: 'Neither credible nor incredible: that ought to mean that the concept of credibility is inappropriate altogether. The trouble is, it is inappropriate to real conduct as well, most of the time.'[37] He is right to claim that the question of credibility arises in our everyday lives much less frequently than the sceptic wants to suggest. But doubting the reality of our impressions is not always wholly inappropriate, and the example Cavell uses to illustrate this is less than convincing. Imagine that we are sitting in a café, watching a couple sipping coffee next to us. 'Suppose the man suddenly puts his hands to the throat of the woman', Cavell says. 'Do I believe or disbelieve that he is going to throttle her? The time for that question, as soon as it comes to the point, is already passed. The question is: What, if anything, do I do?'[38]

I doubt that the question of disbelief is as quickly bypassed here as Cavell attests. Wondering whether someone is actually about to murder his wife might not be such a different matter if it happens in a film set in outer space or on a stage emulating sixteenth-century Venice, but the question surely wants an answer in real life. In real life, what we are witnessing is neither predetermined nor fictional. We sometimes ask ourselves: Is what I think is happening here really happening? Suspending our doubts and simply indulging in the beauty and intensity of the murder at the café would not be pleasurable, unless we know that they are play-acting, or we happen to be psychopaths.[39] The pleasure is made possible by the liberation of the need to ask ourselves whether what we are witnessing is real; and if so, what we should do about it.

But, as Cavell rightly stresses, this problem of reality is tied up with the possibility of interaction. 'What, if anything, do I do?'[40] It is a social or moral, rather than epistemological, matter. As we begin to see, the central problem of reality in relation to fiction does not concern what we know, but whether we are faced with people who can face us. And so we must return to the untouchable Othello.

4.5. Shame and acknowledgement

As the joke with the Southern yokel illustrates, Othello's fictionality makes it impossible for us to stand in any reciprocal relationship to him. No matter how much we would try to disrupt the play, even if we would rush up to the stage and shake him, Othello would remain unaware of our presence (although we would certainly annoy the actor). Since we know this, we usually remain quiet in our seats, moved but unmoving, engaged but undetectable. We are free to blush and laugh and squirm and cry, while being not just untouchable but also invisible to Othello. Besides doubt and responsibility, fiction also protects us from vulnerability. Especially shame.

According to Cavell, tragedy reveals the conditions of acknowledgement. I shall describe how in the end of this section. The general condition of the acknowledgement he describes is that the only alternative to it is not ignorance, but avoidance. We are always faced with others, and this is a problem that cannot be wished away. What is more, we are faced with them being faced with us, and so 'the failure to recognise others is a failure to let others recognise you, a fear of what is revealed to them, an avoidance of their eyes'. The main reason why we would withhold this recognition is shame. 'For shame is the specific discomfort produced by the sense of being looked at, the avoidance of the sight of others is the reflex it produces.'[41]

But comfortably seated in the dark, as a theatre audience, we are protected at the outset from the sense of being looked at. Since Cavell is less interested in the specificity of fiction than its similarity to actual life, he tends to minimize these differences. To understand how the literary art is structured as a liberation from shame, we shall instead turn briefly to Freud. He describes well how plays and poems enable us to enjoy the secret day-dreams of both us and others. Artlessly expressed, the same phantasies would leave us disgusted, cold or ashamed:

> But when a creative writer presents his plays to us or tells us what we are inclined to take to be his personal day-dreams, we experience a great pleasure .... How the writer accomplishes this is his innermost secret; the essential *ars poetica* lies in the technique of overcoming the feeling of repulsion which is undoubtedly connected with the barriers that rise between each single ego and the others.[42]

Literature allows us to connect on another level, since it somehow overcomes the barriers of repulsion that we usually put up between each other. How? The formal beauty of the work gives us a pleasure in its own right, Freud continues, but that is not the only reason. The writer is also 'altering and disguising' his day-dreams. Thus, the fictionality provides an alibi which protects both artist and audience from shame. This alibi (Latin for *at another place*) is experienced almost like an alternative spatiality. As Cavell says about Othello and Desdemona: 'they and we do not occupy the same space'; they are in our presence without us being in theirs, as if we were dreaming them.[43]

This separation gives us a certain sense of relief, which allows us to feel things both within ourselves and the characters that we would not permit ourselves if we were faced with real people. Something deep is indeed shared and communicated when we take these characters seriously. But this something seems to be dependent on our liberation from the demands of actual interpersonal encounters.

Norman L. Holland explains this relief with the Freudian notion of isolation. Isolation is the neurotic's 'taboo on touching'.[44] It entails a prohibition against the possibility of contact with the isolated object, in order to keep our strong drives apart from reality, which is what the convention of art does. Interestingly, Holland brings up the example of the Southern man attempting to save Desdemona to illustrate what it can look like when artistic isolation breaks down. Following this, I would argue that it is this artistic isolation which enables us to share Othello's present. It is only when we respect his untouchability that we can indulge in Othello's dark, tormenting passions as if they were our own. We allow ourselves to share his murderous jealousy thanks to the isolating alibi of fiction.[45]

However, we must also note that Cavell hesitates to call Othello fictional, and almost indicates that it would be a failure to understand him so. 'In failing to find the character's present we fail to make him present', Cavell writes. 'Then he is indeed a fictitious creature, a figment of my imagination, like all the other people in my life whom I find I have failed to know, have known wrong.'[46] Here, he seems to say that seeing fictional characters as imaginary would be as wrong as taking actual people that way, as if finding a character's present would be no different from sharing a present with someone who can gaze back at you.

Indeed, Cavell appears to want to break down the isolation of fiction. This is why the story about the Southern yokel becomes more than a joke to him. The untouchable Othello presents a real problem, since Cavell utilizes him to embody the problem of acknowledgement.

Curiously enough, Cavell argues that acknowledgement can be completed in the theatre. This is done by making the characters' present ours, which requires 'the repudiation of our perception altogether'.[47] We cannot face Othello, so our acknowledgement of him takes place through a kind of identificatory merging of my perception with his, which allows us to share his pain:

> [A]cknowledgement in a theater shows what acknowledgement in actuality is. For what is the difference between tragedy in a theater and tragedy in actuality? In both, people in pain are in our presence. But in actuality, acknowledgement is incomplete, in actuality there is no acknowledgement, unless we put ourselves in their presence, reveal ourselves to them.[48]

Acknowledgement is incomplete in reality, unless we put ourselves in the presence of another (which we can never fully do, because we are embodied and endlessly separate[49]). In theatre, this separateness is established and given beforehand, and so it is not a hinder anymore, we can immerse in it, we 'confirm the final fact of our separateness'.[50] At the same time the difference between mine and Othello's identity is made irrelevant. In Cavell's words: 'What is purged [in theatre] is my difference from others, in everything but separateness.'[51]

But the conditions for acknowledgement in fiction appear to have been severely altered. This deep experience – of sharing feelings which would otherwise be intolerable to us – is dependent on an artistic and fictional isolation which we cannot resort to in actuality. Because we have an alibi, because he is at another place, we can welcome Othello's pained rage as if it were our own. In actuality, Cavell states, acknowledgement requires us to reveal ourselves, but: 'We may find that the point of tragedy in a theatre is exactly relief from this necessity, a respite within which to prepare for this necessity, to clean out the pity and terror which stand in the way of acknowledgement outside.'[52]

Fiction thus becomes an instrumental cleanse, a place where we can enact what acknowledgement should have been. By picturing pity and terror and shame as things that stand in the way of rather than conditioning (or even enabling?) acknowledgement, Cavell is basing his account on a fictive, theatrical model. The fixed separateness and identificatory merging of perceptions in the theatre is not equivalent to meeting the gaze of another person in life. He seems to day-dream that it should be. Thus, Cavell's theatrical fantasy of completed acknowledgement paves the way for an artistic evasion of the problem of sceptical doubt, especially concerning other minds.

4.6. The statue of Othello

Othello refuses to accept what Cavell calls the 'best case' of knowing the other. His doubts in Desdemona's fidelity are ineradicable, because one cannot open another human being completely to the ocular proof, and Othello cannot stand this. He smothers her because he would rather have her dead than unknowable, than endlessly separate, than other, from him.

For Cavell, this fundamental unknowability of any person beyond the 'best case' is expressive of the human condition. Scepticism concerning other minds is an attempt to escape from this condition, by turning the moral problem into an intellectual riddle.[53] Cavell demonstrates this well, and Othello's jealous doubts offer a nice illustration of the problem. Cavell also utilizes fiction effectively to highlight the deficiencies of the epistemological approach. But he goes further than this. He claims that tragedy, and especially the tragedy of Othello, is a more direct expression of what it means to be human. This solution is, I will argue, no less evasive. Tragedy is a genre of fiction, and if Othello can be more opened to the ocular proof for us than Desdemona can be to him, it's because we cannot meet him.

As we have seen, Cavell's account of acknowledgement is not just based on a fictional example, but the premisses of fiction as such. Pity, terror and the instability of our separateness from each other are for him things which stand in the way of acknowledgement outside of theatre. In watching how Othello suffocates Desdemona, Cavell says, 'we know that there is nothing we can do. Tragedy is meant to make sense of that condition.'[54] But what kind of sense-making does fiction offer here, and of what? In actuality, it is rarely a given that we are passive spectators sitting in the dark. Instead, we must constantly redetermine our own level of responsibility; being passive in the face of a real murder would simply be one of the ways we inevitably participate. In the theatre, already before the drama starts, we have given up our agency in relation to what we are witnessing. The suspension of disbelief allows us a relief from these eternal doubts, vulnerabilities and responsibilities. This sounds more like an escape than sense-making to me.

At other times, Cavell almost seems to recognize the escapist character of fiction. For example, he speaks of 'the all but inescapable temptation to think of the past in terms of theater'.[55] Indeed, as we saw earlier about treating real people as fictitious, 'fiction' and 'theatre' seem to Cavell to be derogatory terms, applicable to almost anything but fiction. He even speaks of the theatre as a liberation from the theatricalization of life: 'in giving us a place where our hiddenness and silence and separation are accounted for, [theatre] gives us a chance to stop [theatricalization]'.[56] Theatricalization means seeing the world as a stage, it means taking our existence upon us like a drama, and failing to make others and ourselves real to us; in other words, failing to let ourselves be seen. Again, the spectator cannot fail in this, because nothing he could do would count as self-revelation. He is allowed a momentary escape from the nagging feeling of the performativity of life, by knowing that he is witnessing an actual performance.

But Cavell does not seem to recognize that the theatre in itself gives him the illusion of having the ability to look at life from the outside and grasp it as a story. Murdoch calls this temptation the consolation of form, something I will discuss more at length in the next chapter on tragedy. 'Art', Murdoch writes, 'cannot help changing what it professes to display into something different. ... Hell itself it turns to favour and to prettiness'.[57] This is also true for the pity, terror, vulnerability and shame portrayed in the theatre: it is artificially contained by a charming form. As with the formal or aesthetic bribe that Freud speaks of, fiction allows us to take part of things that would otherwise disgust, frighten or repel us. We engage with it through our imagination, from a hidden place, no matter how deeply or meaningfully it touches us. Fictional characters cannot expose us to ourselves in the eyes of another: an ineradicable part of the human condition.[58]

At the very end of his magnum opus, Cavell presents us with a scene in place of a conclusion. The lived problem had been turned to a statue, a monument or an emblem. We are put in the position of the passive, silent audience, invited to witness the deaths of Othello and Desdemona together with the philosopher, who has taken them in his hand:

> So, they are there, on their bridal and death sheets. A statue, a stone, is something whose existence is fundamentally open to the ocular proof. A human being is not. The two bodies lying together form an emblem of this fact, the truth of skepticism.[59]

But this 'emblem' in itself professes to have opened something to the ocular proof that cannot be opened, except as a fiction. Perhaps Cavell is a bit unsettled by this as well. 'So we are here', he continues, as if to stress our separateness as merely an audience to the scene, 'knowing they are "gone to burning hell"'. They are there. We are here. Hell is in another place and prettified in at least three ways: we are spared from any involvement in it, it has been turned into a graspable story, and been made beautiful to contemplate. But Othello is not a person who can be revealed to us, since we cannot ever be revealed by him. His inner life is only graspable as an instance of the tragedy of human life because he is a fictional character. As Gérard Genette puts it: 'If narrative fiction alone gives us direct access to the subjectivity of another person, this is not by virtue of some miraculous privilege; it is because that other person is a fictitious being.'[60] The fundamental incompleteness of acknowledgement in theatre haunts the closing scene of *The Claim of Reason*.

Stating, as Cavell does, that scepticism is not scepticism but tragedy gives a self-congratulatory sense of having seen through the evasive intellectual manoeuvres of epistemology to the naked facts of life. But what he presents us with instead is a fiction, not an explanation. Perhaps Cavell saw this too, which is why he later softens his conclusion that 'skepticism ... is not skepticism but tragedy' into: 'tragedy is an interpretation of what skepticism itself is an interpretation of.'[61] However, tragedy, and more specifically *Othello*, is not presented by him in *The Claim of Reason* as simply an artistic interpretation, but as what he calls a 'literary fact', offering an illumination of the human condition. '[T]here is no human alternative to the possibility of tragedy', he portentously exclaims,[62] and proceeds to pronounce Othello to be representative of human life in general. In an (even for Cavell) unusually wriggling paragraph, he claims

> to see how his [Othello's] life figures mine, how mine has the makings of his, that we bear an internal relation to one another; how my happiness depends on living touched but not struck by his problems, or struck but not stricken; problems of trust and betrayal, of false isolation and false company, of the desire and fear of both privacy and of union. ... I do not claim to have *explained* how one human being's life (fictional or actual) can be representative of human life generally .... I do claim, for example, that Othello is thus representative, and that to understand that (literary) fact would be the same as to understand what the (philosophical) problem of others is, in particular why its best cases take the forms they take.[63]

Putting Othello in place of an explanation, Cavell gives us an illusion of having demonstrated the problem of other minds. On the last page, he asks whether philosophy can accept Othello and Desdemona *back* at the hands of poetry. But could they ever have been wrestled out of there in the first place? Can a philosopher really do what the Southern yokel gets laughed at for doing, that is, rush up to the stage and attempt to seize the untouchable Othello, and pull him out of his fictional isolation?

To rephrase Cavell's ending question: Can philosophy become fiction and still know itself? It would, at least following Coleridge's notion of poetic faith, require philosophy to suspend its disbelief, and turn its desire to differentiate between the actual and the fantastic into a rejoicing at their momentary sublation. But actual human acknowledgement cannot be modelled on an account of acknowledgement in theatre. Any philosophical attempt to take fiction as directly expressive of the human condition risks misrepresenting life as something as unified, isolated and formally pleasing as a work of art. Seeing through artificial intellectual riddles does not really further our understanding if what we encounter on the other side is a statue, and not a living being.

4.7. Imagining the being of others

This does not mean that it would be meaningless to care about characters. On the contrary: if we appreciate the special status of fiction, characters might have even more to offer us. They may turn out to matter precisely in being imaginary.

Even though Murdoch provides no extensive discussion of the epistemological status of fiction, she repeatedly comments on the importance of fictional characters. 'The main activity and the main difficulty of the writer of fiction is in creation of character', she writes.[64] It is, as Murdoch acknowledges multiple times, very difficult to create a character 'other than oneself who is more than a conventional puppet'.[65] This struggle illuminates how difficult it is to imagine the real and different beings of others. Fiction is not life, but '[t]he work of fiction is not all that self-contained' and 'judgments upon real people ... are not totally unlike judgements which we make upon people in literature'.[66] In reading and writing novels, we engage with the desires and difficulties involved in apprehending other people, with an unavoidable mixture of self-centred fantasies and real curiosity.[67]

Indeed, as Floora Ruokonen notes, this is always a losing battle: 'even the greatest literature can, in her [Murdoch's] opinion, never do justice to the particularity of individuals.'[68] Ruokonen also stresses the duality of Murdoch's moral recognition of character. In judging how a writer treats his characters, we simultaneously react to them as if they were people *and* as products of his imagination. As Murdoch says: 'we naturally envisage a relation between the author and his character as if the character could turn round and say to the author, "You have been unfair to me".'[69] In other words, caring about fictional characters also entails an awareness of their fictional status. That they are made up makes them doubly interesting, in that they are like people but still evidently fantasies. Thus, they remind us of the ambiguous imaginative effort involved in apprehending others. Our disbelief is not cancelled but suspended: we are immersed in a fantasy and at the same time reminded of its artifice. Stories always partly fail to do justice to real human beings, and great stories make us feel this failure. As Maria Antonaccio phrases Murdoch's view: 'The aesthetic unity of the novel is constantly broken by (or breaks against) the reality of the individual person, who resists formal unity and remains endlessly there to be explained, as persons in life do also.'[70] Instead of giving us privileged access to a completed acknowledgement, as Cavell suggests, fiction can more fruitfully be understood as engaging us with both the deep desirability and the insuperable difficulty of rightly imagining the being of others.

We have thus reached the end of our discussion of the problem of fictional characters. If this chapter seems to end a bit abruptly, it is because some of its central concerns will have their continuation in the next one. I will extend my discussion of Cavell into a criticism of using tragedy, a genre of fiction, as philosophy. Problems which have merely been implied here, such as Murdoch's understanding of form and consolation, will be explored in more detail, and I will eventually confront tragedy, the poetic genre of death, with Socrates's description of philosophy as practising dying.

5

Problems purged: *The consolations of tragedy*

5.1. What is the tragic in tragedy?

'The concept of the tragic is obscure, one might be tempted to say confused or incoherent', Murdoch writes. 'Real life is not tragic.'[1]

In the previous chapter, I discussed Stanley Cavell's usage of the fictional character Othello to expose the problems with traditional epistemology and question the boundaries between literature and philosophy. I noted that Cavell suggests that scepticism might be better understood as tragedy. However, although tragedy is expected to do a lot of work in his philosophy, it remains a somewhat indeterminate notion. In this chapter, I shall explore some general and specific problems with utilizing the fictional genre of tragedy as a philosophical argument. Several thinkers shall come into play here, among them Murdoch, Aristotle, Nietzsche, Hegel and Nussbaum.

But let us begin with Cavell. Tragedy is for him the new explanation to be put in the place of scepticism. Scepticism is 'the attempt to convert the human condition … into an intellectual difficulty' – and tragedy 'is the place where we are not allowed to escape the consequences, or price, of this cover'.[2] Tragedy thus holds to power to put us face to face with the human condition, which according to Cavell is that we can never avoid acknowledgement, nor complete it, only be content with the best case of knowing the other.

Cavell's account in 'The Avoidance of Love' is modelled on *King Lear*, and tragedy in *The Claim of Reason* is illustrated by *Othello*. Lear is demanding that his daughter Cordelia speaks her love out of convention and pressure, since (Cavell interprets) he cannot stand the naked fact of her love. Othello is doubting Desdemona's fidelity, or rather (Cavell suggests) refusing to accept that she is another and separate being, whom his probing knowledge can never penetrate fully.

Tragedy, according to Cavell, is a strange mixture of fate and wilfulness. 'It is the enveloping of contingency and necessity by one another, the entropy of their mixture', or the refusal of our own finitude: 'Tragedy is not about the fact that all men are mortal (though perhaps it is about the fact that mortals go to any lengths to avoid that knowledge).'[3] Perhaps? Vagueness and tautology lurk in Cavell's definitions of tragedy. Something is not tragic unless we take it to be tragic, and so 'we are tragic in what we take to be tragic'.[4] It is not that we can never fully know the other that is the tragedy of the human condition, but the fact that we do not seem to be content with this.

Or maybe we are? Even if these are rewarding interpretations of Shakespeare's plays, Cavell does not provide much evidence of how widespread this supposedly essentially human, half-unconsciously voluntary, suffering is. I, for one, am not so sure that I share it. The fact that we can never fully know one another might equally well be a source of delight at the inexhaustibility of interpersonal relations.

This seems to be how the concept of the tragic often functions in philosophy. It is tapered on a specific – but vague and infinitely extendable – case of human suffering and given an aura of universality by being associated with some poetic masterpieces. Jealousy and pettiness can thus be glorified into some kind of unavoidable fate. Or so at least goes one of Plato's main objections to genre. In the *Republic*, Socrates singles out the tragic poets as the most dangerous of all artists, for the wellbeing of the state as well as the pursuit of philosophy. The tragic poets make the strive for goodness appear futile, since they portray noble characters as equally subject to error and misfortunes. Even the gods may be depicted as jealous, mourning or vengeful by them.[5] The tragic poets seem to say that there is no point in making an effort, the human condition is in any case essentially gloomy and contingent and full of suffering. At the same time, they offer us a kind of dramatic and aesthetic pleasure in this, which makes the best parts of the soul relax its guard and welcome these pseudo-truths as enlightenment. In Murdoch's words, tragedy is the most objectionable genre for Plato 'because it would stop the high man from rising higher, by providing intelligent but false consolation, and a sense of achievement and self-satisfaction which impedes the highest vision'.[6]

Aristotle is, as is well known, less judgemental. However, Aristotle does not judge poetry on par with philosophy, but considers it to be an art with its own standard of excellence. His account of tragedy is artistically normative, but morally rather neutral. I shall soon expand upon his description of the form of the genre in his *Poetics*. But let us first attempt to answer the question: What is the tragic in tragedy?

Aristotle thinks that a work in this genre should invoke pity and fear. When do we feel pity and fear? Not when we watch bad people gain fame and money, or good people lose everything from no fault of their own (this only produces disgust, according to Aristotle). Neither do we pity a bad man when he is unlucky, or a good man for whom everything goes well. Thus, tragedy should be about a relatively decent or even fine person, who is held in high esteem, and undergoes bad fortune not through depravity but through some kind of 'error' (*hamartia*).[7] The Greek word *hamartia* has since been associated with sin in Christian theology, but for Aristotle it simply means missing the mark – a mistake which can have its root in a character flaw, an error of judgement or ignorance, but which is not a result of wickedness.[8] In other words, the misfortune of the decent man might have been avoided, but crucially was not. This is tragic to Aristotle – not because it gives a universal account of human life, but because it invokes the feelings he associates with the genre.

Building on an interpretation of Aristotle, Martha Nussbaum gives a very succinct description of the tragic in tragedy:

> Greek tragedy shows good people being ruined because of things that just happen to them, things that they do not control. This is certainly sad; but it is an ordinary fact of human life, and no one would deny that it happens. Nor does it threaten

any of our deeply held beliefs about goodness, since goodness, plainly, can persist unscathed through a change in external fortunes. Tragedy also, however, shows something more deeply disturbing: it shows good people doing bad things, things otherwise repugnant to their ethical character and commitments, because of circumstances whose origin does not lie with them.[9]

Nussbaum takes the tragic to be the vulnerability of human will and intention to forces beyond our control, which may even turn us into agents of badness. Simply put, not even the most perfect goodness is impenetrable. This is not just meant to be a description of the genre, but (as is so astoundingly often the case with tragedy) also of the most fundamental conditions of human life. Nussbaum utilizes Greek tragedy to propose a moral philosophy more open to contingencies, messiness, emotions and fragility than the traditions she traces back to (mainly) Plato and Kant, and therefore questions the distinction between literature and philosophy. I shall quarrel with her on this later in this chapter.

These four accounts of the tragic in tragedy (Cavell's, Plato's, Aristotle's and Nussbaum's) are just a couple of the views that may be cited. I have singled them out here since Plato's and Aristotle's make up the roots of the ancient quarrel, whereas Nussbaum's and Cavell's present some of the most interesting contemporary challenges to the distinction between philosophy and literature. Later, we shall also look at Nietzsche's and Hegel's views of tragedy. The amount of philosophical attention that this literary genre has received is probably unparalleled. Why this is so is a question that would require a dissertation of its own, although it may plausibly be presumed to have something to do with Plato.

While pronouncing his insistent depreciation for the genre, Plato nonetheless based his own dialogues on a modified model of tragic drama. He also explicitly proposed that philosophy was to replace tragedy as a purveyor of wisdom. In the *Laws*, he has the Athenian stranger say that 'we ourselves are poets, who have to the best of our ability created a tragedy that is the most beautiful and the best; at any rate, our political regime is constructed as the imitation of the most beautiful and best way of life, which we at least assert to be really the truest tragedy'.[10] If the tragedians cannot prove that their tragedies are as good and truthful as this discourse, he would not allow them to be performed. Indeed, the self-consciousness of philosophy was initially founded on its rivalry to tragedy, and so it is hardly surprising that philosophers throughout the ages have approached the genre to question the self-image of their discipline, often by returning to the same works that were performed around Plato's time.

Tragedy is generally considered to be a dead genre, although scholars disagree on what works should be counted into the definition and when exactly the time for tragic masterpieces can be said to have passed.[11] It is common to differentiate between classical (ancient Greek) tragedies and modern tragedies (mainly Shakespeare, sometimes also, for example, Racine and Corneille). However, except for Shakespeare, most of the modern tragedies are usually constructed and received in the light of the Greek classics, and the classics continue to be the main focus of philosophical attention.

This chapter will not offer any interpretations of specific tragedies. Instead, I will criticize the philosophical turn to tragedy in relation to Murdoch's notion of form.

Form is one of the main aspects of her distinction between literature and philosophy, and I shall explore the consolations of the form of tragedy and follow the fluctuations in her own philosophical understanding of tragedy to illuminate this difference.

5.2. The consolations of form

Perhaps it should be made clear from the start: The discussion of the form that shall follow will not, as in Aristotle's description of tragedy, provide an index of timespan, peripeteia, climax, chorus, hexameter or any other of the aspects that are usually known as formal. What is meant by form here is indeed something different than that of literary formalism, which looks to structural and linguistic aspects of a text.

Form is one of the most central, difficult and ambiguous concepts in Murdoch's philosophy. It plays a major part in her understanding of moral consciousness, but I shall focus on its importance for her aesthetics, especially concerning the distinction between philosophy and literature. Form may sound like a simple and self-evident concept and has thus received relatively little attention in the scholarship on Murdoch. It is often just contrasted with contingency and particularity. The popular tendency to read her literary and philosophical works together has prompted a co-interpretation of her treatment of characters in her fiction with what form means in her moral philosophy. These readings often compare the art of creating unique and particular characters with how the just perception of others is hindered by our tendency to impose a consoling and false order on the world.[12] However, beyond the problem of imagining the beings of others, that was noted in the previous chapter, these interpretations tend to leave unexplained what exactly form may be, and why Murdoch marked a clear difference between philosophy's and literature's relations to form.

As Murdoch is not a systematic thinker, her usage of concepts does not have a stable and fixed meaning but fluctuates over time and even within the same texts. Form is sometimes exchanged or complemented with unity, order, whole, shape or grasp. We achieve a sense of form when we artificially make something conform to the structure of our own consciousness. This desire for unity, as she calls it, is both a need and a temptation. 'We fear plurality, diffusion, senseless accident, chaos', she states early in *Metaphysics as a Guide to Morals*, 'we want to transform what we cannot dominate or understand into something reassuring or familiar, into ordinary being, into history, art, religion, science.'[13] Her magnum opus opens with a meditation on our intuitive sense of unity in existence, not just regarding our surroundings but also ourselves. 'Oblivious of philosophical problems and paucity of evidence we grasp ourselves as unities, continuous bodies and continuous minds.'[14] She compares this sense of unity with that of the artwork and proceeds to criticize the sceptical impulse in structuralism, which has no respect for this unity in art and instead seeks to deconstruct 'the familiar concepts of individual object, individual person, individual meaning, those old and cherished "limited wholes".[15] Here, unity or form seems to be something good. But then, through a discussion of Plato's and Freud's suspicions of art, she concludes that the unity of art is illusory, or at least not what we think it is.[16] The aesthetic pleasure given from this unity is potentially misleading, and not innocent. 'Kant's definition of art in terms of "purposiveness without a purpose" is [by psychoanalysis] provided with a secret purpose.'[17] This sense of purposiveness gives us satisfaction and consolation. Already from this wide-ranging, fluctuating discussion in the first chapter, we can see how ambiguously charged Murdoch's notion of our form-giving capacity is. Should we cherish it, should we be suspicious of it, can we in any case put up any resistance against it?

The word 'form' is most often used about art, and specifically about tragedy. I shall return to how towards the end of this section. As might already be clear, form in Murdoch is not the Platonic Forms. She speaks of those with a capital F. Instead, her usage of the concept betrays a distinctly Kantian heritage, something that is indicated by the fluctuation with 'unity'.

Kant's aesthetics is widely known as formalist, although what is meant by this term has been the focus of some critical discussion. In an illuminating article, Rachel Zuckert explains that form in Kant is neither the property-formalism (temporal and spatial properties, such as the golden mean), nor the kind-formalism (what makes the object a good exemplar of its kind, such as Aristotle's criteria for tragedies) it has often been taken to imply. Instead, Zuckert advocates for an interpretation of whole-formalism, where everything that contributes to the sense of a unity of the manifold might be considered its formal qualities. As she rephrases Kant, 'the form of a beautiful object is the unity of the manifold in our representation of that object, where it is unclear what that unity is supposed to be.'[18] This is what is meant by purposiveness without a purpose. Everything seems to be ordered in the artwork according to some principle, although no specific principle can be determined. Zuckert points out how other kinds of formalism are dependent on conceptual understandings of art, where we apply external knowledge (the right proportions between lines, or the ideal of a man) to judge its beauty. In contrast, whole-formalism allows for every artwork to be judged on individual terms, non-conceptually, even though we 'use concepts (e.g., parallel line, curve, yellow, etc.) to point out certain properties of this particular object – to indicate the relations that hold "in the given representation" alone'. Furthermore, 'these "properties" are experienced as specific to the individual object, and hence cannot serve to classify objects into general categories.'[19]

In other words, what makes an artwork great is particular to that artwork. No general rules can be made for beauty. This allows for an understanding of formal unity as universal and individual at the same time. We may now see how form is not just a condemnable obfuscation of contingent particulars, but also that which makes an individual into its own unique whole. Murdoch's sprawling initial discussion in *Metaphysics as a Guide to Morals* begins to make more sense. Following this, let us look at why the concept of form is so central to her distinction between philosophy and literature, especially in relation to tragedy. Murdoch brings out the forming character of (the literary) art by comparing and contrasting it to philosophy.

Needless to say, philosophy is not formless. But it has a very different relationship to form than literature. Murdoch explains it thus:

> Philosophy is not exactly entertaining but it can be comforting, since it too is an eliciting of form from muddle. Philosophers often construct huge schemes

involving a lot of complicated imagery. Many kinds of philosophical argument depend more or less explicitly on imagery. A philosopher is likely to be suspicious of the instinctive side of his imagination. Whereas any artist must be at least half in love with his unconscious mind, which after all provides his motive force and does a great deal of his work ... The philosopher must resist the comfort seeking artist in himself. He must always be undoing his own work in the interests of truth so as to go on gripping his problem. This tends to be incompatible with literary art.[20]

In contrast to literature, philosophy 'is continually breaking the forms which it has made'.[21] It may be unpleasantly repetitive, and if it becomes too enamoured with its own forms and images it is likely to turn bad. In literature, 'even what sounds like plain speaking is part of some ulterior formal imaginative structure'.[22] Form, in the sense of a purposeless unity of the manifold, is the organizing principle of art. If philosophy turns to tragedy, it should be aware of this important difference between the disciplines. Form is soothing, pleasing and enchanting.

But tragedy becomes an especially tempting form for the philosophers, since it seems paradoxically defiant of form. Murdoch fell for this temptation herself. As William Schweiker interprets Murdoch's view: 'One needs to shatter form, break the images, for a vision of what is real on its own terms. Tragedy as a form of art is one that enacts this shattering while also rendering lived reality in form.'[23] However, this is only accurate for her early view. I shall now trace some of the shifts in her philosophical understanding of tragedy.

In the essay 'The Sublime and the Good' from 1959, where Murdoch criticizes Kant's aesthetics, she complains that he is aspiring 'to a universal order consisting of a prefabricated harmony'.[24] She quarrels with him precisely because she finds his aesthetics very appealing, and wants to keep certain aspects of it, such as 'a great deal of what Kant has to say about form';[25] but in general, his aesthetics 'will not do because it does not in any way account for the greatness of tragedy'.[26] This is partly, she argues, because he does not find art to be sublime. Not only does Murdoch here miss that Kant allows for the sublime to be combined with beauty in art, and explicitly names tragedies as an example of this;[27] she also ends up constructing her own version of the kind of self-circuiting notion of life as tragic and tragedy as lifelike that I am, from various perspectives, attempting to problematize in this chapter:

> The tragic freedom implied by love is this: that we all have an indefinitely extended capacity to imagine the being of others. Tragic, because there is no prefabricated harmony, and others are, to an extent we never cease discovering, different from ourselves ... Freedom is exercised in the confrontation by each other, in the context of an infinitely extensible work of imaginative understanding, of two irreducibly dissimilar individuals.[28]

This account has a lot in common with Cavell's. Why our endless dissimilarities would be tragic is never really explained. Nor does 'tragic freedom', as authoritative as the concept may sound, ever reoccur in Murdoch's philosophical writings. In this essay, not much more is said about it, except that it is explicitly connected to Greek tragic drama. She also attempts to describe tragedy as a genre which somehow exposes us to the formless and the contingent aspects of life. 'What makes tragic art so disturbing is that self-contained form is combined with something, the individual being and destiny of human persons, which defies form. A great tragedy leaves us in eternal doubt.'[29] Nonetheless, she ends the essay by somewhat doubting her own conclusions. There is a kind of artistic completion to tragedy that the world, 'which is haunted by that incompleteness and lack of form, which is abhorred by art', lacks. As the last sentence enigmatically exclaims: 'Form is the great consolation of love, but it is also its great temptation.'[30]

The longest chapter in *Metaphysics as a Guide to Morals*, published in 1992,[31] is entitled 'Comic and Tragic', and it is almost exclusively about tragedy. Here, the genre and the concept are appearing as much more complex, almost as so paradoxical that they are bordering on the impossible. Murdoch is no longer even sure that tragedy exists: real life is not tragic, she firmly states, and 'tragedy' might just be an ideal conception we use to console us, an imaginary containment of the formless horrors of life.

> Tragedy belongs to art, and only to great art. But perhaps even here one is suffering from an illusion? Are there works of art which are real tragedies, real instances of the form? Or is tragedy just an ideal conception, something we think we need, something which we would like to exist? We feel: *somewhere* it must be justly recorded.[32]

In this great philosophical work, she is indeed holding to her own standard of continuously breaking her own forms in the interest of truth. We are following a winding string of shifting attempts to enlighten both the concept of tragedy and the problematically formal nature of art. Murdoch is clear of its consolatory power: any 'explanatory aesthetic "tragic pattern" gives dignity to aspects of human conduct which might otherwise simply appear base, mean, contemptible, vile, criminally stupid'.[33] I am quoting extensively here in order to illustrate the oscillating, form-resisting character of Murdoch's thought, which relentlessly circles around the same problem:

> It appears then that the concept of tragedy, if considered strictly, is paradoxical. One seems to have in mind some sort of ideal tragic below which actual tragedies usually, or always, fall. Perhaps the concept of tragedy founders … upon the nature of art itself. Art cannot help changing what it professes to display into something different. It magically charms reality, nature, into a formal semblance. Hell itself it turns to favour and to prettiness.[34]

Indeed, she continues later in this long chapter, art is not even prettifying hell; the 'hell' in the psychological material that the artist reworks is not in itself a direct representation of the intolerable. It is a kind of toy-pain compared to real suffering, a narcissistic masochism: 'There is a contrast between absolute (deathly) pain and the kind which can be managed, made part of a story, turned into art.'[35]

At the same time, Murdoch has not given up her quest (also announced in 'The Sublime and the Good') to write an aesthetic theory that does justice to what she considers to be Shakespeare's greatest masterpiece, *King Lear*. 'Tragedy (we feel) is the point where art nearly breaks down but triumphantly does not', she proposes. 'The tragic poet breaks the egoistic illusory unity which is natural to art and is able to look at human evil with a just and steady eye.'[36] And then she asks: 'But is all this really happening, or is it just something that we want to happen?'[37]

Not in most tragedies, she concludes. Not even in many of the greatest ones. The aesthetic force of these plays is more pleasurable than truly tragic. *King Lear* might in fact be the only work that lives up to the impossible standards implicit in the notion of tragedy. 'After witnessing the superb deaths of Othello, Macbeth and Hamlet, we leave the theatre excited, exalted, invigorated, perhaps even persuading ourselves that our pity and fear have been purged. After *Lear* we go away uneasy, chilled by a cold wind from another region.'[38] There is something incomplete about Lear, something that resists the heroism of the genre. Lear is indeed pitiable in a pathetic sense, we hesitate to identify with him, and we even inhibit our pity.

> Othello is a universal tragic character. Shakespeare's highest art attempts to ensure that we cannot see Lear or Cordelia in this light. (They are unattractive.) We are here close to the metaphysical enigma of tragic art, and indeed, by extension, of all art and all discourse. As soon as you talk about it you lose the object.[39]

Art shows something that explanation cannot contain. By criticizing the popular concept of tragedy, Murdoch attempts to discern what she still believes to be the unique truth-conveying potential of art. It consists of some kind of formal self-contradiction, which she unsuccessfully described in 'The Sublime and the Good' as a tragic freedom. Most art, indeed, even most masterpieces, are in *Metaphysics as a Guide to Morals* criticized as more consolatory than truth-conveying. Not that Murdoch sees consolation as something inherently bad: 'Bad art (that is ordinary bad art, not vile pornography) is also in general a sound producer of that unpretentious low-grade happiness (consolation, escape), harmless or not very harmful, which Benthamite utilitarians reasonably regard as a human right.'[40] Indeed, the philosophical disdain for consolation is very much in line with Plato's contempt for ordinary human muddled and fantasy-ridden life. We may tolerate, even applaud, art for its consolatory power. Doing so becomes less counterintuitive if we recognize its evaluative standard to be other than that (or those) of philosophy.

Here, we have seen how Murdoch the philosopher attempts (perhaps not entirely successfully) to 'resist the comfort seeking artist in [her]self' by continuously 'undoing [her] own work in the interests of truth so as to go on gripping [her] problem'.[41] This illustrates what she sees as one of the most significant differences between art and philosophy: that art aims to be formally pleasing, whereas philosophy should stay suspicious of its own form-making desires. We shall now explore this difference further when it comes to the art of tragedy, and the problems with some philosophical attempts to reclaim the genre as something more than 'just' an art. To do that, we must first look a bit closer at the form of tragedy. Since the Kantian concept of form is not applicable to types of beauty, we shall now go elsewhere to find a good description of the genre. What *kind* of unity of the manifold does tragedy typically present us with?

5.3. Serious, complete, great and pleasurable

It is often said that Aristotle's *Poetics* is an attempt to undo Plato's banishment of the poets. However, this does not mean that Aristotle sees poetry in general, or tragedy in particular, as philosophical. He is not defending poetry on the same grounds as Plato, rather states that '[t]he criterion of correctness is not the same in poetry as in ethics, and not the same in poetry as in any other art'.[42] Poetry is free to violate reality in its portrayals, 'for example, to show a horse galloping with both right legs forward', without that counting as any poetic error.[43] The gods need not be portrayed in any edifying or truthful way; the stories about them may simply reflect current practice and imagination.[44] Indeed, in direct contradiction to Plato, Aristotle thinks that truth is less important (in poetry!) than the (perhaps unfounded) opinion of the populace. 'The needs of poetry make what is plausible though impossible preferable to what is possible but implausible.'[45]

Aristotle's main concern in the *Poetics* is to give a normative account of what good poetry should look like, irrespective of its moral, philosophical, educational and/ or political values. The main part of the text describes tragedy, there are a couple of paragraphs on epic, and a second half of the book, on comedy, is assumed to have been lost. This systematic investigation of the dramatic art from 335 BC has, with almost unique durability, remained the key text on the subject, for theoretical as well as practical purposes. Playwrights still use his model to create good plots.

Tragedy is described by Aristotle as a highly ordered art form. His most brief definition goes as follows:

> Tragedy is a representation [*mímêsis*] of an action of a superior [*spoudaios*] kind – grand, and complete in itself [*teleias megethos echouses*] – presented in embellished language, in distinct forms in different parts, performed by actors rather than told by a narrator, effecting, through pity and fear, the purification [*katharsis*] of such emotions.[46]

I shall not attempt to give a complete account of Aristotle's view of tragedy. But let us dwell for a moment on these main characteristics. *Spoudaios* – translated alternatively as superior, heroic, serious or admirable – and *teleias megethos echouses* – having a complete greatness, or being in possession of a complete magnitude – shows us that tragedy is evidently not meant to portray ordinary situations in lifelike ways.[47] Aristotle then devotes an entire paragraph to spell out what he means by completeness, namely that the grand whole must have a beginning, a middle and an end. Well-construed plots should thus not just begin or end anywhere but must depict the cause and the cessation of an action. A tragedy thus becomes, in his account, the artificial, self-contained, heroic playing out of a great event which invokes pity and fear, embellished in an artful language and thus experienced as pleasurable. He explicitly marks this representation as distinct from what the history of a person's life would look like. 'An infinity of things happen to a single individual, not all of which constitute a unity; likewise, a single person performs many actions which do not add up to make a single action.'[48]

According to Aristotle, the art of writing a good tragedy consists in portraying not reality – not even in the sense of uncovering some kind of deep, essential truth about the human condition – but an artistically elevated, isolated and embellished action. This artificially formed imaginative unity may well do violence to reality, as long as it is perceived as plausibly coherent, grand and heroic. Philosophical discussions of Aristotle's description of tragedy do not tend to focus on these imaginative aspects. Instead, many have zoomed in on the concept *katharsis*, usually translated as purification or purgation. It seems to be very central in his account, and yet its meaning is left unexplained. There might have been another part of the *Poetics*, defining the meaning of *katharsis*, that has been lost to us.[49] Or, some scholars argue, *katharsis* might not even have been original to Aristotle's text, but a later insert from one of the many transcriptions.[50] I shall leave the philological discussion to the experts, but as the received view stands, a description of the form of tragedy is not complete without an account of what katharsis may mean.

There exist, roughly, three prominent ways of interpreting katharsis: the medical, the ethical and the cognitive.[51] The medical view sees katharsis as a kind of purgation: the play provides a safe space for the release of harmful or unpleasant emotions and leaves us cleansed. The ethical view seeks to interpret katharsis as moral purification and suggests that tragedies help transform lower passions into virtues. The cognitive view, which, for example, Nussbaum is a proponent of, sees katharsis as a kind of clarification or furthering of the understanding through the dramatization of these emotions. Each of these interpretations seeks to characterize tragedy as beneficial in some way.

However, neither of these interpretations resolves what is known as the paradox of tragedy, namely how we can find such great pleasure in watching something awful happen to good people. Hume was one of the first to point out this problem. Why, he asked, do 'spectators of a well-wrote tragedy receive from sorrow, terror, anxiety and other passions, which are in themselves disagreeable and uneasy', such a delightful pleasure? Aristotle states that it is by rhythm and melody that the language makes the action pleasurable,[52] and Hume's answer is close to his. He says that '[t]his extraordinary effect is produced from that very eloquence, with which the melancholy is portrayed'.[53] Hume also stresses the power of the imagination, which in the finer arts smoothens, softens and mollifies the horrible feelings into entertainment.[54] It is a variant of this imaginative forming that I will present here. A defender of one of the traditional views might argue that medical purgation, ethical purification or the furthering of understanding are pleasurable too; but those pleasures are more like after-effects. Already in the theatre, we are delighted by the drama, no matter how horrible its plot.

In an influential article from 1988, Jonathan Lear refutes the three classical interpretations of katharsis. Through a careful investigation of the overall consistency of the *Poetics*, he dismisses the medical as incomprehensible, since Aristotle views emotions as attitudes to the world, and it would be hard to see what might be meant by purging an attitude; the ethical as invalid, since Aristotle sees tragedy as particularly enjoyable by virtuous people, so it is difficult to see how improvement would be the main aim or effect; and finally the cognitivist as confusing the understanding of a tragedy with the pleasure invoked by it, and as missing that poetry is concerned with plausibility, not with 'the depth of the human condition'.[55] (This is a very condensed summary – many more substantial counterarguments are supplied in the original article.)

Instead, Lear suggests an interpretation of katharsis that is reliant both on the spectators' awareness that they are taking part of a work of art, but also on them being immersed in the drama. It is this self-consciously imaginative dimension of the passions invoked that gives us a certain pleasure. The action portrayed is related to the actual or potential horrors of life, yet distant from them in terms of reality. As Lear puts it: 'We imaginatively live life to the full, but we risk nothing.'[56] Similarly to Murdoch, who says in her chapter on tragedy that '[a]rt offers some consolation, some sense, some form, whereas the most dreadful ills of human life allow of none,'[57] Lear claims:

> Insofar as we do fear that tragic events could occur in our lives, what we fear is chaos … For Aristotle, a good tragedy offers us this consolation: that even when the breakdown of the primordial bonds occurs, it does not occur in a world which is in itself ultimately chaotic and meaningless.[58]

Thus, the kathartic pleasure of tragedy resides in a consolatory exercise of the imagination, bringing the utmost horrors of life closer and at the same time ordering them into self-contained, grand, artificial and well-fashioned unities. A tragedy portrays what would be experienced as most dreadfully chaotic in life through a highly ordered plot. This gives a sense of purposiveness to what is least purposive, which is indeed a high artistic achievement. In what follows, we shall look at how two philosophers utilize this consoling aspect of the form of tragedy.

5.4. Metaphysical consolation and fundamental reconciliation

Philosophical attention to the genre of tragedy has been paid in many different ways. As we have seen, Plato criticized the poets for being questionable moral guides and producing bad thinking; whereas Aristotle, who did not see them as rivals to philosophers, appreciated their art in its own right. Since then, tragedy has become a popular topic for those seeking to question this divide between literature and philosophy. One of the most well-known attempts to pit the tragedies back against Plato's definition of philosophy is Friedrich Nietzsche's youthful work *The Birth of Tragedy* from 1872.[59]

Nietzsche considers what he calls the Socratic view to be guilty of an exaggerated scientific optimism. Will the disciplined search for truth really lead to happiness and a better life, as Plato lets on? Will it even lead us towards truth, since life in itself 'is founded on appearance, art, illusion, optic, the necessity of the perspectival and of error'?[60] Indeed, Nietzsche seems to ask, what kind of truth do we *want*? The austere truth-seeking Plato suggests leads the philosopher to long for something beyond life. Instead of philosophy practising dying, Nietzsche wants it to practise living. How can we be made to feel that life, this contingent flux of miseries and illusions, is nonetheless a self-same and great entity? Here, tragedy comes in as the remedy. Serious, great and complete, tragedy makes us feel 'that life at the bottom of things, in spite of the passing of phenomena, remains indestructibly powerful and pleasurable'.[61] This is the necessary 'metaphysical consolation' with which all true tragedy leaves us. Thus, art does not simply express the truth about the human condition, but shapes and forms it into something more pleasing; art is 'the enchantress who comes to rescue and heal; only she can reshape that disgust at the thought of the horrific or absurd aspects of life into notions with which it is possible to live'.[62]

Consolatory is not commonly used as a compliment in philosophy. One might even say that it is usually regarded as standing in direct opposition to truth, clarity and directness. Religion, a secular philosopher might claim, is consolatory, whereas philosophy is supposed to confront fundamental problems without fear or sentimentality. Early Nietzsche makes a curious exception; but already fourteen years later, in his new foreword to *The Birth of Tragedy* entitled 'Attempt at a Self-Criticism' from 1886, he argues against his own suggestion that it would be 'necessary' to be 'metaphysically consoled'. This now appears to him as a Romantic, Christian weakness.

> 'Would it not be necessary?' ... No, three times no! you young Romantics: it would *not* be necessary! But it is very probable that it will *end* this way, that *you* will end this way, namely, 'consoled', as it is written, in spite of all self-education in seriousness and terror, 'metaphysically consoled', in short, as Romantics end, Christian ...[63]

In *The Birth of Tragedy*, Nietzsche describes how the scientific man, by pursuing his dialectical thinking, ends up staring into an impenetrable darkness, where 'logic coils around itself and finally bites its own tail – then the new form of knowledge breaks through, tragic knowledge, which in order to be tolerated, needs art as a protection and remedy'.[64] One might say that when this tragic knowledge is turned into the art of tragedy, its consolatory form leaves the philosopher purged of his metaphysical problems.

It is only the need for consolation that the later Nietzsche rejects. He still cherishes the impulse of his first work to try to go beyond good and evil, to apply an artistic instead of a moral standard of judgement: 'since before morality (in particular Christian, that is absolute, morality), life *must* continually and inevitably be condemned, because life is something essentially amoral – life, crushed under the weight of contempt and of the eternal No, must finally be felt unworthy of desire, intrinsically without value'.[65] Instead of offering some consolatory conclusion, later Nietzsche thinks that the artist, in contrast to the moralist, stays with 'the riddle of existence' and 'acknowledge[s] of things their terrible, their questionable character' without craving any kind of solution.[66] How has the consolatory 'enchantress' suddenly turned into a heroic confrontation with ambiguity and terror?

As this question is better left to the Nietzsche experts, it suffices for our purposes to note that his early theory of metaphysical consolation echoes well with Murdoch's descriptions of how the formative power of art prettifies even a purposeless hell.

Tragedy gives a semblance of sense to the most senseless horrors of life. In contrast to Nietzsche, who considers the artform important because it does not conform to the standards of rationality, we shall now look at a philosopher who appreciates it because he thinks that it does: Hegel.[67]

Sophocles' *Antigone* is for Hegel the most beautiful of all tragedies because it presents the conflict between two incompatible goods most clearly. Antigone's wish to bury her brother, which represents the old religious order, clashes with the new juridical order in Creon's refusal to grant an enemy of the state a proper burial. Both are absolutely justified according to Hegel, and the tragedy consists in their irreconcilable conflict. However, he sees the conflict as ultimately resolved in the eyes of the audience. Thus, 'finality [does] not lie in misfortune and suffering but in the satisfaction of the spirit'; we are 'shattered by the fate of the heroes but reconciled fundamentally'.[68] The one-sidedness of their pathoses together make up the totality of the play, and thus yield to a larger historical progression of rationality. To put it otherwise, the problems are purged by the audience's von oben-perspective.

Early Murdoch criticizes Hegel for demanding a 'total understanding of a human social situation' and for finding this demand of reason to be completely satisfied by the play. 'Hegel's tragedy does not seem to be tragedy at all, since the spectators are not in the helpless position of the dramatic characters, but comfortably seated at the point of view of totality.'[69]

Indeed, Hegel's rationalization removes something important from tragedy. At the same time, it would be difficult to consistently argue that the audience *is* in the same helpless position as the dramatic characters. As we saw in the previous chapter, Cavell attempts to claim something similar in his interpretation of *Othello*. But the playgoers are not forbidden by the new king to bury their brother. They are not caught doing it anyway and subsequently condemned to death. Neither are they put in the awkward position of Creon, of having to choose between upholding the law and killing the fiancé of their son or ceding their authority to her impossible demands. The playgoers *are* comfortably seated at the point of view of totality. They are free to leave. They are presented with the action as a completed whole with a beginning, a middle and an end. Taking part of a dramatic tragedy does, in that sense, indeed not seem to be very tragic. However, that this would equal the making of a totalizing, rational conclusion out of the incompatible ethical positions is not at all clear.

In this section, we have seen how Nietzsche and Hegel offer two different accounts of how problems can be purged by tragedy. Nietzsche is replacing the problem he argues has been created by an exaggerated philosophical optimism with the enchanting illusion of art, which makes it possible to live with ugly and self-contradictory truths. In contrast to him, Hegel is resolving tragedy's representation of incompatibility with a von oben-synthesis, making the painful clash into a pleasant reconciliation. However different these two accounts may be, they show us two questionable ways in which tragedy has been used philosophically. Either the rational problems are purged by art, or the artistic problems are purged by reason. In the next section, we shall look at a more contemporary attempt to argue for the philosophical importance of tragedy, that paradoxically shares some characteristics of both of these approaches: Nussbaum's *The Fragility of Goodness*.

5.5. Nussbaum's paradox of clarified muddle

Martha Nussbaum (1947–) is one of the most prominent contemporary philosophers seeking to question, or even dissolve, the boundary between philosophy and literature. In *The Fragility of Goodness: Luck and Ethics in Greek Tragedy and Philosophy* (1988), she criticizes dominant methods in and focuses of ethical theorizing by turning to tragedy, a genre which she claims reflects upon the contingency and vulnerability of ethical life. Ever since Plato, she argues, moral philosophy has sought to go beyond much of what it means to be human, inflating our rational self-sufficiency and denying the fragility of reason and goodness. To complicate this picture, we should turn to literature, more specifically tragedies – and not just as complementary illustrations, but as ethical deliberations in their own right:

> [T]ragic drama ... is capable of tracing the history of a complex pattern of deliberation, showing its roots in a way of life and looking forward to its consequences in that life. As it does all of this, it lays open to view the complexity, the indeterminacy, the sheer difficulty of actual human deliberation.[70]

Tragedy thus has a cognitive, ethical value that Plato, according to Nussbaum, with his disembodied and unemotional conception of reason, failed to see. It throws us right into life, but at the same time gives us an overview and a clarification of its inherent complexities. Nussbaum thus presents us with a double account. She indicates that tragedy shows us something similar to what Nietzsche described as logic biting its own tail, an insight into the insufficiencies of reason; but also that it provides us with a kind of von oben-sensemaking akin to Hegel's account. Reason is shown to be insufficient, and yet it gets extended at the same time. I shall now develop my criticism of what I call the paradox of clarified muddle in Nussbaum's reading of tragedy as philosophical.

The title of her book refers to the vulnerability of goodness to causes beyond the power of our reason and will. This is made most evident in tragedy, since it shows 'good people doing bad things'.[71] Vulnerability and fragility are not just detriments to goodness, Nussbaum attempts to show, but valuable parts of it: 'There is a certain valuable quality in social virtue that is lost when social virtue is removed from the domain of uncontrolled happenings.'[72] The best and most valuable things are not invulnerable. Neither is reason purified of emotions the best kind of reason. These fundamental theses are sympathetic, even beautiful. My issue lies not with them, but with how Nussbaum interprets the genre of tragedy as a philosophical clarification of them. In her reading, tragedy functions as a clear presentation of the ambiguous and indeterminate aspects of our moral life. But does not a clear description of these make them precisely *less* ambiguous and *more* determinate? Why should one of the most highly ordered art forms be the best expression of contingency? And is not a vulnerability explained a vulnerability more containable?

In her portrait of Nussbaum for *The New Yorker*, Rachel Aviv seems to suggest that her preoccupation with fragility might be motivated by an urge to contain and control it:

Nussbaum once wrote, citing Nietzsche, that 'when a philosopher harps very insistently on a theme, that shows us that there is a danger that something else is about to "play the master"': something personal is driving the preoccupation. In Nussbaum's case, I wondered if she approaches her theme of vulnerability with such success because she peers at it from afar, as if it were unfamiliar and exotic. She celebrates the ability to be fragile and exposed, but in her own life she seems to control every interaction.[73]

Aviv's text gives a stunning impression of an incredibly disciplined, hyper-rational and controlled individual: someone who begins every day with ninety-minute runs during which she recites opera arias in her head, gives birth without anaesthesia and goes back to work again a week after; who seems completely voided of self-doubt, but nonetheless undergoes careful plastic surgery to maintain her looks. To bring in this kind of biographical portrait into a philosophical discussion might be frowned upon by some: but not by Nussbaum, who not only consistently argues for providing a rich, personal and lived background for thinking, but also gives her own personal account of Murdoch.

In her article on Murdoch's *The Black Prince*, in which she makes a reading of the novel as a direct expression of Murdoch's Platonism, Nussbaum also sees fit to 'connect these vague anxieties about the novel, very tentatively, to my personal experience of Iris Murdoch'.[74] She describes having been invited for lunch to Murdoch's and her husband's house in Oxford. But the meeting does not bring the hoped-for connection. Nussbaum feels uncomfortable, and compares herself to a character in the novel:

More than once I had a Julian-like thought: 'You don't really see *me*' – especially when, being a great lover of food, I found myself offered only two items, neither of which I could eat – a very fatty pâté, which I hate, and a plateful of cherries, to which I have an allergy. (In desperation, I ate some cherries and was sick for the rest of the day.)[75]

The awkwardness of this meeting fuels her accusations of Murdoch as defending a philosophy of love entailing a disregard for the particularity of individuals, a view she has read out of *The Black Prince*.

Even if philosophical questions may have deep roots in our most personal concerns, and it can be fruitful to investigate those motivations and assumptions, I am not convinced that it is the best practice to use private impressions of other philosophers as direct arguments. Nonetheless, in the spirit of Nussbaum, I shall ask: What may her motivation be for turning to tragedies as philosophical reflections on the fragility of reason and goodness? Why is fragility so important for this hyper-controlled individual, and why does she want literature to be considered as philosophy in another form?

Indeed, she herself reflects on the potential dubiousness of her drive. In the acknowledgements, she writes that she has asked herself 'whether the act of writing about the beauty of human vulnerability is not, paradoxically, a way of rendering oneself less vulnerable and more in control of the uncontrolled elements in life', and simply concludes that she leaves the reader with 'the question, what sort of ethical act is the writing of this book?'[76] Let us take her up on this. When she criticizes 'the self-possession' of Plato's dialogues as making us 'feel that it would be highly inappropriate to weep, to feel fear or pity';[77] is it really more emotional imbalance she is after, or just a semblance of it, which would give her the comforting sense that these reactions are neither excluded nor uncontrolled? After all, it seems highly implausible that someone would burst into tears or shudder from pity and fear in the middle of Nussbaum's analysis of Antigone, not to mention her chapter on Aristotle. Rationalizing feelings, that is, drawing them into the argumentative clarity of philosophical discourse, rather than feeling them, seems to be the goal here.

Nussbaum turns explicitly against the prevailing tendency of the analytic tradition to 'assume that the ethical text should, in the process of inquiry, converse with the intellect alone; it should not make its appeal to the emotions, feelings and sensory responses'.[78] Her only named opponent in this context is curiously enough Murdoch, who she quotes as saying that the ideal philosophical style is 'austere', 'unselfish' and 'candid': 'A philosopher must try to say exactly what he means and avoid rhetoric and idle decoration.'[79] Nussbaum expresses disappointment that such a distinguished novelist fails to see the problems with a style which would be 'pure of appeals to emotion and sense',[80] and where 'emotion and imagination play, at best, a decorative and subsidiary role'.[81] But nowhere does Murdoch actually say that she wants to ban imagination and emotion from philosophy. In fact, there are several places where she argues for the opposite: for example, in the very same interview, when she says that '[o]f course philosophy too is an imaginative activity'.[82] Appeals to emotion are also frequent in her work: just look at the central role that love plays, or when she suggests that it is 'always a significant question to ask about any philosopher: what is he afraid of?'[83]

The strive for unbiased, philosophical clarity, to be as Murdoch puts it 'in the front line in relation to [one's] problem'[84] seems, at a closer look, to be more shared by Nussbaum than she cares to let on. For example, she applauds the texts of Aristotle for their 'courageous straightforwardness and directness *vis-à-vis* 'the matter of the practical'; a serene restraint that expresses determination to acknowledge these difficulties'[85], and admits that her own style 'expresses, too, an Aristotelian commitment to explanation, to reading a poetic work so as to ask of it what it is doing and why'.[86] In arguing for the philosophical value of poetry, she is well aware that she is not writing poetry herself, but 'reflective criticism about poetry', and promises that her writing 'will remain always committed to the critical faculties, to clarity and close argument'.[87]

This commitment to explanation applies another standard to poetry than that of aesthetic form. Instead of purposiveness without a purpose, and the inexplicable composition of a manifold into a unity, Nussbaum is looking for what a tragedy is doing and why. As has been mentioned, Murdoch sees both similarities and differences in literature's and philosophy's relations to form. Both are ways to 'elicit form from muddle', but 'the philosopher must resist the comfort seeking artist in himself'.[88] These are important and difficult remarks. Neither literature nor philosophy is a direct expression of 'muddle', but their formal relations to the contingency of life are very different.[89] The poet seeks a pleasing aesthetic form. The philosopher is constantly 'undoing his own work in the interests of truth'.[90] Nussbaum ignores, or perhaps disagrees with, this distinction. There seems to be no place in her work for a purposeless and non-conceptual beauty – everything can also be rendered as an explanation, without any apparent loss in our intuition of the artwork.

Due to lack of space, I refrain from going into Nussbaum's readings of specific tragedies here. I will just say a couple of things about her interpretations generally, many of which I find very rewarding. These long readings show, as all good pieces of literary criticism, a tension between the strive for elucidation and simply letting the work be. When you break up the form of an artwork in the interests of truth, for example, by studying structural or symbolic aspects ripped from the context, you also break up the artwork. Nussbaum seems to have a certain sensitivity to this, and it is why she wants to claim the tragedies to be philosophical in their own right, independently of her analyses. But no matter how careful the explanation of the 'what it [a tragedy] is doing and why'[91] is: what we have in front of us is no longer the artwork, but a clarified philosophical argument.

Many philosophers arguing for the philosophical value of literature seem to assume that complex interpretative activity they perform and report over hundreds of pages is in fact already inherent in the work itself. Perhaps this is because their profession has rendered them incapable of reading in an ordinary spirit. Nussbaum seems, something I also accused Niklas Forsberg of in the second chapter, to have forgotten or put aside the pleasure in going to the theatre: to these thinkers, reading a novel or watching a play becomes almost indistinguishable from making a philosophical interpretation of it. The organizing principle is for them not an aesthetically pleasing form, but a problem, a question, a lack of order or clarity. Nussbaum speaks of Creon in the *Antigone* as gradually 'arriv[ing] at the truth of what he most deeply believes; or at least ... becom[ing] able to acknowledge his own deep perplexity', and says that '[T]he spectator should be engaged in a similar sorting process'.[92] I would say that if it is doubtful that the spectator reaches an insight into what Creon believes, it is even more doubtful whether Creon does so himself.

The paradox of tragedy – the fact that we find pleasure in the portrayal of horrible things – is important to tackle for anyone who wants to claim that tragedies actually present us with 'tragic knowledge' (and not, as early Nietzsche suggested, with a comforting remedy against it). Nussbaum ignores this paradox in *The Fragility of Goodness*. Enjoyment is never in focus in her readings of tragedies, nor in her discussions of literature elsewhere. Instead, she looks to literature mainly for two things: a rich, detailed and inexhaustive account of human lives, in all their confusion and messiness; and a clarification of this contingency.[93]

In Chapter 3 of this book, 'muddle' in Murdoch's fiction was interpreted as an aesthetic idea, in order to exemplify how literature works with concepts in another way than to further conceptual understanding. Aesthetic ideas, understood with Kant, indeterminately and boundlessly enlarge a concept, serving 'really only to animate the mind by opening up for it the prospect of an immeasurable field of related representations'.[94] I demonstrated by examples how 'muddle' in Murdoch's fiction is used to evoke formless and confusing aspects of relationships, time and other things in life that resist narrativization. However, aesthetic ideas are not determinate concepts, but indeterminate representations.

As we have seen, Nussbaum views tragedy as laying 'open to view the complexity, the indeterminacy, the sheer difficulty of actual human deliberation'.[95] But what does this laying open to view actually consist in? 'Interpreting a tragedy', she says, 'is a messier, less determinate, more mysterious matter than assessing a philosophical example'.[96] Nussbaum wants to have her cake and eat it too. As preoccupied with control as she is with vulnerability, she wants to contain unclarity within clear rationality. She criticizes Platonism for appealing 'to an already deep tendency in us towards shame at the messy, unclear stuff of which our humanity is made'.[97] Yet, she also argues that the value of art consists in enhancing our cognitive clarity regarding this (presumably somehow still) 'messy, unclear stuff'. In other words, we can turn to art in order to perceive the messy and unclear in a less messy and unclear way. The obvious paradox is: How can art present us with muddled thinking and clarified muddle at the same time?

This paradox becomes most striking in her cognitivist interpretation of Aristotle's concept of katharsis. She argues that 'the primary, ongoing, central meaning [of katharsis] is roughly one of "clearing up" or "clarification", i.e. of the removal of some obstacle (dirt, or blot, or obscurity, or admixture) that makes the item in question less *clear* than it is in its proper state.'[98] With reference to the sorting out mentioned previously, she sees pity and fear in tragedies as 'sources of illumination or clarification, as the agent, responding and attending to his or her responses, develops a richer self-understanding concerning the attachments and values that support the responses'.[99] Katharsis is thus for Nussbaum simply another name for intellectual clarification of emotions. She recognizes herself that this might seem 'too Platonic', since it 'suggests that emotion is valuable only as an instrumental means to a purely intellectual state'.[100] This is solved by making emotions equal with conceptual understanding: 'the pity and fear are not just tools of a clarification that is in and of the intellect alone; to respond in these ways is itself valuable, and a piece of clarification concerning who we are'.[101]

What exactly 'clarification' is supposed to mean here remains unclear to me: perhaps simply understanding. But I cannot understand how a muddled state of mind would be a kind of clarity in its own right.

Furthermore, the pity and fear we feel when watching the *Antigone* are specific to enjoying a work of art. Elsewhere, Nussbaum argues powerfully for why emotions constitute evaluative judgements, by describing how it is the grief after her mother which makes her understand that she is gone.[102] This is a convincing argument. But the emotions we have in relation to a tragedy are not the same ones that we have in life. Grief is a good example: no matter how much we might feel with Antigone's loss of her brother, we do not even touch upon those stages of rage and denial that constitute real grief. Nussbaum disregards the imaginative, artistic forming of emotions in art, which makes them simultaneously 'larger than life' and posited at a safe distance from our actual lives. Remember Lear's definition of katharsis as the pleasure invoked when we 'imaginatively live life to the full, but we risk nothing'.[103] Rather than being confronted with the messy, self-contradictory emotions of life, the highly ordered art of tragedy offers us a consoling sense of formal containment of them.

Aristotle, Nussbaum's main philosophical paragon, devotes a great deal of attention to describing how tragic drama should be structured: what kind of actions, what kind of people, what timespan it should portray, what sense of awe should be imputed from the whole and even how the events should be ordered in relation to dramaturgical devices such as discovery and peripeteia. Needless to say, this is not how our messy and indeterminate lives are like. So when Nussbaum claims that 'the force of tragedy is ... to warn us of the dangers inherent in all searches for a single form: it continually displays to us the irreducible richness of human value, the complexity and indeterminacy of the lived practical situation',[104] she completely neglects the normative formal model for the genre that Aristotle has outlined in explicit contrast to the indeterminate richness of an actual life.

However, the idea that Plato's banishment of the tragic poets would be bound up with a disdain for the aspects of life they proport to depict is not unique to Nussbaum. The poets may seem to be more occupied with the flaws and fragilities of our finite existence, in contrast to the philosophers' obsessions with eternal truths. This could incline someone who takes themselves to be convinced that there is no eternity to find poetry more truth-conveying than philosophy. In the next section, I shall dig deeper into this problem. That philosophy is described by Socrates as practising dying was provocative already to Nietzsche, who wanted to counter him by defending the philosophical qualities of art as being more deeply connected with life. But what did Plato and Socrates actually mean by calling philosophy a practice of dying? And how is it related to the tragic poets? Why is Socrates so suspicious of their treatment of death?

5.6. Philosophy as practising dying

> Up till this time most of us had been fairly successful in keeping back our tears; but when we saw that he was drinking, that he had actually drunk it, we could do so no longer; in spite of myself the tears came pouring out, so that I covered my face and wept broken-heartedly – not for him, but for my own calamity in losing such a friend.[105]

Socrates, sentenced to death for impiety and corruption of the youth, receives the cup of poison 'quite cheerfully' and empties it 'without a tremor, without any change of colour or expression'.[106] Despite his admonishments to remain calm, his friends are unable to hold back their grief. But with an abnormal courage, or perhaps a cold unworldliness, Socrates does not seem to consider himself pitiable. Why does he not see his own death as a disaster? '[T]rue philosophers', he provocatively says in the *Phaedo*, 'make dying their profession.'[107] There is no wisdom in a life contaminated by the body, and so the work of the philosopher consists in separating and freeing the soul from the body. The body is here equivocated to an attachment to apparent goods and temporary satisfactions. 'So if you see anyone distressed at the prospect of dying', Socrates says, 'it will be proof enough that he is not a lover of wisdom but of the body (this same man would presumably be a lover of money) and of prestige, or both.'[108] A similar argument reoccurs in several other dialogues. In the *Republic*, he states that human life would not be found especially great to a magnificent understanding, and that death would consequently not strike such a man as something terrible.[109] In the *Apology*, Socrates seems proud to face the risk of dying – because 'we are quite mistaken in supposing death to be an evil'.[110]

This contempt for ordinary, bodily human life has troubled many throughout the history of philosophy. Additionally, it is clearly bound up with Socrates' and Plato's disdain for the tragic poets. When Socrates in the *Republic* advocates for their banishment, he is especially criticizing their ability to evoke an enjoyable kind of fear and grief in the face of death. The main concern of the dialogue is how to establish a good state, peopled with good and noble men, who must be 'accustomed to fearing slavery more than death'.[111] But our strivings to be masters of ourselves, truth-seeking and courageous are easily undone by the relaxing enjoyment of poetry:

> When even the best of us hear Homer or any other of the tragic poets imitating one of the heroes in mourning and making quite an extended speech with lamentation, or, if you like, singing and beating his breast, you know that we enjoy it and that we give ourselves over to following the imitation; suffering along with the hero in all seriousness, we praise as a good poet the man who most puts us in this state.[112]

Martin Hägglund, a literary scholar turned philosopher, argues that Plato's hostile attitude to poetry consists in this division between finite, human life and the supposedly eternal truths that the philosopher should be occupied with. 'The philosopher', writes Hägglund with some scorn, 'should not let himself be "disturbed" by the loss of mortal beings; he should rather turn his desire toward the immutable presence of the eternal'.[113] 'Poetry', on the other hand, 'engages the desire for a mortal life that can always be lost'.[114] This interpretation of Plato is merely an introduction to the readings of Proust, Woolf and Nabokov that Hägglund subsequently presents in his book. These readings stay with the finite, sensuous and experiential character of literature, where many scholars have instead tended to look for intimations of timelessness. Hägglund's chapter on Proust is especially illuminating in this regard.

However, Hägglund's departure from what he calls 'the Platonic diagnosis' is too simplified and formulaic: a life rule according to which 'we will overcome the fear of death if we overcome the desire for mortal life and learn to desire immortality in a proper philosophical fashion'.[115] If we take a closer look at Plato's dialogues, concepts like eternity and immortality become less simple, and Socrates' reasons for distrusting the poets might start to make more sense.

First: what are we to make of eternity? That Plato preached detachment from finitude for the sake of eternal truths is popularly assumed, even though what he meant by that which 'does not come into being or perish'[116] is hardly undisputed. Neither time nor eternity is a simple concept. Rather than a radical distinction in kind, as Hägglund would have it, the difference between them is perhaps better understood as a gliding scale between appearances and reality. In the *Timaeus*, time is described as having been created by the Demiurge as a moving image (*eikon*) of eternity.[117] As Wolfgang von Leyden remarks on this passage, there is a difference between an *eikon* and a *phantasma* (semblance): 'As an "*eikon*", at any rate, [time] is not so much in contrast with its model as intimately connected with it.'[118] Finite time is thus not simply unreal but better understood as a moving representation of something that *is* in itself despite our experiences of it. Following this, the distinction Plato makes between finitude and eternity becomes less of a silly fixation on a kingdom of immortal truths and more akin to Kant's distinction between the noumenal and the phenomenal. We cannot know anything beyond time, but we can be critically aware of how our temporal existence limits our knowledge.

Furthermore, what Socrates seeks to safeguard against poetry's affective investment in our mortality is not an eternity he is sure of but a fundamental doubt. In the *Apology*, he repeatedly makes clear that he does not know what kind of change death entails:

> For let me tell you, gentlemen, that to be afraid of death is only another form of thinking that one is wise when one is not; it is to think that one knows what one does not know. No one knows with regard to death whether it is not really the greatest blessing that can happen to a man; but people dread it as though they were certain that it is the greatest evil; and this ignorance, which thinks that it knows what it does not, must surely be ignorance most culpable.[119]

Rather than harbouring any stubborn faith in immortality, Socrates is adamant about his lack of insight into the difference between life and death. He adds: 'if I were to claim to be wiser than my neighbour in any respect, it would be in this: that not possessing any real knowledge of what awaits us in Hades, I am also conscious that I do not possess it'.[120] This not-so-wise neighbour is none other than the poet. With his magical trick mirror, he 'produces earth and heaven and gods and everything in heaven and everything in Hades under the earth',[121] as Homer does.[122] Holding up a mirror to the underworld, the poet even reflects the unknowable and invisible, in what Andrea Capra calls 'the deliberate deficiency of the mirror argument';[123] he provides a semblance of the unrepresentable. Plato did not simply think that the poet is a sophist because he is imitating what is, but because he is also imitating things that he cannot have any idea of whether they exist or not, or what they look like.

Thus, the poets are not simply guilty of caring too much about our finite lives: they also supply us with false whiffs of eternity. Nowhere is this more evident than in the many interpretations of *À la recherche du temps perdu* that Hägglund seeks to refute. In readings by otherwise very diverse scholars, from Beckett to Ricœur, the *Recherche* has consistently been argued to 'transcend temporal finitude'.[124] Even though Hägglund's contrarian interpretation of Proust as fundamentally occupied with finitude is very persuasive and beautiful, the 'timeless essence'[125] that previous scholarship has found in the novels is indeed also implicated there. In the last volume, for example, the narrator reflects upon how 'the eternal man' in him has been roused which enables him to generalize individual impressions of beauty into a 'generalising essence', which is the confirmation he needs in order to complete his artwork.[126] Without sliding into Proust scholarship here, one might find sufficient support for Plato's deliberately deficient mirror argument simply in the fact that so many has looked to these novels for intimations of eternity.

Tragedy is the genre that most of all appears to confront us with finitude, in the sense of death as well as in the sense of the limits of our moral powers. But as Plato reminds us, *appears* is an unpassable keyword here. Art can give us an unfounded sense that we know things, even afford us an illusory grasp of the boundaries of our existence. In an article, Simon Critchley criticizes the turn to tragedy in post-Kantian thought as something which '*disfigures* finitude by making the human being *heroic*'.[127] Critchley shows how the philosophical urge to make death comprehensible has occasioned a widespread wish to treat the genre of tragedy as philosophical. Through tragedy, the confrontation with finitude appears heroic, authentic and affirmed. But Critchley argues that 'finitude cannot be affirmed because it cannot be grasped';[128] an argument which echoes of the Socratic position in the *Apology* that was quoted above. As Critchley says elsewhere, death and dying should instead be viewed as 'the limit of narration'[129] – something which cannot be mastered by any story, since no one can retell their own death.

However, Hägglund's defence of art as an affective investment in mortal life need not be combined with a wish to take this immersive quality as philosophical. If we read Proust not as a critical interpreter of the reality of eternity or finitude, but as a painter concerned with impressions and appearances, none of the greatness of his novels appears to me to be lost. Seeing this affective investment as an undiscerning love for the fleeting and the unfathomable, as well as for the apparent and the illusory, saves art from the sophistry Plato and Socrates seek to accuse it of. If literature is appreciated as literature, that is, as an art with another standard of excellence than philosophy, it becomes lovable instead of misleading.

Socrates means that it would be stupid to value our lives without questioning what is truly valuable and real in them. He is relentless in his doubts, even into death. The artists, on the other hand, are limitless in their celebrations and lamentations of what is, what appears to be and what may only be imagined, dreamt of or feared. A splendid show of this contrast can be found in some of Plato's own dialogues, such as the one quoted in the beginning of this section. In the *Phaedo*, the philosopher gives in to his poetic temptations and fails to contain his grief over his dying teacher.

Socrates himself is in a softened mood towards poetry here. After having provided his famous series of arguments for why we might assume that the soul lives on after death, his conversation partner Simmias confesses to 'still [be] feeling some misgivings'.[130] Socrates answers to him by telling a myth of how a soul is led to Hades by a guardian and gives his own cosmological tale, in which he even quotes Homer to describe one of the deepest cavities of the planet, where the most sinful souls supposedly end up after death. Then, Socrates concludes: 'Of course, no reasonable man ought to insist that the facts are exactly as I have described them.' Nonetheless, he calls his account of the fate of the soul 'a belief worth risking' and adds that 'We should use such accounts to enchant ourselves with'.[131] So, as Socrates himself suggests, we should read the accounts of the afterlife of the soul given in the *Phaedo* as enchanting stories rather than as philosophy.

The sorrowful ending of this dialogue is as captivating as it is infectious – precisely the qualities that made Socrates hold Homer in suspicion. 'Calm yourselves and be brave', the mentor chides his disciples. They are ashamed and contain their tears. But the readers merely intuit this as a still image of the 'storm of passionate weeping that [just] made everyone in the room break down'.[132] We share Plato's grief over precisely that philosopher who criticized the poets for replacing our sense with distraught feelings, and feeding the part of the soul 'that leads to reminiscences of the suffering and to complaints and can't get enough of them'.[133] As Murdoch points out, when Plato is harsh on the poets he is also harsh on his own inclinations, since he 'doubtless had mixed feelings about the great artist inside himself'.[134]

In this chapter, I have described and criticized the widespread philosophical tendency to turn to the genre of tragedy in order to question the distinction between literature and philosophy. I have explained Murdoch's Kantian notion of form and exemplified how the philosopher should always be undoing the forms of his or her own thinking by tracing the development in Murdoch's own philosophical notion of tragedy. Thus, I have illustrated a crucial aspect of what she thought should distinguish philosophy from literature. This chapter has then moved on to consider the form of tragedy according to Aristotle, discussed how Nietzsche and Hegel make different philosophical usage of the genre and at length criticized Martha Nussbaum's contemporary endeavour to argue for the philosophical work of tragedy. Finally, I have looked a bit closer at the Socratic arguments concerning the distinction between poetry and philosophy in their relations to the problem of death, thereby questioning an even more recent attempt by Martin Hägglund to criticize Plato's distinction between the disciplines.

But the unique truth-conveying potential that Murdoch finds in great art still remains to be described. This connects with another central issue in Murdoch, largely ignored in this book so far, namely the relationship between literature and moral philosophy and/or moral improvement. Let us tie up this book by returning to the beginning of the quarrel: why did Plato consider poetry to be immoral, and how could Murdoch think that he was partly right about that?

6

Playing with fire: *The immorality of literature*

6.1. Murdoch's Platonic mistrust of art

6.1.1. Mimesis: As if

There are some obvious ways in which literature can be bad for us. It can make evil or dangerous things, such as murder, rape, adultery, suicide, substance abuse and paedophilia seem interesting and exciting, or simply excusable. It can offer us escape from the hard and difficult facts of life into a comforting dreamworld of wish-fulfilment. It can function like pornography, in stimulating our desires and giving them release without confronting us with other human beings. It can give us the false sense of having understood something, without furthering our minds towards any actual insights. It can provide us with the illusion of being good at empathizing with others, without necessarily rendering us any better at it in life; making us congratulate ourselves on our non-prejudiced perception, simply because we have read a story which makes us feel *as if* we know what it is like (to belong to an oppressed minority, to be a refugee of war, to have lost a child, etc.).

It is this *as if*-character of art that made Plato mistrust it so. In this chapter, I will delve deeper into how the Platonic view of the immorality of art has informed Murdoch's distinction between literature and philosophy. As we will see, Murdoch is often read as stating that art is improving us morally, which in many interpretations become tantamount to taking literature as moral philosophy. Her philosophical and literary work are viewed as two forms of the same struggle: to discover and convey the nature of the good. But these readings, I will argue, do not do justice to many of Murdoch's central notions: the distinction between the interesting and the good, the relation between fantasy and imagination, the desire-based Weilian concept of attention, the erotic nature of inspiration and the accidentalness of art's edifying character. With Murdoch, we shall ask 'the not uninteresting question whether Plato may not have been in some ways right to be so suspicious of art'[1] and explain how art's corruptive power is bound up with its unique truth-conveying potential.

Plato's suspicion of art mainly concerns its mimetic character. What he meant with *mímêsis* is, however, not immediately obvious. The English word is usually simply understood as imitation, and a mimetic view of art then implies that art imitates reality. But the grounds for Plato's mistrust are more complex than that. The Greek concept *mímêsis*, which Plato both enlarged and specified, can be translated as representation, impersonation, imitation or emulation.[2] Mimesis is the production of an imitation of an appearance of something and does not ask what is real or not. It is thus not simply, say, imitating a bad man. There is a corruptive element to mimesis, going deeper than the surface deceptions, which Christopher Janaway explains with Plato's description of actors as both hiding behind their characters and risking to become more like them by playing them.[3] This problematic aspect of theatre is then somehow applied to all of the other arts as well, from painting to poetry, as they are condemned as immoral.[4]

Plato's classic example with the bed in *The Republic* is simple, and therefore easily misunderstood. It is meant to demonstrate not just the fraudulence and uselessness of art, but also art's corruptive influence. God made the form of the bed, the carpenter imitates this blueprint to the best of his abilities when he builds a bed, but the painter only gives us an image of a bed from a certain perspective. It is not immediately obvious from this example why art would be corruptive. One is inclined to wonder, as Stanley Rosen does, 'how the production of a false image of a bed could lead to sexual license on the part of its beholders. If beds are regarded as peculiarly inflammatory artifacts, it must be granted that the carpenter's copy is far more dangerous to sexual continence than the poet's.'[5] At a first glance, art may seem more innocent than Plato would have it.

But the licence given by the painting of a bed is of course not sexual in the simplistic sense of providing the means for copulation. That it is a bed is not a very important aspect of the example, not even symbolically. Plato is attempting to describe the underlying dangers of the 'as if' of art. In imitating the appearance of something, art indulges our perception in a much more fundamental and potentially morally eroding way. The artist is not providing us with anything useful, such as a piece of furniture. He is simply appreciating and possibly even distorting an isolated impression of it. In Murdoch's explanatory summary of Plato's argument, the painter

> does not understand the bed, he could not make it. He evades the conflict between the apparent and the real which stirs the mind towards philosophy. Art naïvely or wilfully accepts appearances instead of questioning them. Similarly a writer who portrays a doctor does not possess a doctor's skill but simply 'imitates doctors' talk. Nevertheless, because of the charm of their work such people are wrongly taken for authorities, and simple folk believe them. Surely any serious man would rather produce real things, such as beds or political activity, than unreal things which are mere reflections of reality.[6]

Plato would probably not even dignify them the name 'reflections of reality'. Reality is not, to Plato, something immediately obvious. Most of the things we take to be real are in fact just our own fantasies or perceptive illusions. But the artist is content with these appearances; indeed, he celebrates them. He sees a straight stick being bent in the water and delights in this illusion instead of seeking an explanation for it.[7] Similarly, the poets do not care if the men they praise really are good and honourable, or if they just seem to be.[8] What's more, they have the audacity to portray the gods as deceitful, vengeful, swayable, greedy, mad with laughter and worn out by tears; inconsistent and blasphemous accounts which make the audience more content with their own human flaws. After all, anyone could forgive themself for sinning if they thought that the gods did it too.⁹

Thus, the general moral import of art becomes: do not try to understand how things really are. Do not occupy yourself with something important, like healing the sick. You could instead cheer up yourself and others by telling consoling but unhelpful stories about how illness is a punishment from the gods, and how a magic rite once has cured someone else. This is not to say that there cannot be any truth or goodness in art. But there does not have to be, and it is this freedom that makes it so troublesome in Plato's eyes. Art is free to be completely insubstantial, useless, uninformative, unproductive and deeply morally ambiguous, without any of this affecting its value as art. Murdoch compares art in general and literature in particular to 'a great hall of reflection'. As such, one might add, it mirrors the world both directly and distortedly. This is why, as Murdoch says, art 'is feared and attacked by dictators, and by authoritarian moralists such as the one under discussion'. As Plato well recognized: 'The artist is a great informant, at least a gossip, at best a sage, and much loved in both roles.'¹⁰

This freedom has made many thinkers turn to art as a potentially liberating, subversive force. Art can, precisely because it lacks a clear purpose, disrupt and disturb our habitual and normative modes of perception, causing confusion in what we take to be good and bad. Indeed, it has often been censured on the same grounds. Today, we congratulate ourselves on appreciating works that have previously been considered immoral and obscene as if this in itself would be a sign of moral progression. As Elisabeth Ladenson writes in *Dirt for Art's Sake: Books on Trial from* Madame Bovary *to* Lolita:

> [S]ubversion and transgression ha[ve] become positive values in themselves. Or at least our ideas of subversion and transgression. … Our culture – especially the academy – pays constant and emphatic lip service to these concepts …. [W]e tend to read books like *Madame Bovary* and *Lolita* for their 'subversive' qualities, but what gets lost in the shuffle is that the subversion in question always concerns values that diverge from our own.¹¹

Literature is seen as good because it challenges a morality we no longer strive to uphold. We want it to break up our moral standards, but only to the extent that they are no longer really *our* moral standards. In other words, we celebrate these novels for being at the same time powerful and harmless.

In this chapter, I intend to stay with the power that Plato so carefully discerned in art. With Murdoch, I believe that it is bound up with its accidentally edifying character and unique (but rarely actualized) truth-conveying potential. In order to see how art may affect us so profoundly, we must recognize how ambiguous its fundamental (im)moral character is. The chapter is divided into three main sections. I shall begin with further explaining Murdoch's moral mistrust of art and its Platonic roots, then discuss her Weilian concept of attention, and finally comment on the accidental truth-conveying potential of art.

6.1.2. Enjoying the cave

As Murdoch explains, Plato judges the artist and his art 'to exhibit the lowest and most irrational kind of awareness, *eikasia*, a state of vague image-ridden illusion; in terms of the cave myth this is the condition of the prisoners who face the back wall and see only shadows cast by the fire'.[12] Art can thus show us what this illusory-ridden awareness consists of: in Murdoch's words, Plato's 'whole criticism of art extends and illuminates the conception of the shadow-bound consciousness'.[13] This heightened awareness of the shadows does not imply a liberation from them. We shall not mistake the fire for the sun here and exaggerate the edifying character of art. 'Enjoyment of art deludes even the decent man by giving him a false self-knowledge based on a healthy egoism: the fire in the cave, which is mistaken for the sun, and where one may comfortably linger, imagining oneself to be enlightened.'[14] But what, exactly, is to be feared from the fire?

As Plato implies, staying in the cave is, or at least appears to be, *nice*. It is cosy and comfortable and familiar. Striving for enlightenment, in contrast, is effortful, lonely and counter-intuitive. What makes art so acutely threatening is not just the illusions it produces, but the intense pleasure it brings about. Homer is enthralling even to Socrates, who calmly refuses the advancements of beautiful boys,[15] but still holds out hope that the poets would make a good case for why their art is beneficial and not just enjoyable.[16] Pleasure, in *The Timaeus* named 'evil's most potent lure',[17] is for Plato intimately tied up with mimetic art. It is not just the simple pleasures of having a good laugh or watching erotic images that he has in mind. As Jessica Moss explains, it is specifically the feeling of recognizing reality in imitations that brings about the relaxing excitement Plato abhorred:

> Here it is crucial to recognize that ... the pleasures poetry offers us are not the cheap thrills of pulp fiction or 'trash'. Imitative poetry offers us compelling portraits of human affairs and human excellence – compelling because they are realistic, that is, they capture these things as they appear. In doing so, such poetry gives us the emotional satisfaction of identifying, grieving, and rejoicing with its heroes.[18]

Realistic literature portrays reality, in the sense of what we perceive, imagine, or even wish to be real. It may even, curiously, make reality seem 'more real'. As Weil writes, 'There is a certain *feeling of reality* which is the very form and colour of the imaginary.'[19] The fantasy makes reality seem easily accessible and leaves us content with appearances.

The poets also show us something we recognize from our lives, namely that bad men can be happy and unjust actions can be applauded. Such affirmations can be relaxing and stimulating in all the wrong ways. It is easy to see how we may become depraved by hearing about how charismatic characters are benefitting from their shady affairs. 'We'll forbid them to say such things', cries Socrates in *The Republic*, 'and order them to sing and to tell tales about the opposites of these things. Or don't you suppose so?'[20]

To thus pay poetry the compliment of threatening it with censorship ('and it is a compliment'[21]) has definitely gone out of style. Pleasure and enjoyment are no longer viewed by most as inherently suspicious, nor even as intrinsic to literature. Our late capitalist digitalized present offers a great bouquet of much more sensually immediate forms of wish-fulfilment in which we may also recognize 'reality'. Novel reading, once likened to opioid abuse,[22] is nowadays seen as demanding an effort, and it is thus closer at hand to expect it to be morally and/or politically edifying and educational.

One of the things that for Murdoch most clearly differs literature from philosophy, both in her own practice and in her aesthetics, is that art is fundamentally enjoyable. 'I think it is more fun to be an artist than to be a philosopher', she says in an interview, adding that: 'We enjoy art, even simple art, because it disturbs us in deep often incomprehensible ways; and this is one reason why it is good for us when it is good and bad for us when it is bad.'[23] The enjoyment is bound up with the edifying as well as the corruptive potential of art, which is as free as it is irresponsible. 'Philosophy and theology have to reject evil in order to explain it', Murdoch writes, 'but art is essentially more free and enjoys the ambiguity of the whole man'.[24] Basking in our general human mediocrity and capacity for evil does indeed form a not contemptible part of the pleasure of novel reading. Perhaps it is this rich ambiguity which has made many moral philosophers turn to literature; but neither, it seems, in order to enjoy it nor to warn against its inherent dangers.

6.1.3. 'Deeper than the level at which we deliberate concerning improvement'

Murdoch is regarded as an important influence in what has come to be known as the 'literary turn' of moral philosophy.[25] The literary turn is a movement characterized by a criticism of the limitations of modern analytic philosophy coupled with an optimism regarding the moral force and complexity of literature. Martha Nussbaum, one of the most prominent figures of the literary turn, goes so far as to argue that 'certain novels are, irreplaceably, works of moral philosophy'.[26] Elaborating on Henry James, Nussbaum claims that moral understanding is not just understanding but also perception. 'It is seeing a complex concrete reality in a highly lucid and richly responsible way; it is taking what is there, with imagination and feeling.'[27]

At face value, it is easy to see how Murdoch's moral theory might be aligned with Nussbaum's view of novels as doing philosophical work. Like Nussbaum, Murdoch is critical of the distinction between fact and value, stresses the moral importance of perception and imagination, and sees morality as intertwined with our ongoing strive to make sense of the world and other people. 'Morality', Murdoch says, 'as the ability or attempt to be good, rests upon deep areas of sensibility and creative imagination, upon removal from one state of mind to another, upon shift of attachments, upon love and respect for the contingent details of the world'.[28] She also frequently draws connections between this characterization of morality and art. 'Literature is soaked in the moral, language is soaked in the moral, fictional characters swim in a moral atmosphere.'[29] In a much-quoted passage, she proclaims art and morals to be

> with certain provisos ... one. Their essence is the same. The essence of both of them is love. Love is the perception of individuals. Love is the extremely difficult realisation that something other than oneself is real. Love, and so art and morals, is the discovery of reality.[30]

Note that Murdoch does not, not even in this early essay, equal art to the good. Nor does she say 'moral philosophy'. The 'extreme difficulties' involved could at first glance seem to imply that a certain amount of effort must be put in. But what kind of effort are we talking about here? What would *an effort to love* look like for a reader or a writer?

To say, as, for example, Nora Hämäläinen does, that literature for Murdoch 'works as a tool for making the appropriate connections' between the striving for the good that is 'manifested in different ways in the particularities of human life and actions'[31] makes this effort sound very instrumental. Hämäläinen's choice of metaphor is not accidental but gets repeated two more times on the same page when she describes art and philosophy in Murdoch's view as 'tools for knowledge and truth', 'tools for fighting the illusions and delusions which are part of our everyday life'.[32]

However, Murdoch is very cautious when it comes to regarding art as instrumental. She is explicitly critical of Sartre's definition of prose as 'the language which we inhabit and which we must treat as a tool'.[33] Art is not a tool like a screwdriver or a hammer; it is more like an immersion or enchantment. 'To say that the essence of art is love is not to say, is nothing to do with saying, that art is didactic or educational', Murdoch adds as provisos to the previously quoted statement on art as love. 'The level at which that love works which is art is deeper than the level at which we deliberate concerning improvement.'[34] At this deep level, we do not make conscious instrumental efforts, we are in the grips of art rather than gripping it as a tool, and the ways in which art changes us could thus be for the worse as well as for the better. 'Even great art', Murdoch says, 'can be a potent source of illusions.'[35]

'Deep' is here meant in the sense of the lower regions of the cave, or the unconscious. Art works at this level; it is, as Murdoch rephrases Plato, 'the base addressing the base',[36] noting that his suspicion of art is 'remarkably Freudian'.[37] Indeed, a great deal of Murdoch's understanding of the morally corruptive potential of art is derived from Plato and Freud, and inspired by two other fierce moralists, Simone Weil and Leo Tolstoy. Plato, the most hostile of them all, is perhaps too suspicious, Murdoch suggests, 'but I think his suspicion comes from a [deep] understanding of what art is like', adding that '[a]rt is to do with sex and the unconscious mind'.[38]

A self-proclaimed Platonist, Murdoch was far from calling herself a Freudian, but some of his central thoughts about art have definitely made a mark on her aesthetics. She claims in an interview that all she agrees on with Freud is what 'he frankly says he's pinched from Plato',[39] but this is a truth with some modification. There are some definite Freudian influences on Murdoch's work.[40] She was very aware of the closeness between literature and the comforting, reality-avoiding stories we tell ourselves, as Freud speaks about in 'Creative Writers and Day-Dreaming'.[41] One of our main pastimes is day-dreaming, she notes, where we immerse ourselves in 'a cloud of more or less fantastic reverie designed to protect the psyche from pain'.[42] Fiction is to this purpose offering us sketches which are 'completed by the ready fantasy of the writer and the reader, that wicked co-operating pair, in an illusory unity and pornography is, again, the pure case of this collusion between the artist and his client'.[43] As I will develop more at length later in this chapter, this 'attempt to achieve omnipotence through personal fantasy'[44] is inseparably tied up with our everyday ways of holding ourselves and our lives together. 'We are all story-tellers and we tell stories about people, and we tell these stories not only to other people but also to ourselves. ... [T]his gives us in return a sense of our own identity, our own separateness, our own self-being.'[45]

But in Murdoch's understanding, these stories can both sustain our individual identities and be attempts to reach out of them. Literature, as art in general, is fundamentally *communication*, and not necessarily of a truthful or rational kind. This notion is informed by Tolstoy, who (in Murdoch's words) 'takes as a paradigm of literature the boy who meets the wolf in the forest and comes home and describes the experience'.[46] In *What Is Art?*, which Murdoch considered 'a very good book',[47] Tolstoy states that we tell about an experience because we want to communicate what we have felt to others. Art is thus, at its most basic level, a transmitter of feelings:

> The activity of art is based on the fact that man, as he receives through hearing or sight the expression of another man's feelings, is capable of experiencing the same feelings as the man who expresses them. The simplest example: a man laughs, and another man feels merry; he weeps, and the man who hears this weeping feels sad.[48]

Plato, who wants to censor all parts of Homer where the gods are laughing or crying in fear of it affecting the audience with uncontrollable emotions, would probably have agreed on this definition. Also for Tolstoy, there is a certain immediacy and amorality to the power of art:

> If the work is good as art, then the feeling expressed by the artist is conveyed to others, regardless of whether the work is moral or immoral. If it is conveyed to others, they experience it, and experience it moreover, each in his own way, and all interpretation is superfluous. If the work does not infect others, then no interpretation is going to make it infectious.[49]

Infectiousness as the measure of the power of art is one way to describe how it affects us on a deeper level than that at which we deliberate concerning improvement. Accordingly, Tolstoy thought that art should be devoted to transmitting the highest religious consciousness of its time, a view that Murdoch professed to feel 'great sympathy' with.[50] This is however rarely the case. Tolstoy deems sexual lust to have been the main topic of all novels from Boccaccio onwards, lamenting that '[a]dultery is not just the favourite but the only theme of all novels'.[51] Be that as it may, it can definitely be said about Murdoch's oeuvre.

Of all her twenty-six novels, there is not a single one which does not contain at least one illicit affair, and usually plenty more than that. These entanglements often constitute the central narrative pull of the fiction, and it must be acknowledged that Murdoch portrays adultery as thrilling, adventurous, pleasurable, fateful and sometimes even as shortcuts to experiencing truth and reality. When, for example, Jean in *The Book and the Brotherhood* goes off from her husband to her lover, there is a distinct sense of divine revelation connected to the state of exception experienced in the affair:

> When Jean, waking when he slept beside her, or waiting for his return home, felt, breathing slowly and deeply, the quietness, the cosmic reality of this joy which now had no term, she thought that surely it was occupation enough to fill the days and hours of her whole life. She had been re-created, given new meaning, new pure flesh, new lucid spirit. She could perceive the world at last, her eyes were cleared, her perceptions clarified, she had never seen such a vivid, coloured, detailed world, vast and complete as myth, yet full of tiny particular accidental entities placed in her way like divine toys. She had discovered breathing, breathing such as holy men use, the breathing of the planet, of the universe, the movement of being into Being.[52]

Those who here want to object – as some Murdoch scholars probably would – that to be taken in by this description would be naïve and careless, and that Murdoch's many portrayals of the attractiveness of adultery serve rather to enlighten us of its dangers than enticing us to experience it for ourselves, are presuming a detached way of reading.[53] The simple, Tolstoian and Platonic view of art as capable of infecting, affecting and changing us in immediate ways – how the actor playing shameful roles on stage loses his dignity in life,[54] or how the audience enjoys 'cruel jokes and bad taste in the theatre, then behave boorishly at home'[55] – is in fact entirely in line with Murdoch's moral philosophy of art. 'Man is a creature who makes pictures of himself', she writes, 'and then comes to resemble the picture.'[56] If pictures and fictions are not innocent, but born out of obscure desires and feeding back into them, if they are oftentimes just the base addressing the base, then fiction in general is far from edifying. In any case, Murdoch is very clear that art does not help us deliberate concerning improvement.

6.1.4. The interesting vs. the good

The main moral problem of literature is that the interesting and the good are opposing poles in our imagination, and thus also in fiction. This is pointed out by Plato, repeated by Weil and developed by Murdoch into her distinction between fantasy and imagination, which I shall get to eventually.

The interesting is another name for what Plato calls the irritable and the various. Murdoch compares it to the Freudian neurotic: the psychological instabilities that are not desirable in life but fascinating in fiction.[57] As Socrates explains in *The Republic*:

> [T]he irritable disposition affords much and varied imitation, while the prudent and quiet character, which is always nearly equal to itself, is neither easily imitated nor, when imitated, easily understood, especially by a festive assembly where all sorts of human beings are gathered in a theater.[58]

It follows from this that 'the imitative poet isn't naturally directed toward any such part of the soul, and his wisdom isn't framed for satisfying it – if he's going to get a good reputation among the many – but rather toward the irritable and various disposition, because it is easily imitated.'[59] As Moss remarks, the word 'multicoloured' (*poikilon*) – here translated as various – is not only used by Socrates to denigrate this neurotically various and falsely seductive beauty, but also by the poets themselves to describe their heroes. 'Homer's Odysseus is *poikilomētēs* – "multicolor-minded" ..., the man of many wiles and many tricks.'⁶⁰

The good is less interesting to (and in) fiction than the bad. As Weil argues, fiction thus reverses the real relationship between the good and the interesting. Good in reality is 'beautiful, marvelous, ever new, ever surprising, so full of sweet and continual delight', whereas evil is 'barren and dismal, monotonous and boring'. But the opposite goes for fictional good and evil. 'Fictional good is boring and flat. Fictional evil is varied, interesting, attractive, profound, and seductive.'⁶¹ All of literature is thus more or less immoral, in her view. In a Freudian-Platonic fashion, Weil adds that literature is a reflection of, rather than an exception to, how we live our lives. Most of our time is spent in such facile amusement-seeking day-dreaming:

> [T]he substance of our life is made nearly entirely of fiction. We tell ourselves tales about our future. Without a heroic love of truth, we recount our past, all the while refashioning it to our taste. Not looking too closely at other people, we tell ourselves stories about what they think, what they are saying, what they are doing. Reality furnishes the elements of these stories, just as romantic novelists often take their plots from the news, but we wrap them in a fog of inverted values, inverted just as they are in all fiction, where evil attracts and good bores.⁶²

The simplicity of the good makes it contrary to the multicoloured expressions that evil has in our imagination; it also makes the good very difficult to represent in the engaging, attractive way it deserves. This poses a serious question to any moral philosopher turning to fiction, a question that many seem to want to duck. Murdoch, however, did not. Informed by Plato, Freud and Weil, as well as her own practice as a novelist, she was well aware of how excruciatingly difficult it is to portray, or indeed to do, anything good in and through fiction.

Several scholars have, since Peter Conradi's early study *The Saint and the Artist*, been quick to identify certain of her characters as 'saintly'.⁶³ These saintly characters are often referred to as moral ideals. One of the most popular examples is Tallis Browne in *A Fairly Honourable Defeat*, which Murdoch confesses to have modelled as a Christ figure,⁶⁴ but in an interview also refers to as 'demonic' and 'with a kind of charm which is illegitimate'.⁶⁵ 'I think Ann in *An Unofficial Rose* is a good character without being demonic', she adds, 'but then, of course, it may be that she's not interesting enough. There is always this problem.'⁶⁶

'Interesting' is indeed an ambiguous word in Murdoch's vocabulary. What is interesting absorbs our attention in an automatic way, and can thus incite as well as suspend further thinking. Tallis is problematic to her because he becomes too interesting. His goodness becomes a spectacle of pathetic suffering (he even, which Conradi good-naturedly points out, 'provides himself with a latter-day stigma by wounding his palm with a screwdriver'⁶⁷). 'Suffering is interesting, our *views* of it are often magically, sexually, charged', Murdoch writes.⁶⁸ Suffering is one of many ways of staying by the fire, that is, the fascinating internal drama of the ego, and the portrayal of it can be very pleasurable, making '[a]lmost all art [into] a form of fantasy-consolation'.[69] What is interesting may easily lead away from the good, also when it appears to confront us with horrible things (as was discussed with tragedy in the previous chapter).

The objection that riveting depictions of vices, such as Murdoch's of adultery, could help us further our self-knowledge would to her have been a meek one. 'Self-knowledge, in the sense of a minute understanding of one's own machinery, seems to me, except at a fairly simple level, usually a delusion'.[70] Digging around in the hot embers of our own psyches does not necessarily bring us closer to the real, no matter if we entertain ourselves with pleasure or pain. Most of the time, this is just a masked narcissism. 'One's self is interesting, so one's motives are interesting, and the unworthiness of one's motives are interesting'.[71] Suffering is also very interesting, and the 'ideas of guilt and suffering can be the most subtle tools of the ingenious self'.[72] This bottomless indulgence in the interesting and the neurotic is indeed a prominent characteristic of much literature, which in Murdoch's view brings it into a problematic opposition with the good.

6.1.5. Reading Murdoch's novels as morally edifying

The problem that the murkiness of interest poses for artistic attention seems mostly overlooked by Murdoch scholars. The received view is (if you permit me a general sketch) that Murdoch thinks that art makes us better, and that her novels are good examples of morally edifying fiction. The power of literature is usually phrased to imply that the writer and the reader are (or should be) both in control and conscious of what they are doing. The descriptions of what Murdoch thinks literature have been phrased as: giving us 'a lesson in how to picture and understand';[73] 'perfect[ing] [our] vision of particular mimetic situations';[74] providing a 'fictional playing out of ideas'[75] which 'embodies and thereby scrutinizes [them]';[76] and presenting us with 'problems in depicting progress towards human consciousness and change'.[77] Literature sounds in these accounts often like a very purposive, dry and unambiguous medium, whereas novels in general rather tend to be quite moist, muddled and dubious.

I shall give more than a couple of evocative adjectives to support my claims. Without engaging in any in-depth dialogue with these scholars or giving anything resembling a full account of current moral philosophical interpretations of Murdoch's fiction, let me just compare a couple of examples which reciprocally highlight the inherent instabilities of their conclusions.

Oftentimes, certain passages from Murdoch's fiction that portray experiences of art are quoted to reinforce what is taken to be her philosophical view of art as morally edifying. One popular scene from *The Bell* is Dora visiting the National Gallery. In front of the great paintings, Dora is faced with something 'which her consciousness could not wretchedly devour, and by making it part of her fantasy make it worthless'. The masterpieces are 'something real outside herself' and their marvellous presence destroys her 'dreary trance-like solipsism'.[78]

Here, Anna Victoria Hallberg claims that Murdoch has a textual intention which 'stands in direct relation to her aesthetic-philosophic objective': to show us what moral change is like, within as well as through the fiction.[79] Her novels are interpreted by

Hallberg both as examples of morally edifying fiction and as explications of how art may be morally edifying. The vocabulary used when Dora is face to face with the painting is according to Hallberg 'identical to the vocabulary she [Murdoch] uses when speaking in her moral aesthetics of how transcendence and consciousness can be retrieved through attention to art'. Consequently, Hallberg concludes that '[g]reat art is an instrument for checking the ego and it gives us access to truth'.[80]

Again, art is described as an intentionally deployed instrument, which brings out reality. Artworks are thought to function as tools, like ropes and climbing axes, which can help us ascend from the cave, and not as shadow theatre. As Gary Browning describes the same scene, quoting Anne Rowe, 'Dora is reassured as she reacts to the loving clarity of the representation and experiences what Rowe terms, "appreciation of the beauty and individuality of others and of the world outside ourselves, to which Murdoch insists we turn our eyes on the Platonic path to goodness"'.[81]

Murdoch did indeed think that art could be morally illuminating, if only rarely and accidentally so, and I shall give my own interpretation of how at the end of this chapter. But she was also very wary of the tendencies, including her own, to view art in too rosy a light. 'This enthusiasm depends upon a certain amount of switching between "art" and "great art". In fact there is very little great art and not all that much good art.'[82] Most scholars take note of her distinction between art and great art in passing, to then turn their undivided attention to the moral significance of great art (a category where they, against her own better judgement,[83] tend to include Murdoch's own novels).[84] But even great art can in her opinion be used to sustain solipsistic fantasy-worlds, and if we look to her fiction to extract illustrative encounters with art, there are plenty of depictions of this as well.

When Charles Arrowby in *The Sea, the Sea* visits the Wallace Collection, he confesses that he 'derive[s] a lot of sheer erotic satisfaction from pictures of women'[85] and proceeds to search for objectified similes of the women in his life in the paintings, finding 'Lizzie by Terborch, Jeanne by Nicholas Maes, Rita by Domenichino, Rosina by Rubens, a perfectly delightful study by Greuze of Clement as she was when I first met her ... '[86] Bradley Pearson in *The Black Prince*, to name another example, imagines himself living in a Platonic-Shakespearian drama and cannot get it up with his beloved Julian unless she is dressed out as Hamlet.[87]

There is no 'proof' and not even any unequivocal indications to be extracted from Murdoch's fiction that great art would function as a tool for an ascent from the cave. As is often the case with art, the opposite interpretation might as well be made. So why does it seem to be so tempting for scholars to regard her novels as works of moral philosophy?[88] Is it out of love for literature, a less and less popular pastime, that people proclaim it to be covert philosophy to make it seem important anew? Indeed, the dwindling popularity of an academic discipline perceived as boring or inaccessible is perhaps also hoped to be raised by the coupling, so that literature and philosophy become like two castaways clinging to each other, imagining that it will stop them from sinking. Perhaps it is also tempting to think that reading an entertaining story might improve one's character. And maybe it can to some extent – but Murdoch sees it more like getting closer to the fire than the sun – a step in the right direction, which might as well be counter-productively taken for a full ascent. 'Even good art makes us feel too much at ease with something less than the best, it offers a sort of spiritual exercise and what looks like a spiritual home, a kind of armchair sanctity which may be a substitute for genuine moral effort.'[89]

Literature dwells upon and swells and enthrals us with ambiguity. A moral ascent in fiction cannot be separated from its own as if-character and might as well be a counter-productive illusion of betterment. This quickly becomes evident when comparing a couple of examples of what is read as moral revelations in Murdoch's fiction.

Taking what is there with imagination and feeling, as Nussbaum calls it, turns out to be very different things for different readers. Sometimes in Murdoch's novels, particular impressions are interpreted as signs by her characters. Stuart in *The Good Apprentice* suddenly sees a mouse on the tracks in the London Underground.[90] He perceives it as a kind of revelation, a sign. Hallberg interprets this as him having a profound moral epiphany: 'The particularity of the revelation transforms Stuart's thought, opening the possibility that "there are signs everywhere, everything is a sign."'[91] In that very moment, the mouse 'becomes the sign that overturns his depression and starts a genuine reversal'.[92] 'This', Hallberg announces, 'is Stuart's particular emerging from the Cave (the Underground) to the sun.'[93]

In contrast to this interpretation, Bran Nicol sees Michael Meade's similar tendency in *The Bell* – to take random things as signs – as symptom and reinforcement of his self-enclosed, egocentric, personal fable.[94] For Nicol, this is an illustration of what Murdoch calls art's 'attempt to achieve omnipotence through personal fantasy'.[95] Contrary to Hallberg, it is for Nicol the meta-awareness of this magical thinking which is the moral of the story: 'because *The Bell* is a narrative itself, and not just about narrative, we do not simply "watch" Michael's narrativization of his life, but become aware that we are engaged in a similar activity'.[96] The message is here not 'notice particulars', but recognize 'how dangerously seductive it is'[97] to order them into a narrative of moral ascent.

The as if-character of literature gets in the way of the morality any reader might want to ascribe to it. A certain kind of irresponsible ambiguity differs mimetic art from rational deliberation, making it *interesting* but not unequivocally good. Arguing that novels like these are doing moral philosophy seems to me fraught, since their open-endedness makes their supposed philosophical work dependent on quite arbitrary and divergent interpretations. The genuinely good cannot be, and is probably not even supposed to be, distinguished from the apparently good in art. As Ted Cohen sums up the ancient quarrel in his chapter on morality in *The Oxford Handbook of Philosophy and Literature*:

> Plato's seeming objection to fiction is that it has nothing to do with knowledge, and thus Aristotle's reply includes the assertion that one can learn from such 'imitations'. The Platonic reply to this, surely, is that there is no guarantee that what may be 'learned' is the truth.[98]

Hämäläinen takes note of this open-endedness in her discussion of the relation between Murdoch's fiction and philosophical work:

> One obvious hazard when reading Murdoch's novels as moral philosophy is that their interpretive openness gives misleading clues for how to read her philosophical

work, leaving us with a muddled rather than clarified picture of what she meant to say in matters of moral philosophy.[99]

It might be more fruitful to take this disturbance as intentional instead of, as another scholar suggests, approaching her novelistic work as a 'fictional playing out of ideas'.[100] As Murdoch puts it herself: 'Literature is a vast scene of confusion, that is of freedom.'[101]

If we look back at Nussbaum's argument for the rich reality-rendering capacity of fiction, we find another involuntary contradiction, expressive of the difficulties involved in interpreting literature as moral philosophy. When she describes how the supposed finely aware and richly responsible moral attention that literature brings takes shape, Nussbaum provides us with directly conflicting metaphors. In her early essay on James, she quotes his metaphorical account of the achievements of fiction, in describing

> the moral contribution of works ... using that 'immense array of terms, perceptional and expressional, that ... in sentence, passage and page, simply looked over the heads of the standing terms-or perhaps rather, like alert winged creatures, perched on those diminished summits and aspired to a clearer air'.[102]

Here, the crisp clarity of a bird's-eye view seems like the epitome of loving attention. In her article on *The Black Prince*, however, Nussbaum criticizes how 'the artist's [Murdoch's] eye, like an eagle soaring above us, look down with something like disdain at the muddled animal interactions of human beings with one another'.[103] She suggests instead that loving vision must entail 'a willingness to be, for a time, an animal or even a plant, relinquishing the sharpness of creative alertness before the presence of a beloved body'.[104]

Literature is of course various and heterogeneous. And even if a coherent general account of its moral import is impossible to make, specific works could still affect our thinking and behaviour profoundly for the better. But if we *are* to make a general claim, and if all of these descriptions are to be applicable – if the love which is art can entail finding magical meaning in random particulars, making us uncomfortably aware of the seductions of finding such magical meaning, lifting off from our habitual discourse to fly in clearer air, and refuse to soar above but instead be suspended in plant-like inertia – the perception and imagination of literature is perhaps better accounted for as a dubious 'as if'. Plato was indeed in some ways right to be so suspicious of art. In order to understand how it might nonetheless offer us rare revelations of reality, we shall now look at a key term in Murdoch's aesthetics: attention.

6.2. Attention

6.2.1. 'Morality is ... not a matter of will.'

Murdoch's moral philosophy is formed as a critical response to the notion of an autonomous, wilful individual, who studies the facts and then makes a decisive choice.[105] In contrast to this, Murdoch suggests a more perception-based, imaginative, relational and consciousness-oriented account. 'Morality', she says, rephrasing Weil, is 'a matter of attention, not of will'.[106] That attention is a central concept in Murdoch's philosophy has hardly escaped anyone studying her work, neither has its Weilian roots.[107] Yet, I believe that some of the most important characteristics of this attention have gotten lost on the way, making it into scarcely more than a new face of the old will.

In this part, I shall seek to do justice to the erotic character of the Weilian-Murdochian attention by tracing it back to the Platonic myth of the origin of Eros, and instead of a voluntary effort describe it as consent to non-consent. In interpretations of Murdoch's aesthetics, attention is often thought to constitute the moral power of art. However, the origins and character of this attention are, I will argue, not unambiguously good. The experience of being 'gripped' by art, both as a client and as an inspired creator, will instead be shown to be foundational for its revelatory and/or deceptive force alike.

Taking the most central problem of morality to be something other than a question of will is, perhaps, so radical as to be almost unassimilable. Hence, in most interpretations of Murdoch's concept of attention, the volitional agent sneaks back in. 'Murdoch defines "attention" as the individual's inner moral effort involved in directing his or her view "outward, away from the self"', writes, for example, Tammy Grinshaw, making attention sound like nothing but a voluntarily directed effort.[108] Rob Hardy describes Murdoch's moral philosophy as 'a coolly rational approach (with no suggestion of working with the unconscious) involving "effort" and "attention"'.[109] To Frits Gåvertsson, attention in Murdoch is 'bringing emphasis to the need for constant revision of our understanding of the world in order for us to fully understand the other'.[110]

Elizabeth Dipple, while recognizing that 'even the greatest art spins from the dangerous unconscious', nonetheless presents the man behind the artwork as a fully self-aware, rational and almost omniscient agent:

> The serious artist nevertheless presents reality because he has soberly and truthfully looked for it through a full examination of the entire range of his materials – the detail of the natural and human world, the work of his fellow artists and the moral discipline required in turning his clear vision lovingly on both the divine and the necessary or random.[111]

Dipple also thinks that '[t]he just reader of Murdoch must ... acknowledge that his task is not simply to get through the pages in a state of greater or less pleasure ... but to *use* the book, to comprehend its intention which has to do with a serious transmission of knowledge and experience'.[112] The attention of both reader and writer sound almost completely like wilfully directed efforts.

In Silvia Panizza's doctoral dissertation *The Importance of Attention in Morality: An Exploration of Iris Murdoch's Philosophy*, a careful account is given of the role of emotions, desire, obedience and other-centeredness in attention. Yet, Panizza repeatedly struggles with locating a volitional agency in Murdoch's philosophy. She recognizes that attention is based on desire, but then shifts the question of agency into a volitional *control of* desire: 'Desire, for Murdoch, is what directs consciousness to particular objects, so it is first of all desire that needs to be controlled and directed properly'.[113] She interprets Weil's by saying that '[t]he only choice offered to man as an intelligent and free creature, is to desire obedience or not to desire it'[114] to mean that human beings 'can choose which way to turn their desires'.[115] Through this subtle rephrasing of an either-or into a freedom of choice, desire sounds like something subject to our will, rather than the other way around. Panizza concludes the chapter on the concept of attention by stating that Murdoch thinks that '[t]he subject is responsible for her "quality of consciousness" and can alter it by altering her desires and the objects of her thoughts'.[116]

Then, turning her focus briefly to literature, Panizza invokes Emma Bovary as 'an extreme example of the self-centred fantasy that is the opposite of attention', describing her as 'the epitome of the daydreamer, whose fantasies lead to destructive actions and a tragic end'.[117] In a footnote, Panizza claims that this is probably not caused by her voracious reading, and if it is, it is because the books were bad and the reader faulty:

> The negative influence of bad literature is not, I believe, the central question here. Emma does tend to read poor quality books (i.e. books that lack imagination and realism, aimed at satisfying specific desires in the readers, themselves lacking in the moral quality of attention to reality on the part of the authors), but even more important is the attitude of the reader, who only focuses on what gratifies her in the fiction and fails to learn what she could from it; the books are not read attentively but … they are themselves props for her fantasies.[118]

As several commentators on Flaubert have pointed out, the negative influence of novel-reading can indeed be said to be the central cause of Emma's demise, since she dies with a distinct and symbolic taste of ink in her mouth.[119] In any case, it is interesting to note that Panizza here contrasts reading and writing attentively with reading and writing rapturously and hungrily. Desire-driven writers and readers, like Emma, envelop themselves in their own fantasies, and fail to pay proper attention; that is, they fail to exercise the right volitional control of their own attractions.[120]

The problem of agency in a non-wilful notion of attention is of course a very complex one, and I shall not attempt to do it full justice here. My focus is on art and literature. Effort does have a place in Murdoch's moral philosophy, but I believe it has been over-emphasized at the cost of the erotic other-centeredness of attention, which has skewed the view of the moral power of art.

In 'Against Dryness', Murdoch describes a general Zeitgeist in which the self-image is that 'we are all rational and totally free', which 'engenders a dangerous lack of curiosity about the real world, a failure to appreciate the difficulties of knowing it'.[121] Difficulty is indeed the key word here, which she keeps hammering on:

> [W]hat we require is a renewed sense of the difficulty and complexity of the moral life and the opacity of persons. … Simone Weil said that morality was a matter of attention, not of will. We need a new vocabulary of attention.[122]

What kind of difficulty and opacity is this? How can the experience of attending to it be described? 'Through literature', Murdoch adds, 'we can re-discover a sense of the density of our lives.'¹²³ Literature is here not to be expected to provide us with any answers, but rather to remind us of how difficult this re-discovery is.¹²⁴ How is this supposed to be achieved, if not (as was suggested in the interpretations of Murdoch referred to above) through an effortful, careful, reflective revision of our perception? Is there perhaps instead a sense in which the enrapturing quality of art, the enjoyment and desire which eventually fill the mouth of Emma Bovary with a taste of ink, make up the very character of its revelatory capability?

6.2.2. Eros and his non-consensual origins

That attention is a fundamentally erotic concept for Murdoch is recognized by most, but this is often modified into taking Eros as a source of energy rather than as a name for attention as such. Panizza, for example, draws on Murdoch's adjectival phrasing 'loving attention' to claim that 'love is an element of attention, rather than another name for it'; it is 'a way of looking at things qualified by love'.¹²⁵

Kate Larson, on the other hand, in explaining the Platonic background to Murdoch's notion of a loving gaze, draws a parallel to a passage in the *Theaetetus* where '[t]he eye is filled with sight; at that moment it sees, and becomes not indeed sight, but a seeing eye'¹²⁶ and comments: 'The Greek term used for the meeting between the eye and its object is *homilia*, it could be translated as a meeting but has the more erotic connotation of intercourse, a mingling the fruit of which the particular object is.'¹²⁷ Lovemaking and seeing, penetration and perception, attention and desire, here become one and the same.

Weil unequivocally says, 'Attention is intimately related to desire – not to the will, but to desire.'¹²⁸ At the same time, '[a]ttention is an effort, the greatest of all efforts perhaps, but it is a negative effort'.¹²⁹ The negativity here indicates not just abstention but also loss of agency and overview. Like sight as intercourse in the Theaetetus, we give ourselves over to perception. 'It is a question, in fact, of losing perspective.'¹³⁰ Beauty is for Weil the paradigm case of attention, since it attracts us, and not the other way around. 'It *tears us away* from the point of view.'¹³¹ Enchanted, we stumble into something other than ourselves, submitting to it, soon to be lost:

> The beauty of the world is the mouth of a labyrinth. The unwary individual who on entering takes a few steps is soon unable to find the opening. Worn out, with nothing to eat or drink, in the dark, separated from his dear ones, and from everything he loves and is accustomed to, he walks on without knowing anything or hoping anything, incapable even of discovering whether he is really going forward or merely turning round on the same spot. ... [I]f he does not lose courage, if he goes on walking, it is absolutely certain that he will finally arrive at the center of the labyrinth. And there God is waiting to eat him.¹³²

Attention to beauty is here very far from being, or leading to, a clear-sighted, rational self-revision. However, also in Weil studies, explanations of the concept of attention tend to privilege metaphors of light over those of abduction and rape,¹³³ even though there is plenty of imagery in her work which illustrates the painful, humiliating muddle involved when the otherness of reality mingles with our sensibilities. 'Attention consists of suspending our thought, leaving it detached, empty, and ready to be penetrated by the object,' she writes.[134] Here, the agent's accomplishment of emptying her mind is often stressed by scholars, rather than the otherness of the object penetrating it. But this emptiness is less of a self-conscious detachment and more of an aching lack – Larson connects the word attention to the French *attendre*, to wait and long for – 'not seeking anything, but ready to receive in its naked truth the object that is to penetrate it'.[135]

Among Murdoch scholars, Larson dwells perhaps most successfully on the difficulty of describing the negative effort attention describes. She spells out the difference between will and desire:

> Will, considered as a motivational force, is connected to already decided objects of desire; they are desired because they are already known in their consequences. Desire in the erotic understanding of lack, reach[es] out to [objects] not already known but not even possible to [fathom] as being possessed; it is a desire transcending the desiring subject.[136]

Understanding attention as erotic lack makes the kind of effort involved into an exposure rather than a reaching out.[137] If we compare it to the quote by Henry James with which Nussbaum begins her ground-breaking essay of the literary turn, '[t]he effort really to see and really to represent is no idle business in face of the constant force that makes for muddlement',[138] we can now discern an important difference between this attention and the Weilian-Murdochian one. As Nussbaum continues: 'We live amid bewildering complexities. Obtuseness and refusal of vision are our besetting vices. Responsible lucidity can be wrested from that darkness only by painful vigilant effort, the intense scrutiny of particulars.'[139]

Rather than giving us a detailed overview of particulars, Murdochian attention is more akin to submitting to muddle; getting, as it were, sensuously closer to the world. In Larson's words: 'A meeting is what is about to occur, not a categorization.'[140] Falling in love is, as Larson also demonstrates, a prime case of this kind of attention, 'the capability to so lose and decentre oneself'.[141] It can be painful and difficult, but it is not really the product of a vigilant effort. Falling in love is involuntary, even if it can be affirmed and affected by choices. Thus, attention can be described as a kind of consent to non-consent, something which is also mirrored in the origin myth of Eros.

In Plato's *Symposium*, Eros is described as the illegitimate child of Poros (plenty, resourcefulness) and Penia (poverty, lack). At the party celebrating the birth of Aphrodite, Poros got drunk on nectar and fell asleep in the grass. Penia then raped him – or, as it is put in the dialogue, 'lay down beside him and became pregnant'.[142] Their son, Eros, is accordingly sprung out of non-consent. When Weil says that attention is related to desire, she adds in a parenthesis: 'Or more precisely to consent; it constitutes consent', she is describing a consent to something unwilled, which we cannot replace or change, only reject or embrace: attention is consent to non-consent. The very existence of desire cannot be freely chosen, nor can its direction or object, which it is bound up with.

6.2.3. Inspiration: The otherness within oneself

It follows from this that neither the consumption nor the production of art is an entirely wilful endeavour, since both are desire-driven. The unconscious aspect of desire hinders the good artist from being a moralistic teacher because he is driven by an otherness within himself.[143]

For Plato, beauty is the attractive quality of reality which, in stirring our desire for it, directs our attention out of ourselves. But there is also a multitude of false, apparent beauties, and our attraction to something is not in itself proof of the object's worthiness, nor is our desire any guarantee for a just discernment. Nonetheless, desire is something inside us reaching out to something outside of ourselves. This is the sense in which we must understand Murdoch's statement that art and morals become one in love: through the trickster Eros, who might as well make us blind and crazy as gentle and just. Murdoch brings up the *Phaedrus*, in which Plato says that the 'manic condition' of falling in love 'proves to be of all inspirations the best and of the best ancestry'.[144] The two contradictory speeches Socrates makes in this dialogue together describe Eros as a revelatory but irrational, corruptive and even half-mad kind of attention. In Murdoch's words:

> 'Falling in love', a violent process which Plato more than once vividly describes (love is abnegation, abjection, slavery) is for many people the most extraordinary and revealing experience of their lives, whereby the centre of significance is suddenly ripped out of the self, and the dreamy ego is shocked into awareness of an entirely separate reality.[145]

The shock is proof that we do not create the attractiveness of reality; it has agency over us. A careful revision of one's own perception of reality can perhaps be good, but the painful revelation of another being as the incarnated centre of one's world is certainly more powerful than any willed intention. An unwilled, half-mad sexual desire is always one ingredient of falling in love, the paradigm of paying attention.

The desire-based consent to non-consent of attention also describes the character of artistic inspiration. Larson takes note of Murdoch's occupation with the myth of Marsyas, a flute-playing satyr who challenged the god Apollo to a musical contest. Naturally, Marsyas was defeated, and the punishment for his arrogance was to be flayed alive. '"Why do you tear me out of myself", Marsyas, according to Ovid, cries in pain when he suffers his failure', Larson quotes.[146] In Murdoch's fiction, she argues, '[t]he "flaying" is a violent metaphor for the overturning and possibly transforming experience of the recognition of another centre of attention than the self.'[147] By following his artistic hubris and playing his flute, Marsyas is torn out of himself. Symptomatically, one might add, Socrates states in *The Republic* that he prefers Apollo and his lyre before Marsyas and his flute, the sound of which is way too mixed up and various.[148] Compared to the god, the mortal artist is uncontrolled, various and unstable. He is and becomes other to himself.

Plato is much worried by the fact that the poet does not know what he is doing and cannot explain or defend it. In the *Ion*, Socrates asks the rhapsode whether he is in his right mind, 'or outside yourself?', perhaps even in the grips of something divine.[149] As Murdoch comments, '[t]he genius of the poet is left unanalysed under the heading of madness, and the ambiguous equation "insanity – senseless intuition – divine insight" is left unresolved.'[150] Beauty (but not art, even though he, as Murdoch argues, leaves the door somewhat ajar there) is *anamnesis* for Plato, in Larson's words 'a short glimpse of something strange and other within ourselves',[151] and Murdoch wants to connect this to mimesis. 'Art is mimesis and good art is, to use another Platonic term, anamnesis, "memory" of what we did not know we knew.'[152]

We can here also recall Kant's notion of genius, the artist who gives the rules to art but 'does not know himself how the ideas for it come to him, and also does not have it in his power to think up such things at will or according to plan'.[153] Through an inborn otherness within himself, the genius becomes the vehicle for nature giving the rules to art, which thus becomes something more than simply mimetic (Kant sees the art of genius as 'entirely opposed to the spirit of imitation'[154]). The world speaks through an artist who cannot control his inspiration and does not really know what he is doing. And, as Murdoch comments, '[g]eniuses are not necessarily good'.[155] Weil too, even though she considered genius the only 'remedy of the immorality of letters', recognizes the existence of what she calls 'demonical genius'.[156]

In this kind of inspiration, these shocks of otherness, there is no way of deciding what is mad and what is divine. We would all, like Ion, prefer to be the latter. As Agathon is mocked in the *Symposium* for thinking that touching Socrates could be a shortcut to wisdom,[157] art can in Plato's and Murdoch's eyes be 'a sort of dangerous caricature of *anamnesis*'.[158] Art treats appearances as real, it plays with the fire and is fascinated by its whirling shadows.[159] But as such, Murdoch also claims, it can accidentally be one of the most illuminating things we have. How do these two things go together?

6.2.4. Necessary fiction: Fantasy or imagination

As was touched upon before, Murdoch sees image-making as an irreducible part of our perception of reality. The image-making activity, imagination, is what ultimately holds our experiences together. The foundational character of imaginative activity is examined from a wide range of perspectives in her magnum opus, *Metaphysics as a Guide to Morals*.

The first philosopher mentioned in this book is curiously seldom discussed by Murdoch scholars: David Hume. On the very first page, Murdoch notes that we all grasp ourselves as unities, oblivious of the philosophical problems of metaphysics, and then quotes Hume, who 'was prepared to say that some of our most cherished unities, the self, the material object, were illusions fostered by imagination, by association of ideas, by "habit and custom"'.[160] 'If a fiction is necessary enough', she adds, 'it is not a lie.'[161] This is a startling remark. It is also a very eccentric reversal of Hume's scepticism. Murdoch often returns to the piquant fact that Hume, even though he took the self to be a senseless bundle of sensations, professed to fall back upon his habitual associations as soon as he left his study,[162] and it is these unavoidable, provisional and imaginative unities for experiences she calls necessary. But if some fictions are truly necessary for holding our lives together, how can we distinguish those from our phantasmatic self-deceptions? Are they even that different in kind, or do the necessary and the frivolous blend in fiction?

Let us begin with clarifying what necessary may indicate here. In the chapter on imagination, Murdoch returns to Hume, explaining his view of imagination as the faculty which holds

> the transcendental function of providing those 'habits and customs without which human nature would perish and go to ruin'. Our objects, our casual links, our sense of space and time, all our apprehension of an objective world, are based upon strong (very strong) imaginative associations, which by operating upon somehow-given discrete data save us from chaos.[163]

In fact, the Humean phrase 'perish and go to ruin' reoccurs six times in *Metaphysics as a Guide to Morals*, suggesting that it has been a central brooding point for Murdoch in developing her moral philosophy. Picture and fiction-making, storytelling and imagination, are something we continuously rely on, not because they are true, but so as not to lose ourselves in chaos. Necessary means 'of necessity for sanity' here, not 'necessarily true'.

Necessary fictions are not lies. But if they are not strictly speaking true, either, but products of the imagination, how should we describe them? Even Plato 'speaks of a return to the cave', as Murdoch points out,[164] because the cave is where our life together is lived. Plato is to her the prime example of a philosopher dismayed by ordinary human consciousness, who was 'well aware of the lying fantasising tendency of the human mind and that it would be hard to exaggerate our capacity for egoistic fabrication. The mind is indeed besieged and crowded by selfish dream life.'[165] Egoistic fantasy is blocking us from living in the truth. But, Murdoch claims, 'Plato makes a place for "metaphorical moral thinking" when he says in the Cave myth that a higher moral level appear to us first, at our own lower level, as an image, reflection or shadow.'[166] These shadows of our imagination are not unconnected to the sun, and so the artist's playing with the fire could be brushing against and stirring up things both foundational and true.

The problem of distinguishing between good and bad imaginings is formed by Murdoch against the background of her reading of Weil. Imagination for Weil is almost equal to sin. It manufactures a substitute for us when we cannot put up with reality, and it is this very avoidance that sin consists of.[167] Larson points out that '[t]he first endnote in Iris Murdoch's copy of the English translation of Simone Weil's notebooks reads: "What of creative role of imagination?"'[168] Larson shows how this question to Weil forms the foundation of a distinction that has been much discussed in Murdoch studies, but perhaps more often taken as an explanation rather than an open-ended question: the distinction between imagination and fantasy.

In *Metaphysics as a Guide to Morals*, Murdoch states: '[W]e need, for purposes of discussion, two words for two concepts: a distinction between egoistic fantasy and liberated truth-seeking creative imagination.'[169] Immediately afterwards, she posits the alarming question: 'Can there not be high evil fantasising forms of creative imaginative activity?'[170] Fantasy, she explains, is something that 'somewhat mechanically [is] generating narrowly banal false pictures (the ego as all-powerful)', whereas imagination is 'freely and creatively exploring the world, moving toward the expression and elucidation (and in art celebration) of what is true and deep.'[171] However, this conceptual distinction does not make the difference in practice evident.

It is easy to assume when reading Murdoch that imagination is an effortful striving, working with a resistance. But it is not primarily a difference of effort, will, intention or even level of consciousness that she seeks to describe.[172] For example, she is contrasting the mechanical character of neurotic, erotic and vengeful fantasies with 'the amazing inventiveness of some sleeping dreams'.[173] 'Imagination', she writes, 'is an (inner) activity of the senses, a picturing and a grasping, a stirring of desire.'[174] It is sensuous and erotic, and thus has the same source as our self-enclosed fantasies. Murdoch notes that '[t]he role of "personal fantasy" in "high art" (for instance) is a subject which merits consideration.'[175] Unfortunately, she does not offer much consideration herself on this topic. 'The ego is passionate', she writes; 'yet without passion no high work.'[176] And Eros himself 'is a great artist, not a pure being.'[177] In an interview, she admits that 'creative imagination and obsessive fantasy may be very close almost indistinguishable forces in the mind of the writer"', adding that '[t]he serious writer must "play with fire"'.[178]

Hanna Marije Altorf, who explicates Murdoch's concept of imagination in her dissertation, claims that the main difference between imagination and fantasy resides in what might be called the continual revision of imagination. '[F]antasy stops at egoistic imagery and imagination constantly moves on', she writes, and it is precisely this progress that she understands to be moral in Murdoch's view.[179] Building on Altorf's account, we can say that imagination is not necessarily more willed than fantasy, rather more humble and dissatisfied with itself; frustrated by its own limitations. This echoes with Murdoch's view of the writer as being

> conscious of a tension between himself and something utterly other than himself, and he is also conscious of the obsessive, self-enclosing strength of his fantasy. Imagination, as opposed to fantasy, is the ability to see the other thing, what one might call, to use those old-fashioned words, nature, reality, the world.[180]

But what propels imagination to be dissatisfied with itself? What makes it want to seek out that which is utterly other? Here, the attention of art which is love might be understood in analogy to falling in love with a person. We can perhaps never draw any final lines between our romantic projections and a just perception of the beloved. But when we are in love, we are not satisfied with remaining within our own fantasies. However misguidedly and madly we seek to get closer to the other (e.g. as Bradley Pearson in Murdoch's *The Black Prince*), we want to *meet* her. This is another way of understanding the poet as a divine madman, who greets beauty with the mimetic impulse, where the attempt to imitate is driven by a feeling of the insufficiency of habitual imaginings, evoked by falling in love with the world. The necessity of a fiction is thus tested by desire.

Weil, who would never speak of necessary fictions, places necessity in sharp contrast to imagination. Necessity is a central concept for her and usually designates material reality, forces beyond our control, such as mortality and gravity. Beauty is to Weil the 'concordance between harmony and necessity'.[181] Seeking completion, we are tempted to create too harmonious a picture, which in Weil's eyes always becomes merely subjective and thus not truly beautiful. We cannot decide completely for ourselves what a great artwork should look like. 'The appropriateness corresponding to our desire', Weil writes in her *Notebooks*, 'is subjective unless necessity places an impassable barrier to our fixing that appropriateness ourselves.'[182] To Murdoch, desire is such an impassable barrier in itself because what we really desire is something other than ourselves, and so we are dissatisfied until this other thing is allowed to meet and enter us.[183]

Attention, understood as consent to non-consent, becomes the realization that the world is other than our habitual imaginings of it. It is *difficult* to remember this. We normally do not notice the otherness of the world unless we are terribly hurt or unless we are driven half-mad by desire, and then we usually try to wrap this shock into some narcissistic purposive fantasy. In Murdoch's words: 'We fear plurality, diffusion, senseless accident, chaos, we want to transform what we cannot dominate or understand into something reassuring and familiar, into ordinary being, into history, art, science.'[184] These reassuring and familiar unities may also be understood as stories. 'The story is a way of thinking, it is a fundamental mode of consciousness, or self-being.'[185] Without these 'fictions', we would perish and go to ruin, and good imaginings differ from bad in that they are frustrated by their own insufficiencies: they are open and incomplete.

So, when Nussbaum speaks of wrestling 'responsible lucidity' from darkness by 'painful vigilant effort, the intense scrutiny of particulars',[186] Murdoch in contrast argues for a part surrender to what we cannot make sense of, which also entails a part surrender to our inability to resist turning this overwhelming chaos of particulars into stories. Art can approximate reality precisely because we do not live by truth alone. We *need* fiction, and so it is not simply lies, if still our own moving fabrications. The activity of imagination is never completed, nor ever finally separated from fantasy.

Art stays with appearances and threatens philosophy because it reminds us that we must live by appearances. As such, it can make us too content with the fictions that sustain us and protect us from suffering, from perishing, from going mad.[187] It can make frivolous and distortive fictions appear necessary. The imagination answers simultaneously to our real need for fabricated unities and our base wishes to avoid a senseless or painful reality. In other words, what is illuminated by the myth of the ascent to the sun is perhaps primarily that our lives take place within the cave. The fire in the middle between the prisoners and the sun symbolizes for Murdoch the source of the fictions we live by. Playing with the fire is, in a way, becoming aware of the necessity as well as the arbitrariness of fantasies. But to the extent that this play can be edifying it is also always potentially corruptive.

6.3. Accidentally educational

6.3.1. Contingency

'It is of course a fact that if art is love then art improves us morally', Murdoch writes, 'but this is, as it were, accidental.'[188] It is immediately apparent that the use of the word 'accidental' here contradicts many of the interpretations of Murdoch's view of the morality of literature that were quoted before.[189] For example, Dipple's claim that '[t]he serious artist ... presents reality because he has soberly and truthfully looked for it through a full examination of the entire range of his materials'[190] suggests an almost omniscient and conscientious craftsman, well aware of what he is doing and why. Dipple also, among others, argues that the reader must make a conscious effort to learn from what she is reading. In those accounts, there is nothing accidental about how literature improves us morally, neither in writing nor reading.

The role of accident, chance and contingency in Murdoch's philosophy is, again, a distinctly Weilian legacy. Everything in this world is subject to chance, according to Weil.[191] When Murdoch is setting out to formulate her aesthetic theory, the inability to tolerate contingency is one of her prime accusations against earlier thinkers: 'Kant is afraid of the particular, he is afraid of history' and he 'shares this fear with Plato, ... [whose] mistrust of art was a mistrust of something which was hopelessly concerned with the senses, with the particular.'[192] The particular in conjunction with history is how Murdoch understands contingency: as the accidental happenings and impressions that cannot be sorted into a coherent, primary order. There is also a Sartrean inheritance here: an understanding of existence as fundamentally contingent, in the sense that what exists need not exist, and does not have a stable metaphysical foundation.

Literature, especially the novel, is in this sense for Murdoch the epitomal art form, being a vast scene of confusion and particularities. 'The great novelist', she states, 'is not afraid of the contingent.'[193] This brings out an inherent tension in her view of literature, noted by several scholars. David Gordon writes, for example:

> There is evidently a logical complication here since the novel as well as the drama is an artifice and at best only an imitation of the heterogeneity and randomness of life itself. It may be a looser form but it cannot lack form and can only imitate randomness. The complication is epitomized in that Sartrean word contingency, dear to Murdoch from the beginning of her career and the most difficult concept in her work.[194]

The same problem is troubling Bran Nicol, who attacks the concept of contingency in Murdoch's work as a fetish supposed to maintain the distinction between philosophy and literature. He claims that 'the libidinal energy of Murdoch's fiction comes from the currency of ideas circulating within.'[195] Following this, it is not difficult to see how he might conclude:

> [T]he contingent in her work is essentially an idea about contingency. Although she refers continuously to the value of the particular, a representation of it is in fact

very difficult to find in her writing (though of course this is not exactly a failure on her part, given the nature of fiction). What we have instead is a simulacrum of the contingent, made possible by Murdoch's philosophical supplement. Her fascination with the contingent is a fantasy of, rather than a nostalgia for, the particular.[196]

Nicol is not content with an experiential illusion of contingency. What, exactly, a direct representation of contingency or particularity might look like is indeed a difficult philosophical problem. But art need not give us anything more than simulacrum and imaginations – it may still be *concerned* with the senses, the particular and the contingent. The Sartrean link pointed out by Gordon is a key here. What does Murdoch make of his artistic depiction of contingency?

As was discussed in the second chapter, Murdoch describes the central focus of Sartre's novel *La Nausée* as 'a certain discovery, of metaphysical interest': 'that the world is contingent, and that we are related to it discursively and not intuitively'.[197] The lack of purpose of the Sartrean contingency is, I argued, by Murdoch both regarded as pleasing (through the beauty of the prose composition which gives a sense of purposiveness without a purpose) and unpleasurable (in that it invokes the sublime terror of what imagination cannot hold together). The senselessness of Roquentin's perceptions is presented within an illusion of sense. Literature is thus not to be expected to be a straightforward *representation* of contingency. Rather, it can (as in the case of Sartre's novel) challenge, transmit and transform our *experiences* and *imaginings* of it, in an interplay of pleasure and displeasure.[198]

Another discussion of the role of contingency in Murdoch's fiction and philosophy can be found in Julia Jordan's dissertation *Chance and the Modern British Novel*. Rather than looking for straight-forward representations of contingency, Jordan finds the concept charged with an extraordinary ambiguity in Murdoch's oeuvre. Contingency, Jordan argues, is by Murdoch seen as both horrible and good: 'our confrontation of the contingent nature of things generates an element of genuine fear, an heir of the existential horror which is seen as a natural reaction to chance's power to subvert and render meaningless the belief that there exists value and purpose in the universe'.[199] Since contingency is an experience of reality, and goodness is perception of reality, purpose and value are put into opposition to the good. 'Goodness, she [Murdoch] contends, gives up the search for meaning; it coexists with meaninglessness, is illusionless, and thus brave.'[200] But again, the difficulty to comprehend 'that life is contingent, messy, unpredictable' is according to Jordan considered by Murdoch to be 'antithetical to the artistic impulse – the temptation to create form, narrative, myth, story'.[201]

So, it appears that Murdoch at the same time thinks that literature should be the prime scene for contingency, but mistrusts the artistic impulse as antithetical to this purpose. How do these two things go together? Through this central paradox, we begin to glimpse the extreme difficulties involved in the loving feat of imagination proper to great art.

6.3.2. Reinterpreting the Kantian sublime

Murdoch's understanding of the artistic impulse to console oneself by imposing form on the formless was described in the previous chapter as a Kantian legacy.[202] But something that clearly separates Murdoch from Kant is her view of the erotic character of aesthetic attention. This is also intimately bound up with the problem of contingency and form, as her accusation that 'Kant is afraid of the particular, he is afraid of history'[203] is connected with her later statement that 'Plato's fear of art, and theirs [Tolstoy's and Kant's] too, is to some extent a fear of pleasure.'[204] Fearing desire, enjoyment, contingency and chance is for Murdoch tantamount to fearing human relationship, especially erotic ones. Throughout her fiction, Murdoch displays a never-ceasing fascination with the fact that almost anyone seems capable of suddenly falling in love with almost anyone else. Never are we as completely enthralled by something contingent, and never are we as tempted to escape from it into the wish-fulfilments of fantasy.

As has been discussed before, Murdoch does not reinterpret Kant as much as she thinks when she reads together the beautiful and the sublime.[205] Nor does her view diverge much in relation to the disinterested pleasure Kant describes as proper to the aesthetic judgement. Disinterested for Kant does not mean devoid of feeling. Rather, it means contemplating something in its unique existence without intending to change or use it: without imagining an end for it or thinking that it can be reproduced.[206] One aspect of Murdoch's notion of art as love can frictionlessly be aligned with Kant here: to let the loved one be. But where Murdoch clearly deviates from Kant is in her understanding of the aesthetic feelings of pleasure and displeasure as also deeply related to desire. This is most clearly shown in her reinterpretation of the Kantian sublime.

The sublime is in Murdoch's interpretation 'an experience of formlessness and limitlessness, combined with a thought of, or desire for, limit (conceptualisation)'; it is 'a (thrilling, frightening) apprehension of reason confronting contingency, devoid of the mediating, shaping, soothing power of the object-making imagination'.[207] This is still more or less in line with Kant. However, the prime example of the sublime is for Murdoch the endless contingent particularity of other individuals. It is thus, as Altorf points out, for her a much more ordinary occurrence of the failure of imagination than Kant's rare thrill in the alps:

> The experience of the sublime, and of the limitations of imagination is then for Murdoch what can accompany perceiving other people. In perceiving other people one can experience the failure of imagination to encompass this individual. The individual transcends any image formed by the imagination. What for Kant is an exceptional experience, for Murdoch becomes an important element in her moral philosophy, encountered in the perception of other people. Moreover, this experience of the failure of the imagination is for Murdoch not redeemed by any hope for grasping the whole.[208]

In our ongoing interactions with the irreducible particularity of the world and other people, we rely on our necessary fictions without which we would perish and go to ruin. But we also long to perceive more than these well-rounded images. Even if we strive to really see and really represent, the difference between imagination and fantasy is not a matter of effort as much as the love in which *imagination experiences itself as insufficient*. In Altorf's words, '[i]t is while imagining ... that one finds the reality which is not completely imagined'.[209] The accidental morality of art is bound up with this failure, rather than a success of seeing and representing; with the strain of artifice and impossibility which characterizes the pictorial placeholder for a totalizing grasp.

It is the same as if-character of art that made Plato so suspicious which allows us a way of staying with and cherishing images of reality *as images*. Thus, the loving attention of art can be understood as a kind of celebratory failure of the imagination. This ambiguous thrill is what the merging of the beautiful with the sublime eventually entails for Murdoch. Desire, in its painful restless longing for the other and its pleasure-seeking want for completion, is central here. Indeed, Murdoch even says that 'if we consider what may be actual occasions of sublime feelings, these feelings are not at all easy to interpret, and we may suspect them to have to do, in their real complexity, not only with morals but also with sex'.[210]

6.3.3. Sublime sublimation

An exciting mix of frustration and pleasure characterizes our enjoyment of art. What Murdoch takes issue with in Freud is not his view of artistic endeavour as driven by covert sexual desire, but that his understanding of sex is too simplistic and deterministic. It is not a masked drive to procreate, but an all-pervasive Eros she has in mind.[211] '"[E]xplanation by sex" tends to have for us a kind of intuitive obviousness, as if we perfectly knew what sex was.'[212] Instead, Murdoch sees sex as 'fundamentally jumble; not even roulette as much as mishmash'.[213] Following this definition of sex as 'jumble', she states that art is not discredited if we recognize that it is based on this confusing mishmash. 'Great art, especially literature, ... carries a built-in self-critical recognition of its incompleteness. It accepts and celebrates jumble, and the bafflement of the mind by the world. The incomplete pseudo-object, the work of art, is a lucid commentary upon itself.'[214] In other words, artistic attention is a self-aware erotic bafflement. In what follows, I shall define this bafflement as a *sublime sublimation*.

As Freud describes sublimation in *Civilisation and Its Discontents*, the instinctual aims are shifted so that 'satisfaction is obtained from illusions, which are recognized as such without the discrepancy between them and reality being allowed to interfere with enjoyment', and '[a]t the head of these satisfactions through phantasy stands the enjoyment of works of art'.[215] Murdoch's view of art is concordant with this. She appreciatively cites Freud's description of art's illusory 'omnipotence of thought'[216] and concludes somewhat hesitantly: 'It begins to look as if, where the art object is a mechanical stimulus to personal fantasy, pornography is the end point. All art aspires to the condition of pornography? It may be true at least that more does than meets the eye.'[217]

But what Freud describes for art in general cannot be reconciled completely with Murdoch's view of great art. Sublimation must be combined with something that is not simply an illusory satisfaction: a kind of unwilled (self-)awareness. In great art, sublimity and sublimation coincide. Sublimation is for Freud a case of sexual fantasies transformed into decently enjoyable artworks, whereas the sublime, in Kant's words, is 'as it were doing violence to our imagination'; it is a 'bewilderment or sort of embarrassment' which makes us feel the inadequacy of our imagination and thus attempt to extend it to the point until it 'sinks back into itself, but is thereby transported into an emotionally moving satisfaction'.[218]

Sublime sublimation would then describe the oscillating excitement when satisfaction is obtained from what we know to be illusions, while at the same time making us feel the inadequacy of our imagination, and then transporting us back into an emotionally moving satisfaction. To put it briefly, great art presents us with imagination's delight in its own defeat. There is a fundamentally deceptive character to this accomplishment: '[w]e intuit in art a unity, a perfection, which is not really there'.[219] This makes Murdoch ask herself:

> Is the work of art a kind of hoax, something which seems complete but is really incomplete, completed secretly by the private unacknowledged fantasies of the artist and his conniving client? A consideration of this question can also throw light on the nature of virtue, so that art can turn out to be an image of good, though in a sense different from that which might at first occur to one.[220]

What is the sense that might at first occur to one? Here, we may remember Murdoch's much-quoted earlier attempt to read together art and love, when she stated that art and morals 'is the discovery of reality' through 'the extremely difficult realization that something other than oneself is real'.[221] In *Metaphysics as a Guide to Morals*, the difficulty involved may no longer be interpreted as simply dropping one's egoism and looking to others. It is precisely as a false unity, as 'the product of a mortal man who cannot entirely dominate his subject matter and remove or transform contingent rubble and unclarified personal emotions and attitudes',[222] that art becomes illuminating. It is only 'as if' it shows us the world; and at the same time, it shows us the fundamental character of this as if, the very picture-making activity we live by, in all its insufficiency.

'The art object as false unity is an image of the self', says Murdoch.[223] It is thus not entirely correct to say, as for example Panizza does, that Murdoch has a more benevolent attitude to the self than Weil has.[224] She explicitly considers it a false unity. The difference might be better stated in the words of Gabriele Griffin: 'Where Weil wanted to experience the reality of God Murdoch wants the reality of this world to be accurately perceived. Both demand an internal process of self-negation.'[225] Murdoch is just as harsh as Weil in judging our comfy illusion-making egos. But seeking the reality of the world, and not its transcendent other through it, she is much more interested in the *stuff* of this illusion-making than Weil, and art is the dubious mirror of this:

> [G]ood art mirrors not only the (illusory) unity of the self but its real disunity. The pseudo-object need not mislead: though in a sense it proclaims its incompleteness and points away. Good art accepts and celebrates and meditates upon the defeat

of the discursive intellect by the world. Bad art misrepresents the world so as to pretend there is no defeat.[226]

In bad art, there is sublimation without sublimity: imagination is never exposed to its own limitations. In great art, success and failure are intertwined, since the art object is always a kind of hoax, just like the self is a loose and contingent fabric of superfluous and necessary fictions. Thus, it sometimes becomes an 'intense showing' which can illuminate 'accident and contingency and the general muddle of life, the limitations of time and the discursive intellect, so as to enable us to survey complex or horrible things which would otherwise appal us'.[227] Driven by desire, art delights in illusions and makes us frustrated with them as illusions at the same time. Great art, at least, can make us feel the sublime edges of our imagination in the very sublimated fantasies it offers. A clear-headed purposive and effortful strive to represent reality would never have the same immersive and baffling effect. To put it differently, art will fail to teach us anything about the shadows if it does not play with the fire.

6.3.4. 'On se tue pour des mensonges'

How do these flickers of shadows become accidentally illuminating? Murdoch gives a good example of what it may look like when imagination rubs up against its own boundaries in her discussion of Proust in *Metaphysics as a Guide to Morals*. The narrator of *À la recherche du temps perdu* has random experiences charged with mysterious meaning. He stumbles over some cobble stones, and suddenly experiences a jolt of unclear values, a surge of magical presence, which unfolds as an involuntary memory. By struggling to stay with these jolts, and working them out into a novel, the narrator gives his memories a form that simultaneously affirms their ephemeral character and sustains them. Murdoch uses the flash-like illuminations of Proust to emphasize the distinction between the loving attention of art and moral philosophy:

> Proust's examples concern and illustrate a particular way in which reality is suddenly apprehended in the midst of illusion, an experienced contrast of dead impure time with live pure time, serial time with lived time, which may lead toward a recovery or 'redemption' of life through art. ... [This can be seen as] Simone Weil's perception without reverie, but it is also unlike. Proust's essential illuminations are involuntary, gifts from the gods, not experiences or states which could be attained or prolonged by a (morally, spiritually) disciplined way of living. Proust is here celebrating, as capable of a truthful 'recovery' or vision of his own life, the artist in the ordinary sense (an exceptional person) not in the 'we are all artists' sense. ... But the narrator's final revelation is not ... a general guide or pointer to a good or spiritual way of life .... We have here to be our own moralists if we want to use Proust's states of pure consciousness as part of a moral, or moral philosophical, argument.[228]

Literature does not improve us morally, nor does it help us understand morality in any philosophical fashion. If moral improvement was our goal, 'we ought to be out helping our neighbour rather than reading Proust or Tolstoy'.[229] Neither does *La Recherche* provide us with an illustration of what a good life would be like. Illuminated from within by the Proustian jolts is a life where we live in illusions to the point of being ready to die for them, *on se tue pour des mensonges*. In writing, Proust says, one attempts to be truthful,

> Mais tant qu'il ne s'agit que de la vie, on se ruine, on se rend malade, on se tue pour des mensonges. Il est vrai que c'est de la gangue de ces mensonges-là que … on peut seulement extraire un peu de vérité.[230]

> But when it is only a question of our own lives, we ruin ourselves, make ourselves ill, kill ourselves for the sake of lies. Of a truth, it is only out of the matrix of those lies … that we can extract a little truth.[231]

It is the trivial illusions and suffering-induced lies that we live by, and the artist cannot look for truth outside of them. A novelist must be occupied with these lies and take them as seriously as his characters do: that is, pay little attention to their untruthfulness, and stay with our affective investment in these semblances.

Plato's harshest dismissal of art departs, Murdoch suggests, from an unwillingness to accept human life as it is. Plato 'never thought that we were μεγα τι [*mega ti*], anything much.'[232] We are base creatures, playthings of the gods, ruled by necessary passions. '*The Republic* seems to assume a world where what is really real is harmonious, and we can reasonably attempt to know ourselves and the world.'[233] Contrastingly, in *The Laws* and *The Timaeus*, this view 'gives way to a more realistic picture of the mind confronting a confused world'.[234] This is akin to her own understanding. In Jordan's words: 'Murdoch believes that mess and muddle is the natural state of the universe when it is perceived by a good, ego-less consciousness that does not seek to distort what it perceives'[235] – although what the artist who does not seek to distort perceives is also the dubious, egocentric, internal mess and muddle of his own consciousness.

It is by staying with this irreducible contingency that art can be seen as educational. This does not just describe the representational content of art, but also the ambiguity of its medium. 'Art is far and away the most educational thing we have', Murdoch even claims, 'far more so than its rivals, philosophy and theology and science. The pierced nature of the work of art, its limitless connection with ordinary life, even its defencelessness against its client, are part of its characteristic availability and freedom.'[236] As unstable, fraudulent and vulnerable, the artwork is educational because, in Stanley Rosen's paraphrase of Plato, 'human life plainly belongs to those things that have come to be, are coming to be, and will come to be, that is, to the continuously changing or perishing, about which precise knowledge is impossible'.[237]

In Plato's republic, Rosen says, 'the poets become superfluous, not because they do not understand the soul at all but because they are skilled at eliciting the heterogeneity of human nature', and capable of creating 'a much more accurate imitation of actual life than … philosophy'.[238] It is precisely this similarity to life which makes art so dubious to the philosopher king of Socrates's ideal city, who 'wishes to restrict the heterogeneity and plasticity of human nature, not to celebrate or portray it'.[239]

6.3.5. The pointlessness of virtue and art

We may now be better equipped to understand the deep connection Murdoch sees between morality and art, while remaining adamant that we should not be confusing art (or more specifically literature) with philosophy. The mimetic arts, she writes,

> especially literature and painting, show us the peculiar sense in which the concept of virtue is tied on to the human condition. They show us the absolute pointlessness of virtue while exhibiting its supreme importance; the enjoyment of art is a training in the love of virtue. The pointlessness of art is not the pointlessness of a game; it is the pointlessness of human life itself, and form in art is properly the simulation of the self-contained aimlessness of the universe. Good art reveals what we are usually too selfish and too timid to recognise, the minute and absolutely random detail of the world, and reveals it together with a sense of unity and form.[240]

In this quote, we find Murdoch's moral aesthetics in a nutshell. It betrays a distinctly Weilian heritage. As Weil states, 'All human creations are adjustments of means in view of determinate ends, except the work of art, in which there is adjustment of means, where obviously there is completion, but where one cannot conceive of an end.'[241] There is no 'point' of art. Artworks do not explain, argue or transform the world: they simulate a self-contained aimlessness.

Absence of point, aim or end is not the same as a lack of meaning. Weil continues: 'In a sense the end is nothing but the very arrangement, the assembling itself of the means employed; in another sense the end is completely transcendent.'[242] For Murdoch, the ultimate meaning of art is not the divine revelation it is for Weil, even if it is still a revelation of sorts. But we must tread carefully here. Although great art 'is the most educational of all human activities and a place in which the nature of morality can be *seen*',[243] it does not impart any necessary or useful knowledge. Even great art is 'an extra', it must 'in a sense be detached from good because art is not essential'.[244] Helping our neighbour is better than reading Proust. But Proust may be uniquely revelatory in another sense: his prose simulates the pointlessness of life, while at the same time inducing us to love it.

Murdoch's view of art entails a paradoxical moralism, in that it makes instrumentality inimical to it. Art's 'for nothing' character is precisely what makes it capable of being 'for life'.[245] Through its freedom to be completely insubstantial, useless, uninformative, unproductive and deeply morally ambiguous, art 'invigorates us by a juxtaposition, almost an identification, of pointlessness and value'.[246] Thus, great art can make it possible to enjoy and celebrate what Kant and Plato both feared so much, the endlessly particular unfair chaos of existence.

It is indeed in contrast to Kant, who saw beauty as a symbol for morality in its lawful harmony with the understanding, that Murdoch stresses the contingency and pointlessness of art. The aesthetic and the ethical points about pointlessness are inseparable here. Murdoch's secular concept of virtue consists in a love of good without the notion of a God; without any final harmony. For Kant, the postulate of God is necessary, since it makes it imaginable for us that the good and our happiness eventually shall coincide. There is a point to it all: the good we do eventually results in an eternal happiness. This is, according to him, what makes morality possible.

In an aside in the third Critique, Kant provides us with a (for him) unusually vivid description of a man who takes himself 'to be firmly convinced that there is no God'.[247] This man would, in Kant's opinion, probably have to give up morality as impossible because

> his effort is limited; and from nature he can, to be sure, expect some contingent assistance here and there, but never a lawlike agreement in accordance with constant rules .... Deceit, violence, and envy will always surround him, even though he is himself honest, peaceable, and benevolent; and the righteous ones besides himself that he will still encounter will, in spite of all their worthiness to be happy, nevertheless be subject by nature, which pays no attention to that, to all the evils of poverty, illnesses, and untimely death, just like all the other animals on earth, and will always remain thus until one wide grave engulfs them all together (whether honest or dishonest, it makes no difference here) and flings them, who were capable of having believed themselves to be the final end of creation, back into the abyss of the purposeless chaos of matter from which they were drawn.[248]

When Murdoch questions the Kantian notion of beauty as harmonious and lawful, she accuses him of being afraid of contingency, chaos and tragedy. This is an aesthetic and a moral argument in one. Art, in Murdoch's view, can be truthful precisely because it does not provide ethical manuals, but rather shows us how heroes die, conmen triumph and empty appearances suffice to please. Furthermore, art is to her the ontological proof that it is nonetheless 'worth it'. It is in this sense she suggests that '[p]erhaps in general art *proves* more than philosophy can'.[249]

Verging on the edge of not just immorality, but amorality, art is celebrating the very stuff which makes us want to pronounce the good to be an illusion. Socrates wants to ban the poets from telling us about things like the senseless sufferings of men because such sayings 'are neither holy, nor advantageous for us, nor in harmony with one another'.[250] That is only logical if one demands literature to be moral in any instrumental sense; that is, change us or the world. The loving attention which is art is uncomfortably tolerant. Murdoch speaks of 'the almost insuperable difficulty of looking properly at evil and human suffering ... without falsifying the picture in some ways while making it bearable. ... Only the very greatest art can manage it, and that is the only public evidence that it can be done at all.'[251]

On the same page, however, she admits that of course one is 'afraid that the attempt to be good might turn out to be meaningless, or at best something vague and not very important, or turn out to be as Nietzsche described it, or that the greatness of great art might be an ephemeral illusion.'[252] Here, meaninglessness is looming. If art is a proof, it is not a very stable one: it cannot go beyond the 'as if'. 'Looking properly' means nothing more than this. Yet, art can make us feel like there is something more, some meaning to the pointless, and this experience, 'if it is not to be corrupted by some sort of quasi-theological finality, must remain a very tiny spark of insight .... But it seems to me that the spark is real, and that great art is evidence of its reality.'[253]

The semblance of 'as if there is something more' is obvious in great art but impossible to pin down. The hoax is never transformed into understanding. If we seek to magnify this tiny spark, we might say that it is the appreciation which separates art from pornography. Art entertains and pleases us, but when art is great there is also something about it that we admire and love. The core of that something evades our understanding, since it lacks a discernible point. As Plato demonstrates, it is thus extremely easy to question the importance and truth value and goodness of art. Art must remain vulnerable to those objections. In Adorno's words:

> There is no answer that would convince someone who would ask such questions as 'Why imitate something?' or 'Why tell a story as if it were true when obviously the facts are otherwise and it just distorts reality?' Artworks fall helplessly mute before the question 'What's it for?' and before the reproach that they are actually pointless.[254]

This muteness is part of the specific eloquence of art. It does not elucidate like philosophy. For Adorno, this makes art into a rare site of political resistance. 'Art is pre-emptively mediated by its as if-character', Adorno writes. 'If it were completely intuitable, it would become part of the empirical world that it resists.'[255]

In a kindred anti-instrumental spirit, Murdoch describes the moral freedom and force of art. By virtue of its pointlessness, art can immerse us in our own mixed-up nature. Temptations, untruth, illusions and confusion are the stuff art consists of and invites us to enjoy. The murkiness of the interest involved is part of art's rare revelatory quality, in that it refuses us the distance of a dispassionate observer and thus never claims to show a clarified or unmediated image of the world.

In Platonic terms, art can be described as a double-edged *pharmakon*, a drug or a remedy.[256] If it is a cure, it is also an intoxication. Like the sophist, Murdoch notes, the artist 'glories in image-making without knowledge, and, living in a world of fictions, blurs the distinction between true and false'.[257] But, as she also points out, the artist is ranked slightly higher than the sophist precisely because he might be expected to admit that he does not really know what he is talking about. Art and love are alike in this. Elsewhere, Murdoch notes that it is interesting that Diotima in the *Symposium* describes Eros as a *pharmakeus* ('spiritual chemist') as well as a sophist.[258] 'Eros is a great artist', she adds, 'not a pure being.'[259]

Rosen suggests that the Platonic remedy to the immorality of mimesis consists of understanding what mimesis is. Art is after all allowed a place in Socrates's ideal state: in the hands of the guardians, that is, people who know what they are doing with it: 'all types of mimesis ... are an outrage or destruction of the discursive intellect of those who listen to them ..., if they do not possess the remedy (*pharmakon*): namely, knowledge of what mimetic art actually is.'[260] Philosophically, art should be put in its place. Knowing that art is, in Murdoch's words, 'a shameless collaborator',[261] that it 'accepts and enjoys the ambiguity of the whole man, and [that] great artists can seem to "use" their own vices for creative purposes without apparent damage to their art',[262] we are better equipped to recognize its rare revelatory power. But the drug must remain ambiguous. Art cannot be instrumentalized and still be great. The true genius is like a divine madman who does not know and cannot explain what he is doing. Indeed, if the guardians were purposively employing mimesis, they would only be acting like sophists (and probably also make mediocre art). It would be as meaningless as an instrumentally conceived love.

In Murdoch's view, art holds a unique moral potential, which is completely dependent on its most probable immorality. If we know the place of art, we also know that what art does is *not* knowing. It is – with an ineradicable 'as if' – showing. As she says towards the end of *The Fire and the Sun*:

> Art as the great general universal informant is an obvious rival, not necessarily a hostile one, to philosophy and indeed to science, and Plato never did justice to the unique truth-conveying capacities of art. ... The spiritual ambiguity of art, its connection with the 'limitless' unconscious, its use of irony, its interest in evil, worried Plato. But the very ambiguity and voracious ubiquitousness of art is its characteristic freedom.[263]

The revelatory power masterpieces sometimes possess can make us tempted to treat them as tools for betterment or understanding, or even declare them to be works of moral philosophy in their own right. I believe that Murdoch had good reasons for advising against that. The truth that art presents us with is at best a spark, and at worst a complete deception. It mirrors virtue in its pointlessness and is therefore always on the verge of frivolity. There is no way of counterproving its claims, since art's way of being right consists in playing with all of the ways in which we often are wrong. As such, it can at times make us see the paradoxical good in the existence of ourselves and the world, however unjust, meaningless and wicked we and it may be.

For better or worse, art is playing with fire, that is, the muddled human psyche. 'A recognition of its power may be a step towards escape from the cave; but it may equally be taken as an end-point. The fire may be taken for the sun, and self-scrutiny taken for goodness.'[264]

Concluding remarks

1. Summary

Why is literature not philosophy? Any philosophical attempt to answer this question must, somehow, provide a definition of what literature is and does. But as Murdoch says, literature 'does many things'.[1] She repeatedly stresses that we 'have so many kinds of relation to a work of art. A literary work is an extremely heterogeneous object which demands an open-minded heterogeneous response.'[2]

This book has sought to describe only some of these heterogeneous aspects: those that seemed to me most prominent in regards of what makes literature distinct from philosophy. On no account should my explications be taken as complete, definitive or absolute. An exhaustive definition of what literature is and does would luckily be impossible to make. Instead, I have been speaking in general terms about the distinction between two long-standing, various, shifting and permeable disciplines. I have sought to describe more carefully some of the characteristics that I with Murdoch take to be specific for literature, the art form which uses words. This has entailed discussing art generally, as well as dwelling on some aspects of literature that are specific to certain genres. Everything said in this book is not applicable to all literary works, but most may nonetheless be applicable to many.

A condensed summary of my description of literature as distinct from philosophy could sound like this.

Literature presents a sensory illusion of sense. This is not best understood as a form of indirect communication, but as a form of sense-making that is reflective rather than determining. That means that it is the semblance of a whole, rather than a determinate concept, which provides a unity of the manifold for our impressions in art. Literature may still at times make a common case with philosophy, but the aesthetic mode of presentation brings a certain vagueness which makes the discursive functionality of philosophy-as-fiction rather limited. Even when literature seemingly is 'about' philosophy, it might be more occupied with enchanting, sensuous illusions than sensemaking.

The aesthetic judgement is non-conceptual. So how are we to understand literature, an art which obviously makes use of concepts? As an art, literature is more concerned with conveying a feeling of a state of mind, than to make determinate judgements. Conceptual understanding may, in various ways, play into our experiences of art, but it does not constitute their aesthetic character. The way concepts work in literature is better understood with the notion of aesthetic ideas, which boundlessly enlarge the imagination in relation to a given concept, such as hell or eternity, rather than bringing determinate conceptual understanding.

Another central aspect of much literary writing is its fictionality. Even though the epistemology of fiction has been very discussed, fictionality might not be best understood as a problem of knowledge. Rather, fiction brings an important challenge to the entire epistemological approach, since we engage with it without asking what is real or not. We suspend our disbelief, which gives a heightened immersion into the real and the phantasmatic alike. But relating to fictional characters is different from reacting to the presence of actual people. Since we cannot in any way interact with the characters, we can indulge in feelings and attitudes towards and with them that we would normally censor from interpersonal relations. Although this can make fiction deeply meaningful to us, it also makes it difficult to use fiction as philosophy; especially if one looks to it as expressive of fundamental human concerns, since the conditions for interpersonal relations are severely altered in fiction.

Tragedy, a genre of fiction, has been given a prominent role in many attempts to question the divide between literature and philosophy. How this highly ordered form of drama can be expressive of real miseries, or some essentially tragic aspect of the human condition, is, however, far from evident. The genre creates an artificial form for rather than presents us with suffering and death. As art, it gives a pleasing sense of purposiveness to even the most purposeless of experiences, an appearance of order to things that in life may be chaotic and senseless, and a consolatory imaginative feeling of having confronted these horrors. Thus, tragedy does not present us with the muddled and self-contradictory ethical problems of life; rather, it brings the artistically pleasing illusion of doing so. Philosophy may in contrast to this metaphysical consolation be understood as a refusal of letting go of doubts: as a practice of dying in the sense of remaining open to the unknowable.

Art is mimetic. This means that it does not need to go beyond its own as if-character: it may show us what appears to be goodness, divinity or courage, without inducing us to ask what is real or not. Morally, this is especially troublesome, since art invites us to enjoy the basest parts of ourselves. It stays in the cave and plays with the fire. The good, which is simple and stable, might not appear attractive in fiction – the evil and neurotic is more various and interesting. Reading novels as morally edifying, or even as works of moral philosophy in their own right, thus becomes problematic. The attention of art is based on desire, not will, and is inherently dubious. Since artistic inspiration springs from unconscious sources, we lack volitional control of its power. We are all storytellers – we live our lives within approximate imaginings and fantasies. Art celebrates these aspects of being human and might thus risk make us content with the second best. But it also has the rare ability of letting us rub against the limits of our imagination: when art reflects upon its own imaginative limitations. This unique truth-conveying potential of art is accidental and bound up with its pointlessness: it is not by striving for betterment, but by being radically non-instrumental, that art can mirror the good. Virtue may not have a point, but great art can be the ambiguous and flickering proof that it is nonetheless meaningful.

2. Implications for future research

All of this – the beauty, dubiousness, illusoriness, fictionality, funniness, muddled thinking, pointlessness, immorality and consolatory purging of problems – does not preclude works of literature from also being and doing other things. Literature may of course be read and used in a wide variety of ways, for didactic, sociological, juridical, theological, political and, yes, philosophical purposes. Using literature in those ways can nonetheless be considered as distinct from appreciating it as an art. But there are also literary works that independently of interpretation are doing other things than 'just' being art: conveying a rich historical knowledge, for example, or challenging oppression. I do not wish to deny that: in the second chapter, I discussed Sartre's novel *La Nausée* as what Murdoch calls a rare example of a properly philosophical novel. But if my book is a defence of literature, it is so in the sense of propagating for a removal of the 'just' in the sentence above. Literature is marvellous as literature. No external purpose needs to be added for our appreciation of it to be justified or interesting. Murdoch was not attempting to sell her own novels short by refusing to call them philosophical novels. She was asking us to appreciate them artistically.

In Murdoch scholarship, there has been a widespread unwillingness to accept her firm distinction between literature and philosophy. Several attempts have been made to question it, many in order to read her own novels as philosophical, and some of those attempts have been discussed and refuted in this book. As such, this text is intended as a challenge to the continuing research on Murdoch's aesthetics as well as her fiction. Murdoch claimed that literature is not philosophy: I have endeavoured to explicate some of the main reasons why. Hopefully, I have thus made it more difficult for those seeking to ignore or dispute Murdoch's insistence on the distinction.

Perhaps it should here be mentioned again that the account of literature presented in this book is not meant to be blueprint of Murdoch's. As I said in the Introduction, I have intended to follow her backwards and forwards where I think that she was right, a method which has entailed a number of deviations from the more narrow path of interpreting her arguments. At times, this method may appear to have left the image of Murdoch's aesthetics somewhat skewed. With her interpretation of Kant, for example, I have (in contrast to the main tendency in Murdoch scholarship) relied more on her later work, where she has grown more appreciative of Kant's aesthetics, than on the explicit rebuttal in her earlier essays (a rebuttal that is, as I showed in Chapter 3, largely based on a misreading of Kant). Oftentimes, I have found that the relevance of Kant's aesthetics for the problem at hand, as well as the most central aspects of Murdoch's inheritance from Kant, can be better explained by going straight to Kant. Murdoch wavers somewhat in her interpretation of him, and I have not spent much time on discussing her deviations from him in detail. But I have attempted to be clear about where she makes a valuable new use of some of the most central aspects of his aesthetics, especially regarding the problem of form[3] and the relationship between art and morality.[4]

It would also be pertinent to admit that I have to some extent avoided to quote from the parts where Murdoch may come across as over-optimistic, even idealistic, regarding the moral power of art (by which she usually means masterpieces).[5] I have instead chosen to highlight those passages in her work where she advised a certain caution regarding this idealizing tendency, since this aspect has been largely neglected by the previous scholarship. In relation to the research on Murdoch, this book is to be read more as a corrective contribution to the general understanding of the distinction between literature and philosophy, than a complete account of Murdoch's views on art. It mainly seeks to argue for why literature is not philosophy.

Finally, a few words on the ancient quarrel at large. In the Zeitgeist we are currently in – in literary studies, artistic research, continental philosophy and the kind of analytic philosophy which seeks to challenge its methods from within – there is a nearly dogmatic aversion to making firm distinctions between philosophy and literature. After having made an initial account of the history and current state of that dogma, I have written the rest of this book in polemical resistance to it. I have done so not just in order to pick a fight, but because I believe that important and valuable artistic aspects of literature are skewed and disvalued by the well-meant attempts to appreciate literature on philosophical grounds. I also think that a philosophical turn to literature may risk making us forget how difficult philosophy is. If any wider influence of this book might be imagined, it is to induce reflection on the often-presupposed virtue in questioning the distinction between the disciplines.

3. A personal note

I began this book by describing my personal reasons for wanting to emphasize the distinction between philosophy and literature. Over the years, this work has certainly alleviated my worries, but in a rather different way than I had assumed. I am now less, rather than more, afraid to let philosophy 'get into' my fiction. This does not mean that I am now writing philosophical novels; but having worked on this book engrossedly for a long time, I have become more aware of what kind of effort that must be involved to even come close to producing anything of minute philosophical value. Having looked more closely at the non-philosophical aspects of literature, I am also more convinced than ever that any 'philosophy' in my fiction may be just that: philosophy in quotation marks, a mimesis of actual thinking. This strikes me as a splendid aspect of literature, and art in general: that it may disrespectfully play around with everything, without any need for critical self-scrutiny to strengthen one's case. I also feel more free in my 'simple' enjoyments of literature – hopefully, any reader of this book may have felt such an alleviating whiff. Literature may be profound, deep and meaningful, without clarifying or furthering our thinking. Whatever a novel is about, it is not best understood by philosophical analysis, but through the pleasure it brings us as art.

It seems appropriate to give the last word to Iris Murdoch. When asked at the end of her career what effect she would like her books to have, she answered the following:

I'd like people to enjoy reading them. A readable novel is a gift to humanity. It provides an innocent occupation. Any novel takes people away from their troubles and the television set; it may even stir them to reflect about human life, characters, morals. So I would like people to be able to read the stuff. I'd like it to be understood too; though some of the novels are not all that easy, I'd like them to be understood, and not grossly misunderstood. But literature is to be enjoyed, to be grasped by enjoyment.[6]

Notes

Preface

1. LP, 4.
2. LP, 6.
3. Murdoch does of course not agree completely with Plato's view of literature – she does not, for example, suggest that we should banish every poet who does not agree to be censored – even though she thinks that he was right to distinguish art from philosophy. See Chapter 6 for a fuller discussion of her Platonic inheritance.
4. *MGM*, 292.
5. FS, 387.
6. The ordinary reader is a frequent figure in Murdoch. As Hanna Marije Altorf describes it, 'Murdoch heeds to voices outside the academic debate, even when they are more like a cry and less like a fully fledged argument.' Altorf connects Murdoch's ordinary man to the Arendtian notion of common sense: not a general agreement, but a vulnerable assumption of reality put in contrast to the sometimes alienating activity of theorizing. Hanna Marije Altorf, 'Iris Murdoch and Common Sense or, What Is It Like to Be a Woman in Philosophy', *Royal Institute of Philosophy Supplements* 87 (2020): 215–19.

Chapter 1

1. A.N. Whitehall, *Process and Reality: An Essay in Cosmology*, ed. David Ray Griffin and Donald W. Sherburne (New York: Free Press, 1978), 39.
2. Plato, *The Republic*, trans. Allan Bloom (New York: Basic Books, 1991), 398A.
3. FS, 393.
4. Plato, *The Republic*, 607B.
5. Ibid., 607B-C.
6. Andrea Wilson Nightingale, *Genres in Dialogue: Plato and the Construct of Philosophy* (Cambridge: Cambridge University Press, 1995), 60.
7. Glenn W. Most, 'What Ancient Quarrel between Philosophy and Poetry?', in *Plato and the Poets*, ed. Destrée and Herrmann (Leiden: Brill, 2011), 12.
8. Plato, *The Apology*, in *The Last Days of Socrates*, trans. Hugh Tredennick and Harold Tarrant (Middlesex: Penguin Books, 1969), 18A–19C.
9. Most, 'What Ancient Quarrel between Philosophy and Poetry?', 18.
10. Martha C. Nussbaum, *The Fragility of Goodness: Luck and Ethics in Greek Tragedy and Philosophy* (Cambridge: Cambridge University Press, 2001), 123.
11. Nussbaum, *The Fragility of Goodness*, 124.
12. Ibid., 129.
13. See 5.5.

14 Nightingale, *Genres in Dialogue*, 60.
15 Catherine Rowett, 'Murdoch and Plato', in *The Murdochian Mind*, ed. Silvia Caprioglio Panizza and Mark Hopwood (Abingdon, Oxon: Routledge, 2022), 250.
16 Debra Nails, 'Mouthpiece Schmouthpiece', in *Who Speaks for Plato?: Studies in Platonic Anonymity*, ed. Gerald Press (Lanham, MD: Rowman & Littlefield, 2000), 20.
17 Please note that I am not relying on an institutionalist definition of the disciplines. These remarks are merely illustrative of the ordinary understanding: library sorting as a symptom rather than the cause of the distinction.
18 See 2.1.1, 5.1 and 5.6, and more at length in Chapter 6.
19 Friedrich Nietzsche, *The Birth of Tragedy*, trans. Douglas Smith (New York: Oxford University Press, 2000), 9.
20 Nietzsche, *The Birth of Tragedy*, 78.
21 See Christopher Janaway, 'Beauty Is False, Truth Ugly: Nietzsche on Art and Life', in *Nietzsche on Art and Life*, ed. Daniel Came (New York: Oxford University Press, 2014), 48.
22 Friedrich Nietzsche, *On the Genealogy of Morality*, trans. Carol Diethe, ed. Keith Ansell-Pearson (New York: Cambridge University Press, 2007), 113, italics original.
23 For a more detailed discussion of this, see David Farrell Krell, 'Art and Truth in Raging Discord: Heidegger and Nietzsche on the Will to Power', *boundary 2*, no. 4, *Martin Heidegger and Literature* (1976): 378–92.
24 See, for example, my discussion in 5.6: 'Plato did not simply think that the poet is a sophist because he is imitating what is, but because he is also imitating things that he cannot have any idea of whether they exist or not, or what they look like.'
25 Martin Heidegger, 'The Origin of the Work of Art', in *Poetry, Language, Thought*, trans. Albert Hofstadter (New York: Harper & Row, 1975), 152.
26 Heidegger, 'The Origin of the Work of Art', 197.
27 David A. White, 'Poetry and Thinking: Heidegger and the Question of Rightness', *Revue Internationale de Philosophie* 43, no. 168(1) (1989): 67.
28 Martin Heidegger, *Introduction to Philosophy: Thinking and Poetizing*, trans. Phillip Jacques Braunstein (Bloomington: Indiana University Press, 2011), 6.
29 Heidegger, *Introduction to Philosophy*, 12.
30 Ibid., 50.
31 White, 'Poetry and Thinking', 67.
32 Ibid., 65.
33 Iris Murdoch's 'Heidegger Manuscript', 1993, KUAS6/5/1/4, Iris Murdoch's writings, Peter Conradi Archive, Kingston University, London, United Kingdom, 55–6.
34 Iris Murdoch's 'Heidegger Manuscript', 75.
35 Aristotle, *Poetics*, trans. Anthony Kenny (Oxford: Oxford University Press, 2013), e-book, 1460B 20.
36 Aristotle, *Poetics*, trans. Malcolm Heath (London: Penguin, 1996), 1451B10–15.
37 See, for example, Gregory Scott, 'Purging the Poetics', *Oxford Studies in Ancient Philosophy* 25 (2003): 233–63.
38 Plato, *The Republic*, 607D.
39 Stephen Halliwell, *Aristotle's Poetics* (London: Duckworth, 1998), 1.
40 Halliwell, *Aristotle's Poetics*, 2.
41 See, for example, Nussbaum, *The Fragility of Goodness*, 378–94.
42 See Chapters 5 and 6.
43 Plato, *The Republic*, 606–7.
44 Aristotle, *Poetics*, trans. Malcolm Heath, 1451B 10–15.

45 See 2.3.3 and 5.5.
46 Ibid.
47 Jonathan Lear, 'Katharsis', *Phronesis* 33, no. 3 (1988): 312.
48 Lear, 'Katharsis', 313.
49 'aesthetic (n.)', *Online Etymology Dictionary*, accessed 25 February 2022, https://www.etymonline.com/word/aesthetic
50 Rosalind Thomas, *Literature and Orality in Ancient Greece* (Cambridge: Cambridge University Press, 2010), 6.
51 Charles H. Kahn, 'Writing Philosophy: Prose and Poetry from Thales to Plato', in *Written Texts and the Rise of Literate Culture in Ancient Greece*, ed. Harvey Yunis (Cambridge: Cambridge University Press, 2003), 159, 139–61.
52 Nickolas Pappas, 'Aristotle', in *The Routledge Companion to Aesthetics*, ed. Berys Gaut and Dominic McIver Lopes (London: Routledge, 2013), 21.
53 *CJ*, 5:320.
54 *CPR*, A21, note.
55 See 2.2.4, 2.3.2 and the entirety of Chapter 3 for a longer discussion of Kant's aesthetics.
56 G.W.F. Hegel, *Aesthetics: Lectures on Fine Art*, trans. T.M. Knox (Oxford: Clarendon Press, 1998), 977.
57 Ibid., 977.
58 Hegel, *Aesthetics*, 975.
59 Ibid., 976.
60 See 2.2.1 for a further Hegelian discussion of the sensuousness of literature.
61 G.W.F Hegel, F.W.J. Schelling, and Friedrich Hölderlin, 'Oldest System Programme of German Idealism', trans. Andrew Bowie, in Andrew Bowie, *Aesthetics and Subjectivity: From Kant to Nietzsche* (Manchester: Manchester University Press, 2003), 334.
62 F.W.J. Schelling, Sämmtliche Werke, I Abtheilung Volume 3, 351. Quoted and translated by Andrew Bowie, *Aesthetics and Subjectivity,* 111.
63 See Bowie, *Aesthetics and Subjectivity*, 110–12.
64 See Emil L. Fackenheim, 'Schelling's Philosophy of the Literary Arts', *The Philosophical Quarterly* 4, no. 17 (1954): 325–6.
65 Plato, *Republic*, 379C-380D, 391A-E.
66 Raymond Barfield, *The Ancient Quarrel between Philosophy and Poetry* (Cambridge: Cambridge University Press, 2011), 74.
67 Barfield, *The Ancient Quarrel between Philosophy and Poetry*, 97.
68 Ibid., 120.
69 See 2.2.3 for more on Kierkegaard's notion of indirect communication.
70 Søren Kierkegaard, 'The Sickness unto Death: A Christian Psychological Exposition for Upbuilding and Awakening (30 July 1849), By Anti-Climacus, Edited by S. Kierkegaard', in *The Essential Kierkegaard*, ed. and trans. Howard V. Hong and Edna H. Hong (Princeton: Princeton University Press, 2000), 367.
71 Søren Kierkegaard, 'The Seducer's Diary', in 'Either/Or, A Fragment of Life (20 February 1843), Edited by Victor Eremita, Part 1 Containing A's Papers', in *The Essential Kierkegaard*, 63.
72 Søren Kierkegaard, 'On My Work as an Author (7 August 1851), The Point of View for My Work as an Author (Written 1848, Published 1859), By S. Kierkegaard', in *The Essential Kierkegaard*, 451.
73 See, for example, Kate Larson, '*Everything Important Is to Do with Passion*': *Iris Murdoch's Concept of Love and Its Platonic Origin* (Uppsala: Uppsala University,

2009); Gabriele Griffin, *The Influence of the Writings of Simone Weil on the Fiction of Iris Murdoch* (San Francisco: Mellen Research University Press, 1993); and Silvia Panizza, *The Importance of Attention in Morality: An Exploration of Iris Murdoch's Philosophy* (Norwich: University of East Anglia, 2015).

74 See Simone Pétrement, *Simone Weil: A Life*, trans. Raymond Rosenthal (New York: Pantheon Books, 1976).
75 See 6.1.4.
76 Simone Weil, 'Literature and Morality', in *Late Philosophical Writings*, trans. Eric O. Springsted and Lawrence E. Schmidt, ed. Eric O. Springsted (Notre Dame: University of Notre Dame Press, 2015), 146.
77 Simone Weil, 'Divine Love in Creation', in *Intimations of Christianity among the Ancient Greeks*, trans. Elisabeth Chase, (London: Routledge, 1998), 90.
78 Simone Weil, *The Notebooks of Simone Weil*, trans. Arthur Wills (London: Routledge, 2004), 627.
79 Patrick Sherry, 'Simone Weil on Beauty', in *Simone Weil's Philosophy of Culture*, ed. Richard H. Bell (Cambridge: Cambridge University Press, 1993), 267.
80 Weil, 'Literature and Morality', 148.
81 Weil, *The Notebooks of Simone Weil*, 417. For a discussion of Weil's concept of attention, see 6.2.
82 Weil, *The Notebooks of Simone Weil*, 548.
83 Ibid., 472.
84 Plato, *The Phaedrus*, trans. James H. Nichols JR (Ithaca: Cornell University Press, 1998), 245A.
85 Sigmund Freud, *Three Essays on the Theory of Sexuality*, trans. and ed. James Strachey (New York: Basic Books, 2000), xxx.
86 Sigmund Freud, *Civilization and Its Discontents*, trans. James Stracthey (New York: W.W. Norton & Company, 2010), 53.
87 Lionel Trilling, 'Freud and Literature', *Horizon: A Review of Literature & Art* XVI, no. 92 (1947): 188–9.
88 As Murdoch puts it: 'Both Plato and Freud wish to heal by promoting awareness of reality. Only Freud holds that we grasp reality through the ego and not through the "critical punishing agency" of the ideal; whereas Plato holds that, above a reasonable egoism, there is a pure moral faculty which discerns the real world and to which sovereignty properly belongs.' FS, 418–19.
89 Plato is not entirely consequent here. The *Phaedrus* presents, as many have noted, an interesting exception in the Platonic mistrust of the mad poet.
90 Jonathan Lear, *Freud* (Hoboken: Taylor & Francis Ltd, 2005), 13.
91 See 4.5. and 6.3.3.
92 Trilling, 'Freud and Literature', 193.
93 Not everyone would agree with Trilling here. Neil Hertz writes for example, quoting Freud, that 'what interpreting meant to him was less assigning meanings to a work of art than accounting for why the reader or viewer had been "so powerfully affected" by it.' (Neil Hertz, 'Foreword', in Sigmund Freud, *Writings on Art and Literature* (Stanford, California: Stanford University Press, 1997)), xi. Quote from page 123 in the same book.
94 Sigmund Freud, 'Creative Writers and Day-Dreaming', in *Collected Papers, vol. 4*, trans. Joan Riviere (New York: Basic Books Inc., 1959), 421.
95 There are sixteen of his titles included among the books in her archive, several of them annotated.

96 See, for example, *MGM*, 86.
97 See the discussion of pointlessness in 6.3.5.
98 Karl Marx, 'Theses on Feuerbach', in *The German Ideology* (Amherst, N.Y.: Prometheus Books, 1998), 571.
99 To soften my conscience over this neglect, I echo Terry Eagleton's reproach: 'No doubt we shall soon see Marxist criticism comfortably wedged between Freudian and mythological approaches to literature, as yet one more stimulating academic "approach", one more well-tilled field of inquiry for students to tramp. Before this happens, it is worth reminding ourselves of a simple fact. Marxism is a scientific theory of human societies and of the practice of transforming them; and what that means, rather more concretely, is that the narrative Marxism has to deliver is the story of the struggles of men and women to free themselves from certain forms of exploitation and oppression. There is nothing academic about those struggles, and we forget this at our cost.' Terry Eagleton, *Marxism and Literary Criticism* (London: Routledge, 2003), i.
100 Benjamin J.B. Lipscomb claims that this 'interest' of Murdoch's was far from innocent: 'She offered herself as a low-level spy for the Communist Party, copying Treasury documents and leaving them in a hollow tree in Kensington Garden for a fellow agent to collect.' Benjamin J.B. Lipscomb, *The Women Are Up to Something: How Elizabeth Anscombe, Philippa Foot, Mary Midgley, and Iris Murdoch Revolutionized Ethics* (New York: Oxford University Press, 2022), e-book, 91.
101 Existentialism is sometimes understood as a broader category than simply the French strand, including thinkers as diverse as Heidegger, Kierkegaard and Martin Buber. Henceforth, the word will refer to French Existentialism in this dissertation.
102 Murdoch did, however, consider Sartre's *La Nausée* to be a rare example of a successful philosophical novel. See 2.3.
103 The influence of psychoanalysis on Existentialism is complicated, although arguably forceful. For example, Sartre denies the existence of the Freudian unconscious and seeks instead to replace it with his notion of bad faith. As Hazel E. Barnes says in her introduction to *Being and Nothingness*: 'While still deeply indebted to Freud, Sartre has effected a sharper break with the Freudian tradition than any other contemporary psychologist.' (Hazel E. Barnes, 'Translator's Introduction', in Jean-Paul Sartre, *Being and Nothingness: An Essay on Phenomenological Ontology*, trans. Hazel E. Barnes (New York: Citadel Press, 1956), xxxvi.)
104 Simone de Beauvoir, 'Literature and Metaphysics', in *Philosophical Writings*, trans. Veronique Zaytzeff and Frederick M. Morrison, ed. Margaret A. Simons (Urbana: University of Illinois Press, 2004), 273.
105 Jean-Paul Sartre, 'Introducing *Les Temps modernes*', trans. Jeffrey Mehlman, in *'What Is Literature?' and Other Essays*, ed. Steven Ungar (Cambridge, MA: Harvard University Press, 1988), 251.
106 de Beauvoir, 'Literature and Metaphysics', 270.
107 Jean-Paul Sartre, *What Is Literature?*, trans. Bernard Frechtman (New York: Philosophical Library, 1949), 22.
108 See Sartre, *What Is Literature?*, 35.
109 Iris Murdoch, *Sartre: Romantic Rationalist* (London: Vintage, 1999), 36.
110 Theodor W. Adorno, *Negative Dialectics*, trans. E.B. Ashton (New York: Continuum, 2007), xx.

111 Stewart Martin, 'Literature and the Modern System of the Arts: Sources of Criticism in Adorno', in *Adorno and Literature*, ed. David Cunningham and Nigel Mapp (London: Continuum, 2006), 16.
112 Adorno, *Aesthetic Theory*, 78.
113 Ibid.
114 Ibid., 347.
115 A helpful discussion on this is provided by Tony Milligan, who exposes the flaws of her offhanded dismissal of Derrida as a technocratic determinist. Tony Milligan, 'Murdoch and Derrida: Holding Hands under the Table', in *Iris Murdoch: Texts and Contexts*, ed. Anne Rowe and Avril Horner, (Houndmills, Basingstoke: Palgrave Macmillan, 2012), 77–90.
116 *MGM*, 189–90.
117 *MGM*, 205.
118 *MGM*, 207.
119 *MGM*, 185.
120 Jacques Derrida and Derek Attridge, '"This Strange Institution Called Literature": An Interview with Jacques Derrida', in *Acts of Literature*, trans. Geoffrey Bennington and Rachel Bowlby, ed. Derek Attridge (London: Routledge, 1992), 39.
121 Jacques Derrida, 'The First Session', in *Acts of Literature*, ed. Derek Attridge (London: Routledge, 1992), 142.
122 See, for example, Leslie Hill, *The Cambridge Introduction to Jacques Derrida* (Cambridge: Cambridge University Press, 2007), 33–40, and Derrida, 'The First Session'.
123 Hill, *The Cambridge Introduction to Jacques Derrida*, 37.
124 Derrida and Attridge, 'This Strange Institution Called Literature', 60. This interview is done about a year before the publication of *Gender Trouble*. It is possible that Derrida was already aware of Butler's work.
125 Ibid., 45.
126 Ibid., 36–7.
127 Rita Felski, *Uses of Literature* (Malden, Mass: Blackwell Pub, 2008), 2.
128 Felski, *Uses of Literature*, 2.
129 Ibid., 4.
130 Ibid., 3.
131 Amanda Anderson, Rita Felski and Toril Moi, *Character: Three Inquiries in Literary Studies* (Chicago, IL: The University of Chicago Press, 2019), 1. See also 4.1.
132 Anderson, Felski and Moi, *Character*, 5.
133 Murdoch's antedating of this critique is described more at length in 4.1 and 4.7.
134 See, for example, the chapter on 'Knowledge' in Felski, *Uses of Literature*, 77–104. Felski says about Edith Warton: 'Emancipated from criteria of verifiable accuracy, her writing is free to register fleeting expressions, penumbral perceptions, shifting foci of attention, subconscious motions of affinity and distancing: all the ephemeral and barely registered forms of consciousness and communication that help make up the stuff of social interaction' (91). A 'knowledge' that is 'emancipated from criteria of verifiable accuracy' can never be counterproved or validated and may as well be made up. A similar paradox in Martha Nussbaum's view of literature will be discussed at length in 5.5.
135 See, for example, Helga Nowotny, 'Foreword', in *The Routledge Companion to Research in the Arts*, ed. Michael Biggs and Henrik Karlsson in collaboration with Stiftelsen Riksbankens Jubileumsfond, Stockholm (Oxon: Routledge, 2011), xix.

136 Henk Borgdorff, *The Debate on Research in the Arts*, vol. 2 (Bergen, Norway: Kunsthøgskolen i Bergen, 2006), 10.
137 Nowotny, 'Introduction', xviii.
138 Ibid., xxi.
139 Borgdorff, *The Debate on Research in the Arts*, 7–8.
140 *MGM*, 205.
141 A proper justification of this gut feeling would have to take the form of a thorough discussion of several individual works of artistic research, something I fortunately lack the time and space to pursue here.
142 LP, 4.
143 Wittgenstein did not write explicitly about the relationship between literature and philosophy and is thus left out from this chapter. Some discussion of his importance for Murdoch's thought can be found in Nora Hämäläinen, 'What Is a Wittgensteinian Neo-Platonist? Iris Murdoch, Metaphysics and Metaphor', *Philosophical Papers* 43, no. 2 (2014): 191–225 and Anne-Marie Søndergaard Christensen, 'Murdoch and Wittgenstein', in *The Murdochian Mind*, ed. Silvia Caprioglio Panizza and Mark Hopwood (Abingdon, Oxon: Routledge, 2022), 318–29.
144 Stanley Cavell, *The Claim of Reason: Wittgenstein, Skepticism, Morality, and Tragedy* (New York: Oxford University Press, 1999), xvii.
145 Cora Diamond and Silver Bronzo, 'Philosophy in a Realistic Spirit: An Interview with Silver Bronzo', *Iride* 26, no. 2 (2013): 277.
146 Nussbaum, *The Fragility of Goodness*, 15.
147 I will discuss my issues with Cavell's attempt to question the distinction in Chapter 4, and Nussbaum's interpretation of tragedy as a philosophical genre in 5.5.
148 To name just a few examples: Walter Benjamin, Hélène Cixous, Friedrich Hölderlin, and Mikhail Bakhtin.

Chapter 2

1 FS, 450.
2 See 1.2.
3 FS, 392.
4 FS, 393.
5 Ibid.
6 Plato, *The Ion*, in *Ion, Hippias minor, Laches, Protagoras*, trans. Reginald E. Allen (New Haven: Yale University Press, 1996), 542A.
7 Plato, *The Ion*, 541E.
8 There is even some indication that she had an idea for a longer study on the relationship between philosophy and poetry. One of her notebooks begins with the headline 'Poets and philosophers', which is followed by 'Plato's old quarrel bet. poetry & philosophy. Why Plato banished poets', and a great flora of names of philosophers and poets, such as Hölderlin, Heidegger, Derrida, Blake, Ricœur, Valery and many more. (Iris Murdoch's 'Untitled Notebook', Undated (est. early-mid 1990s), KUAS202/4/5, Iris Murdoch Archive, Kingston University, London, UK.)
9 LP, 18.
10 Harold Hobson, 'Lunch with Iris Murdoch', in *From a Tiny Corner in The House of Fiction: Conversations with Iris Murdoch*, ed. Gillian Dooley Dooley (Columbia: University of South Carolina Press, 2003), 2.

11 Hobson, 'Lunch with Iris Murdoch', 3.
12 Frank Kermode, 'Interview from "The House of Fiction: Interviews with Seven English Novelists"', in *From a Tiny Corner in The House of Fiction: Conversations with Iris Murdoch*, ed. Gillian Dooley Dooley (Columbia: University of South Carolina Press, 2003), 12.
13 W.K. Rose, 'Iris Murdoch, Informally', in *From a Tiny Corner in The House of Fiction: Conversations with Iris Murdoch*, ed. Gillian Dooley Dooley (Columbia: University of South Carolina Press, 2003), 20.
14 Stephen Glover, 'Iris Murdoch Talks to Stephen Glover', in *From a Tiny Corner in The House of Fiction: Conversations with Iris Murdoch*, ed. Gillian Dooley Dooley (Columbia: University of South Carolina Press, 2003), 36.
15 Jack I. Biles, 'An Interview with Iris Murdoch', in *From a Tiny Corner in The House of Fiction: Conversations with Iris Murdoch*, ed. Gillian Dooley Dooley (Columbia: University of South Carolina Press, 2003), 58.
16 Simon Price, 'Iris Murdoch: An Interview with Simon Price', in *From a Tiny Corner in The House of Fiction: Conversations with Iris Murdoch*, ed. Gillian Dooley Dooley (Columbia: University of South Carolina Press, 2003), 152.
17 Glover, 'Iris Murdoch Talks to Stephen Glover', 36.
18 LP, 4.
19 LP, 19.
20 Biles, 'An Interview with Iris Murdoch', 58.
21 Jeffrey Meyers, 'Two Interviews with Iris Murdoch', in *From a Tiny Corner in The House of Fiction: Conversations with Iris Murdoch*, ed. Gillian Dooley Dooley (Columbia: University of South Carolina Press, 2003), 225.
22 LP, 10–1.
23 SGO, 85.
24 Hobson, 'Lunch with Iris Murdoch', 3.
25 Niklas Forsberg, *Language Lost and Found: On Iris Murdoch and the Limits of Philosophical Discourse* (London: Bloomsbury Academic, 2013), 18.
26 Forsberg, *Language Lost and Found*, 71.
27 Maria Antonaccio, 'The Virtues of Metaphysics: A Review of Iris Murdoch's Philosophical Writings', *The Journal of Religious Ethics* 29, no. 2 (2001): 320.
28 Gary Browning, *Why Iris Murdoch Matters: Making Sense of Experience in Modern Times* (London: Bloomsbury Academic, 2018), vi.
29 Anna Victoria Hallberg, *Novel Writing and Moral Philosophy as Aspects of a Single Struggle: Iris Murdoch's Hybrid Novels* (Örebro: Örebro universitet, 2011), 34.
30 Anne Rowe and Avril Horner, 'Introduction: Art, Morals and "The Discovery of Reality"', in *Iris Murdoch and Morality*, ed. Anne Rowe and Avril Horner (New York: Palgrave Macmillan, 2010), 1.
31 Sofia de Melo Araújo, 'Introduction', in *Iris Murdoch, Philosopher Meets Novelist*, ed. Sofia de Melo Araújo and Fatima Vieira (Newcastle upon Tyne: Cambridge Scholars Publishing, 2011), 3.
32 John Haffenden, 'John Haffenden Talks to Iris Murdoch', in *From a Tiny Corner in The House of Fiction: Conversations with Iris Murdoch*, ed. Gillian Dooley Dooley (Columbia: University of South Carolina Press, 2003), 128.
33 LP, 10.
34 LP, 11.
35 LP, 5.
36 *MGM*, 2.

37 *MGM*, 3, italics original.
38 Hegel, *Aesthetics*, 1035.
39 Ibid.
40 Forsberg, *Language Lost and Found*, see especially: 'The received view and its complications', 15–22.
41 Ibid., 4.
42 Martha Nussbaum, '"Faint with Secret Knowledge": Love and Vision in Murdoch's *The Black Prince*', in *Iris Murdoch, Philosopher: A Collection of Essays*, ed. Justin Broackes (Oxford: Oxford University Press, 2012).
43 Michael Weston, *Philosophy, Literature and the Human Good* (London: Routledge, 2001).
44 Iris Murdoch, *The Black Prince* (Harmondsworth: Penguin, 1975), 266. Quoted by Forsberg in *Language Lost and Found*, 227.
45 Forsberg, *Language Lost and Found*, 27.
46 Ibid., 224.
47 AD, 290. Quoted by Forsberg in *Language Lost and Found*, 223.
48 Forsberg, *Language Lost and Found*, 228.
49 Ibid., 11.
50 Ibid., 226.
51 Ibid., 13.
52 Ibid., 12.
53 Forsberg, *Language Lost and Found*, 185.
54 See 1.7.3.
55 de Beauvoir, 'Literature and Metaphysics', 270.
56 Ibid., italics added.
57 Forsberg, *Language Lost and Found*, 34.
58 Ibid., 227.
59 Murdoch, *The Black Prince*, 266.
60 Charles Bernstein, 'Artifice of Absorption', in *A Poetics* (Cambridge, MA: Harvard, 1992), 16.
61 Forsberg, *Language Lost and Found*, 158.
62 Ibid., 12.
63 Ibid., 185, italics original.
64 Forsberg, *Language Lost and Found*, 5.
65 Forsberg, *Language Lost and Found*, 225.
66 Ibid., 224.
67 Ibid., 185.
68 Ibid., 110–1.
69 See Forsberg, *Language Lost and Found*, for example 9, 11, 151, 183.
70 Forsberg, *Language Lost and Found*, 152.
71 Forsberg, *Language Lost and Found*, 34.
72 Ibid., 156.
73 Murdoch, *The Black Prince*, 207.
74 Forsberg, *Language Lost and Found*, 34.
75 Ibid., 172.
76 For an explication of suspension of disbelief, see 4.4.
77 Forsberg, *Language Lost and Found*, 151.
78 Ibid., 153.

79 Understanding the concept of God would be equivalent to having true faith. Forsberg evades the problem of the fundamentally theological structure of Kierkegaard's notion of illusion of sense and brings it straight into a language-philosophical reading of a novel, something which creates further problems that I due to lack of space refrain from discussing here.
80 Forsberg, *Language Lost and Found*, 94.
81 Kierkegaard, 'On My Work as an Author', 452, footnote.
82 Ibid., 451, italics original.
83 Ibid., 459.
84 Forsberg, *Language Lost and Found*, 77.
85 *MGM*, 87, italics added.
86 Forsberg, *Language Lost and Found*, 123.
87 Ibid.
88 Kierkegaard, 'On My Work as an Author', 464.
89 Forsberg, *Language Lost and Found*, 186. Quoting Murdoch, *The Black Prince*, 308.
90 There is some mention of 'self-sufficient beauty' (*selbstständige Schönheit*), (*CJ* §16 endnote 36, 371) a somewhat unclear and rare phrase in Kant, which the translators in §16 translate with 'self-subsisting' and in an endnote suggest 'seems more like what he here calls adherent or dependent beauty rather than free beauty'.
91 Forsberg, *Language Lost and Found*, 5.
92 Ibid., 65.
93 The matter might be further complicated by the fact that what Forsberg means with concepts and what Kant means with the same word do not necessarily overlap. The word 'concept' should, in other words, not be mistaken for the concept here.
94 Immanuel Kant, *Critique of Pure Reason*, trans. Norman Kemp Smith (Houndmills: Palgrave Macmillan, 2007), A51/B75. Quoted by Forsberg in *Language Lost and Found*, 66.
95 Forsberg, *Language Lost and Found*, 66.
96 Ibid., 67.
97 This will be explained at length in Chapter 3.
98 *CJ*, 20:206.
99 For the autonomy of the judgement of taste, see, for example, *CJ*, 5:350. As Casey Haskins points out, Kant nowhere speaks of art as autonomous, only the judgement of taste. ('Kant and the Autonomy of Art', *The Journal of Aesthetics and Art Criticism* 47, no. 1 (1989): 43.) And strictly speaking, Kant says, the judgement of taste is heautonomous (lawgiving for itself) and not autonomous (lawgiving for nature or freedom). See the First introduction (*CJ*, 20:225).
100 *CJ*, 20:207.
101 *CJ*, 5:203 (§1).
102 Ibid., italics added.
103 For a further discussion of Kant's (and Murdoch's) notion of form, see 5.2.
104 Hegel, *Aesthetics*, 4.
105 Ibid., 9, brackets added by the translator.
106 Ibid., 1236.
107 See, for example, SG, 214.
108 Forsberg, *Language Lost and Found*, 226.
109 Ibid., 157.
110 Ibid., 158.
111 Forsberg, *Language Lost and Found*, 34.

112 Fictional city similar to Le Havre. A homonym of *Boue-ville*, mud-town. See the introduction by Hayden Carruth in Jean-Paul Sartre, *Nausea* (New York: New Directions, 1964), v–xiv.
113 Jean-Paul Sartre, *Nausea*, trans. Robert Baldick (London: Penguin, 2000), 15–16.
114 D.H. Lawrence, 'Art and Morality', in *The Bad Side of Books: Selected Essays*, ed. Geoff Dyer (New York: New York Review Books, 2019), 223.
115 *CPR* A:77, B:103.
116 *CPR*, A:69, B:94.
117 *CJ*, 26.
118 Howard Caygill, *A Kant Dictionary* (Oxford, UK: Blackwell Reference, 2000), E-book, 264.
119 Caygill, *A Kant Dictionary*, 79.
120 *CPR*, A:45, B:63.
121 *CPR*, A:45–46, B:63.
122 *CJ*, 20:213–14.
123 LP, 20.
124 Ibid.
125 Iris Murdoch, 'The Existentialist Hero', in *Existentialists and Mystics*, 115.
126 LP, 21.
127 Murdoch, *Sartre*, 39.
128 Murdoch, *Sartre*, 41.
129 Ibid., 42.
130 Ibid.
131 Iris Murdoch, 'The Novelist as Metaphysician', in *Existentialists and Mystics*, 107.
132 Murdoch, *Sartre*, 47.
133 Ibid.
134 Ibid., 48.
135 Sartre, *Nausea*, 16.
136 Jean-Paul Sartre, *La nausée* (Paris: Gallimard, 1980), 10.
137 Murdoch, *Sartre*, 146. Quoted by Miles Leeson in *Iris Murdoch: Philosophical Novelist* (London: Continuum, 2011), 31.
138 Murdoch, *Sartre*, 145–6.
139 Ibid., 40.
140 Leeson, *Iris Murdoch*, 31.
141 Hallberg, *Novel Writing and Moral Philosophy as Aspects of a Single Struggle*, 29–30. Peter Lamarque, *The Philosophy of Literature* (Oxford: Blackwell Publishing, 2009), 3.
142 Hallberg, *Novel Writing and Moral Philosophy as Aspects of a Single Struggle*, 29, footnote 62.
143 *L'Être et Le Néant* is not a collection of essays, but a book presenting a highly structured argumentation. Among Sartre's more famous claims is that shame is the disclosure of subjectivity as being among others, which might perhaps, with some goodwill, be interpreted as 'hell is other people'. But this sentiment can hardly be said to be central for *La Nausée*; with some goodwill, it might be applicable to *Les Chemins de la Liberté*.
144 Jean-Paul Sartre, *Huis clos: suivi de Les mooches* (Paris: Gallimard, 1947), 93.
145 LP, 21.
146 Ibid.
147 Nora Hämäläinen, *Literature and Moral Theory* (New York: Bloomsbury Academic, 2016), 30.

148 Ibid.
149 Ibid., 31.
150 Ibid., 158.
151 See also the discussion of Aristotle's statement that 'poetry is more philosophical […] than history' because poetry 'tends to express universals, and history particulars' in 1.4.1.
152 Forsberg, *Language Lost and Found*, 69-70.
153 Ibid.
154 LP, 6.
155 LP, 4. She names them as examples of 'great individual thinkers who are great writers, whom I would not call philosophers'.
156 Ibid.
157 One could easily argue that this definition does not hold for Murdoch's own philosophical writings, which are more essayistic than technical.
158 SG, 205.
159 LP, 20.
160 Cavell, *The Claim of Reason*, 130.
161 Ibid., 139-40, italics original.
162 Robert Mankin, 'An Introduction to *The Claim of Reason*', *Salmagundi* 67 (1985): 70.
163 Cavell, *The Claim of Reason*, 140-2.
164 Ibid., 143.
165 The generic object of the traditional epistemologist is the envelope, hand or table he uses as an example for the whole world in asking us whether we can be really certain that what we have in front of us really exists. See Cavell, *The Claim of Reason*, 135-8.
166 Ibid.
167 Forsberg, *Language Lost and Found*, 134.
168 Ibid., 221.
169 Anthony J. Cascardi, '"Disowning Knowledge": Cavell on Shakespeare', in *Stanley Cavell*, ed. Richard T. Eldrige (Cambridge and New York: Cambridge University Press, 2003), 197.
170 Ibid.
171 Whether this situation is actually tragic is another matter. The philosophical notion of tragedy will be discussed in Chapter 5, and Cavell's related view of the relationship between literature and philosophy in Chapter 4.
172 Cavell, *The Claim of Reason*, 45.
173 Ibid., 493.
174 Immanuel Kant, *Critique of Pure Reason*, trans. N.K. Smith (New York: The Humanities Press, 1950), 7. Quoted by Cavell, *The Claim of Reason*, 127.
175 Cavell, *The Claim of Reason*, 241-2.
176 Murdoch, *Sartre*, 44.
177 Ibid., 110.
178 Sartre, *Nausea*, 133.
179 CJ, 112.
180 Sartre, *Nausea*, 133.
181 For a discussion of Murdoch's interpretation and usage of the Kantian sublime, see 3.5 and 6.3.3.
182 Murdoch, *Sartre*, 51.
183 Iris Murdoch, 'On "God" and "Good"', in *Existentialists and Mystics*, 359.
184 Murdoch, *Sartre*, 146.

185 Ibid., 47.
186 These two accounts for the same word have, despite their differences, often been read together. It is simply taken for granted that Sartre's fictional and philosophical work makes up a coherent whole, that his novels are representations of his ideas. See, for example, Hazel E. Barnes introduction to her English translation of *Being and Nothingness*, who takes the concept of nausea from *L'Être et Le Néant* to be the theme of the novel ('Translator's Introduction', xvii).
187 Richard Kamber, 'Sartre's Nauseas', *MLN* 98, no. 5 (1983), 1280.
188 Sartre, *Being and Nothingness*, 338.
189 Kamber, 'Sartre's Nauseas', 1281.
190 Ibid., 1282.
191 Ibid.
192 Ibid.
193 For a further discussion of suspension of disbelief and the epistemology of fiction, see Chapter 4.
194 The manuscript for Murdoch's unpublished book on Heidegger contains many reflections on how 'poeticized' language may or may not aid metaphysical thinking: 'Philosophy need not be systematic. The later work of Wittgenstein is not, much philosophical writing in the empiricist tradition is not. When do "reflections" qualify as philosophy, is Simone Weil a philosopher?' (Iris Murdoch's 'Heidegger Manuscript', 83). Her arguments are here more concerned with the relationship between metaphysics and mysticism, than philosophy and literature. 'Heidegger's philosophy, throughout, lacks this sort of clarity, indeed as he increasingly says later, deliberately shuns it, condemns it as cut and dried "logical" argument which cannot touch the deeper matters, which can only be reached by more "poeticized" or in effect (he does not use the word) mystical mode of thought' (ibid., 103). Murdoch is not categorically opposed to the use of poetic or literary language for philosophy, but she is, ultimately, critical: 'Late Heidegger suggests a poeticization of philosophical thinking. This is another way to kill philosophy' (ibid., 130).
195 Kamber, 'Sartre's Nauseas', 1283–4.
196 Jean-Paul Sartre, *Sartre: Un film réalisé par Alexandre Astruc et Michel Contact* (Paris: Gallimard, 1977), 57–8. Quoted in Kamber, 'Sartre's Nauseas', 1284, my trans.
197 David Pole, 'Literature as Prophecy: Sartre's "Nausea"', in *Philosophy and Literature*; Spring 1981; vol. 5, no. 1: 38.
198 Pole, 'Literature as Prophecy', 44, italics added.
199 Cavell, *The Claim of Reason*, 496. I shall return to this question in Chapter 4.
200 Murdoch, *The Sovereignty of Good*, 49.
201 Iris Murdoch, *The Philosopher's Pupil* (London: Vintage Books, 2000), 97.
202 Murdoch, *The Philosopher's Pupil*, 83.
203 Mentioned by for example Leeson, *Iris Murdoch*, 120, and Nicol, *Iris Murdoch*, 155.
204 LP, 19: 'I think as soon as philosophy gets into a work of literature it becomes a plaything of the writer, and rightly so.' Haffenden, 'John Haffenden Talks to Iris Murdoch', 124–5: 'And yet the character, John Robert Rozanov, has covered something of the same ground as your own work in philosophy, including Platonism … Murdoch: In a very rough way, yes, but that's not particularly significant.'
205 Leeson, *Iris Murdoch*, 113.
206 Ibid., 115.
207 Bran Nicol, *Iris Murdoch: The Retrospective Fiction* (Basingstoke: Palgrave Macmillan, 2004), 162.

208 Nicol, *Iris Murdoch*, 155.
209 Ibid., 163.
210 Murdoch, *The Philosopher's Pupil*, 132.
211 Ibid., 137.
212 Murdoch, *The Philosopher's Pupil*, 138.
213 Ibid., 139.
214 LP, 6.
215 Murdoch had some contempt for this approach. In her margin notes on Simone Weil's Notebooks, Murdoch comments: 'This seeing of meaning in things – often a bit mad.' 'One understands interest in astrology!' Simone Weil, *The Notebooks of Simone Weil Vol 2* (London: Routledge and Kegan Paul, 1956) IML 932, Iris Murdoch's Libraries, Kingston University, London, UK, 474–5.
216 Murdoch, *The Philosopher's Pupil*, 220.
217 Ibid., 143.
218 Nicol, *Iris Murdoch*, 166. But as Nicol also mentions, the dialogues between Rozanov and the priest are much richer. I would however suggest that these are more theological than philosophical in nature, exploring the mystery of apophatic faith. This is a separate concern which I do not have the space for discussing here.
219 Murdoch, *The Philosopher's Pupil*, 147.
220 Ibid., 142.
221 Murdoch, *The Philosopher's Pupil*, 256.
222 Haffenden, 'John Haffenden Talks to Iris Murdoch', 125: 'Haffenden: You didn't intend the novel to be an indictment of a certain kind of philosophy? Murdoch: Yes, but I think philosophy is a subject which does lead some people to despair, it's much too difficult for the human mind.'
223 Plato, *Timaeus*, 44D-E: 'In other words, not wanting the head to roll around on the ground without the ability to climb over the various rises and out of the various dips, [the gods] gave it the body to be its vehicle and means of transport.'
224 See 1.5.2 and 2.2.1.
225 Hegel, *Aesthetics*, 961–3.
226 Ibid., 965.
227 Ibid., 976.
228 Heidegger's view of truth as disclosure prompts him to propose a more poeticized philosophical language. But there is nonetheless a kind of abstract systematicity to his thinking. A further discussion of this would benefit from a closer look at the unpublished manuscript for Murdoch's book on Heidegger, where she repeatedly attempts to describe why she considers his plea for poeticized thinking to be problematic.
229 Hegel, *Aesthetics*, 977. See also for example 981: 'To cling to what […] can only have a relative value, seems therefore to the Understanding to be useless and wearisome. But, in a poetic treatment and formulation, every part, every feature, must be interesting and living on its own account, and therefore poetry takes pleasure in lingering over what is individual, describes it with love, and treats it as a whole in itself.'
230 Murdoch, *The Philosopher's Pupil*, 298.
231 Forsberg, *Language Lost and Found*, 225.
232 Bran Nicol, 'Murdoch's Mannered Realism: Metafiction, Morality and the Post-War Novel', in *Iris Murdoch and Morality*, ed. Anne Rowe and Avril Horner (New York: Palgrave Macmillan, 2010), 23.

233 Again, Sartre's first novel might be a rare exception here.
234 LP, 8.
235 Murdoch, *The Philosopher's Pupil*, 308.
236 Ibid., 455.
237 Ibid., 558.
238 Nicol, 'Murdoch's Mannered Realism', 23.
239 Nicol, *Iris Murdoch*, 153.
240 Ibid., 165.
241 Ibid., 154.
242 Ibid., 156.
243 As Anna Enström says, 'the sublime for Kant does not constitute the opposite of the beautiful, but its counter-weight', in *Sinnesstämning, skratt och hypokondri: om estetisk erfarenhet i Kants tredje Kritik* (Huddinge: Södertörn University, 2021), 22, my transl.
244 See 3.5 and 6.3.3.
245 See 6.2.4.
246 Bran Nicol, 'Philosophy's Dangerous Pupil: Murdoch and Derrida', *MFS Modern Fiction Studies* 47, no. 3 (2001): 599.
247 Nicol, *Iris Murdoch*, 156.
248 Nicol, 'Philosophy's Dangerous Pupil', 591.
249 LP, 4.
250 Hegel, *Aesthetics*, 12.
251 Haffenden, 'John Haffenden Talks to Iris Murdoch', 125.
252 I am, of course, not suggesting that these aspects should be hermetically sealed off from the pure thoughts of a detached, ahistorical, disembodied mind – but most people would agree that there is a sense in which Kant's very slight height (156 centimetres) is largely irrelevant to his view of space and time as *a priori* categories. If, furthermore, one is to consider a philosopher's appearance relevant, such a discussion would hopefully not take shape as minute emotionally infused depictions of his or her ugliness.
253 Murdoch, *The Philosopher's Pupil*, 534.
254 See, for example, Malcolm Bradbury, 'Introduction', in Murdoch, The Philosopher's Pupil, ix–xx and Barbara Stevens Heusel, *Patterned Aimlessness: Iris Murdoch's Novels of the 1970s and 1980s* (Athens: U of Georgia P, 1995).
255 Haffenden, 'John Haffenden Talks to Iris Murdoch', 128. 'The only tension involved there is that both pursuits take up time.'

Chapter 3

1 SG, 210.
2 *CJ*, 5:203.
3 SG, 209.
4 For a further explication of why Kant's aesthetics is not mainly a theory of art, see 1.5.1.
5 *CJ*, 5:320.
6 *MGM*, 312.
7 Immanuel Kant, *Kant's Critique of Aesthetic Judgement* (Oxford: Clarendon Press, 1911), IML 996, Iris Murdoch's Libraries, Kingston University, London, UK. The

notes that form the background for *SG* are made in the back of this volume, whereas the later annotations are made directly in the margin, with a different pen and style. It is also worth noting that this volume is only the first half of the third Critique – the latter half, on the teleological judgement, may not have been in Murdoch's possession, or has at least not been kept in her archive.

8   *MGM* is based on an expanded and amended version of Murdoch's Gifford Lectures from 1982.
9   *MGM*, 313.
10 A good discussion of Murdoch's Kantian heritage is provided by Melissa Merritt in 'Mudoch and Kant', in *The Murdochian Mind,* ed. Silvia Caprioglio Panizza and Mark Hopwood (Abingdon, Oxon: Routledge, 2022), 253–65. However, Merritt does not bring up the change in Murdoch's interpretation but stays with her earlier views. She discusses Murdoch's reasons for objecting to the Kantian sublime as bringing consolation, but fails to acknowledge that Kant, too, discussed the sublime as pertaining to art.
11 See 2.2.4.
12 In §16, he makes a distinction between pure beauty and adherent beauty. Murdoch is of course aware of this but confuses not only pure beauty with 'pure art', but also conceptual content in general with determining or governing concepts, see 3.3.
13 Like Niklas Forsberg does in his philosophical interpretation of *The Black Prince,* see 2.2.2. Another example will be discussed in the next section of this chapter.
14 Angela Breitenbach, 'One Imagination in Experiences of Beauty and Achievements of Understanding', *The British Journal of Aesthetics* 60, no. 1 (2020): 72.
15 Note also that Breitenbach bases her arguments on Kant's judgement of taste and beauty. In his account of the sublime, there is some more support for seeing the aesthetic as purposive for intellectual progression, although that would still have entailed leaving the properly aesthetic behind. See 3.5.
16 Breitenbach, 'One Imagination in Experiences of Beauty and Achievements of Understanding', 74.
17 *CJ*, 5:315.
18 Ibid.
19 Breitenbach, 'One Imagination in Experiences of Beauty and Achievements of Understanding', 73.
20 Ibid.
21 Ibid., 74; *CJ*, 5:326.
22 Breitenbach, 'One Imagination in Experiences of Beauty and Achievements of Understanding', 78.
23 An extensive and illuminating account of why this pleasure *is* the aesthetic judgement and neither a preliminary stage to it nor a symptom of it can be found in Hannah Ginsborg's elaboration on §9 of the *CJ*, in *The Role of Taste in Kant's Theory of Cognition* (New York and London: Garland Publishing, 1990), 20–40.
24 *CJ*, 5:326.
25 *CJ*, 5:328.
26 *CJ*, 5:327.
27 Ginsborg, *The Role of Taste in Kant's Theory of Cognition,* 87.
28 See 3.5.
29 Immanuel Kant, 'The False Subtlety of the Four Syllogistic Figures', in *Theoretical Philosophy 1755–1770* (New York: Cambridge University Press, 2002), 2: 60, 104.
30 Caygill, *A Kant Dictionary,* 120.

31 *A priori* or pure concepts are also called categories in Kant.
32 *CJ*, 5:203.
33 *CJ*, 5:218–19.
34 Ginsborg, *The Role of Taste in Kant's Theory of Cognition*, 21.
35 *CJ*, 20:232.
36 *CJ*, 5:169.
37 CPR A:51, B:75. See 2.2.4 for a preliminary discussion of why this does not apply to the aesthetic judgement.
38 CPR A:52, B:76.
39 Robert Hanna, 'Kant and Nonconceptual Content', *European Journal of Philosophy* 13, no. 2 (2005): 256, italics original.
40 Hanna, 'Kant and Nonconceptual Content', 257.
41 CPR A:90, B:122.
42 CPR A:297, B:254.
43 Hanna, 'Kant and Nonconceptual Content', 263, italics original.
44 Ibid., 278.
45 For an explanation of the difference between the determining and the reflective judgement, see 2.3.2.
46 On the place of the reflective judgement in Kant's critical philosophy as a whole, see Angelica Nuzzo. 'Reflective Judgment, Determinative Judgment, and the Problem of Particularity', *Washington University Jurisprudence Review* 6, no. 1 (2013): 7–25.
47 Andrea Kern, 'Reflecting the Form of Understanding: The Philosophical Significance of Art', in *Kant after Derrida*, ed. Philip Rothfield (Manchester: Clinamen, 2004), 110.
48 *CJ*, 5:204.
49 Kant never used the term 'aesthetic experiences' but spoke solely about the aesthetic judgement. Aesthetic experience is, however, a quite frequently used term in the literature on Kant and means (just as in the epistemological use) the empirical instances of applied judgement.
50 *CJ*, 5:229.
51 Hanna, 'Kant and Nonconceptual Content', 266.
52 Ibid.
53 *MGM*, 312, italics added.
54 *CJ*, 5:285.
55 *CJ*, 5:300.
56 *CJ*, 5:299.
57 *CJ*, 5:300, bold original.
58 *CJ*, 5:302.
59 *CJ*, 5:303.
60 §43 On art in general, §44 On beautiful art, §45 Beautiful art is an art to the extent that it seems at the same time to be nature, §46 Beautiful art is art of genius.
61 *CJ*, 5:306.
62 Adorno, *Aesthetic Theory*, 62.
63 Ibid., 66.
64 *CJ*, 5:300.
65 Breitenbach, 'One Imagination in Experiences of Beauty and Achievements of Understanding', 73.
66 See also Andrea Kern's description of the aesthetic as the paradoxical experience of something philosophically undevelopable: 'From the point of view of philosophical

reflection, the cooperation of these two faculties of ours [imagination and understanding] possesses the status of a transcendental condition, that is, the status of something one cannot "experience" in the same sense as one experiences objects, for it is the condition of possibility for the givenness of objects of experience in general. Therefore, according to Kant, aesthetic experience is the paradoxical experience of something that, from the perspective of philosophical reflection upon our experience, cannot be experienced at all.' Kern, 'Reflecting the Form of Understanding', 110.

67 SG, 213.
68 SG, 214.
69 *CJ*, 5:325. Murdoch takes note of this later in *MGM*, 99–100: 'Kant tells us that tragedy joins the sublime and the beautiful together.'
70 *CJ*, 5:244.
71 *CJ*, 5:245.
72 *CJ*, 5:345.
73 *CJ*, 5:246.
74 *CJ*, 5:248.
75 *CJ*, 5:250, bold original.
76 *CJ*, 5:270, bold original, italics added.
77 See 2.3.3–4.
78 *MGM*, 88. Again, Murdoch appears confused as to whether Kant allowed for art to be sublime or not.
79 Kirk Pillow, *Sublime Understanding: Aesthetic Reflection in Kant and Hegel* (Cambridge, MA: MIT Press, 2003), 77.
80 Murdoch, 'The Sublime and the Good', 216.
81 *CJ*, 5:259.
82 *CJ*, 5:260.
83 Merritt, 'Murdoch and Kant', 261.
84 For a further discussion of morality and the sublime, see 6.3.2 and 6.3.3.
85 *MGM*, 88.
86 *CJ*, 5:314.
87 Ibid.
88 Ibid.
89 *CJ*, 5:316.
90 *CJ*, 5:315.
91 Pillow, *Sublime Understanding*, 68.
92 Ibid.
93 Pillow, *Sublime Understanding*, 84.
94 Ibid., 83–4.
95 Simone Weil, *Lectures on Philosophy*, trans. Hugh Price (Cambridge: Cambridge University Press, 1978), 187.
96 *CJ*, 5:314.
97 'muddle (v.)', *Online Etymology Dictionary*, accessed 31 August 2020, https://www.etymonline.com/word/muddle#etymonline_v_19212
98 'muddle', *Cambridge Dictionary*, accessed 31 August 2020, https://dictionary.cambridge.org/dictionary/english/muddle
99 'muddle', *Dictionary.com*, accessed 31 August 2020, https://www.dictionary.com/browse/muddle?s=t

100 'muddle', *Oxford English Dictionary*, accessed 31 August 2020, https://www.oed.com/view/Entry/123242#eid35881665
101 *MGM*, 88, italics added.
102 *FS*, 460, italics added.
103 Iris Murdoch, *The Time of the Angels* (London: Chatto & Windus, 1989), 121–2, italics added.
104 Murdoch, *The Time of the Angels*, 122, italics added.
105 *The Philosopher's Pupil* is also discussed in 2.4.
106 *MGM*, 88.
107 Murdoch, *The Philosopher's Pupil*, 60, italics added.
108 Ibid., 486, italics added.
109 Murdoch, *The Philosopher's Pupil*, 531, italics added.
110 *FS*, 460.
111 Iris Murdoch, *A Severed Head* (London: Vintage Books, 2001), 42, italics added.
112 Iris Murdoch, *The Nice and the Good* (St Albans: Panther Books, 1997), 80, italics added.
113 Murdoch, *The Nice and the Good*, 27.
114 Communication is here not to be confused with a narrow idea of intentionally conveyed information between sender and receiver. See Ginsborg's comment on the German word 'mitteilen' on page 79.
115 *CJ*, 5:316.
116 *MGM*, 8.
117 Iris Murdoch, *An Unofficial Rose* (London: Penguin Books, 1962), 39, italics added.
118 Ibid.
119 *CJ*, 5:314.
120 *CJ*, 5:315.
121 William Shakespeare, 'Romeo and Juliet', in *The Complete Works of William Shakespeare* (London: Spring Books, 1958), 901.
122 Gertrude Stein, 'Sacred Emily', in *Geography and Plays. Poems* (Boston: Four Seas Co., 1922), 178.

Chapter 4

1 Toril Moi, 'Rethinking Character', in Anderson, Felski, Moi, *Character*, 27–76.
2 Rita Felski, 'Identifying with Characters', in Anderson, Felski, Moi, *Character*, 85.
3 Characters may of course also be non-fictional, as they point out; the boundaries between fictionality and reality are also increasingly being challenged in contemporary autofiction.
4 Moi, 'Rethinking Character', 60. Moi states that the problem of how to understand fiction would 'clearly [be] a different question'. In contrast, I believe that our relation to characters is bound up with our understanding of fiction, and I will discuss these two issues as intertwined in this chapter.
5 I have also commented on this in the Introduction, 1.8.2.
6 *AD*, 294.
7 *MGM*, 189.

8   Stanley Cavell, 'The Avoidance of Love', in *Must We Mean What We Say?: A Book of Essays* (New York: Scribner, 1969), 268.
9   Cavell, *The Claim of Reason*, xxii–xxiii.
10 A proper recap of the debate can be found in Damien Freeman, 'The Paradox of Fiction', in *The Routledge Companion to the Philosophy of Literature*, ed. Noël Carroll and John Gibson (London: Routledge, 2015), 247–58.
11 Arthur C. Danto, 'Philosophy as/and/of Literature', *Proceedings and Addresses of the American Philosophical Association* 58, no. 1 (1984): 9.
12 Danto, 'Philosophy as/and/of Literature', 9.
13 Ibid., 10.
14 John R. Searle, 'The Logical Status of Fictional Discourse', *New Literary History* 6, no. 2 (1975): 324.
15 Kendall L. Walton, 'Appreciating Fiction: Suspending Disbelief or Pretending Belief?' *Dispositio* 5, no. 13–14 (1980): 2.
16 Walton, 'Appreciating Fiction', 9.
17 Cavell, *The Claim of Reason*, 496.
18 Stanley Cavell, 'Aesthetic Problems of Modern Philosophy', in *Must We Mean What We Say?* (Cambridge: Cambridge University Press, 2002), 80.
19 Cavell, 'The Avoidance of Love', 328.
20 Here, one might wonder whether this man has *really* failed to comprehend the status of fiction, or whether his objections to the scene is instead expressive of racist indignation at having to witness a Black man murder a White woman; something symbolically rather than epistemologically intolerable to him. A great field of political and social problems of imagination and representation appears here to have been covered over by the philosophical problem of fictionality; problem which unfortunately fall outside the scope of my dissertation. I shall instead follow Cavell's perspective in order to explain my problems with his understanding of fiction. But I owe Catherine Wheatley and Hugo Strandberg thanks for drawing my attention to how Cavell ignores the problem of bigoted rage, an ignorance which renders the problem of the incomprehension of the Southern man somewhat artificial.
21 Cavell, 'The Avoidance of Love', 328–9.
22 Ibid., 330.
23 Ibid., 319–20.
24 Ibid., 327.
25 See, for example, Eva Schaper, 'Fiction and the Suspension of Disbelief', *The British Journal of Aesthetics* 18, no. 1 (1978): 31–44; Searle, 'The Logical Status of Fictional Discourse'; Walton, 'Appreciating Fiction'.
26 Freeman, 'The Paradox of Fiction', 256.
27 Ibid.
28 Samuel Taylor Coleridge, *Biographia Literaria*, ed. Adam Roberts (Edinburgh: Edinburgh University Press, 2014), 208.
29 Coleridge, *Biographia Literaria*, 208.
30 Stanley Cavell, *The World Viewed: Reflections on the Ontology of Film* (Cambridge, MA: Harward University Press, 1979), 40.
31 Cavell, *The Claim of Reason*, 455.
32 Ibid.
33 Cavell, *The World Viewed*, 40.
34 Cavell, 'The Avoidance of Love', 323.

35 Ibid., 324.
36 Cavell, *The Claim of Reason*, 457.
37 Cavell, 'The Avoidance of Love', 329.
38 Ibid.
39 Cavell largely ignores the old aesthetic problem of how tragedy can be so pleasurable to watch, known as the paradox of tragedy. This will be revisited in the next chapter.
40 Ibid.
41 Cavell, 'The Avoidance of Love', 277–8.
42 Freud, 'Creative Writers and Day-Dreaming', 427–8.
43 Cavell, 'The Avoidance of Love', 334. 'We could also say: there is no distance between us, as there is none between me and a figure in my dream' (ibid.).
44 Freud quoted in Norman N. Holland, 'The "Willing Suspension of Disbelief" Revisited', *Centennial Review* 11, no. 1 (1967): 10.
45 Holland calls these feelings 'weaker' and argues that the artistic isolation breaks down when they become too strong. I think that the reasons the Southern man has for attempting to stop Othello are quite different (see endnote 20). Art can make us feel very strongly indeed; at times (perhaps thanks to the licence of fiction) more strongly than in life.
46 Cavell, 'The Avoidance of Love', 337.
47 Ibid., 337.
48 Ibid., 332–3.
49 See, for example, Cavell, *The Claim of Reason*, 369: 'We are endlessly separate, for *no reason*'.
50 Cavell, 'The Avoidance of Love', 339.
51 Ibid., 338.
52 Ibid., 333.
53 Cavell, *The Claim of Reason*, 493.
54 Cavell, 'The Avoidance of Love', 334.
55 Ibid., 337.
56 Cavell, 'The Avoidance of Love', 334.
57 *MGM*, 122.
58 Here, live action role playing (larp) offers a very interesting exception, which falls outside the scope of my discussion.
59 Cavell, *The Claim of Reason*, 496.
60 Gérard Genette, *Fiction & Diction*, trans. Catherine Porter (Ithaca: Cornell UP, 1993), 65.
61 Cavell, *Disowning Knowledge*, 5–6.
62 Ibid., 453.
63 Ibid., 453.
64 AIN, 253.
65 Murdoch, 'The Sublime and the Beautiful Revisited', 283.
66 AIN, 257.
67 For a further discussion of Murdoch's distinction between fantasy and imagination, see 6.2.4.
68 Floora Ruokonen, 'Iris Murdoch and the Extraordinary Ambiguity of Art', *Journal of Value Inquiry* 42, no. 1 (2008): 88.
69 AIN, 254.
70 Maria Antonaccio, *A Philosophy to Live By: Engaging Iris Murdoch* (New York: Oxford University Press, 2012), 60.

Chapter 5

1. *MGM*, 93.
2. Cavell, *The Claim of Reason*, 493.
3. Cavell, 'The Avoidance of Love', 341.
4. Cavell, *The Claim of Reason*, 493.
5. Plato, *Republic*, 379C–380D, 391A–E.
6. *MGM*, 92.
7. Aristotle, *Poetics*, 1453A 20.
8. The exact meaning of *hamartia* is much debated. Malcolm Heath provides an overview of the discussions in his 'Introduction' in Aristotle, *Poetics*, trans. Malcolm Heath, xxxii–xxxiii.
9. Nussbaum, *The Fragility of Goodness*, 25.
10. Plato, *The Laws*, trans. Thomas L. Pangle (Chicago: University of Chicago Press, 1988), vii, 817B.
11. See, for example, George Steiner, *The Death of Tragedy* (London: Faber and Faber, 1995).
12. See, for example, Andrzej Gasiorek, 'A Renewed Sense of Difficulty': E. M. Forster, Iris Murdoch and Zadie Smith on Ethics and Form', in *The Legacies of Modernism: Historicising Postwar and Contemporary Fiction*, ed. David James (Cambridge: Cambridge University Press, 2011); William Schweiker, 'The Moral Fate of Fictive Persons: On Iris Murdoch's Humanism', in *Iris Murdoch and Morality*, ed. Anne Rowe and Avril Horner (New York: Palgrave Macmillan, 2010), and Antonaccio, *A Philosophy to Live By*, 52–68.
13. *MGM*, 1–2.
14. *MGM*, 1.
15. *MGM*, 5.
16. *MGM*, 21.
17. *MGM*, 21.
18. Rachel Zuckert, 'The Purposiveness of Form: A Reading of Kant's Aesthetic Formalism', *Journal of the History of Philosophy* 44, no. 4 (2006): 617. *CJ* §15.
19. Zuckert, 'The Purposiveness of Form', 618.
20. LP, 7.
21. LP, 7.
22. LP, 11.
23. Schweiker, 'The Moral Fate of Fictive Persons', 184.
24. SG, 216. See also the discussion in Chapter 3.
25. SG, 210.
26. SG, 211.
27. See my discussion in 3.5, and *CJ*, 5:325.
28. SG, 216.
29. SG, 219.
30. SG, 220.
31. The first version, which is slightly shorter, was delivered as the Gifford Lectures in 1982.
32. *MGM*, 94.
33. *MGM*, 111.
34. *MGM*, 122.
35. *MGM*, 131.

36 *MGM*, 116–17.
37 *MGM*, 117.
38 *MGM*, 121.
39 *MGM*, 125.
40 *MGM*, 86.
41 LP, 7.
42 Aristotle, *Poetics*, trans. Anthony Kenny, 1460B 20. See also 1.4.
43 Ibid.
44 Ibid., 1460B 35–1460A 5.
45 Ibid., 1461B 15.
46 Ibid., 1449B 25.
47 My thanks to Rebecka Kärde for helping me with the original Greek.
48 Aristotle, *Poetics*, trans. Anthony Kenny, 1451A 25–30.
49 Malcolm Heath, 'Introduction', in Aristotle, *Poetics*, trans. Malcolm Heath (London: Penguin, 1996), xxxvii.
50 See, for example, Scott, 'Purging the Poetics', 233–63.
51 Julian Young, *The Philosophy of Tragedy from Plato to Žižek* (Cambridge: Cambridge University Press, 2013), 26–34.
52 Aristotle, *Poetics*, 1449B 30.
53 'Of Tragedy', in *Four Dissertations,* ed. David Hume (London: printed for A. Millar, 1757), 190.
54 Hume, 'Of Tragedy', 197.
55 Lear, 'Katharsis', 314.
56 Ibid., 325.
57 *MGM*, 93.
58 Lear, 'Katharsis', 325.
59 For an introduction to Nietzsche's position in the ancient quarrel, see 1.3.1.
60 Nietzsche, *The Birth of Tragedy*, 9.
61 Ibid., 45.
62 Ibid., 46.
63 Ibid., 12.
64 Ibid., 84.
65 Ibid., 9.
66 Friedrich Nietzsche, *The Will to Power: Selections from the Notebooks of the 1880s*, trans. R. Kevin Hill and Michael A. Scarpitti, ed. R. Kevin Hill (London: Penguin Books, 2017), $852.
67 For an introduction to Hegel's position in the ancient quarrel, see 1.5.2.
68 Hegel, *Aesthetics*, 1215.
69 SG, 214.
70 Nussbaum, *The Fragility of Goodness*, 14.
71 Ibid., 24.
72 Ibid., 420.
73 Rachel Aviv, 'The Philosopher of Feelings', *The New Yorker*, 18 July 2016.
74 Martha Nussbaum, '"Faint with Secret Knowledge": Love and Vision in Murdoch's *The Black Prince*', *Poetics Today* 25, no. 4 (2004): 707.
75 Ibid.
76 Nussbaum, *The Fragility of Goodness*, xliii.
77 Ibid., 131.
78 Ibid., 15.

79 LP, 4.
80 Nussbaum, *The Fragility of Goodness*, 16.
81 Ibid.
82 LP, 11.
83 Murdoch, 'On "God" and "Good"', 359. See also LP, 7.
84 LP, 5.
85 Nussbaum, *The Fragility of Goodness*, 392.
86 Ibid., 394.
87 Ibid., 17.
88 LP, 7.
89 See also the discussion of 'muddle' in Murdoch's fiction as a Kantian aesthetic idea in 3.7.
90 LP, 7.
91 Nussbaum, *The Fragility of Goodness*, 394.
92 Ibid., 129.
93 This is also an aspect of Nussbaum's reading of Henry James, which will be mentioned in the next chapter: 5.1.3, 5.1.5 and 5.2.2.
94 *CJ*, 5:315.
95 Nussbaum, *The Fragility of Goodness*, 14.
96 Ibid.
97 Ibid., 260.
98 Ibid., 389.
99 Ibid., 388.
100 Ibid., 390.
101 Ibid., 391.
102 Martha Nussbaum, 'Emotions as Judgements of Value and Importance', in *Thinking about Feeling: Contemporary Philosophers on Emotions*, ed. Robert C. Solomon (New York: Oxford University Press, 2004).
103 Nussbaum, *The Fragility of Goodness*, 325.
104 Ibid., 134.
105 Plato, *The Phaedo*, in *The Last Days of Socrates*, trans. Hugh Tredennick and Harold Tarrant (Middlesex: Penguin Books, 1969), 117C–D.
106 Plato, *The Phaedo*, 117B.
107 Ibid., 67E.
108 Ibid., 68B–C.
109 Plato, *Republic*, 486A–B.
110 Plato, *The Apology*, 40B.
111 Plato, *The Republic*, 387B.
112 Plato, *The Republic*, 605C–D.
113 Martin Hägglund, *Dying for Time: Proust, Woolf, Nabokov* (Cambridge: Harvard University Press, 2012), 1–2.
114 Hägglund, *Dying for Time*, 2.
115 Ibid., 10.
116 Plato, *The Symposium*, 21A. Hägglund quotes this passage in claiming that 'Socrates argues that temporal objects do not answer to what we really desire. The proper destination of desire is rather an eternity that "neither comes into being nor passes away" and thus transcends temporal finitude'. Hägglund, *Dying for Time*, 2.
117 Plato, *The Timaeus*, in *Timaeus and Critias*, trans. Robin Waterfield, ed. Andrew Gregory (Oxford: Oxford University Press, 2008), 37D.

118 Wolfgang von Leyden, 'Time, Number, and Eternity in Plato and Aristotle', *The Philosophical Quarterly* 14, no. 54 (1964): 38.
119 Plato, *The Apology*, 29A–B.
120 Ibid.
121 Plato, *The Republic*, 596C.
122 Ibid., 386.
123 Andrea Capra, 'Seeing through Plato's Looking Glass: *Mythos* and *Mimesis* from *Republic* to *Poetics*', *Aisthesis: Pratiche, linguaggi e saperi dell'estetico* 10, no. 1 (2017): 83.
124 Hägglund, *Dying for Time*, 22.
125 Ibid.
126 Marcel Proust, *Time Regained*, trans. Andreas Mayor and Terence Kilmartin (London: Vintage, 1996), 190.
127 Simon Critchley, 'Comedy and Finitude: Displacing the Tragic-Heroic Paradigm in Philosophy and Psychoanalysis', *Constellations* 6, no. 1 (1999): 110.
128 Critchley, 'Comedy and Finitude', 119.
129 Simon Critchley and Carl Cederström, *How to Stop Living and Start Worrying: Conversations with Carl Cederström* (Oxford: Polity, 2010), 49.
130 Plato, *The Phaedo*, 107b.
131 Ibid., 114d–e.
132 Ibid., 117D.
133 Plato, *The Republic*, 604D.
134 FS, 396.

Chapter 6

1 FS, 387.
2 Nickolas Pappas, 'Plato's Aesthetics', in *The Stanford Encyclopedia of Philosophy*, ed. Edward N. Zalta. Fall 2020 Edition. https://plato.stanford.edu/archives/fall2020/entries/plato-aesthetics/
3 Christopher Janaway, 'Plato', in *The Routledge Companion to Aesthetics*, ed. Berys Gaut and Dominic McIver Lopes (London: Routledge, 2013), 4.
4 See also Andrea Capra's description of the 'deliberate deficiency of the mirror argument' in 'Seeing through Plato's Looking Glass', discussed in 5.6.
5 Stanley Rosen, 'The Quarrel between Philosophy and Poetry', in *The Quarrel Between Philosophy and Poetry: Studies in Ancient Thought* (New York: Routledge, 2014), e-book, 19.
6 FS, 390.
7 Plato, *The Republic*, 602C.
8 Ibid., 364A.
9 Ibid., 391E.
10 FS, 461.
11 Elisabeth Ladenson, *Dirt for Art's Sake: Books on Trial from Madame Bovary to Lolita* (Ithaca: Cornell University Press, 2007), xx.
12 FS, 389–90.
13 FS, 389–90.
14 FS, 244.

15 It is almost painful to partake of the pretty Alcibiades's drunken monologue about his failed attempts to seduce Socrates. Inviting him to dinner, wrestling with him, forcing him to stay the night on the bed right next to him … all in vain. Plato, *The Symposium*, 217.
16 Plato, *The Republic*, 607D-E.
17 Plato, *The Timaeus*, 69D.
18 Jessica Moss, 'What Is Imitative Poetry and Why Is It Bad?', in *The Cambridge Companion to Plato's Republic*, ed. G.R.F. Ferrari (Cambridge: Cambridge University Press, 2007), 441–2.
19 Weil, *The Notebooks of Simone Weil*, 327.
20 Plato, *The Republic*, 392B.
21 FS, 393.
22 Ladenson, *Dirt for Art's Sake*, 11.
23 LP, 10.
24 FS, 449.
25 See Hämäläinen, *Literature and Moral Theory*, 153: 'she is correctly considered a central figure in creating an interest in narrative literature in analytic moral philosophy and beyond, inspiring, for example, Nussbaum, Diamond, Blum and Goldberg.'
26 Martha Nussbaum, 'Finely Aware and Richly Responsible', *The Journal of Philosophy* 82, no. 10 (1985): 516.
27 Nussbaum, 'Finely Aware and Richly Responsible', 521.
28 *MGM*, 337.
29 AIN, 254.
30 SG, 215.
31 Hämäläinen, *Literature and Moral Theory*, 171.
32 Ibid.
33 Murdoch, 'The Sublime and the Beautiful Revisited', 277. Murdoch criticizes him for claiming that prose 'must give information', but what Sartre is trying to describe with the tool metaphor in *What Is Literature?* is part of a more complex argument about transparency, where prose language is described as using and at the same time transforming words into sensory, prosthetic extensions of the body. Sartre, *What Is Literature?*, 20.
34 SG, 218.
35 *MGM*, 9.
36 Iris Murdoch, 'Salvation by Words', in *Existentialists and Mystics*, 238.
37 Ibid.
38 AIN, 247.
39 John Haffenden, 'John Haffenden Talks to Iris Murdoch', 132: 'The doctrine of *anamnesis* is a doctrine of the unconscious mind, and the idea of *eros* as fundamental energy, a drive which includes sex and which can be good and can be bad: that's all in Plato.' It is clear even from the chiasmic structure of reference in this quote, however, that Murdoch's reading of Plato has been affected by Freud, as was Weil's.
40 For a thorough discussion of the Freudian influence on Murdoch's fiction and literary theory, see Bran Nicol, *Iris Murdoch: The Retrospective Fiction* (Hampshire: Palgrave Macmillan, 2004). Among other things, Nicol claims that Freud's understanding of how compulsions and fantasies drive our artistic endeavours are important for Murdoch, even though she parts company with him 'because art for Freud remains a disguised expression of selfish impulses no matter its *quality*, while for Murdoch,

the better the art the further away it is from personal desire' (171). The quality distinction is an important point of difference, although I would not phrase it as a matter of distance from desire.
41 Freud, 'Creative Writers and Day-Dreaming', 419–514.
42 SGO, 364.
43 AIN, 251.
44 Ibid.
45 AIN, 253.
46 AIN, 252. Leo Tolstoy, *What Is Art?* trans. Richard Pevear (London: Penguin Books, 1995), 39.
47 AIN, 248. She adds 'though it is certainly an extremely eccentric book', which is not difficult to agree with. For example, Tolstoy provides a supplement where he sums up Wagner's Ring Cycle with the explicit purpose of sparing his readers of having to take part of it.
48 Tolstoy, *What Is Art?*, 38.
49 Ibid., 94.
50 LP, 19. Tolstoy, *What Is Art?*, 123–38.
51 Tolstoy, *What Is Art?*, 62.
52 Murdoch, *The Book and the Brotherhood*, 167–8.
53 I shall not devote more space here to discussing the moral value of Murdoch's own literary work, since the focus of this chapter concerns her view of literature in general. However, it may also be interesting here to take note of how Murdoch's eventual personal vices might have been generative for her fiction, despite her view that a good writer should aim to be absent from her own work. Nicol comments that new 'biographical material has transformed not simply our perception of Murdoch's personality, but her writing', so that '[t]he impression that she maintained of a disciplined detachment from her own fiction now seems less persuasive' (Bran Nicol, 'Iris Murdoch's Aesthetics of Masochism', *Journal of Modern Literature* 29, no. 2 (2006): 149). Indeed, the statement that a good writer should be absent from their own work has for her functioned as a clever way of distracting her readers from seeking biographical inspirations in her fiction. As she states in AIN: 'Writers try to conceal their obsessions' (251).
54 Plato, *The Republic*, 395D.
55 FS, 391.
56 Iris Murdoch, 'Metaphysics and Ethics', in *Existentialists and Mystics*, 75.
57 Murdoch, 'Salvation by Words', 238.
58 Plato, *The Republic*, 604E.
59 Ibid., 605A.
60 Moss, 'What Is Imitative Poetry and Why Is It Bad?', 436.
61 Weil, 'Literature and Morality', 145.
62 Ibid., 147.
63 Peter J. Conradi, *The Saint and the Artist: A Study of the Fiction of Iris Murdoch* (London: Macmillan, 1986).
64 According to Conradi, a 'draft for the novel makes clear that [...] Tallis was born, Christ-like, on 25 December'. Conradi, *The Saint and the Artist*, 205. For the virtuousness of Tallis, see, for example, Browning, *Why Iris Murdoch Matters*, 106, and Scott H. Moore, 'Murdoch's Fictional Philosophers: What They Say and What They Show', in *Iris Murdoch and Morality*, ed. Anne Rowe and Avril Horner (New York: Palgrave Macmillan, 2010), 107–8.

65 Bellamy, 'An Interview with Iris Murdoch', 51.
66 Ibid.
67 Conradi, *The Saint and the Artist*, 220-1.
68 *MGM*, 130.
69 Murdoch, 'On "God" and "Good"', 352.
70 Ibid., 355.
71 Ibid.
72 Ibid.
73 Hämäläinen, *Literature and Moral Theory*, 168. Hämäläinen also adds: 'But it does not, primarily, give us philosophical answers or illustrate philosophical positions.' Nonetheless, I find the lesson-metaphor problematic. It is a word which, to my knowledge, Murdoch never uses in relation to art. On the contrary, she often says things like 'I think a novelist should be wary of being a teacher in a didactic sense.' Meyers, 'Two Interviews with Iris Murdoch', 227.
74 Hallberg, *Novel Writing and Moral Philosophy as Aspects of a Single Struggle*, 50.
75 Mark Luprecht, 'Death and Goodness: Bruno's Dream and "The Sovereignty of Good over Other Concepts"', in *Iris Murdoch and Morality*, ed. Anne Rowe and Avril Horner (New York: Palgrave Macmillan, 2010), 113.
76 Luprecht, 'Death and Goodness', 123.
77 Elizabeth Dipple, *Iris Murdoch: Work for the Spirit* (London: Methuen, 1982), 6.
78 Iris Murdoch, *The Bell* (London: Vintage, 1999), 190.
79 Hallberg, *Novel Writing and Moral Philosophy as Aspects of a Single Struggle*, 55.
80 Ibid., 5.
81 Browning, *Why Iris Murdoch Matters*, 74; quoting Anne Rowe, *The Visual Arts and the Novels of Iris Murdoch* (Lewiston, N.Y.: E. Mellen Press, 2002), 194.
82 *MGM*, 9.
83 Murdoch never thought she had produced any masterpieces but was instead inclined to say things like 'one is always discontented with what one has done' (Meyers, 'Two Interviews with Iris Murdoch', 228). This may of course be dismissed as an expression of English humility – although I dare say that there is more of self-doubt than hubris in her diaries as well.
84 Frits Gåvertsson is one of the few who devotes any lengthy attention to bad art, although he claims that it in Murdoch's aesthetics is 'sharply distinguished' from great art. Frits Gåvertsson, *Perfection and Fiction: A Study in Iris Murdoch's Moral Philosophy* (Lund: Lund University, 2018), 197. See also 164–76.
85 Iris Murdoch, *The Sea, the Sea* (London: Vintage, 1999), 182.
86 Ibid., 183.
87 Priscilla Martin also points out some of the negatively charged visions of art in Murdoch's novels in 'Houses of Fiction: Iris Murdoch and Henry James', in *Iris Murdoch: A Reassessment*, ed. Anne Rowe (Hampshire: Palgrave Macmillan, 2007), 128, but only the scenes in which the characters fail to see the greatness of the works because they are under some kind of explicit external negative influence. The artworks are, of course, innocent of any negative impact on their viewers.
88 For Murdoch, moral philosophy should be normative, that is, conducted for purpose of moral improvement. The ideal of a 'neutral' moral philosophy is misguided to her: 'since an ethical system cannot but commend an ideal, it should commend a worthy ideal. Ethics should not be merely an analysis of ordinary mediocre conduct, it should be a hypothesis about good conduct and about how this can be achieved. How can we make ourselves better? is a question moral philosophers should at least

attempt to answer.' SGO, 364. Thus, a certain amount of switching between 'moral improvement' and 'moral philosophy' is permitted in this chapter.
89 *MGM*, 91.
90 Iris Murdoch, *The Good Apprentice* (London: Vintage, 2000), 447.
91 Murdoch, *The Good Apprentice*, 508; Hallberg, *Novel Writing and Moral Philosophy as Aspects of a Single Struggle*, 58.
92 Hallberg, *Novel Writing and Moral Philosophy as Aspects of a Single Struggle*, 58.
93 Ibid.
94 Bran Nicol, 'The Curse of *The Bell*: The Ethics and Aesthetics of Narrative', in *Iris Murdoch: A Reassessment*, ed. Anne Rowe and Avril Horner (New York: Palgrave Macmillan, 2010), 105.
95 AIN, 251.
96 Nicol, 'The Curse of *The Bell*', 106.
97 Ibid., 109.
98 Ted Cohen, 'Literature and Morality', in *The Oxford Handbook of Philosophy and Literature*, ed. Richard Eldridge (New York: Oxford University Press, 2009), 487. This interpretation of Aristotle conforms to what I in 1.4.1 refer to as the received view.
99 Hämäläinen, *Literature and Moral Theory*, 154.
100 Luprecht, 'Death and Goodness', 113.
101 *MGM*, 189. Creating confusion could perhaps be considered a philosophical achievement, as suggested by Niklas Forsberg's metaphor of literature as the 'contrast fluid' of philosophy. But this is implying that the aim and achievement of literature would be subservient to a subsequent philosophical sorting out or clarification (or else that confusion would be a philosophical aim in itself, something very few practitioners would agree on).
102 Nussbaum, 'Finely Aware and Richly Responsible', 517, quoting Henry James, *The Golden Bowl* (New York: Penguin Modern Classics, 1966), 17/8.
103 Nussbaum, 'Faint with Secret Knowledge', 708.
104 Ibid. See also my discussion of what I call Nussbaum's paradox of clarified muddle, in 5.5.
105 See, for example, Murdoch, 'Metaphysics and Ethics', 67–70.
106 AD, 293.
107 Weil's concept of attention as desire-based is much inspired by the ladder of desire in Plato's *Symposium*, where to desire and to desire the good are shown to be interrelated. To sum up Plato: being gripped by affection for a beautiful boy may lead towards a love of truth.
108 Tammy Grinshaw, 'Do not Seek God outside Your Own Soul: Buddhism in The Green Knight', in *Iris Murdoch and Morality*, ed. Anne Rowe and Avril Horner (New York: Palgrave Macmillan, 2010), 174.
109 Rob Hardy, 'Stories, Rituals and Healers in Iris Murdoch's Fiction', in *Iris Murdoch and Morality*, ed. Anne Rowe and Avril Horner (New York: Palgrave Macmillan, 2010), 44.
110 Gåvertsson, *Perfection and Fiction*, 20.
111 Dipple, *Iris Murdoch*, 101. 'Sober' is by the by an odd word to associate with Murdoch's fiction, in which almost every character seems to be drinking like a fish, suggesting an at least relaxed attitude to intoxication on part of the author. In the caricature list 'How to Tell if You Are in an Iris Murdoch Novel', the third point is 'Powerful claret and lots and lots of it and also whiskey and you're drunk and where's

some more, be a peach and bring us a bottle, won't you?' *The Toast*, accessed 5 August 2021, https://the-toast.net/2013/09/05/tell-iris-murdoch-novel/

112 Dipple, *Iris Murdoch*, 6.
113 Panizza, *The Importance of Attention in Morality*, 81.
114 Simone Weil, *Waiting for God*, trans. Emma Craufurd (London: Fontana Books, 1959), 88.
115 Panizza, *The Importance of Attention in Morality*, 98.
116 Ibid., 103.
117 Ibid., 184.
118 Ibid., 185, footnote 202.
119 See an account of some of these interpretations in Ladenson, *Dirt for Art's Sake*, 28.
120 At the obscenity trial for Flaubert's novel, its author was charged with infecting his reader with these dangerous fantasies. Here, the question about the relationship between mimesis and morality becomes exceedingly interesting and muddled. As Ladenson remarks, the fate of the novel itself is 'inextricably bound up with the question of fiction's failure to perform its assigned role of providing consolation and moral uplift, of serving as an antidote to reality rather than a reflection of it'. Ladenson, *Dirt for Art's Sake*, 27.
121 AD, 293.
122 Ibid.
123 AD, 294.
124 Statements like these have, by for example Peter Conradi, been taken to suggest that literature might help us cure the ailments of philosophy. As Altorf points out, 'The ills are, contrary to what Conradi's question implies, not only philosophical but also literary. One would then be mistaken to think of philosophy as the problem and literature as the answer. Rather, Murdoch considers both contemporary philosophy and contemporary literature to be suffering from the same ill: a "far too shallow and flimsy an idea of human personality"'. Hanna Marije Altorf, *Iris Murdoch and the Art of Imagination: Imaginative Philosophy as Response to Secularism* (Glasgow: University of Glasgow, 2004), 57–8.
125 Panizza, *The Importance of Attention in Morality*, 115.
126 Plato, *The Theaetetus*, in *Theaetetus and Sophist*, transl. and ed. Christopher Rowe (Cambridge: Cambridge University Press, 2015), 156E. In this translation: 'now it sees, having become, certainly not sight, rather a seeing eye'. Larson is quoting a translation by M.J. Lewett.
127 Larson, 'Everything Important Is to Do with Passion', 86.
128 Weil, *The Notebooks of Simone Weil*, 527.
129 Weil, *Waiting for God*, 111.
130 Weil, *The Notebooks of Simone Weil*, 19.
131 Ibid., 232, italics original.
132 Weil, *Waiting for God*, 163–4.
133 For example, in her interpretation of the myth of Kore/Persephone, Weil writes: 'Kore is the soul which sees a beautiful flower and is seized and carried against its will into the other world'. *The Notebooks of Simone Weil*, 375.
134 Weil, *Waiting for God*, 111.
135 Ibid. Larson, 'Everything Important Is to Do with Passion', 67.
136 Larson, 'Everything Important Is to Do with Passion', 91. Spelling mistakes have been corrected in the quote.

137 Frits Gåvertsson also connects the problem of attending to the other with 'the difficulty of letting our guard down' in *Perfection and Fiction*, 78.
138 Henry James, *The Art of the Novel* (New York: Scribners, 1934), 149. Quoted by Nussbaum.
139 Nussbaum, '"Finely Aware and Richly Responsible"', 516.
140 Larson, 'Everything Important Is to Do with Passion', 68.
141 Ibid.
142 Plato, *The Symposium*, 203B.
143 Murdoch occasionally speaks about the novelist as a moralist, but this is somewhat misleading, since what she means by this is not something didactic. She says about Proust, for example, that he 'as every great novelist does, [reveals himself] as a great moralist as well as a great artist'. Then she adds, which I shall return to in 6.3.4, that '[w]e have here to be our own moralists if we want to use Proust's states of pure consciousness as part of a moral, or moral philosophical, argument'. *MGM*, 263.
144 FS, 416–17; *MGM*, 497. Plato, *The Phaedrus*, 249E.
145 FS, 417.
146 Larson, 'Everything Important Is to Do with Passion', 98.
147 Ibid., 99.
148 Plato, *The Republic*, 399E.
149 Plato, *The Ion*, 535B and 536C.
150 FS, 393.
151 Larson, 'Everything Important Is to Do with Passion', 124.
152 LP, 12.
153 *CJ*, 5:308.
154 *CJ*, 5:308.
155 *MGM*, 313.
156 Weil, 'Literature and Morality', 148.
157 Plato, *The Symposium*, 175D.
158 FS, 422.
159 FS, 425.
160 *MGM*, 1.
161 Ibid.
162 LP, 8; AIN, 253; *MGM*, 160, 166.
163 *MGM*, 309. As far as I can tell, Murdoch misquotes Hume somewhat here. He speaks of 'the principles [of the imagination] which are permanent, irresistable, and universal; such as the customary transition from causes to effect [...] [which are] the foundation of all our thoughts and actions, so that upon their removal human nature must immediately perish and go to ruin'. David Hume, *A Treatise of Human Nature* (Oxford: Clarendon Press, 1888), 225. What Murdoch has in mind with necessary fictions is something far more wide-reaching than causality.
164 SGO, 379.
165 *MGM*, 317.
166 *MGM*, 183.
167 See, for example, Weil, *The Notebooks of Simone Weil*, 150: 'The imagination is continually working to stop up all the fissures through which grace might pass.'
168 Larson, 'Everything Important Is to Do with Passion', 87.
169 *MGM*, 321.
170 Ibid.
171 Ibid.

172 Altorf also recognizes that 'imagination [to Murdoch] is operative at both an unconscious and a conscious level' (Altorf, *Iris Murdoch and the Art of Imagination*, 105). However, she also identifies 'the imagination of genius' with the conscious level, which I do not find entirely accurate, especially not when it comes to art.
173 *MGM*, 322.
174 *MGM*, 325.
175 *MGM*, 321.
176 *MGM*, 326–7.
177 *MGM*, 343.
178 LP, 11.
179 Altorf, *Iris Murdoch and the Art of Imagination*, 91.
180 AIN, 255.
181 Weil, *The Notebooks of Simone Weil*, 514.
182 Ibid.
183 This might be said to be true of Weil as well, but what we really desire, according to her, lies beyond the personal and interpersonal sphere: divine grace.
184 *MGM*, 1–2.
185 AIN, 252.
186 Nussbaum, 'Finely Aware and Richly Responsible', 516.
187 Hume did indeed fear going mad from his scepticism, or what he called the 'disease of the Learned'. Richard H. Popkin, 'David Hume', in *The Columbia History of Western Philosophy*, ed. Richard H. Popkin (New York: Columbia University Press, 1999), 454.
188 SG, 218.
189 Forsberg, one of the few who has taken note of the keyword 'accidental' here, interprets this as a claim that literature is 'doing philosophy', by working as a 'contrast fluid' on philosophy: 'One might say, with Murdoch, that literature is only accidentally philosophical in the sense that it challenges our philosophical conceptions and presuppositions the most when it shows us something about ourselves, our language, our culture, that we had not considered, seen or pondered.' Forsberg, *Language Lost and Found*, 12; see also 74–5. Even if one would agree with Forsberg's extremely wide definition of philosophy ('philosophy is everywhere', 12), the sensuousness, desire and enjoyment of art are pushed out of the picture when he describes how literature is forcing us to ask questions. See the criticism of Forsberg in 2.2.
190 Dipple, *Iris Murdoch*, 6.
191 For example, Weil dismisses all theories of genius which understands it as a self-conscious achievement, since these 'proceed from the fact that it is intolerable to imagine what is most precious in the world being delivered up to chance. It is because this notion is intolerable that it has to be contemplated'. *The Notebooks of Simone Weil*, 271.
192 SG, 214.
193 Murdoch, 'The Sublime and the Beautiful Revisited', 271.
194 David J. Gordon, 'Iris Murdoch's Comedies of Unselfing', *Twentieth Century Literature* 36, no. 2 (1990): 127.
195 Nicol, *Iris Murdoch*, 166.
196 Ibid., 162.
197 Murdoch, *Sartre*, 39.
198 See 2.3.

199 Julia Jordan, *Chance and the Modern British Novel* (London: University College London, 2013), 160.
200 Ibid.
201 Jordan, *Chance and the Modern British Novel*, 165.
202 See 5.2.
203 SG, 214.
204 FS, 400.
205 See 3.5.
206 See, for example, Nick Zangwill, 'Kant on Pleasure in the Agreeable', *The Journal of Aesthetics and Art Criticism* 53, no. 2 (1995): 167–76; and Thomas Hilgers, *Aesthetic Disinterestedness: Art, Experience, and the Self* (New York: Routledge, 2017). Even though these two do not completely agree with each other on how disinterestedness is to be interpreted, taken together they give a good general account of the Kantian concept.
207 MGM, 311–2.
208 Altorf, *Iris Murdoch and the Art of Imagination*, 102.
209 Ibid., 89.
210 SG, 213.
211 Mudoch's criticism of Freud might here be closer to Freud than she thinks. Freud proposes an enlarged concept of sexuality, and also criticizes the simplistic notion that 'the normal sexual aim is regarded as being the union of the genitals in the act known as copulation'. Freud, *Three Essays on the Theory of Sexuality*, 15.
212 MGM, 21.
213 Murdoch, 'Salvation by Words', 240.
214 Ibid.
215 Freud, *Civilization and Its Discontents*, 50.
216 MGM, 20.
217 MGM, 21.
218 CJ, 5:252.
219 MGM, 19.
220 MGM, 85.
221 SG, 215. See also 6.1.3.
222 MGM, 87.
223 MGM, 86.
224 'The difference between Murdoch and Weil lies in their conception of the self, which Murdoch considers with a little more benevolence than Weil does.' Panizza, *The Importance of Attention in Morality*, 98.
225 Griffin, *The Influence of the Writings of Simone Weil on the Fiction of Iris Murdoch*, 196.
226 MGM, 88.
227 MGM, 8.
228 MGM, 263.
229 MGM, 86.
230 Marcel Proust, *À la recherche du temps perdu*, vol. 4 (Paris: Gallimard, 1989), 488.
231 Proust, *Time Regained*, 184.
232 FS, 438.
233 FS, 451.
234 Ibid.
235 Jordan, *Chance and the Modern British Novel*, 199.

236 FS, 461.
237 Plato, *The Philebus*, transl. J.C.B. Gosling (Oxford: Clarendon Press, 1975), 58E–59B. Rosen, 'The Quarrel between Philosophy and Poetry', in *The Quarrel between Philosophy and Poetry*, 37.
238 Stanley Rosen, *Plato's Republic: A Study* (New Haven: Yale University Press, 2005), 104.
239 Ibid.
240 SGO, 371.
241 Weil, 'Divine Love in Creation', 90. See also 1.6.3.
242 Ibid.
243 SGO, 372.
244 FS, 453.
245 SG, 218: 'Art is for life's sake, in the sense in which I have tried to indicate, or else it is worthless.'
246 SGO, 371.
247 *CJ*, 5:453. Kant names in a parenthesis the type of man he has in mind: '(like Spinoza)'.
248 *CJ*, 5:453.
249 FS, 458.
250 Plato, *The Republic*, 380C.
251 Murdoch, 'On "God" and "Good"', 359.
252 Ibid.
253 Murdoch, 'On "God" and "Good"', 359–60.
254 Adorno, *Aesthetic Theory*, 166.
255 Ibid., 131.
256 Derrida's essay 'Plato's Pharmacy' explains how writing works as a double-edged pharmakon: 'Plato maintains *both* the exteriority of writing *and* its power of maleficent penetration, its ability to affect or infect what lies deepest inside. The *pharmakon* is that dangerous supplement that breaks into the very thing that would have liked to do without it yet lets itself *at once* be breached, roughed up, fulfilled, and replaced, completed by the very trace through which the present increases itself in the act of disappearing.' Derrida, 'Plato's Pharmacy', in *Dissemination*, trans. Barbara Johnson (London: Athlone, 1981), 110. Contrary to her usual suspicion to Derrida, Murdoch states her great appreciation of this essay in FS, 413.
257 FS, 413.
258 *MGM*, 343.
259 Ibid.
260 Rosen, 'The Old Quarrel', 21. Plato, *The Republic*, 595B.
261 FS, 449.
262 FS, 458.
263 FS, 461.
264 SGO, 383.

Concluding remarks

1 LP, 4.
2 LP, 24.

3   See 5.2.
4   See 6.3, especially the discussion of contingency and sublime sublimation.
5   Although they have not been emphasized, these aspects of her thought have not been ignored. See, for example, 4.7 and 6.1.3.
6   Meyers, 'Two Interviews with Iris Murdoch', 230.

Bibliography

Works by Iris Murdoch

Metaphysics as a Guide to Morals. London: Chatto & Windus, 1992.
Sartre: Romantic Rationalist. London: Vintage, 1999.
From *Existentialists and Mystics*. Edited by Peter Conradi. London: Chatto & Windus, 1997:
    'Against Dryness'. 287–95.
    'Art Is the Imitation of Nature'. 243–57.
    'Literature and Philosophy: A Conversation with Bryan Magee'. 3–30.
    'Metaphysics and Ethics'. 59–75.
    'On "God" and "Good"'. 337–62.
    'Salvation by Words'. 235–42.
    'The Existentialist Hero'. 108–15.
    'The Fire and the Sun'. 386–463.
    'The Novelist as Metaphysician'. 101–7.
    'The Sovereignty of Good over Other Concepts'. 363–85.
    'The Sublime and the Beautiful Revisited'. 261–86.
    'The Sublime and the Good'. 205–20.

Novels by Iris Murdoch

A Severed Head. London: Vintage Books, 2001.
An Unofficial Rose. London: Penguin Books, 1962.
The Bell. London: Vintage, 1999.
The Black Prince. Harmondsworth: Penguin, 1975.
The Good Apprentice. London: Vintage, 2000.
The Nice and the Good. St Albans: Panther Books, 1997.
The Philosopher's Pupil. London: Vintage Books, 2000.
The Sea, the Sea. London: Vintage, 1999.
The Time of the Angels. London: Chatto & Windus, 1989.

Archive material

Peter Conradi Archive, Kingston University, London, United Kingdom.
Iris Murdoch Archive, Kingston University, London, United Kingdom.
Iris Murdoch's Libraries, Kingston University, London, United Kingdom.

Printed books, articles and e-books

Adorno, Theodor W. *Aesthetic Theory*. Translated by Robert Hullot-Kentor. London: Continuum, 2002.
Adorno, Theodor W. *Negative Dialectics*. Translated by E.B. Ashton. New York: Continuum, 2007.
Altorf, Hannah Marije. 'Iris Murdoch and Common Sense or, What Is It Like to Be a Woman in Philosophy'. *Royal Institute of Philosophy Supplements*, 87 (2020): 201–20.
Altorf, Hanna Marije. *Iris Murdoch and the Art of Imagination: Imaginative Philosophy as Response to Secularism*. Glasgow: University of Glasgow, 2004.
Anderson, Amanda, Felski, Rita and Moi, Toril. *Character: Three Inquiries in Literary Studies*. Chicago, IL: The University of Chicago Press, 2019.
Antonaccio, Maria. *A Philosophy to Live By: Engaging Iris Murdoch*. New York: Oxford University Press, 2012.
Antonaccio, Maria. 'The Virtues of Metaphysics: A Review of Iris Murdoch's Philosophical Writings'. *The Journal of Religious Ethics* 29, no. 2 (2001): 307–35.
Araújo, Sofia de Melo. 'Introduction'. In *Iris Murdoch, Philosopher Meets Novelist*. Edited by Sofia de Melo Araújo and Fatima Vieira. Newcastle upon Tyne: Cambridge Scholars Publishing, 2011. 1–10.
Aristotle. *Poetics*. Translated by Anthony Kenny. Oxford: Oxford University Press, 2013. E-book.
Aristotle. *Poetics*. Translated by Malcolm Heath. London: Penguin, 1996.
Aviv, Rachel. 'The Philosopher of Feelings'. *The New Yorker*, 18 July 2016.
Barfield, Raymond. *The Ancient Quarrel between Philosophy and Poetry*. Cambridge: Cambridge University Press, 2011.
Barnes, Hazel E. 'Translator's Introduction'. In Sartre, Jean-Paul. *Being and Nothingness: An Essay on Phenomenological Ontology*. Translated by Hazel E. Barnes. New York: Citadel Press, 1956. viii–xliii.
de Beauvoir, Simone. 'Literature and Metaphysics'. Translated by Veronique Zaytzeff and Frederick M. Morrison. In *Philosophical Writings*. Edited by Margaret A. Simons. Urbana: University of Illinois Press, 2004. 269–77.
Bellamy, Michael O. 'An Interview with Iris Murdoch'. In *From a Tiny Corner in the House of Fiction: Conversations with Iris Murdoch*. Edited by Gillian Dooley Dooley. Columbia: University of South Carolina Press, 2003. 44–55.
Bernstein, Charles. 'Artifice of Absorption'. In *A Poetics*. Cambridge, MA: Harvard University Press, 1992. 9–89.
Biles, Jack I. 'An Interview with Iris Murdoch'. In *From a Tiny Corner in the House of Fiction: Conversations with Iris Murdoch*. Edited by Gillian Dooley Dooley. Columbia: University of South Carolina Press, 2003. 56–69.
Borgdorff, Henk. *The Debate on Research in the Arts*. Vol. 2. Bergen, Norway: Kunsthøgskolen i Bergen, 2006.
Bowie, Andrew. *Aesthetics and Subjectivity: From Kant to Nietzsche*. Manchester: Manchester University Press, 2003.
Bradbury, Malcolm. 'Introduction'. In Murdoch, Iris. *The Philosopher's Pupil*. London: Vintage Books, 2000. ix–xx.
Breitenbach, Angela. 'One Imagination in Experiences of Beauty and Achievements of Understanding'. *The British Journal of Aesthetics* 60, no. 1 (2020): 71–88.
Browning, Gary. *Why Iris Murdoch Matters: Making Sense of Experience in Modern Times*. London: Bloomsbury Academic, 2018.

Capra, Andrea. 'Seeing through Plato's Looking Glass: *Mythos* and *Mimesis* from *Republic* to *Poetics*'. *Aisthesis: Pratiche, linguaggi e saperi dell'estetico* 10, no. 1 (2017): 75–86.
Carruth, Hayden. 'Introduction'. In Sartre, Jean-Paul. *Nausea*. Translated by Lloyd Alexander. New York: New Directions, 1964. v–xiv.
Cascardi, Anthony J. "Disowning Knowledge': Cavell on Shakespeare'. In *Stanley Cavell*. Edited by Richard T Eldrige. Cambridge, UK and New York: Cambridge University Press, 2003. 190–205.
Cavell, Stanley. 'Aesthetic Problems of Modern Philosophy'. In *Must We Mean What We Say?* Cambridge: Cambridge University Press, 2002. 68–90.
Cavell, Stanley. 'The Avoidance of Love'. In *Must We Mean What We Say?: A Book of Essays*. New York, Scribner, 1969. 295–381.
Cavell, Stanley. *The Claim of Reason: Wittgenstein, Skepticism, Morality, and Tragedy*. New York: Oxford University Press, 1999.
Cavell, Stanley. *The World Viewed: Reflections on the Ontology of Film*. Cambridge, MA: Harvard University Press, 1979.
Caygill, Howard. *A Kant Dictionary*. Oxford, UK: Blackwell Reference, 2000. E-book.
Cohen, Ted. 'Literature and Morality'. In *The Oxford Handbook of Philosophy and Literature*. Edited by Richard Eldridge. New York: Oxford University Press, 2009. 486–95.
Coleridge, Samuel Taylor. *Biographia Literaria*. Edited by Adam Roberts. Edinburgh: Edinburgh University Press, 2014.
Conradi, Peter J. *The Saint and the Artist: A Study of the Fiction of Iris Murdoch*. London: Macmillan, 1986.
Critchley, Simon. 'Comedy and Finitude: Displacing the Tragic-Heroic Paradigm in Philosophy and Psychoanalysis'. *Constellations* 6, no. 1 (1999): 108–22.
Critchley, Simon and Cederström, Carl. *How to Stop Living and Start Worrying: Conversations with Carl Cederström*. Cambridge: Polity, 2010.
Danto, Arthur C. 'Philosophy as/and/of Literature'. *Proceedings and Addresses of the American Philosophical Association* 58, no. 1 (1984): 5–20.
Derrida, Jacques. 'Plato's Pharmacy'. In *Dissemination*. Translated by Barbara Johnson. London: Athlone, 1981. 61–171.
Derrida, Jacques. 'The First Session'. In *Acts of Literature*. Edited by Derek Attridge. London: Routledge, 1992. 127–80.
Derrida, Jacques and Attridge, Derek. '"This Strange Institution Called Literature": An Interview with Jacques Derrida'. Translated by Geoffrey Bennington and Rachel Bowlby. In *Acts of Literature*. Edited by Derek Attridge. London: Routledge, 1992. 33–75.
Diamond, Cora and Bronzo, Silver. 'Philosophy in a Realistic Spirit: An Interview by Silver Bronzo'. *Iride* 26, no. 2 (2013): 239–82.
Dipple, Elizabeth. *Iris Murdoch: Work for the Spirit*. London: Methuen, 1982.
Eagleton, Terry. *Marxism and Literary Criticism*. London: Routledge, 2003.
Enström, Anna. *Sinnesstämning, skratt och hypokondri: om estetisk erfarenhet i Kants tredje Kritik*. Huddinge: Södertörn University, 2021.
Fackenheim, Emil L. 'Schelling's Philosophy of the Literary Arts'. *The Philosophical Quarterly* 4, no. 17 (1954): 310–26.
Farrell Krell, David. 'Art and Truth in Raging Discord: Heidegger and Nietzsche on the Will to Power'. *boundary 2*, no. 4, *Martin Heidegger and Literature* (1976): 378–92.
Felski, Rita. *Uses of Literature*. Malden, MA: Blackwell Pub, 2008.

Felski, Rita. 'Identifying with Characters'. In Anderson, Felski, Moi. *Character: Three Inquiries in Literary Studies*. Chicago, IL: The University of Chicago Press, 2019. 77–126.

Forsberg, Niklas. *Language Lost and Found: On Iris Murdoch and the Limits of Philosophical Discourse*. London: Bloomsbury Academic, 2013.

Freeman, Damien. 'The Paradox of Fiction'. In *The Routledge Companion to the Philosophy of Literature*. Edited by Noël Carroll and John Gibson. London: Routledge, 2015. 247–58.

Freud, Sigmund. *Civilization and Its Discontents*. Translated by James Strachey. New York: W.W. Norton & Company, 2010.

Freud, Sigmund. 'Creative Writers and Day-Dreaming'. In *Collected Papers, vol. 4*. Translated by Joan Riviere. New York: Basic Books Inc., 1959. 419–514.

Freud, Sigmund. *Three Essays on the Theory of Sexuality*. Translated and edited by James Strachey. New York: Basic Books, 2000.

Gasiorek, Andrzej. '"A Renewed Sense of Difficulty": E.M. Forster, Iris Murdoch and Zadie Smith on Ethics and Form'. In *The Legacies of Modernism: Historicising Postwar and Contemporary Fiction*. Edited by David James. Cambridge: Cambridge University Press, 2011. 170–86.

Genette, Gérard. *Fiction & Diction*. Translated by Catherine Porter. Ithaca: Cornell University Press, 1993.

Ginsborg, Hannah. *The Role of Taste in Kant's Theory of Cognition*. New York: Garland Publishing, 1990.

Glover, Stephen. 'Iris Murdoch Talks to Stephen Glover'. In *From a Tiny Corner in the House of Fiction: Conversations with Iris Murdoch*. Edited by Gillian Dooley Dooley. Columbia: University of South Carolina Press, 2003. 33–43.

Gordon, David J. 'Iris Murdoch's Comedies of Unselfing'. *Twentieth Century Literature* 36, no. 2 (1990): 115–36.

Griffin, Gabriele. *The Influence of the Writings of Simone Weil on the Fiction of Iris Murdoch*. San Francisco: Mellen Research University Press, 1993.

Grinshaw, Tammy. 'Do not Seek God outside Your Own Soul: Buddhism in The Green Knight'. In *Iris Murdoch and Morality*. Edited by Anne Rowe and Avril Horner. New York: Palgrave Macmillan, 2010. 168–79.

Gåvertsson, Frits. *Perfection and Fiction: A Study in Iris Murdoch's Moral Philosophy*. Lund: Lund University, 2018.

Haffenden, John. 'John Haffenden Talks to Iris Murdoch'. In *From a Tiny Corner in the House of Fiction: Conversations with Iris Murdoch*. Edited by Gillian Dooley. Columbia: University of South Carolina Press, 2003. 124–38.

Hallberg, Anna Victoria. *Novel Writing and Moral Philosophy as Aspects of a Single Struggle: Iris Murdoch's Hybrid Novels*. Örebro: Örebro universitet, 2011.

Halliwell, Stephen. *Aristotle's Poetics*. London: Duckworth, 1998.

Hanna, Robert. 'Kant and Nonconceptual Content'. *European Journal of Philosophy* 13, no. 2 (2005): 247–90.

Hardy, Rob. 'Stories, Rituals and Healers in Iris Murdoch's Fiction'. In *Iris Murdoch and Morality*. Edited by Anne Rowe and Avril Horner. New York: Palgrave Macmillan, 2010. 43–55.

Haskins, Casey. 'Kant and the Autonomy of Art'. *The Journal of Aesthetics and Art Criticism* 47, no. 1 (1989): 43–54.

Heath, Malcolm. 'Introduction'. In Aristotle. *Poetics*. Translated by Malcolm Heath. London: Penguin, 1996. vii–lxxi.

Hegel, G.W.F., Schelling, F.W.J. and Hölderlin, Friedrich. 'Oldest System Programme of German Idealism'. Translated by Andrew Bowie. In Bowie, Andrew. *Aesthetics and Subjectivity: From Kant to Nietzsche*. Manchester: Manchester University Press, 2003. 334–5.

Heidegger, Martin. *Introduction to Philosophy: Thinking and Poetizing*. Translated by Phillip Jacques Braunstein. Bloomington: Indiana University Press, 2011.

Heidegger, Martin. 'The Origin of the Work of Art'. In *Poetry, Language, Thought*. Translated by Albert Hofstadter. New York: Harper & Row, 1975. 17–87.

Hegel, G.W.F. *Aesthetics: Lectures on Fine Art*. Translated by T.M. Knox. Oxford: Clarendon Press, 1998.

Hertz, Neil. 'Foreword'. In Freud, Sigmund. *Writings on Art and Literature*. Stanford, CA: Stanford University Press, 1997. ix–xx.

Heusel, Barbara Stevens. *Patterned Aimlessness: Iris Murdoch's Novels of the 1970s and 1980s*. Athens: University of Georgia Press, 1995.

Hilgers, Thomas. *Aesthetic Disinterestedness: Art, Experience, and the Self*. New York: Routledge, 2017.

Hill, Leslie. *The Cambridge Introduction to Jacques Derrida*. Cambridge: Cambridge University Press, 2007.

Hobson, Harold. 'Lunch with Iris Murdoch'. In *From a Tiny Corner in the House of Fiction: Conversations with Iris Murdoch*. Edited by Gillian Dooley Dooley. Columbia: University of South Carolina Press, 2003. 1–8.

Holland, Norman N. 'The "Willing Suspension of Disbelief" Revisited'. *Centennial Review* 11, no. 1 (1967): 1–23.

Horner, Avril, and Rowe, Anne. 'Introduction: Art, Morals and "The Discovery of Reality"'. In *Iris Murdoch and Morality*. Edited by Anne Rowe and Avril Horner. New York: Palgrave Macmillan, 2010. 1–14.

Hume, David. *A Treatise of Human Nature*. Oxford: Clarendon Press, 1888.

Hume, David. 'Of Tragedy'. In *Four Dissertations*. London: Printed for A. Millar, 1757.

Hägglund, Martin. *Dying for Time: Proust, Woolf, Nabokov*. Cambridge: Harvard University Press, 2012.

Hämäläinen, Nora. *Literature and Moral Theory*. New York: Bloomsbury Academic, 2016.

Hämäläinen, Nora. 'What Is a Wittgensteinian Neo-Platonist? Iris Murdoch, Metaphysics and Metaphor'. *Philosophical Papers* 43, no. 2 (2014): 191–225.

Janaway, Christopher. 'Beauty Is False, Truth Ugly: Nietzsche on Art and Life'. In *Nietzsche on Art and Life*. Edited by Daniel Came. New York: Oxford University Press, 2014.

Janaway, Christopher. 'Plato'. In *The Routledge Companion to Aesthetics*. Edited by Berys Gaut and Dominic McIver Lopes. London: Routledge, 2013. 3–12.

Jordan, Julia. *Chance and the Modern British Novel*. London: University College London, 2013.

Kahn, Charles H. 'Writing Philosophy: Prose and Poetry from Thales to Plato'. In *Written Texts and the Rise of Literate Culture in Ancient Greece*. Edited by Harvey Yunis. Cambridge: Cambridge University Press, 2003. 139–61.

Kamber, Richard. 'Sartre's Nauseas'. *MLN* 98, no. 5. (1983): 1279–85.

Kant, Immanuel. *Critique of the Power of Judgment*. Translated by Paul Guyer and Eric Matthews. Cambridge: Cambridge University Press, 2000.

Kant, Immanuel. *Critique of Pure Reason*. Translated and edited by Paul Guyer and Allen W. Wood. Cambridge: Cambridge University Press, 1998.

Kant, Immanuel. 'The False Subtlety of the Four Syllogistic Figures'. In *Theoretical Philosophy 1755–1770*. Translated and edited by David Walford and Ralf Meerbote. New York: Cambridge University Press, 2002. 85–105.

Kermode, Frank. 'Interview from "The House of Fiction: Interviews with Seven English Novelists"'. In *From a Tiny Corner in the House of Fiction: Conversations with Iris Murdoch*. Edited by Gillian Dooley Dooley. Columbia: University of South Carolina Press, 2003. 9–13.

Kern, Andrea. 'Reflecting the Form of Understanding: The Philosophical Significance of Art'. In *Kant After Derrida*. Edited by Philip Rothfield. Manchester: Clinamen, 2004. 106–26.

Kierkegaard, Søren. 'On My Work as an Author (August 7, 1851), The Point of View for My Work as an Author (Written 1848, Published 1859), By S. Kierkegaard'. In *The Essential Kierkegaard*. Translated and edited by Howard V. Hong and Edna H. Hong. Princeton: Princeton University Press, 2000. 449–81.

Kierkegaard, Søren. 'The Seducer's Diary'. In *Either/Or, A Fragment of Life* (February 20, 1843), Edited by Victor Eremita, Part 1 Containing A's Papers'. In *The Essential Kierkegaard*. Translated and edited by Howard V. Hong and Edna H. Hong. Princeton: Princeton University Press, 2000. 62–5.

Kierkegaard, Søren. 'The Sickness unto Death: A Christian Psychological Exposition for Upbuilding and Awakening (July 30, 1849), By Anti-Climacus, Edited by S. Kierkegaard'. In *The Essential Kierkegaard*. Translated and edited by Howard V. Hong and Edna H. Hong. Princeton: Princeton University Press, 2000. 350–72.

Ladenson, Elisabeth. *Dirt for Art's Sake: Books on Trial from Madame Bovary to Lolita*. Ithaca: Cornell University Press, 2007.

Lamarque, Peter. *The Philosophy of Literature*. Oxford: Blackwell Publishing, 2009.

Larson, Kate. '*Everything Important Is to Do with Passion*': Iris Murdoch's Concept of Love and Its Platonic Origin. Uppsala: Uppsala University, 2009.

Lawrence, D.H. 'Art and Morality'. In *The Bad Side of Books: Selected Essays*. Edited by Geoff Dyer. New York: New York Review Books, 2019. 222–9.

Lear, Jonathan. 'Katharsis'. *Phronesis* 33, no. 3 (1988): 297–326.

Lear, Jonathan. *Freud*. Hoboken: Taylor & Francis Ltd, 2005.

Leeson, Miles. *Iris Murdoch: Philosophical Novelist*. London: Continuum, 2011.

von Leyden, Wolfgang. 'Time, Number, and Eternity in Plato and Aristotle'. *The Philosophical Quarterly* 14, no. 54 (1964): 35–52.

Lipscomb, Benjamin J.B. *The Women Are Up to Something: How Elizabeth Anscombe, Philippa Foot, Mary Midgley, and Iris Murdoch Revolutionized Ethics*. New York: Oxford University Press, 2022. E-book.

Luprecht, Mark. 'Death and Goodness: Bruno's Dream and "The Sovereignty of Good over Other Concepts"'. In *Iris Murdoch and Morality*. Edited by Anne Rowe and Avril Horner. New York: Palgrave Macmillan, 2010. 113–25.

Mankin, Robert. 'An Introduction to *The Claim of Reason*'. *Salmagundi* 67 (1985): 66–89.

Martin, Priscilla. 'Houses of Fiction: Iris Murdoch and Henry James'. In *Iris Murdoch: A Reassessment*. Edited by Anne Rowe. Hampshire: Palgrave Macmillan, 2007. 124–35.

Martin, Stewart. 'Literature and the Modern System of the Arts: Sources of Criticism in Adorno'. In *Adorno and Literature*. Edited by David Cunningham and Nigel Mapp. London: Continuum, 2006. 9–25.

Marx, Karl. 'Theses on Feuerbach'. In *The German Ideology*. Amherst, NY: Prometheus Books, 1998. 569–71.

Merritt, Melissa. 'Murdoch and Kant'. In *The Murdochian Mind*. Edited by Silvia Caprioglio Panizza and Mark Hopwood. Abingdon, Oxon: Routledge, 2022. 253–65.

Meyers, Jeffrey. 'Two Interviews with Iris Murdoch'. In *From a Tiny Corner in the House of Fiction: Conversations with Iris Murdoch*. Edited by Gillian Dooley Dooley. Columbia: University of South Carolina Press, 2003. 218–34.

Milligan, Tony. 'Murdoch and Derrida: Holding Hands under the Table'. In *Iris Murdoch: Texts and Contexts*. Edited by Anne Rowe and Avril Horner. Houndmills, Basingstoke: Palgrave Macmillan, 2012. 77–90.

Moi, Toril. 'Rethinking Character'. In Anderson, Felski, and Moi. *Character: Three Inquiries in Literary Studies*. Chicago, IL: The University of Chicago Press, 2019. 27–76.

Moore, Scott H. 'Murdoch's Fictional Philosophers: What They Say and What They Show'. In *Iris Murdoch and Morality*. Edited by Anne Rowe and Avril Horner. New York: Palgrave Macmillan, 2010. 101–12.

Moss, Jessica. 'What Is Imitative Poetry and Why Is It Bad?' In *The Cambridge Companion to Plato's Republic*. Edited by G.R.F. Ferrari. Cambridge: Cambridge University Press, 2007. 415–44.

Most, Glenn W. 'What Ancient Quarrel between Philosophy and Poetry?' In *Plato and the Poets*. Edited by Destrée and Herrmann. Leiden: Brill, 2011. 1–20.

Nails, Debra. 'Mouthpiece Schmouthpiece'. In *Who Speaks for Plato?: Studies in Platonic Anonymity*. Edited by Gerald Press. Lanham, MD: Rowman & Littlefield, 2000. 15–26.

Nicol, Bran. 'Iris Murdoch's Aesthetics of Masochism'. *Journal of Modern Literature* 29, no. 2 (2006): 148–65.

Nicol, Bran. *Iris Murdoch: The Retrospective Fiction*. Houndmills, Basingstoke: Palgrave Macmillan, 2004.

Nicol, Bran. 'Murdoch's Mannered Realism: Metafiction, Morality and the Post-War Novel'. In *Iris Murdoch and Morality*. Edited by Anne Rowe and Avril Horner. New York: Palgrave Macmillan, 2010. 17–30.

Nicol, Bran. 'Philosophy's Dangerous Pupil: Murdoch and Derrida'. *MFS Modern Fiction Studies* 47, no. 3, (2001): 580–601.

Nicol, Bran. 'The Curse of *The Bell*: The Ethics and Aesthetics of Narrative'. In *Iris Murdoch: A Reassessment*. Edited by Anne Rowe. Hampshire: Palgrave Macmillan, 2007. 100–111.

Nietzsche, Friedrich. *On the Genealogy of Morality*. Translated by Carol Diethe. Edited by Keith Ansell-Pearson. New York: Cambridge University Press, 2007.

Nietzsche, Friedrich. *The Birth of Tragedy*. Translated by Douglas Smith. New York: Oxford University Press, 2000.

Nietzsche, Friedrich, *The Will to Power: Selections from the Notebooks of the 1880s*. Translated by R. Kevin Hill and Michael A. Scarpitti. Edited by R. Kevin Hill. London: Penguin Books, 2017.

Nightingale, Andrea Wilson. *Genres in Dialogue: Plato and the Construct of Philosophy*. Cambridge: Cambridge University Press, 1995.

Nowotny, Helga. 'Foreword'. In *The Routledge Companion to Research in the Arts*. Edited by Michael Biggs and Henrik Karlsson in collaboration with Stiftelsen Riksbankens Jubileumsfond, Stockholm. Oxon: Routledge, 2011. xvii–xxvi.

Nussbaum, Martha. 'Emotions as Judgements of Value and Importance'. In *Thinking about Feeling: Contemporary Philosophers on Emotions*. Edited by Robert C. Solomon. New York: Oxford University Press, 2004.

Nussbaum, Martha. '"Faint with Secret Knowledge": Love and Vision in Murdoch's The Black Prince'. *Poetics Today* 25, no. 4 (2004): 689–710.

Nussbaum, Martha. '"Finely Aware and Richly Responsible": Moral Attention and the Moral Task of Literature'. *The Journal of Philosophy* 82, no. 10 (1985): 516-29.

Nussbaum, Martha C. *The Fragility of Goodness: Luck and Ethics in Greek Tragedy and Philosophy*. Cambridge: Cambridge University Press, 2001.

Nuzzo, Angelica. 'Reflective Judgment, Determinative Judgment, and the Problem of Particularity'. *Washington University Jurisprudence Review* 6, no. 1 (2013): 7-25.

Panizza, Silvia. *The Importance of Attention in Morality: An Exploration of Iris Murdoch's Philosophy*. Norwich: University of East Anglia, 2015.

Pappas, Nickolas. 'Aristotle'. In *The Routledge Companion to Aesthetics*. Edited by Berys Gaut and Dominic McIver Lopes. London: Routledge, 2013. 13-24.

Pappas, Nickolas. 'Plato's Aesthetics'. In *The Stanford Encyclopedia of Philosophy*. Edited by Edward N. Zalta. Fall 2020 Edition. https://plato.stanford.edu/archives/fall2020/entries/plato-aesthetics/

Pétrement, Simone. *Simone Weil: A Life*. Translated by Raymond Rosenthal. New York: Pantheon Books, 1976.

Pillow, Kirk. *Sublime Understanding: Aesthetic Reflection in Kant and Hegel*. Cambridge, Mass: MIT Press, 2003.

Plato. *The Apology*. In *The Last Days of Socrates*. Translated by Hugh Tredennick and Harold Tarrant. Middlesex: Penguin Books, 1969. 37-67.

Plato. *The Ion*. In *Ion, Hippias minor, Laches, Protagoras*. Translated by Reginald E. Allen. New Haven: Yale University Press, 1996. 1-22.

Plato. *The Laws*. Translated by Thomas L. Pangle. Chicago: University of Chicago Press, 1988.

Plato. *The Phaedo*. In *The Last Days of Socrates*. Translated by Hugh Tredennick and Harold Tarrant. Middlesex: Penguin Books, 1969. 109-85.

Plato. *The Phaedrus*. Translated by James H. Nichols JR. Ithaca: Cornell University Press, 1998.

Plato, *The Philebus*. Translated by J.C.B. Gosling. Oxford: Clarendon Press, 1975.

Plato. *The Republic*. Translated by Allan Bloom. New York: Basic Books, 1991.

Plato. *The Symposium*. Translated by M.C. Howatson. Edited by Frisbee C.C. Sheffield. Cambridge: Cambridge University Press, 2008.

Plato, *The Theaetetus*. In *Theaetetus and Sophist*. Translated and edited by Christopher Rowe. Cambridge: Cambridge University Press, 2015.

Plato, *The Timaeus*. In *Timaeus and Critias*. Translated by Robin Waterfield. Edited by Andrew Gregory. Oxford: Oxford University Press, 2008.

Pole, David. 'Literature as Prophecy: Sartre's "Nausea"'. *Philosophy and Literature* 5, no. 1 (1981): 33-48.

Popkin, Richard H. 'David Hume'. In *The Columbia History of Western Philosophy*. Edited by Richard H. Popkin. New York: Columbia University Press, 1999. 454-62.

Price, Simon. 'Iris Murdoch: An Interview with Simon Price'. In *From a Tiny Corner in the House of Fiction: Conversations with Iris Murdoch*. Edited by Gillian Dooley Dooley. Columbia: University of South Carolina Press, 2003. 148-54.

Proust, Marcel. *À la recherche du temps perdu*, vol. 4. Paris: Gallimard, 1989.

Proust, Marcel. *Time Regained*. Translated by Andreas Mayor and Terence Kilmartin. London: Vintage, 1996.

Rose, W.K. 'Iris Murdoch, Informally'. In *From a Tiny Corner in the House of Fiction: Conversations with Iris Murdoch*. Edited by Gillian Dooley Dooley. Columbia: University of South Carolina Press, 2003. 16-29.

Rosen, Stanley. 'The Quarrel between Philosophy and Poetry'. In *The Quarrel between Philosophy and Poetry: Studies in Ancient Thought*. New York: Routledge, 2014. E-book. 14–38.

Rowett, Catherine. 'Murdoch and Plato'. In *The Murdochian Mind*. Edited by Silvia Caprioglio Panizza and Mark Hopwood. Abingdon, Oxon: Routledge, 2022. 239–52.

Ruokonen, Floora. 'Iris Murdoch and the Extraordinary Ambiguity of Art'. *Journal of Value Inquiry* 42, no. 1 (2008): 77–90.

Sartre, Jean-Paul. *Huis clos: suivi de Les mooches*. Paris: Gallimard, 1947.

Sartre, Jean-Paul. 'Introducing *Les Temps modernes*'. Translated by Jeffrey Mehlman. In *'What Is Literature?' and Other Essays*. Edited by Steven Ungar. Cambridge, MA: Harvard University Press, 1988. 247–67.

Sartre, Jean-Paul. *La nausée*. Paris: Gallimard, 1980.

Sartre, Jean-Paul. *Nausea*. Translated by Robert Baldick. London: Penguin, 2000.

Sartre, Jean-Paul. *Sartre: Un film réalisé par Alexandre Astruc et Michel Contact*. Paris: Gallimard, 1977.

Sartre, Jean-Paul. *What Is Literature?* Translated by Bernard Frechtman. New York: Philosophical Library, 1949.

Schaper, Eva. 'Fiction and the Suspension of Disbelief'. *The British Journal of Aesthetics* 18, no. 1 (1978): 31–44.

Schweiker, William. 'The Moral Fate of Fictive Persons: On Iris Murdoch's Humanism'. In *Iris Murdoch and Morality*. Edited by Anne Rowe and Avril Horner. New York: Palgrave Macmillan, 2010. 180–93.

Scott, Gregory. 'Purging the Poetics'. *Oxford Studies in Ancient Philosophy* 25 (2003): 233–63.

Shakespeare, William. 'Romeo and Juliet'. In *The Complete Works of William Shakespeare*. London: Spring Books, 1958. 893–922.

Sherry, Patrick. 'Simone Weil on Beauty'. In *Simone Weil's Philosophy of Culture*. Edited by Richard H. Bell. Cambridge: Cambridge University Press, 1993. 260–76.

Searle, John R. 'The Logical Status of Fictional Discourse'. *New literary history* 6, no. 2 (1975): 319–32.

Stein, Gertrude. 'Sacred Emily'. In *Geography and Plays*. *Poems*. Boston: Four Seas Co., 1922. 178.

Steiner, George. *The Death of Tragedy*. London: Faber and Faber, 1995.

Søndergaard Christensen, Anne-Marie. 'Murdoch and Wittgenstein'. In *The Murdochian Mind*. Edited by Silvia Caprioglio Panizza and Mark Hopwood. Abingdon, Oxon: Routledge, 2022. 318–29.

Thomas, Rosalind. *Literature and Orality in Ancient Greece*. Cambridge: Cambridge University Press, 2010.

Trilling, Lionel. 'Freud and Literature'. *Horizon: A Review of Literature & Art* XVI, no. 92 (1947): 182–200.

Tolstoy, Leo. *What Is Art?* Translated by Richard Pevear. London: Penguin Books, 1995.

Walton, Kendall L. 'Appreciating Fiction: Suspending Disbelief or Pretending Belief?' *Dispositio* 5, no. 13–14 (1980): 1–18.

Weil, Simone. 'Divine Love in Creation'. In *Intimations of Christianity among the Ancient Greeks*. Translated by Elisabeth Chase. London: Routledge, 1998. 89–105.

Weil, Simone. *Lectures on Philosophy*. Translated by Hugh Price. Cambridge: Cambridge University Press, 1978.

Weil, Simone. 'Literature and Morality'. In *Late Philosophical Writings*. Translated by Eric O. Springsted and Lawrence E. Schmidt. Edited by Eric O. Springsted. Notre Dame: University of Notre Dame Press, 2015. 145–50.
Weil, Simone. *The Notebooks of Simone Weil*. Translated by Arthur Wills. London: Routledge, 2004.
Weil, Simone. *Waiting for God*. Translated by Emma Craufurd. London: Fontana Books, 1959.
Weston, Michael. *Philosophy, Literature and the Human Good*. London: Routledge, 2001.
White, David A. 'Poetry and Thinking: Heidegger and the Question of Rightness'. *Revue Internationale de Philosophie* 43, no. 168 (1) (1989): 64–79.
Whitehall, A.N. *Process and Reality: An Essay in Cosmology*. Edited by David Ray Griffin and Donald W. Sherburne. New York: Free Press, 1978.
Young, Julian. *The Philosophy of Tragedy: From Plato to Žižek*. Cambridge: Cambridge University Press, 2013.
Zangwill, Nick. 'Kant on Pleasure in the Agreeable'. *The Journal of Aesthetics and Art Criticism* 53, no. 2 (1995): 167–76.
Zuckert, Rachel. 'The Purposiveness of Form: A Reading of Kant's Aesthetic Formalism'. *Journal of the History of Philosophy* 44, no. 4 (2006): 599–622.

Internet sources

'aesthetic (n.)', in *Online Etymology Dictionary*, accessed 25 February 2022, https://www.etymonline.com/word/aesthetic
'muddle (v.)', *Online Etymology Dictionary*, accessed 31 August 2020, https://www.etymonline.com/word/muddle#etymonline_v_19212
'muddle', *Cambridge Dictionary*, accessed 31 August 2020, https://dictionary.cambridge.org/dictionary/english/muddle
'muddle', *Dictionary.com*, accessed 31 August 2020, https://www.dictionary.com/browse/muddle?s=t
'muddle', *Oxford English Dictionary*, accessed 31 August 2020, https://www.oed.com/view/Entry/123242#eid35881665
'How to Tell If You Are in an Iris Murdoch Novel', *The Toast*, accessed 5 August 2021, https://the-toast.net/2013/09/05/tell-iris-murdoch-novel/

Index

À la recherche du temps perdu 129, 160–1
A Severed Head 91
absurd 19, 20, 26, 28, 58, 60, 96, 120
   literature 28
academia 1, 32, 35
academic 12, 20, 25, 172 n.6, 176 n.99
   discipline 63, 143
   institutions 32
   philosophy 2, 56
academics 3
accident 89, 112, 155, 160 (*see also*
   contingency)
accidental 58, 133, 135, 138, 140, 154, 158,
   168 (*see also* contingency)
accidentally (*see also* contingency)
   educational 36, 155–65
   edifying 135
   illuminating 143, 151, 160
Adorno, Theodor W. 23, 25, 27–9, 83–4,
   164
aesthetic
   attention 157
   bribe 106
   comprehension 87
   description 1
   enjoyment 76
   experience 40, 74, 81, 84–5, 87, 93
   feeling 77, 84, 86, 157
   force 116
   form 51, 89, 124–5
   idea 75–6, 78, 87–94, 125, 168
   illusion of sense 62
   imagination 92
   judgement 13, 47–8, 52, 60–1, 74,
     75–87, 93, 157, 167
   perspective 16, 18
   -philosophic 142
   philosophy 17
   pleasure 77, 79, 81, 110, 112
   state of mind 84, 87, 89, 93
   theory 115, 155
   thinker 74
   unity 108
aestheticism 2
aesthetics
   Adorno 27–9
   Aristotle 11–11
   Freud 23, 138
   Hegel 14–16, 41, 49
   Kant 12–14, 22, 47–9, 71, 75–94,
     113–14, 157, 162–3
   moral 143, 163
   Murdoch 40, 47, 71, 90–1, 112–14,
     137–8, 143, 145–6, 155, 162–5, 169
   Plato 7, 11, 34, 133–7, 140, 144, 164
   Weil 20–3, 88, 136, 140–1, 151–2,
     154–5, 162, 201 n.133, 202 n.167,
     203 n.191
Altorf, Hannah Marije 153, 157–8,
   172 n.6, 201 n.124, 203 n.172
An Unofficial Rose 92, 141
analytic philosophy 1, 34–6, 96–7, 100,
   124, 137, 170, 197 n.25
anamnesis 151, 197 n.39
Anderson, Amanda 31, 95
Anna Karenina 53, 57, 95
Antonaccio, Maria 39, 108, 193 n.12
Araújo, Sofia de Melo 40
Aristotelian 124
Aristotle xii, 4, 9–12, 109–13, 117–19, 124,
   126–7, 131, 144
artistic research 32–4, 170, 178 n.141
attention
   aesthetic (*see under* aesthetic)
   artistic/of art 142, 153, 158, 160, 168
   concept of 65, 133, 135, 142–54, 168
   loving 145, 148, 158, 160, 163
   moral 145
Augustine, St. 18–19

bad art 34, 72, 116, 160
   and good/great art 21, 87, 160, 199 n.84

218 Index

Barfield, Raymond 18–19
Bernstein, Charles 43
Borgdorff, Henk 33
Breitenbach, Angela 77–8, 84, 187 n.15
Browning, Gary 40, 143, 198 n.64

Cavell, Stanley 2, 35, 38, 57–63, 95–111, 114, 121
Christ 141, 198 n.64
Christian 18–21, 46, 110, 120
　Judeo- 2
Cinema (*see* film *and* movie)
cognition 41, 48, 51, 75, 79–84, 88, 92–3
cognitive 52, 75–8, 80–1, 84, 88, 118, 122, 126
Coleridge, Samuel Taylor 96, 99–102, 107
concepts 10, 16, 43–8, 53, 62, 70, 74–5, 78–80, 85–8, 93–4
　central 24, 112
　philosophical 65
　use of 92, 112, 167
conceptual
　clarity 49, 90
　content 43, 75–94, 187 n.12
　judgement 47–8, 74
　non- 48, 74, 75–94, 113, 125, 167
　understanding 14, 61, 75–94, 113, 126, 168
Conradi, Peter J. 141, 198, 201 n.64
consciousness 53, 55, 66, 79–82, 87, 112, 136, 142–3, 146–7, 152–4, 160–1, 177 n.134
　Existentialist/Sartrean 26–7, 53, 55, 62
　false/inauthentic 23, 29
　Hegel 14–16
　moral 112
　psychoanalysis 23
　pure 202 n.143
　religious 139
　self- (*see* self-consciousness)
　uncanny 84
　Weil 22
continental philosophy 1, 34–6, 170
contingency 26–7, 53–4, 86, 89, 109, 112, 122–5, 155–7, 160–3 (*see also* accident, accidental, accidentally *and* particularity)
Critchley, Simon 130

Danto, Arthur C. 97
de Beauvoir, Simone 1, 21, 25–7, 43–4, 53
deconstruction 29–31, 33–4
Derrida, Jacques 7, 29–31, 36, 72, 177 n.115, 178 n.8, 205 n.256
determining judgement (*see* judgement)
Diamond, Cora 35, 197 n.25
didactic 11, 23, 138, 169, 199 n.73, 202 n.143 (*see also* educational)
Dipple, Elizabeth 146, 155
divine 19, 22, 23, 38, 65, 139–40, 146, 151, 162, 203 n.183
　madman 153, 165
divinity 168
dramaturgy 9
dramaturgical 127
dream 153, 192 n.43
　day- 24, 103, 105, 138, 141, 147
　-like 91
　life 152
　of 26–7, 85, 97, 130
　world 133
dreaming 58, 98, 103
dreamy 150

educational 10, 39, 117, 137–8, 162 (*see also* didactic)
　accidentally 36, 155–62
emotion 14, 35, 43, 46, 68, 72–3, 75, 86, 92, 111, 117–18, 122, 124, 126, 139, 146, 159
emotional 30, 50, 55, 63, 68, 92, 124, 137
　un- 5, 122
emotionally 44, 159, 186 n.252
epistemological 54, 57, 63, 74, 95–102, 105, 108, 168, 188 n.49, 191 n.20
epistemologist 57–9, 98, 100–2, 183 n.165
epistemology 23, 58, 107, 109
　of fiction 95–103, 168
Eros (*see also* love) 22, 150, 153, 158
　in/of Plato 23, 146, 148–50, 164, 197 n.39
　low and high 71
erotic 21, 36, 56, 133, 136, 143, 146–9, 153, 157–8
Existentialism 25–6, 71, 176 n.101, 176 n.103
Existentialist 19, 21, 26–7, 31, 35, 43, 55
　novel 1, 53, 55

fantastic 36, 107, 138
fantasy 101, 105, 108, 116, 136, 141–2, 147, 152–4, 156–7
  and imagination 71, 133, 140, 151–4, 158
  personal 138, 144, 153, 158
  world 143
Felski, Rita 31–2, 95, 177 n.134
fictional character 5, 95–7, 104, 106, 107–9, 137, 168
film 99, 101–2 (*see also* movie)
formal 50, 80, 87, 106, 108, 112–16, 124, 126–7
  beauty 89, 103
  experiments 22, 51
formalism 112–13
  Kant (*see under* Kant)
Forsberg, Niklas 39, 41–9, 51, 58–9, 70, 74, 125, 187 n.13, 200 n.101, 203 n.189
free will 13
freedom 3, 13, 15–16, 26, 64, 78, 135, 145, 147, 161–2, 164–5, 181 n.99
  tragic 114, 116
Freud, Sigmund 29, 96
  aesthetics (*see under* aesthetics) 23–5, 34, 103–4, 138, 158–9, 175 n.93
  influence on Murdoch 25, 106, 112, 138, 140–1, 158–9, 175 n.88, 197 n.39–40, 204 n.211
  influence on Weil 22, 141, 197 n.39
Freudian 34, 104, 138, 140–1, 176 n.99, 176 n.103, 197 n.40

Gåvertsson, Frits 146, 199, 202 n.137
Genette, Gérard 107
genius 11, 14, 17, 21–2, 76, 83–4, 151, 165, 203 n.172
Ginsborg, Hannah 78–9, 187 n.23
God 17–20, 22, 46, 134, 148, 159, 163, 181 n.79
god(s) 18, 40, 110, 117, 129, 134–5, 139, 150, 160–1, 185 n.223
great art 7, 22, 115, 131, 138, 143, 156, 158–60, 162–4, 168
  and bad art (*see under* bad art)
  -ist 81, 131, 153, 164–5, 202 n.143
  -work 64, 154
Griffin, Gabriele 159

Hägglund, Martin 128–31
Hallberg, Anna Victoria 40, 55–6, 142–4
Halliwell, Stephen 10
Hämäläinen, Nora 56, 138, 144, 178 n.143, 197 n.25, 199 n.73
Hamlet 24, 45, 102, 116, 143
Hanna, Robert 80–1
Hegel, G.W.F. 14–17, 27, 38, 41, 43, 46, 48–9, 68–9, 72, 74, 109, 111, 121–2, 131
Heidegger, Martin 6–9, 17, 26, 30, 35–6, 176 n.101, 178 n.8, 184 n.194, 185 n.228
Heusel, Barbara Stevens 186 n.254
high Eros (*see under* Eros)
historicity 3
Holland, Norman N. 104, 192 n.45
Horner, Avril 40
Hume, David 101, 118, 151–2, 202 n.163, 203 n.187

ideological 12
ideology 23, 27, 28, 71
illusion 2, 7, 23, 56, 60, 78, 80, 95, 106–7, 115, 119, 121, 133–4, 136, 144, 156, 159, 160, 163, 168
  of sense 37–49, 51, 59, 61–4, 71–4, 156, 167, 181 n.79
illusory 20, 28, 44, 61, 63, 65, 78, 112, 130, 136, 158
  unity 116, 138, 159
imagination
  and fantasy (*see under* fantasy)
  immoral (*see under* moral)
ironic 19–20
irony 19, 31, 165

Jewish 20–1
Jordan, Julia 156, 161
judgement 14, 38, 57, 79, 108, 120, 143
  aesthetic (*see under* aesthetic)
  capacity to make 13
  conceptually determinate 92
  determining 15, 47–8, 51–2, 56, 74, 80
  error of 110
  evaluative 126
  logical 41, 82, 83, 85–6
  of beauty 14, 56, 82, 84

of taste 13, 48, 75–9, 81–2, 85,
  181 n.99, 187 n.15
objectively valid 80, 84, 89
power of 51, 85
reflective 47, 51, 52, 56, 60, 80, 188
  n.46
teleological 14, 186–7 n.7
universal 82
value 96

Kamber, Richard 62–3
Kant
  aesthetics (*see under* aesthetics)
  concepts 78–81
  determining and reflective judgement
    51–2
  formalism 113–14
  genius 151
  God 163
  influence on Murdoch 35, 40, 45, 65,
    75–7, 93, 112–16, 125, 155, 157,
    162–3, 169
  moral philosophy (*see under* moral
    philosophy)
Kern, Andrea 80, 188–9 n.66
Kierkegaard, Søren 1, 17–20, 22, 35, 44–7,
  57, 74, 176 n.101, 181 n.79
King Lear 75, 81, 87, 109, 116

La Nausée 1, 38, 49–64, 72, 74, 86, 156,
  169, 176 n.102, 182 n.112
Ladenson, Elisabeth 135, 201 n.120
Lamarque, Peter 55
language 7, 15, 18, 27–9, 35, 60, 63, 69,
  86–9, 117–18, 137–8, 203 n.189
  ancient 9
  ordinary (*see under* ordinary)
  medium of 42, 89
  metaphorical 33
  -philosophical 181 n.79
  philosophical 185 n.228
  poetic 184
  prose 197 n.33
  written 41
Larson, Kate 148–52, 174 n.73
Lawrence, D.H. 51–2
Lear, Jonathan 10, 24, 118–19
Leeson, Miles 54–5, 65
linguistic 35, 60, 65, 78–9, 87, 112

Lipscomb, Benjamin J.B. 176 n.100
literary
  critic 32, 96
  criticism 53, 95, 125
  fact 96–7, 102, 107
  history 72
  scholar 25, 128
  studies 1, 29, 31–2, 34, 56, 95, 170
  turn 137, 149
love (*see also* Eros)
  art as 138, 157
  being in 42, 45, 70, 114, 153
  falling in 55, 149–50, 153–4, 157
  of good 163
  of truth 141, 200 n.107
  of virtue 162
  philosophy of 123
lover 23, 82, 123, 127, 139
low Eros (*see under* Eros)
loving
  attention (*see under* attention)
  clarity 143
  feat of imagination 156
  gaze 148
  nature- 83, 89
  vision 145

mad 22, 65–7, 134, 151, 154, 175 n.89,
  185 n.215, 203 n.187
  half- 150, 154
madness 23, 59, 151
Marx, Karl 25, 29, 176 n.99
Marxist 23, 25–7, 34
Merritt, Melissa 87, 187 n.10
metaphor 1, 52, 56, 138, 145, 148, 150,
  197 n.33, 199 n.73, 200 n.101
metaphorical 33, 89, 145, 152
  language (*see under* language)
metaphysical 7–8, 13, 17, 26, 30–1, 53–4,
  59, 63, 72, 81, 116, 155–6, 184
  anti- 7, 17, 26
  consolation 7, 119–20, 168
metaphysics 3, 6–9, 11, 13, 17, 19, 22, 23,
  26, 35, 72, 151, 184 n.194
mimesis 7, 30, 117, 133–4, 151, 164–5,
  170, 201 n.120
mimetic 42, 44, 47, 83, 133, 142, 154, 168
  art 136, 144, 162, 164
Moi, Toril 31, 95, 190 n.4

moral
- a- 120, 139
- aesthetics (*see under* aesthetics)
- im- 6, 21, 22, 51, 131, 133–5, 139, 141, 151, 164–5, 169
- improvement 131, 155, 160, 199–200 n.88
- -ist 120, 135, 138, 160, 202 n.143
- -istic 21, 150
- -ity of art 158
- -lly edifying xii, 142–3, 168
- philosopher 40, 137, 141, 199–200 n.88
- power of art 146–7, 170

moral philosophy 111, 122, 131, 137, 144–5, 160, 165, 168
- Kant 13
- Murdoch 95, 112, 133, 137–8, 140, 143–7, 152, 157, 199–200 n.88

Moss, Jessica 136, 140
Most, Glenn W. 4
Movie (*see also* film) 98, 101
mystic 20
- -al 21, 184 n.194

mysticism 8, 71, 184 n.194

narration 9, 130
narrative 15, 47, 92, 107, 139, 144, 156, 176 n.99, 197 n.25
narrator 50, 61, 71, 117, 129, 160
- unreliable 42, 46, 71

Nicol, Bran 65–7, 70–2, 144, 155–6, 185 n.218, 197–8 n.40, 198 n.53
Nietzsche, Friedrich 1, 6–9, 18, 30, 32, 57, 65–6, 109, 111, 119–23, 125, 127, 131, 163
Nietzschean 65
non-conceptual (*see under* conceptual)
nonsense 58, 61
nonsensical 50, 80
novel
- form 15, 74
- philosophical (*see* philosophical novel)
- writing 55

novelist 26, 38–40, 44, 54, 64, 71, 91, 124, 141, 155, 161
- philosophical (*see* philosophical novelist)

Nussbaum, Martha 4–5, 35, 42, 109, 110–11, 118, 121–7, 131, 137, 144–5, 149, 154, 197 n.25
Nuzzo, Angelica 188 n.46

objective 27, 32, 47, 48, 49, 79, 84, 152
ontological 63, 97, 163
ordinary
- consciousness 23, 76, 152
- discourse 22
- life 1, 91, 110, 112, 116–17, 128, 154, 161
- man 91
- meaning 62
- reader 29–30, 33, 71, 95, 172 n.6
- speech 27
- spirit 125
- thinking 15–16

ordinary language 8
- philosophy 43–4, 58

Othello 95–7, 99–100, 102–7, 109, 116, 121, 192 n.45

Panizza, Silvia 146–8, 159, 204 n.224
particularity 10, 17, 56, 86, 108, 112, 123, 144, 156–7 (*see also* contingency)
particulars 10, 15, 49, 51, 56, 113, 144–5, 149, 154, 183 n.151
philosophical novel 38–40, 45, 49, 56, 72–4, 169
- existentialist 26–7, 49–64
- non- 38, 65, 72

philosophical novelist 38–9, 54, 64
Pillow, Kirk 87–8, 91
Plato
- aesthetics (*see under* aesthetics)
- dialogues (form of) 5–6, 111, 124, 127–8, 130 (*see also specific titles*)
- Eros (*see under* Eros)
- influence on Murdoch 2, 6, 21, 42, 65, 133–7, 140, 143, 148–51, 164
- influence on Weil 22, 65, 141

Platonic 126, 128
- Forms 113

Platonism 7, 39, 65, 123, 126, 184 n.204
- neo- 2, 6, 21, 65

poet 40, 65
- inspiration of 23–4, 153
- Kant 88
- philosopher 8, 17, 20, 29, 178 n.8
- Plato 3, 38, 129, 140, 150–1, 172 n.3, 175 n.89
- tragic 116, 124, 128–9

poetics 71
pointless 26, 28, 34, 164
   -ness 162–5, 168–9
Pole, David 63
political 11–2, 21, 25–6, 28, 30, 111, 117, 135, 164, 169, 191 n.20
pornography 116, 133, 138, 158, 164
postcritique 31–2, 34, 95
Protestant 20
Proust, Marcel 1, 56, 128–30, 160–2, 202 n.143
Proustian 92
psyche 138, 142, 165
psychoanalysis 23–6, 34, 113, 176 n.103
psychological 13, 50, 59, 63, 77, 115, 140

reader, ordinary (*see under* ordinary)
reflective judgement (*see under* judgement)
religion 3, 14, 112, 120
religious 12, 15, 17–22, 53, 121, 139
rhapsode 3, 11, 37–8, 65, 73, 150
Romeo and Juliet 94
Rosen, Stanley 134, 161, 164
Rowe, Anne 40, 143
Rowett, Catherine 5
Ruokonen, Floora 108

Sartre, Jean-Paul 25–9, 31, 176 n.103, 182 n.143, 184 n.186
   influence on Murdoch 35, 38, 52–7, 72, 138, 155–6, 197 n.33
   influence on Weil 21
   La Nausée (see *La Nausée*)
Sartrean 155–6
sceptic 57, 65, 98, 99, 102 (*see also* epistemologist)
sceptical (*see also* epistemological)
   doubt 50, 58, 62, 74, 97–8, 101–2, 105
   impulse 61, 112
scepticism 9, 57–9, 70, 102, 105, 107, 109, 151, 203 n.187 (*see also* epistemology)
self-consciousness 14–16, 25–6, 62, 91, 111

sensory 15, 35, 40–1, 43, 46, 50, 54, 56, 63, 66, 74, 83, 124, 197 n.33
   illusion of sense (*see* illusion of sense)
sex 134, 138, 158, 197 n.39
sexual 22–3, 65, 134, 139, 141, 159
   desire 23–4, 150, 158
sexuality 22, 204 n.211
Shakespeare, William 57, 75, 87, 94, 96–7, 102, 110–1, 116
Stein, Gertrude 94
subjective 13, 19, 32, 43, 48, 77, 79, 84, 154
   inter- 44
subjectivity 28, 41, 95, 107, 182 n.143
sublimation 22, 24, 158–60
sublime, the 12, 48, 61, 71, 75, 80, 84–8, 91, 114, 156–60, 186 n.243, 187 n.10, 187 n.15, 189 n.69
sublimity 13, 85–8, 159–60
subversion 33, 135
suspension of disbelief 46, 63, 71, 96, 100–2, 105

taste (*see under* judgement)
The Apology 128–30
The Bell 142, 144
The Black Prince 38, 40–9, 70, 74, 123, 143, 145, 153, 187 n.13
The Good Apprentice 144
The Ion 23, 37–8, 48, 65–6, 73, 150–1
The Laws 111, 161
The Nice and the Good 92
The Phaedo 127, 130–1
The Phaedrus 150, 175 n.89
The Philosopher's Pupil 38, 64–74, 91
The Republic 5, 10, 18, 29, 38, 110, 127–8, 134, 136, 140, 150, 161
The Sea, the Sea 143
The Symposium 5, 22, 149, 151, 164, 195 n.116, 197 n.15, 200 n.107
The Theaetetus 148
The Timaeus 68, 128, 136, 161, 185 n.223
The Time of the Angels 90–1
theatre 4–5, 100, 102–7, 116, 118, 125, 134, 140, 143
theatrical 81, 105
   -ization 106

Tolstoy, Leo 53, 57, 138–9, 157, 161,
    198 n.47
transcendence 47, 143
transcendent 17
    beauty 22
    end 21–2, 162
    essence 57
    love 22
    other 159
    reading 30
    truth 6, 9, 22, 30
transcendental
    criticism/critique 13–16, 76
    condition 189
    function 152
    object 52

unreliable narrator (*see under* narrator)

vision 42, 63, 65, 72, 110, 114, 142, 149, 160
    loving 145–6

Walton, Kendall L. 98
Weil, Simone 19–22, 200 n.107
    aesthetics (*see under* aesthetics)
    influence on Murdoch 25, 27, 35, 65,
        138, 140–1, 146–9, 151–2, 154–5,
        159–60, 162, 184 n.194, 185 n.215,
        197 n.39, 203 n.183, 204 n.224
Weilian 27, 133, 135, 146, 149, 155,
    162
Wittgenstein, Ludwig 32, 35, 99,
    178 n.143, 184 n.194
Wittgensteinian 95
    post- 35–6

Zuckert, Rachel 113

www.ingramcontent.com/pod-product-compliance
Lightning Source LLC
Chambersburg PA
CBHW071833300426
44116CB00009B/1527